I Saw It in THE BUDGET

Elmer S. Yoder

1990

Published by
Diakonia Ministries
3511 Edison St. NE
Hartville, Ohio

First Printing - 1990
Second Printing - 1991
Third Printing - 1991

I Saw It in *The Budget*

Printed by Schlabach Printers of Sugarcreek, Ohio.

Dedicated

To the scribes whose writings

appear in this volume, and all who

contributed to THE BUDGET during its

one hundred years of publication.

Contents

Dedication

Table of Contents

Preface

"I Saw it in THE BUDGET" must have been heard tens of thousands of times in Amish, Amish Mennonite and Mennonite circles during the past one-hundred years. It was heard in both the English form as given in the title and in its Pennsylvania German equivalent, of which the English form is a literal translation (Ich haab es sckeenah in Die Budget). The news items mentioned in the letters became the subject of an untold number of conversational topics during the century that THE BUDGET has been published.

Far too many people only superficially acquainted with the weekly newspaper, THE BUDGET, brush it aside with some stereotypes. The most common one is that its only value is to find out where people were for Sunday dinner, the location of singings, who is traveling, and who is suffering from illness or was involved in an accident. They think of THE BUDGET as a paper to find out what type of work is "the order of the day", be it housecleaning, canning, hay making, plowing or the annual butchering. They have stereotyped THE BUDGET as little more than a means to find out in whose home Amish church services were held and which family would host the services the next time, or to find out the location of the all-important farm sales. THE BUDGET did all of the things mentioned but much more.

The author maintains that most readers of THE BUDGET in the 1980's are unaware of the kind of paper it was during its century of publication and the services it rendered. Few readers realize its value to the dozens of widely scattered Amish, Amish Mennonite and Mennonite communities, as well as to the larger and more stable ones. THE BUDGET was far more than a paper devoted to reporting church services by fellow Amish or Amish Mennonites. The larger Amish, Amish Mennonite and Mennonite community was influenced, molded, and held together to a degree understood and appreciated by very few, and this by the very paper so readily dismissed in an air of superiority by some who consider themselves as having graduated from its level of exchange, as they mistakenly perceive it.

Another stereotype is that of THE BUDGET as a paper abounding with substandard grammar, homespun Pennsylvania German expressions, misplaced modifiers, homemade spelling, and hilarious bloopers. All of these can be found on its pages, but substandard grammar, misspelled words and bloopers can be found in other papers as well. The stereotype usually finds expression in remarks about one of the above items followed by a chuckle which has an air of sophistication in it offensive to true humility. The really well-educated person is one who accepts THE BUDGET and its letters as a medium of communication and appreciates the services it rendered to tens of thousands of persons, individually and collectively, during the past century.

The previous paragraph is not a justification or defense of inferior work. It is, however, a recognition that the number of persons among the readers of THE BUDGET who graduated from high school was very small, especially during the early years of publication. In fact, many did not complete elementary school and most never entered high school. Eighth grade education is still standard among the Old Order Amish. In spite of their limitations, the scribes and readers served their generation in a commendable manner.

This volume is not intended to be a historical overview of the one-hundred year history of THE BUDGET. It is hoped that someone will make available such a volume during its centennial in the year of 1990, or at some later time. Some facets of its history will be included in this book, but these are secondary to its main purpose. The primary purpose of this book is to gain insight into Amish and Amish Mennonite life during the one-hundred years of its publication. To accomplish this the author personally scanned most of the letters appearing in THE BUDGET since it was first published on May 15, 1890.

THE BUDGET from its first year of publication included letters from scribes in Amish, Amish Mennonite and Mennonite communities outside of the Sugarcreek and Millersburg area. The number of scribes and the variety of communities was a reflection of life and practice in the Amish and Amish Mennonite communities. It must be remembered that the first editor, John C. Miller, also known as "Budget" John, was Amish Mennonite, and he piloted the paper through its first two decades. Editor Samuel H. Miller, 1913-1920, was an Amish Mennonite minister, serving what was then the Walnut Creek

Amish Mennonite Church. These editors had a great impact on the course the paper would take in its illustrious first century. Editor S. A. Smith (1920-1936), who succeeded Miller, was a friend of the Amish and continued, but refined, the kind of paper it was during the early decades. Longest at the helm of the paper was George R. Smith, son of S. A. Smith, who was Editor from 1936 to 1969, and still serves as Associate Editor. George Smith's influence on the paper and its readers covers more than fifty years. He performed an invaluable service to the larger Amish, Amish Mennonite and Mennonite community and to many readers of other circles. He was an able diplomat and walked that fine line between respecting the beliefs and culture of the readers and the requirements of good journalism.

THE BUDGET is a reflection of life in the scattered and sometimes isolated Amish and Amish Mennonite settlements on the American frontier and the emerging areas of the Midwest, particularly. The established area of Lancaster County in Pennsylvania was not brought into THE BUDGET family as easily and completely, as those west of the Allegheny Mountains. This is based on circulation statistics by regions and post offices which appeared at intervals in THE BUDGET.

Sorry to say, the value of THE BUDGET as a source of historical information on Amish and Amish Mennonite life has been largely untapped, or perhaps ignored. Within the past decade some have begun utilizing its value as a major source. One example is the book by David Luthy and published by Pathway Publishers in 1986. It is entitled *The Amish in America: Settlements that Failed, 1840 - 1960*. It is likely that if THE BUDGET were indexed it would be used more extensively for historical purposes.

The extensive use of THE BUDGET by missionaries such as J. A. Ressler of India, and by organizations such as Mennonite Board of Missions and Charities, Mennonite Central Committee, and even Goshen College is something of which most current readers are unaware. Sunday School lesson helps, columns on national and world news, and articles to assist farmers could be found in most issues during the early decades of this century. In addition, there were syndicated columns on a variety of topics, and even continued stories, some of which were fiction. A National Edition and Home Edition were unknown during the first fifty years of its existence. It was a single edition which served those near Sugarcreek, those living in sod houses on the plains of North Dakota or Kansas, and those adapting to the south on the gulf coast of Alabama and Florida, and those establishing new settlements in Oregon.

THE BUDGET provided a means of helping to unite the Amish and Amish Mennonites in a manner not possible through a religious periodical. A periodical of a particular viewpoint, representing one of the three groups - - Old Order Amish, Amish Mennonite, or Mennonite, would have had limited circulation even within the group it represented, but in addition, very few copies would have found their ways into the other two circles. THE BUDGET was a medium by which communication took place across the lines of the numerous groups of Amish and Mennonites to a degree impossible by any other type of paper. J. C. Miller and Amish Mennonite Minister S. H. Miller deserve recognition for the paper they pioneered and molded, and the Smith's deserve recognition for competently continuing the tradition and early purposes of the paper, and Mr. Spector for the indication he has given for its continuation.

The intention and purpose of this volume is to provide a sampling of Amish and Amish Mennonite life during the past century, from the pages of THE BUDGET itself. Hundreds of excerpts will be included along with the geographical location of the writer and the date of the paper in which it appears. This is done so the reader can enter first-hand into the descriptions and perceptions of the writers, and experience their feelings, values and outlook, in ways not possible through someone's interpretation of them. The running commentary by the author is provided to give continuity, explanation and hold the voices of the scribes together in a cohesive manner.

"I Saw it in THE BUDGET" was sometimes stated emphatically during the past century to settle an argument. Sometimes it was an exclamation of surprise about some developments in church affairs or community events. Sometimes it was used in rejoicing with others as information was conveyed about baptisms, weddings and family gatherings. On other occasions, "I Saw it in THE BUDGET" was used of news about tragedy, sorrow and disappointment.

Giving a historical overview of the one-hundred year history of THE BUDGET is secondary to providing a sampling of Amish, Amish Mennonite and Mennonite life during the one-hundred years. To provide this sampling more than two thousand excerpts from the letters of scribes are used. In this way the reader will be able to understand better what was said and how it was said than if it would be given second-hand. These excerpts are designed to be "windows" to catch the best possible glimpse. Because of its purpose as a sampler, the running commentary is kept at a minimum.

The information gleaned from the pages of THE BUDGET was placed in one of fifty two categories. A deliberate attempt was made to give a fair representation of viewpoints expressed on a wide variety of topics. The author sought to be objective in the selection and presentation of excerpts. There were areas not mentioned in the letters, and it is understandable why. For instance, there have been many divisions of congregations during the one-hundred years, but the basic and underlying reasons for the divisions were not addressed directly by the scribes. The differences in understanding and application of The Ordnung, the personality conflicts and generational differences were some of the matters that scribes did not relate other than by an umbrella-type of statment, such as "church difficulties".

The reader should also be aware of the fact that the scribes represent only a small percentage of the total membership of the larger Amish and Amish Mennonite community. How well the scribes represented the position and beliefs of the "silent majority" in the comments and positions taken in their letters is a question that is impossible to assess with the information at hand. It is very probable that the scribes were more vocal on church and community matters than most who did not write. By the phrase "more vocal" is not meant that they were engaged in gossip and spreading of rumors. It simply means that they were more ready to express themselves publicly than most fellow-members of their communities. Keeping this important fact in perspective is imperative as one reads the many excerpts.

The reader is invited to peruse the chapter "Historical Highlights" for some additional facts about the one-hundred year history of THE BUDGET. To discover how the scribes evaluated the paper, you are invited to read the chapter "Historical Significance of THE BUDGET."

The author presents this book with the hope that it will add enough to a greater understanding and appreciation of Amish and Amish Mennonite life to justify the effort and time invested.

The author wants to acknowledge and thank some people who have made this volume possible. Mr. Albert Spector of Sugarcreek Budget Publishers, Inc. deserves acknowledgement and thanks for granting permission to use the excerpts from THE BUDGET. Fannie Mae Erb, Business Manager, THE BUDGET, and the staff are to be commended for "putting up" with the author who spent many days in the building engaged in research. Mary Jeanette King of Hartville deserves due recognition for the cover design. And finally, my wife Esther, deserves recognition for the many errands she performed and the encouragement given during the time-consuming research and preparation of the manuscript.

Elmer S. Yoder
October, 1989

Historical Introduction
To Amish, Amish Mennonites and Mennonites

A brief introduction to the historical background and context of Old Order Amish and Amish Mennonites will be given. For some who have made a careful study this would not be needed. However, most of the readers will be able to benefit from such an introduction, and will be better able to understand the excerpts from THE BUDGET if their perspective of the historical and social context is enlarged.

The Mennonites trace their origin to events early in the year 1525 near Zurich, Switzerland. The Religious Reformation, which surfaced abruptly in Germany in 1517, had spread to Switzerland. Some leaders sought a more thorough reformation and did not believe that changes were being made rapidly enough by Ulrich Zwingli and the state church leaders. These so-called radicals were essentially pushed out of leadership roles in the state church because of their beliefs. Rather than be untrue to their beliefs and conscience, they cast their lives and destinies together by forming a new group. They referred to themselves as the Swiss Brethren. The members in the initial group baptized each other and embarked upon what they believed was the proper response to the call of full discipleship as followers of Christ. This included obedience to the Great Commission, which is the mandate of Christ to evangelize the world. The best known leaders among them were Felix Manz, Conrad Grebel and George Blaurock.

The state church leaders did not recognize the name these radicals gave themselves. Instead of honoring the name Swiss Brethren, they were given the nickname Anabaptist. This name was offensive to the Swiss Brethren, because it meant to "baptize again". The nickname was designed as mockery of believer's baptism, which the Swiss Brethren held as one of their foundational beliefs. The Swiss Brethren did not believe infants should be baptized. They believed that only a person who voluntarily seeks baptism should be baptized. Other basic beliefs of the Swiss Brethren were nonresistance, religious liberty, separation of church and state, and the final authority of the Word of God, the Bible.

The Anabaptist movement had its beginning in Holland in the late 1520's. Menno Simons joined the group in 1536 and soon became one of the leaders. It is from his nearly two decades of leadership in the low countries of northern Europe that the name Mennonite had its origin.

The origin of the Amish is usually given as the year 1693. The failure of ministers Jakob Ammann and Hans Reist to come to agreement on several matters led to a division in 1693 in Alsace, southern Germany and in Switzerland. The division and the failure of attempts at reconciliation in the 1690's is referred to as the Mennonite/Amish Schism. The Amish withdrew from the Mennonites, rather than the Mennonites from the Amish.

The first Mennonites reached North America in 1683, settling at Germantown, Pennsylvania. The Amish began emigrating in 1736. Between 1736 and 1755 the first wave of Amish emigrants reached North America, emigrating from the Palatinate, and numbering less than 500. These Amish settled in eastern Pennsylvania in what are now Berks and Chester Counties. From there they scattered to Lancaster, Mifflin and Somerset Counties.

The second wave of Amish reached North America between 1815 and 1860. About 3000 arrived from Bavaria, Alsace, and Hesse. These did not settle in the communities of eastern Pennsylvania, but moved directly to Ohio, Indiana, Illinois, upper New York and Canada.

The differences between the first wave of Amish and the second wave led to some open problems. The early arrivals tended to be more conservative, having established themselves on the frontier and being isolated to the momentous events in Europe, such as the French Revolution and the Napoleonic wars. The ones who had remained in Europe longer were more inclined to some changes. These differences led to a series of meetings of ministers between 1862 and 1878. The meetings were called Amish Diener-Versammlungen.

In spite of well-conducted and well-recorded meetings they did not resolve the issues sufficiently for them to remain together as a single group. Out of this failure came two major groups of Amish. For purposes of identification, the conservatives began to be called Old Order Amish, because they wanted to maintain

12

the Ordnung and practices as they had been, in other words, maintaining the old order. Prior to this division all the Amish went by the name Amish. But after 1880 there were two groups. The conservatives were known as Old Order Amish and the progressives as Amish Mennonites. This latter name indicated that they borrowed from the Mennonites and became more like them. This use of names is important to understand many of the excerpts in this volume. Amish Mennonite as part of a formal name is often abbreviated A.M.

One of the things borrowed from the Mennonites by the Amish Mennonites was the organization of conferences. Four Amish Mennonite Conferences were formed within thirty years after 1880. The Indiana-Michigan Amish Mennonite Conference was organized in 1888; the Western Amish Mennonite Conference in 1890; the Eastern Amish Mennonite Conference in 1893; and the Conservative Amish Mennonite Conference in 1910. Three of these eventually merged with Mennonite Conferences. The Indiana-Michigan A.M. Conference merged with the Indiana-Michigan Mennonite Conference in 1917. The Western A.M. Conference merged with several Mennonite conferences in the west and midwest in 1920. The Eastern A.M. Conference merged with the Ohio Mennonite Conference in 1927. The Conservative A.M. Conference is still an independent conference, although it dropped the name Amish in 1954. A graphic presentation has been included to help clarify these events.

The first issue of what is now the weekly paper, THE BUDGET, appeared on May 15, 1890. In the one-hundred years of its existence, the pages of THE BUDGET were used much more extensively by the Old Order Amish and Amish Mennonites than by the Mennonites. It must be emphasized, however, that there were also many scribes from Mennonite congregations, with their numbers considerably greater prior to World War II than since.

An attempt will be made to use terminology consistent with the above explanations in the running commentary in this volume. Some of the subtleties used by scribes revolve around these distinctions, and understanding the statements depends upon one's understanding of the nuances of the names.

Elmer S. Yoder   1987

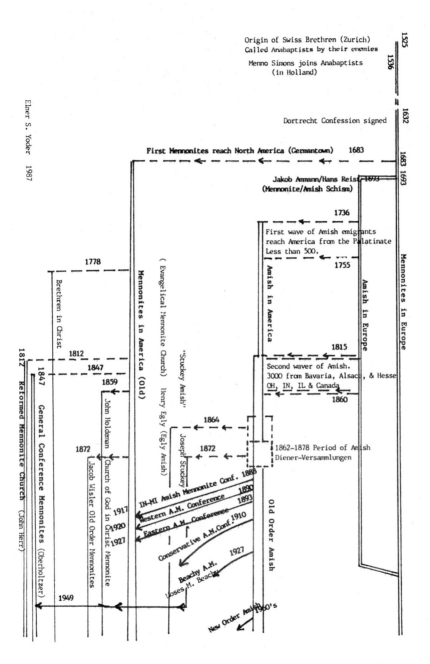

A Word to Readers

Two things are essential to glean the fullest value from the excerpts in this volume. One is a constant awareness of the *date* of publication. A second is to notice carefully the *geographic location*.

Keeping both the date and geographic location in focus will in most cases make the difference between understanding what the scribe was intending to communicate, or failing to comprehend the meaning, and wondering why it was included in this volume. For instance, the year becomes very important in understanding the significance of any discussion of technological matters. A comment about an automobile in 1908 has a meaning different from that of one in 1980. The farm silo did not come into use until the 1890's, and early references to them are not clear without checking the date of the excerpt. The location becomes very important in discussions about agricultural matters. Rice growing, citrus fruit production, large wheat acreages, or raising turnips for dairy cows all refer to a specific region of the North American continent.

It was the intention of the author to reproduce the excerpts as they appeared in THE BUDGET. The two most likely changes made by the author were in spelling and punctuation. Very few spelling corrections were made. The author believed that a great deal of the "flavor" would be lost by such corrections. Most words were always spelled as written by the scribes. Whatever form they used for threshing was retained; which was mostly thrashing. Bratwurst was not changed, nor was Braucha. The spelling used by the scribes for Menno Simons and Jakob Ammann was used, regardless of how they were spelled.

Some scribes put together paragraphs similar to the Greeks of the classical period, without punctuation. In only a few exceptional cases did the author make editorial changes in punctuation.

Many scribes failed to capitalize the names of languages and nationalities such as English, German and Spanish. Capital

15

letters were supplied for these, as well as the names of states and territories.

Comments appearing in [brackets] are those of the author when some explanation or transition statement was in order. The introductory material at the beginning of each chapter is not placed in brackets. Where (parentheses) appear, they were used by the scribe.

In translations of Pennsylvania German into English, meaning is given priority over grammar.

And finally, to obtain the fullest benefit of this volume, employ both the Table of Contents and the index to locate excerpts by topics.

The "Home Edition" of *The Budget* during the late 1970's.

The Budget offices in Sugarcreek prior to remodeling.

Accidents and Mishaps 1

A whole volume could be written about the many mishaps and accidents reported by the hundreds of scribes during the past century. Nearly every issue included an account of accidents with driving horses and the horsedrawn vehicles, such as buggies. These ranged from horses "spooking" to runaways completely out of control. The excerpts used are only representative of the sixteen subheadings under which they have been placed.

Auto-truck: Bud Stoll had the misfortune of breaking his arm last week when trying to crank his car.
Nov. 9, 1933   Mylo, ND   Gladys and Freeda

Pete Shrock broke his arm by cranking his car.
Dec. 7, 1933   Shelbyville, IL   Nettie M. Eash

A very sad accident occurred on Sunday, May 25th, at 9 P.M. when five young Mennonite people were instantly killed when a small sedan in which they were riding crashed against the speeding locomotive of the west bound North Shore Central Limited express, at the New York Central railroad crossing in Crittenden.
June 5, 1930   Akron, NY   A Reader

On last Wednesday morning while Crist K. Smoker was driving his dear little Ford down east Main Street, enroute for Lewistown with some produce for market the car left the road and in trying to straighten it up, she turned turtle alighting on top with Mr. Smoker and produce pinned beneath, neighbors were soon on the scene stopped the machinery and assisted the driver from his position. The top and shield were considerably smashed but otherwise not much damage was done, nevertheless the chauffeur gathered up, alighted in his car and went on his journey none the worse for his thrilling experience.
June 16, 1915   Belleville, PA   Rudy J. Kanagy

Beard: It was very interesting to my husband to read of the misfortune of the fellow in Canada who wanted to cool the end of a drill bit. A number of years ago he had the same experience, also instantly getting rid of his beard. It happened on Sat. and it took a lot of nerve to go to church the next day, even though he wasn't a minister! A few years later he got a good part of his beard removed again when he lit a gas furnace and it puffed out!

Nov. 5, 1986   Halfway, Mo.   Mrs. John D. Blosser

Daniel J. Gingerich thought he heard a strange rattling noise somewhere on his jointer while working with it in the shop. He bent down to examine it and all at once he got an awful bump across his head and lo and behold there was some of his beard wound around the line shaft at the pulley. Now Dan is walking around with a lopsided beard.

Oct. 26, 1977   Ethridge, Tenn.   Jacob M. Yoder

Children: A freak accident occurred last Thursday while the hired girl was caring for the small baby of Jacob E. Schwartzes. A small golden safety pin dropped from the girl's dress into the baby's mouth as it was crying. The pin was open and lodged in the baby's throat with the point upwards. The pin could be reached with a finger but were unable to remove it and it had to be taken to a specialist at Fort Wayne, where they tried to remove the pin with a magnet, but when touched it slipped down in the stomach and was later removed by an operation.

Dec. 11, 1947   Bluffton, Ind.   Sarah Schwartz

Jacob E. Schrock's two year old child drowned in a sewer, where they poured in their waste, which was stopped up.

April 26, 1923   Winesburg, Ohio   No Name

Church: Quite an excitement happened this week, at the Albright Church. The floor gave way and they all ran out as fast as they could, but no one was hurt.

Mar. 8, 1900   Geistown, Pa.   Moses J. Mishler

Farmyard: John L. Yoder of Farmerstown fell 18 ft. down his silo chute Saturday p.m. He was knocked unconscious and also received other injuries.

Aug. 14, 1947   Berlin, OH   Sara Weaver

The writer's brother attempted to ride a mule thru a mud hole while working for Elmer Kauffman and naturally got off in the deepest place. Ananias Miller also tried to ride a colt and was sent headfirst into a mud hole. Both per-

18

formers were covered with mud when they waded out. Luckily no one was hurt.

July 28, 1920   Greentown, Ind.   Menno J. Ebersole

A sad mishap occurred Thursday, Sept. 9th when Daniel B. Fisher fell at a barn raising. He died Friday morning at 5:30. He was 54. About 12 men were standing on a joist and were helping to push up the purlin when the joist suddenly broke and left them all drop to the floor except about 3 or 4 who caught themselves. Three or four others received injuries also.

Sept. 16, 1948   Gordonville, Pa.   Amos K. Lapp

David Fisher had the misfortune to fall while carrying a crate of eggs on Wednesday. The result was a lot of broken eggs.

Feb. 13, 1902   Gordonville, Pa.   John H. Kauffman

[On Oct. 7, 1964, a young life was suddenly snuffed out. Elva Mae, eight-year old daughter of Menno and Alma Yoder, lost her life in a farm accident.] In some unexplained way she was caught in the shaft of the power take-off while the tractor was idling, awaiting the arrival of another load of silage from the field. No one witnessed the tragedy in full, but her 13-year-old brother Elmer heard that the tractor was pulling a load and looked in time to see her being flung around in opposite directions, luckily not having entered the conveyor. The upper part of her body was hurled some feet, but was not badly damaged, which may indicate that the body was not balanced on the shaft, thereby saving the head.

Oct. 15, 1964   Montezuma, Ga.   Mrs. Enos W. Yoder

Animals: Seth Byler had the misfortune of a cow jumping over him while he was working in the field where the cows were. The cow threw him over and tramped on him, cut his eye lid and a few other scratches. He had to have three stitches in his eye lid. The dog chased the cow and the cow made a run for him. His eye pained pretty badly for two days.

Aug. 24, 1933   Uniontown, Ohio   Eli Lapp

Jacob Lapp, of this place lost a bull in a peculiar way on Thursday morning. He was taking it away and had it fastened to the rear end of a two-horse wagon, and when he got as far as Elias Smokers the animal grew stubborn and fell and being unable to get it upon its feet. They dragged

19

it to the barnyard where it died soon after. It was supposed to have broken its neck.

Oct. 31, 1901   Gordonville, Pa.   John H. Kauffman

Peter Stoll had bad luck; a week or two ago he went to the woods to haul wood, and a strange dog followed him and finally the dog ran ahead of the horses and bit one of his best mares in the nose; last night the mare got mad and they had to kill her; she was worth $150.

Feb. 19, 1903   Montgomery, Ind.   Noah J. Stutzman

Robert Yoder had quite an experience this morning as he caught the bull in the pasture to take to the barn for the T.B. test. Had a chain on a nose ring. The bull knocked him down, he got up and was knocked down again. Robert got him by the ring and twisted it while lying on his back, which held the bull with his head and nose to the ground. Dr. Royer clubbed the bull, with no results so he ran and got his car, ran through the fence and drove up to the bull which gave Robert time to get into the car and saved his life. Robert is laid up with both legs hurt.

Dec. 20, 1962   Rustburg, Va.   Willis C. Glick

On Saturday an infuriated sheep butted Mrs. J. C. Miller to the ground the second time and as a result she is laid up and unable to visit her husband in the hospital.

Apr. 15, 1943   Lynnhaven, Va.   Mrs. Enos W. Yoder

The other day when Irvin Kurtz was driving a hog that had escaped from the pen, the hog turned on him and bit him in the leg which has laid him up for a little while.

Nov. 3, 1932   Fentress, Va.   S. D. Kurtz

Mose Stahl lost a valuable horse last week. It fell in a 40 foot well. The well was located in the garden and was unknown to Mose, having been put there by former owners. It was covered with boards and dirt, making it invisible.

May 6, 1909   Clarksville, Mich.   Cor.

Dave Yoder was attacked by the bull recently. The bull gave him a pitch and when Dave looked around the dog was after the bull so he made his getaway.

April 1, 1987   Inola, Okla.   Eli & Mary Schrock

Fieldwork: Dan Wengerd had a narrow escape a week ago when his team started to run off in the corn planter. He ran in front of them to stop them and the horses ran over him, and also the planter. He had quite a bit of pain, but by the latter part of the week he was at work again.

July 17, 1952   Conewango Valley, NY   Mrs. Menno E. M.

Another sad accident happened Tuesday evening while Jonas Hershberger was cutting wheat. They thought the children had all gone to the house, but instead little William had laid himself in the wheat and went to sleep and was struck on the back of the head with the big wheel of the binder. Mrs. Hershberger was driving the tractor while Mr. Hershberger was on the binder. He saw the child but of course she could not hear him calling with the noise of the tractor so he jumped off in time yet to avoid the wheel from going over him, but his head was already partly crushed, he was rushed to the hospital but died early the next morning.

June 27, 1935   Norfolk, Va.   Jemimia Yoder

Dennis Miller started out to plow this morning and came across a soft place when all at once the horse went down and all that would have been needed would be a few shovels of dirt and he would have been covered up.

April 14, 1927   Kalona, Ia.   Miss Katie Miller

Friday, May 21, a very sad accident happened while Noah, little son of Eli Kinsinger was out in the field working with the roller. He wanted to whip one of the horses that was so slow and he fell off and the roller went over him up to his breast and then stopped. When the father seen that his team was stopping he went to see what was wrong, but he was dead already.

June 3, 1926   Arthur, Ill.   A Few Readers

Fire: David L. Yoder had quite an experience late Mon. when he got gas on his clothes which caught fire. He buried himself in hay and smothered the flames. It is a great wonder that the hay didn't start to burn. He got a few burns on his neck and lost some hair and whiskers, but his clothes aren't damaged much.

Jan. 30, 1964   Medford, Wis.   Mrs. David Hostetler

A very sad accident occurred on March 22, when the three children of Roy and Malinda Troyer Miller perished in the flames of the burning barn where the three children were playing. No one knew just how the barn was set afire....

April 18, 1946   Greenwich, Va.   Mrs. Ira M. Zook

Mr. and Mrs. Henry Schrock and one of their children had

the misfortune of getting burned one day last week when they were spraying their brooder house with gasoline and there was just a little fire in the stove which they thought was out, causing a sudden fire. They were burned quite badly, but were up and around the last we heard.

May 15, 1930   Middlefield, Ohio   Two Readers

J. S. Overholt had quite an excitement last week. One of his boys took matches out and wanted to burn some straw near the barn. Two big stacks of feed were burned but by hard work they saved the barn, which was only about 10 ft. away.

April 25, 1907   Bucklin, Kans.   Noah J. Stutzman

Firearms: A serious accident occurred near the home of David King last week. While his son, Daniel T. was in the act of shooting a dog for a neighbor when part of the charge blew out of the rear end of the gun, into his face and eyes, which were badly burned. A piece of the gun struck him near the nose, making a painful wound. He was nearly blind but is recovering his sight and is getting along as well as can be expected.

Feb. 22, 1900   Gordonville, Pa.   John H. Kauffman

Daniel Chupp shot three fingers off of his right hand last Sunday.

Jan. 2, 1902   Goshen, Ind.   Miss Lydia Miller

A sad accident occurred yesterday at the wolf chase, near Haven. A boy was shot through the head with a B.B. shot at about three oclock p.m. and died about 9 the same day....

Feb. 8, 1906   Haven, Kans.   Amos J. Miller

Dismemberment: Dan Delagrange who had the misfortune of losing both eyes this spring, is now learning to weave baskets and is doing real well. He has made a number of different kinds.

July 9, 1931   Ft. Wayne, Ind.   Lillian & Rosa Chupp

Ira Yoder, who had the misfortune of losing both his hands while working on the sawmill, is getting along as well as can be expected. We who have hands can scarcely realize how it is to raise a family of six children without hands. Mrs. Yoder said if he cannot work with his hands, he can sing and talk and help raise the children for the Lord.

July 22, 1910   Nineveh, Ind.   Miss Mary S. Hochstetler

Lewis Hochstetler had the four fingers of his left hand

severed March 1 when he caught his hand in a roller on his corn picker.

March 15, 1945   Kalona, Ia.   Eliza M. Miller

Drowning: Today our community was saddened when two of Joe Overholt's girls were drowned in their farm pond. Their names and ages are: Lillie, 17, and Caroline, 12, a twin. Their brother, Rudy, had gone out on the ice, and broke through, and in trying to rescue him the sisters met their death. The Orange Rescue Squad came in time to save Rudy who clung to the edge of the ice.

Feb. 8, 1962   Madison, Va.   Noah A. Keim

On Wednesday, while Isaac Peachey and wife were visiting at the Katie Yoder home, near Allensville, their little son, Menno, opened the trap door to the cistern and fell in. When the little boy was missed a search was made and was found floating on the water; he was quickly pulled out, but no signs of life were there for about half an hour, after which he was revived.

April 21, 1904   Belleville, Pa.   M. P. Zook

Explosives: A very sad accident occurred last week when Chester and Lester Miller, twin brothers, were dynamiting . . . A stone hit Chester in the face and killed him almost instantly.

May 2, 1946   Burton, Ohio   Noah O. Hershberger

Horse and buggy: On their way to the Yoder home they saw a car coming towards them and when not far from the buggy the driver of the car deliberately swerved against the buggy, breaking the rear axle, then hurriedly left the scene. The jar threw Edna out into the road but none were seriously injured. A few similar buggy accidents have occurred lately by hit-skip drivers, which seemed to be done intentionally, and could have caused serious injury.

Sept. 4, 1947   Berlin, Ohio   Sara Weaver

Rufus Gingerich and Bud Yoder had the misfortune of tipping over with a wagon load of calves Saturday night. I wonder if they went to sleep.

Nov. 9, 1933   Mylo, N.D.   Gladys and Freeda

The sad news reached this place on Monday of the accident which befell Jacob Zook of Eden, Lancaster County. While on their way to partake of a wedding dinner, Mr. Zook and his two daughters were caught on a crossing by a trolley car, where one of the girls met her death, and the other girl and Mr. Zook were seriously injured. [See p. 356]

[See p. 356]

Jan. 15, 1903   Belleville, Pa.   M. P. Zook

Samuel Beiler's horse was frightened by an automobile last Saturday evening, throwing Samuel out and damaging the buggy considerably, but Samuel stuck to the lines like glue and kept the horse from getting away. Mr. Beiler recovered some damages from the party.

Aug. 23, 1906   Arthur, Ill.   Lewis D. Yutzy

Mrs. S. H. Miller is suffering a black eye, skinned nose, and other severe bruises as a result of a pony running off and upsetting the buggy on Sunday afternoon. The daughters Pauline and Grace were in the upset, but escaped without injury.

June 9, 1915   Walnut Creek, Ohio   Local news

Household: Joe Stutzmans had quite an explosion, but it happened to be just a strawberry can, the berries flew up to the ceiling and made quite a mess.

July 18, 1935   Jessup, Iowa   Mrs. Ida Gingerich

Miss Lydia C. Bontrager fell out of a cherry tree last week one day and bruised her left elbow badly. She has her arm in a sling.

July 9, 1931   Plain City, Ohio   Mr. & Mrs. Andrew J. Yoder

Remedies / Drugs: Last Saturday Paul Beachy had a close call. He had sent for some tablets which had been put up for horses, and he not being able to see the fine print in the advertisement, thought they were for humans; having a headache, he thought they might be good for that and swallowed one. He soon became very sick, and told the family what he had taken and a doctor was quickly called, but before he arrived Paul had to vomit severely, which no doubt saved his life. The doctor thought the dose was large enough for 18 men. He was stirring around on Monday but not quite well yet.

June 30, 1915   Elk Lick, Pa.   Mrs. John D. Yoder

Unclassified / humorous: One of her sisters once climbed to an upper cupboard, then when jumping off, her dress caught on a lower door handle. There she hung arms and legs flying until one of the family recovered from laughing to unhook her.

April 5, 1989   Panama, N.Y.   Mrs. Joe Bricker

Eli Raber had the misfortune of getting a chicken bone in his throat. He was taken to the hospital where it was removed and was obliged to stay at the hospital over Sunday.

Feb. 6, 1947   Uniontown, Ohio   Ada J. Helmuth

The other week an elephant made hash out of Mrs. Jacob D. Weaver's shopping bag and its contents. He grabbed it out of her hand with his trunk while she was watching the elephants perform. For a while she thought he had also swallowed her purse that was in the bag but in some lucky way the pocket book dropped out of the elephant's mouth.

March 15, 1945   Sarasota, Fla.   No name

I will not give the name of the young man that I know, who had a set of teeth for which he paid $100, and one day when he was working away from home he took them and wrapped them in a paper and put them in his lunch box to carry home. When his wife emptied the box of its contents, she three the contents into the stove not knowing that his teeth were in the box.

Nov. 14, 1929   Denbeigh, Va.   Mrs. S. P. Yoder

. . . like it went with Eli Dave, when his wife went on a visit and told him to churn while she was gone. Dave thought the cream was too cold, so he put it in the oven and baked it awhile; he thought he would do quick work; and you bet he did, too. When he got through churning, instead of having butter, he had cheese.

Mar. 13, 1902   Milford, Neb.   J. M. Schlegel

Milo Yoder found out lately that sorghum molasses don't work the same in a motor, as motor oil does, when he put some in the water pump motor instead of oil, by mistake of course!

Feb. 11, 1987   Marion, Ky.   Amos A. Mast

We are anxious to know how A.B.B.'s toes are getting along by this time; he got pinched when he kicked through the window. Never mind, the scribe was also nursing a sore toe from a rat bite during his sleep.

Oct. 11, 1906   Dodge City, Kans.   Aaron A. Yoder

25

Advertising   2

Uneasiness and dissatisfaction with the amount and content of advertising was frequently expressed by both scribes and in the letters to the Editor during the first fifty years. What many of the persons objecting failed to realize, based on their comments, was the fact that THE BUDGET depended on advertising revenue to keep subscription costs at an affordable price. The Editor attempted at various times to defend, via the Editor's Corner, the use of advertisements. Since WWII comments by scribes about advertising have subsided gradually.

Charles Pierson, a watch repairman, expressed his satisfaction with advertising, stating that it brought him trade from eighteen states. In one advertisement he included the following: "I received 17 watches today for repairs from a distance. I am getting new agents everyday or two to send me watches for repairs, I give them 25 cents for their trouble and pay the express charges one way if they send 3 watches at a time." June 14, 1900 Arcola, Ill.

Local merchants ran ads regularly. The following are some ads of interest, both local and distant.

Daniel & Polly Troyer: Homemade Amish clothes
    Sugarcreek,   1909-1912
Bunnie Hat Co. of Reading, Pa.: "Plain Hats" for Amish, Dunkards and Mennonites   1925
Smuckers of Orrville: Apple Butter   1906
Circular Standard Colony Brooder house: 1917
The Odell Type Writer: 1891   Cost - - $20
I. W. Johnson of Etna Green, Ind.: The Grave Robber, a remedy that supposedly arrested cancer.
Shoo Fly insect killer advertised by local merchants.
Scott's Emulsion of Cod Liver Oil was advertised by the company in 1900, with the following:
    Don't Get Thin
    Get fat: get nice and plump;

there is safety in plumpness.

500 tumblers at the Racket Store at 2 for 5 cents. ₁₉₁₂

Some church agencies used the pages of THE BUDGET for publicity, and some paid for advertising.

> Chicago Home Mission on Jan. 23, 1902 used + 1 column for its Christmas dinner. A. H. Lehman, Supt.
>
> Mennonite Publishing House, Elkhart, Ind. used nearly five inches of column two columns wide, June 20, 1901
>
> Elkhart Institute (forerunner of Goshen College) advertised its offerings June 14, 1900. Courses of study were listed as: Latin-Scientific, Normal, Bible, Commercial, Elocution, Stenographic, Physical Culture and Vocal Music.

Some other examples of advertisements worthy of space are the following:

> Will call sales in any locality. Can speak the German, English and Swiss language.
> P. W. Andrews, Auctioneer   May 15, 1902

> I have a few Whitely Mowers and Tedders and Thomas hayrakes on hand; will sell them at less than wholesale prices, on easy terms.
> Geo. Smith   Shanesville, Ohio

> The Star Woven Fence Machine was advertised with the following qualities: Take it right into the field or any place. Make a woven wire fence where you want it. More than 50 styles. Can make them horse high, bull strong, pig and chicken tight.
> Geo. Smith   Shanesville, Ohio

> A movement is now on foot around Plain City, Ohio to organize "The Amish Farming Company" to buy 12,995 acres of Black Land, 4 miles south of Moyock N.C. ($31 per acre)
> May 5, 1920

> It would be hard to convince a man suffering from bilious colic that his agony is due to a microbe with an unpronounceable name. But one dose of DeWitt's Colic and Cholera Cure will convince him of its power to afford instant relief. It kills pain.
> June 25, 1896   Weaver Bros. of Sugarcreek

27

Agriculture and Farming   3

Agriculturally related occupations were predominant among the readers of THE BUDGET. There has, however, been a slow but steady decrease throughout the Amish communities. In some communities it is quite pronounced. Some Ohio congregations in the Middlefield area, have only half of their wage earners on farms. One prominent Ohio Amishman has said that the lunchbucket is the biggest threat to their way of life.

The predominance of agriculture during the past century accounts why it ranks as one of the most reported subjects in THE BUDGET. Its rivals are weather, health, church services and perhaps social affairs, such as visiting.

The excerpts in this chapter were not selected to cover the routine work of the farmers, whether it be chores, field work, or the seasonal work. A whole volume could be written just on agriculture. What is included here is a sampling of excerpts which shed some light on the size and type of operations, priorities, and the variety and scope of the animals and equipment, but above all, the outlook and philosophy of the scribes.

Beasts of burden: When I was at home with my folks in Colorado, Father had a steer and a bull about half grown, and as good horsepower was scarce, most horses being wild-west broncos, father decided to break these young animals. So he set out to find a yoke for an ox team, but that being plains country, he found it a difficult matter. So, as I remember it, he managed to get a piece of timber large enough to carve out a yoke, and soon the team was broken to work, and we used them to haul water for our house use, as we didn't have any soft water on our claim. At one time, when I wanted to do some harrowing and the ox team was quite young, I hitched a little grey mare that was slow-gaited along side of the oxen, so I had a three hoss team, and they worked together very well. Quite a combination - - a bull, a

steer and a mare.
Mar. 17, 1949   Hutchinson, Kans.   D. A. Hostetler

Recently 17 horses in the Melba country died from eating frozen potatoes. Boiled potatoes have proven very good food for hogs. It is almost a daily occurrence that the veterinary is called out to unchoke a cow that has tried to swallow a potato. Sometimes the farmer in excitement, has tried to give the poor animal relief by using a broomstick, but only to make matters worse. Usually the gullet is broken and the animal dies.
Feb. 18, 1923   Nampa, Ida.   Mrs. F. H. Hostetler

Local farmers want an enormous price for a mated team of horses. Wonder what they will bring at farm sales. Those that have good young and well broke horses for sale are asking from $350 to $400 per pair.
Feb. 1, 1940   Gap, Pa.   John F. Glick

Next Wednesday there will be another wild-horse sale in town. The horses sell at from $1 to $15.
Mar. 1, 1900   Nampa, Ida.   A Reader

There are quite a few sick horses around here. J. K. Reno lost a valuable mule nearly two weeks ago. Andrew Hostetler lost a good horse this morning. The number of stock that the Amish lost last winter was 22 head of horses, 22 head of cattle and 26 head of hogs.
Aug. 15, 1901   Grass Lakes, N.D.   E. D. Wierich

Crop report for 1901: [In 1901 eighty crop reports were submitted at the request of the editor. They were listed in two issues. To check the locations and the correspondents reporting see Chapter 25.]
Aug. 22 and 29, 1901

Dairy farms: Noah E. Yoders were having some trouble with garlic milk but by putting the cows out of pasture at 12 o'clock it seems to be unnoticeable. The cows seem to like garlic when it is young and tender.
April 5, 1928   Norfolk, Va.   Simon D. Hershberger

John D. Yoder, of near Springs, is quite extensively engaged in the dairy and poultry business. He has twenty-five cows and about eight hundred chickens. He is now getting over four hundred eggs a day.
April 5, 1910   Meyersdale, Pa.   A. L. Beiler

The farmers have just finished filling the milk station ice

house, where they have stored away about 800 tons of ice for milk purposes.
Feb. 22, 1900   Ronks, Pa.   Miss Sarah B. Fisher

Daniel Hershberger, of Canton, Ohio, I would think that you would get tired till you get 28 cows milked.
April 7, 1907   Middlebury, Ind.   Noah S. Yoder

Some dairy farmers are buying cream separators and ship the cream to the city, claiming they realize as much for the cream as they would selling the milk, beside feeding the skim milk to their calves and hogs.
April 27, 1905   Mantua, Oh.   No name

Cow sales are numerous and cows sell high. Good ones readily sell for from sixty to sixty five dollars. A great deal of milk is shipped to Philadelphia.
Nov. 9, 1905   Gordonville, Pa.   John H. Kauffman

Possibly it may surprise some of the readers if I tell them what many of the dairy men do with their calves. They give them away when they know of anybody that wants them, and if not they knock them in the head and feed them to their hogs. Some only kill the male calves and raise the others. You will say, such a waste, why not veal them. Because it does not pay. Or why not raise them in such a grass country? Because they don't think it pays. In the first place a cow ought to give from one dollar to three dollars worth of cream or butter, and it is considered that a calf will drink at least one dollars worth of milk per week, and at seven weeks old it brings only about five dollars, and beef cattle have been only two cents per pound. There are no regular stock buyers here; occasionally one comes from Minneapolis; so you can see there is very little money in calves, except such as make good dairy cows.
April 16, 1908   Mora, Minn.   Samuel B. Miller

Animal diseases: Hog cholera is making its rounds in this neighborhood. One farmer has lost 4 brood sows and about 30 pigs this past week. Everyone in the vicinity has vaccinated.
Aug. 26, 1943   Sturgis, Mich.   Salome Chupp

Hog cholera is prevailing in this locality and they are dying by the hundred.
Dec. 17, 1896   Bertrand, Neb.   Levi S. Yoder

Farmers are getting pretty well excited with the recent

T.B. testing as some lost all or nearly all of their cows with only a meager compensation for the condemned cows. It is at least the most important topic of discussion, more so even than politics.

Nov. 6, 1924   Burton, Ohio   Levi Miller

Hogs for butchering are scarce in the neighborhood on account of nearly all died of cholera.

Dec. 11, 1912   Lagrange, Ind.   E. A. Mishler

Quite a good many farmers in this locality had to buy hogs this fall for their own meat, as some kind of a disease killed a great many hogs for the farmers thru here, some lost all they had others saved a few, but a very small percent was saved of those that were not vaccinated. The writer did not have much faith in vaccinating hogs, but is now convinced that the vaccinating is the right thing to do, if it is done with the right serum.

Jan. 6, 1921   Arthur, Ill.   David S. Beachy

Farm fowl: Raising turkeys is a good business here; some people raise from 400 to 500 turkeys in one season.

May 21, 1909   Portersville, Calif.   Mrs. J. A. Gingerich

John Kropf has 1200 young chicks and some others have a few home set ones too. I have an incubator set but so many eggs are not fertile.

Mar. 17, 1927   Harrisburg, Ore.   Mrs. Andrew Yoder

[One party had trouble with their 10,000 birds running and flying.] On Saturday evening when they were especially bad, husband Stanley found a way to calm them, by standing on a stool in the middle of the building and singing at the top of his voice they were quiet until bedtime. It brought to mind the scripture where Adam was to have dominion over the fowl of the air.

Oct. 5, 1977   Dallas Center, Iowa   Mrs. Stanley Funk

Mr. Summy, 114 chickens are not many, Mr. Webster had over 1200 already, sometime ago.

June 15, 1899   Hutchinson, Kans.   N. Helmuth

Dan A. Schwartz's are taking care of 600 baby chicks since Tuesday. Seems like there is no demand for chicks this spring as feed is so high and so many have to buy all their feed. Hatcheries have turned down lots of eggs for quite a while. Some places they electrocute the little chicks they can't sell.

April 29, 1937   Monroe, Ind.   Sarah Schwartz

We have not been away for one month, about next Sunday or the following we will be able to go again. It was on account of the little chicks.

July 7, 1932　　Harrisburg, Ore.　　Mrs. Andrew Yoder

In these days of forcing egg production, perhaps some of our poultry fanciers may experience the truthfulness of the following rhyme:

"Mary had a little hen
That acted very queer;
She always laid when eggs were cheap,
But quit when they were very dear.

Jan. 22, 1919　　Manchester, In.　　J. Albert Zepp

Poultry is not doing very well as they have no green grass to eat and must be fed.

Aug. 2, 1911　　Latour, Mo.　　Sarah E. Hershberger

Farm crops: People are coming home from the hop yards. Hops were a fair crop this year. Prunes are about all dried.

Sept. 27, 1900　　Albany, Ore.　　James Troyer

Farmers are putting out from 10 to 20 acres of sugar beets this season.

Mar. 13, 1902　　Elkton, Mich.　　H. E. R.

Peanuts are a good crop this year, and people are busy harvesting them.

Oct. 24, 1901　　Gibson, Miss.　　Moses & Rebecca Hershberger

At Moyock, the men folks were busy planting mint plants. They had quite a lot of rain while I was there. Seth Slabach made $1700 from one acre of mint last year.

April 29, 1926　　Norfolk, Va.　　J. K. Fisher

The beet company was around getting acreage for the coming year.

Jan. 10, 1907　　Nampa, Ida.　　Andrew G. Kauffman

Some farmers are still busy planting corn. Several farmers here are putting out 250 acres each. I think some people don't know when they have enough.

June 7, 1900　　Plain City, Ohio　　Mrs. Anna K. Yoder

There has been a large acreage of sugar beets sown this spring which are doing nicely and the Mexicans are busy thinning them. The farmers are to receive $13 per ton for the sugar beets.

June 9, 1920　　LaJunta, Colo.　　Mrs. C. T. Kauffman

Now would be a good time for the northern people to come and see how the rice is flooded by artificial irrigation, how the fields are prepared with levees step by step to hold water, 8 inches at the deepest. The leveler the field the less levees are required. The best of the levees are made by plowing two rounds with a 12 inch plow, throwing the furrows together, than going one round with a "V" grader and grade up the last furrow. If you get too many levees in the field to be convenient in cutting the rice you take a team and plow and turn a furrow back on both sides then it is easy to run across with the binder. This is done after the water is let off, before cutting.

June 21, 1900   Iowa, La.   C. C. Schrock

C. C. Schrock threshed about 120 acres of his rice, which averaged about 7½ sacks to the acre, or 896 sacks from the 120 acres.

Oct. 24, 1901   Iowa, La.   J. J. Keim

Making levees and fence is all the go among the farmers as the fields are all new and were never leveed before.

June 21, 1900   Iowa, La.   C. C. Schrock

The people are very busy cutting tobacco this week. Hands are scarce and hard to get.

Sept. 13, 1900   Gordonville, Pa.   John H. Kauffman

[The following excerpt followed a report of searching for a potential area for a new settlement in the Carolinas.] If I am informed correctly, the land is favorable for raising of the higher priced tobacco, which is used in the manufacture of cigarettes. One would think that the soil could be used to better advantage than for the raising of the filthy weed, especially since we see so many women and girls smoking, deliberately ruining their health....

Feb. 15, 1940   Lynnhaven, Va.   Mrs. E. W. Yoder

Farm land: Our folks were pulling stumps, having pulled 292 in all.

Oct. 4, 1911   Fairview, Mich.   Mrs. M. S. Zook

The two large steam breaking outfits, which were breaking in this neighborhood, have moved farther north and northeast. They are about forty or forty-five horsepower engines, pulling twelve plows each.

May 27, 1910   Bloomfield, Mont.   Enos D. Yoder

In places the steam breakers are still turning over the sod

at the rate 18 to 30 acres a day per outfit.
> July 5, 1910   Miller, S. D.   P. J. N. Miller

Our population is growing by leaps and bounds. . . . In the not too distant future we will need all our land to feed and clothe our population. It behooves us as city dwellers and farmers alike, to do all we can to protect, nourish, and be good stewards, over the land on which we all are dependent.
> Aug. 1, 1963   Enon Valley, Pa.   Mr. J. S. Byler

Farm workers: Farm help is getting scarce here as so many of the boys are leaving the farms to work in shops. Lots of farmers have to sell on account of not having help.
> May 1, 1941   Cochranton, Pa.   Mr. E. E. Schrock

There are quite a number of Mexicans here already to care for the sugar beet crop.
> June 12, 1924   Midland, Mich.   Mrs. Mabel Kauffman

Garden and truck crops: Farmers are planting truck crops at present.
> Dec. 20, 1911   Mission, Tex.   C. J. Schlabach

Farmers are sowing their turnips.
> June 14, 1900   Shakespeare, Ont.   Jacob Iutzi

Working cabbage is in full blast.
> Mar. 28, 1901   Kempsville, Va.   Simon D. Hershberger

Watermelon shipping is over for this season. They sold at from $50 to $100 a car. A number of cars were shipped north, but no returns yet.
> July 26, 1910   Tuleta, Tex.   C. C. Schrock

Our housewives are still going to the garden for their cabbage, turnips, beets and lettuce, and someone said that over by Brownsville is a field of oats just heading out.
> Jan. 25, 1911   Albany, Ore.   S. D. Yoder

Garden truck is very plentiful this year. L. B. Yoders have sold 200 quarts of currants for fifteen cents per quart.
> Aug. 7, 1912   Minot, N.D.   Mollie A. Yoder

Garden trucks are looking nice.
> Aug. 7, 1912   Exland, Wis.   Miss Katie Gingerich

The truckers are very busy cultivating and working at their spinach, kale, cabbage, etc.
> Nov. 13, 1912   Norfolk, Va.   Iddo D. Yoder

Harvesting: Cotton picking has started. It is a pretty good crop, and nice weather to open up the cotton, but not so pleasant for the picker as it is quite warm to work out in the sun.

Sept. 9, 1948   Aberdeen, Miss. .   Mrs. D. A. Miller

Harvest is about over on the binding part anyway. The combines are in full swing and the threshing machines will start out threshing shocks any day.

July 1, 1937   Haven, Kans.   William D. Yoder

A young farmer, David K. King, farming the Henry Lantz farm, was hauling in his fourth crop of hay. For all the joking remarks of passers-by and neighbors he continued hauling till it was all brought in.

Oct. 24, 1940   Lancaster County Briefs   Jonathan B. Fisher

I am digging my peanuts at present which are fine.

Nov. 1, 1916 .   Fentress, Va.   Sol King

Pulling and topping onions is the order of the day among the farmers.

Aug. 30, 1911   Hartville, Ohio   Fannie & Katie Kuhns

The writer has cut 1467 shocks of corn this fall among the farmers.

Oct. 11, 1911   Grabill, Ind.   Aaron L. Beiler

Putting up praire hay is the go now a days and is a good crop.

Aug. 14, 1912   Garnett, Kans.   C. J. Miller

The writer's father has been shocking grain for the last three weeks, can say everyday and is not done yet.

Sept. 11, 1912   Bloomfield, Mont.   Mrs. May Slabach

Wm. Schrock had his clover hulled yesterday, and it yielded 6 bushels to the acre.

Sept. 13, 1906   Comins, Mich.   Misses Annie Schlabach & Eva Yoder

I wish a good threshing outfit would come in here; there are nothing but "rattle traps" here.

July 12, 1900   Centralia, Mo.   J. D. Guengerich

Flax cutting has commenced and yields are very good.

Aug. 9, 1900   Petersburg, Ont.   M. J. Schlabach

Cutting broom corn is all the go now; it is a fair crop; some sold at $100 per ton. Broom corn hands are receiving $1.50 per day.

Sept. 6, 1900   Arthur, Ill.   M. G. Stoltzfus

Herman Freeman is cutting 50 acres with a combined outfit. . . .

July 31, 1924   Dodge City, Kans.   Mrs. Ida Gingerich

Insects & insecticides: Army worms were very destructive at places, and now that they have disappeared, the Japanese beetles are showing up.
June 21, 1951   Bayside, Va.   Mrs. Enos W. Yoder

Grasshoppers are raiding the countryside. Are more numerous this year than usual. Makes a person's mind wander to the plagues in the days of King Pharaoh.
Sept. 4, 1947   Berlin, Ohio   Sara Weaver

The muck farmers are having trouble with a new kind of worms, they just eat everything up where ever it is dry, the wet spots they don't bother so much.
·June 7, 1934   Uniontown, Ohio   Sarah & Cathryn Miller

Spray your young trees to keep them from blighting, and shake your plum trees every morning to keep off the insects.
June 14, 1900   Berlin, Ohio   Local news item

The Japanese beetles have done a lot of damage to the corn crop the previous summer. Some farmers report only a 50 per cent crop. Some of our farmers have planted hybrid and had a successful crop. S. J. would better take salesmanship for hybrid, because the famous Lanc. Co. Sure Crop is losing fight in this community. We had a hybrid salesman today and he was successful in making quite a few sales.
Oct. 26, 1939   Gap, Pa.   No name

The crop of oats bugs is larger than the crop of oats.
July 21, 1932   West Liberty, Ohio   Maude E. Peachey

Oats look exceedingly well at present, but the army worms are in this locality, doing a great deal of damage. Some fields they have almost cleaned up, leaving nothing but the bare stems....
July 23, 1896   Oakland, Md.   D. C. Schlabach

Don't know how much good it will do the people to plant their crops, as the grasshoppers seem to be terribly thick around here.
May 22, 1947   Campo, Colo.   Mrs. Delbert Miller

[The following excerpt was included in "Editor's Corner", but the farmer was not identified.] Please find enclosed 50 cents to renew my subscription which expires April 1. If God will let us have a wheat crop I may be able to send you a two-year subscription. We Kansas people had grasshoppers and drouth last year so we get short at both ends,

sometimes in $$ and sometimes in eatables, between crops. I don't like to be without your good, newsy paper."
Mar. 25, 1937

Marketing and sales: A big herd of cattle passed by our house yesterday. There were 256 head, which they loaded in the big city of Yoder to ship them to market. A man bought them in Texas and drove them north and pastured them on wheat pasture for the few months till now.
Jan. 24, 1935   Hutchinson, Kans.   Mrs. Sam R. Borntrager

Corn is selling at 12 cents a bushel, oats at 10 cents a bushel, and wheat at 35 cents a bushel. Eggs are 10 cents a dozen and cream is 15 cents a pound.
Mar. 9, 1933   Arthur, Ill.   Budget Readers

Quite a few chickens are going to market this morning paying 20 cents for old hens, 35 cents for young.
July 17, 1918   Fairview, Mich.   Mrs. M. S. Zook

In Sept. 1928, Lando Gingerich started to sell milk with one cow, a coaster wagon, and two customers. During the 18 years his dairy increased to 10 cows and approximately 125 customers.
Oct. 2, 1946   Kalona, Ia.   No name

Mechanization and new methods: Horse farmers have started to plow sod. I have not heard any tractors humming yet. We are living in a community which is becoming industrialized so fast each year there is less farming than the year before. Yes, even among our own people. It is also increasingly hard to make ends meet on the farm. When you think you can just about make it, someone moves the ends.
April 4, 1963   Middlefield, Ohio   Enos Miller

It was quite amusing to read about the horses vs tractors for farming. One I do know is the fleas do not take the sap out of a tractor, and another thing, a tractor cannot be used unmercifully as I have seen some horses being used.
April 27, 1961   Hutchinson, Kans.   Delila Nisly

Farming practices over these years have changed dramatically. Several thousand chickens and a dozen milk cows would not be considered practical at all. In fact, a decent egg market would not even be available today for a small operator. Back in the early 60's farmers in Lancaster County started building cage layer houses for some side income and the usual size flock was from 6,000 to 10,000 layers. They did quite well most years with a few dull, or should we say bad, years mixed in until around 1983. In the past three to five years most of these chicken houses have been cleared out and are being used for other purposes. Purchase of feed was at a premium for operators with less than a trailer load orders while egg prices were docked on houses with less than truck load shipments. Thus these farmers were being hit from both sides and could no longer compete. Taking their place in the market are some million bird operations with several being built right now. In a 25-year span we've seen the so-called Amish cage houses layer operations come and go again.

November 19, 1986   Ronks, Pa.   Levi A. Esh

When this modern method of farming came into practice, we lost much of the neighborly method of working together. I have some mighty fine English and Mennonite neighbors, (only one Amish land joiner) but we don't need each other so much anymore. My! how I used to enjoy working together threshing and filling silo, and gathering around the table the women had prepared for us hungry men. The fellowship we had together and the ideas we gleaned by working with our neighbors is now being replaced by State College and machines.

Mar. 9, 1961   Belleville, Pa.   Ezra Kanagy

You know I am too young to quit working and too old for the new systems. We live right in the heart of no-till country. Now, having been taught that one must cultivate corn to make it grow, I just can't believe that no-till can work, but it does.

July 2, 1980   Gambier, Ohio   Melvin L. Yoder

Weather: We didn't have any wheat to harvest this year as all of it was blown out this spring.

July 21, 1920   Kingsdown, Kans.   Miss Barbara Stutzman

Stock water is still somewhat scarce, but we are in hopes of plenty when the snow melts.

Feb. 27, 1902   East Lynne, Mo.   Eli Hostetler

Corn will be a total failure; it is all in tassels and is nice and green yet but has no ears on the stalk. It will soon be cut for fodder.

Aug. 1, 1901   Yoder, Kans.   D. M. Yoder

Weeds: Farmers were about all busy raking and burning Rus-

38

sian thistles all winter and some have started to put up ice now.

Feb. 17, 1921   Bloomfield, Mont.   Mrs. Isaac J. Coblentz

Destroying Canada thistles and potato bugs is the order of the day; it seems they come through the cold winter nicely.

June 29, 1899   Baden, Ont.   A Baden Boy

Vocabulary: Most of the oats *stooled* out after the hail....

July 11, 1917   Wainwright, Okla.   J. D. Yoder

The Goshen Hole orator called a meeting of the stock growers last Saturday, and it was decided to run a *shotgun wagon* again this year to gather up lost cattle, which got away from the ranchmen the past year.

Sept. 17, 1896   Bear Creek, Wyo.   W.M.

The work among the farmers is planting tobacco and *shovel harrowing* corn.

June 18, 1925   Leola, Pa.   Mrs. M. P. Stoltzfus

Farmers are busy making hay, cutting wheat and *laying by* corn.

July 3, 1902   Milford, Neb.   Susan L. Conrad

Unclassified: Farm sales are soon to start, and according to newspapers they will be   numerous the coming spring. Most everything is still at a high level in line of milk cows and farm machinery. Eggs, however, are on the decline and many farmers complain of sick chickens. My chickens are taking a long vacation, in fact, I have them only for barnyard pets, but they are expensive pets. No doubt the continuous change in the weather would be a good answer to our chicken troubles here.

Feb. 2, 1950   Gap, Pa.   John F. Glick

We are in the piggy business right now. Have 8 gilts with little ones but aren't doing too good. We lost quite a few already. Have them in our buggy shed and isn't very warm in there. So every so often Milo brings some in the house and sure doesn't smell too good around here.

April 5, 1989   Fredericktown, Ohio   Mrs. Milo J. Byler

There is quite a land boom here and land has gone up from $5 to $10 per acre. One farm of 320 acres, about 4 miles from here, bought 3 months ago for $30 was sold last week for $40 per acre to an Illinois man.

May 29, 1902   Centralia, Mo.   J. D. Guengerich

Some farmers in this and Stark Counties are very particular about keeping everything in the dry; they even keep the manure in the barn all winter, especially when they are going to move away in the spring. The writer succeeded one of these "particular" farmers. Peter Miller, who moved from Geauga Co., had some similar experience. I understand he hauled nine wagon loads out of one box-stall.

April 11, 1907   East Akron, Ohio   P. V. Yoder

It may be of interest to some of my friends in the United States if I describe a little what the people raise here. Very little corn is raised here; cattle do not run out in the corn fields all winter, and at night make shelter around the straw-stacks, like in Nebraska and Kansas, they are tied up in the barns and get their attention three times a day. Besides hay they get meals of chaff and turnips, bran mixed with salt to it which is a delicious food. Hogs are fed on peas; they have better pork here than in the states, because peas make more solid meat than corn.

Oct. 18, 1900   Tavistock, Ont.   L. S. Yoder

Ben C. Yoder is in trouble this year; he has already all his cribs full, the garret in the hog barn is full, and one large rail pen, and he is not near done husking. He says he can hardly scrape up enough rails and lumber to build cribs to hold all his corn.

Nov. 9, 1899   Kokomo, Ind.   G. W. North

We noticed that Ben C. Yoder of Kokomo, Ind. is in trouble in regard to his big crop. Mr. Yoder, let me just give you one word of consolation. You need not worry at all in regards to finding a place to put your corn, with which God has blessed you so abundantly. Perhaps if you look you can find some room in the cribs of poor neighbors, whom God has not prospered as he has you, to store some in, which if you will, you will have laid up treasures above, where you need not worry about. Should you not find such room, you again need not worry, sell your corn and put the proceeds in the usury (not for self) of God and let him use it as He and His cause will receive most glory therefrom, and remember, "a little in the fear of the Lord is better than great treasures and trouble therewith." (Prov. 15:16)

Nov. 23, 1899   Smithville, Ohio   Lucy A. Yoder

Amish, Amish Mennonite and Mennonite

To someone not initiated to the distinctions within the larger Amish, Amish Mennonite and Mennonite community the grouping named in the heading of the chapter may appear cumbersome and rather pointless. The differences, however, are very important to understanding some of the things scribes included in their letters as well as in the way the groups function and relate to each other. At the time THE BUDGET was first published, in 1890, the name Amish began to be limited to the "Old Order Amish" and closely related groups. Amish Mennonite came to be used of those who had strong Amish characteristics as far as appearance is concerned but had, in addition, adopted some of the features of Mennonites, especially in the kind and types of church services, use of meetinghouses, and technological features. Mennonite was a broad term covering many groups, from some quite conservative to others very progressive, or even quite liberal, according to some of the judgments expressed.

For more clarification on these distinctions read the Historical Introduction at the beginning of this volume.

Amish or Mennonite: In regard to the name of the denomination to which we belong, I find we differ.   To illustrate: In a certain county history are some of the names of our brethren, giving their occupation, religion, etc., some as belonging to the Amish, some to the Amish Mennonites and others to the Mennonite Church; three names and yet these brethren all belong to one church, and worship at the same place. Brethren, these things ought not to be so.

I hope the readers of the Budget are all Christians, (at least ought to be) but we are designated by some denominational name, let us have the same name. Our denominational name is *Mennonite*, not *Amish*, as some say, from the name Jacob Ammon. He (Jacob Ammon) was a Mennonite, as were all of his congregation; a strong defender of the same faith that Menno Simmons advocated, as it was in Christ Jesus; also of the Eighteen Articles of Faith, formed by the Mennonite people at Dort, A.D. 1632.

As there are several branches of Mennonites, it sometimes becomes necessary to state to which branch we hold; to which we reply, "Amish Mennonite." We think, however, that this name was given to us in derision; I think the sooner we conclude to omit the name *Amish*, the better, and have only the name *Mennonite*, to which we think we are entitled to, as much if not more so than any other people. While it sometimes becomes necessary to speak of our denominational name, let us not lose sight of Him who died for us, and of the "all things."

June 14, 1900   Ligonier, Ind.   Jonathan Kurtz

First, Jonathan Kurtz of Ligonier, Ind. writes to the Budget ... about the good old name, "The Amish Church." He says it is the "Mennonite Church." Now I do not like that, and no good Amish person likes it; it is not right. The Amish Church was formed before your grandfather was born. It is the name of one of the best churches in America. The Mennonite Church is entirely separate from it, and is a very good Christian Church, but no better than the Amish. When Jacob Aman separated from the Mennonite Church he did so from good reasons and his fellowmen were named there after him, and it has been loved and revered by many thousands since. Now, why should an upstart be made in this present day and question the right of these true Christian people to call themselves "The Amish Church?" Where would you find a better people; a more honest, true and religious people than the old Amish church? Every true Amish church member is proud of this venerable name, and in my candid opinion, that every member who does not like this honorable name ought to get out. The old Amish Church is just the same as the Methodist or any other church. Let me ask every true Amishman to scorn with the utmost contempt every effort to add or to take away from this good old name.

June 28, 1900   Chehalias, Wash.   Moses Yoder

In regards to what Moses Yoder ... says in regard to the Amish church, I would say, if he can give a good lawful reason for staying away from Amish Church privileges for over 30 years, then no doubt the Budget readers can have more faith in his profession of love and veneration for the church of his choice. I have nothing to say against the Amish Church; I believe the articles of faith adopted by the Mennonites and Amish as their creed are the nearest to the truth of the gospel of any church creed I know of. Those articles of faith were drawn up and adopted as a church creed in 1632. . . . They were believed in and taught by Menno Simons and afterwards by Jacob Aman. The good book does not teach us that we can get salvation through a church name, but only through the name of Jesus. Paul in his chapter to the Corinthians, reproves them for calling themselves after men. The Mennonites and Amish were so-called by their enemies, and it is well enough to have a name to distinguish between denominations, but we should not build on a man's name. [Hostetler corrected his mistaken statement that Menno Simons taught the 1632 Dortrecht Confession of Faith. Menno died in 1561. July 26, 1900.]

> July 12, 1900   East Lynne, Mo.   Eli Hostetler

To Moses Yoder . . . I would say, there is some written and a great deal of unwritten history of the Mennonite and Amish Churches since 1867, that has not come under your observation. [Kurtz had reference to the Amish division in the 1880's. See the Historical Introduction of this book.]

> July 12, 1900   Smithville, Ohio   A. K. Kurtz

We see what a discussion was brought forth by those having different opinions of church names. This is only an index of what would follow, were these columns open to the discussioin of the different religious denominations of the present, and also what endless complications the editor would get into, were he to publish all that was sent to him for publication touching religious subjects.

> Aug. 2, 1900   Smithville, Ohio   A. K. Kurtz

In the spirit that some of the letters on the subject were written, it has done more harm than good, and if anyone has anything further to say on the subject, let him do so by private correspondence, as these columns will not be open for its further discussion.

> Aug. 2, 1900   Editor's Corner

She was a peaceable member in the Old Amish Church. . . .

[He was writing about the passing of Malinda Yoder Wingard.]
Mar. 1, 1916   Thomas, Okla.   M. K. Yoder

Amish-Mennonite: The Amish and Mennonite congregations are getting considerably scattered over the whole North American continent, and we wish them all luck, happiness and prosperity; not only in temporal affairs, but most of all in their spiritual welfare, so that when the time arrives for the transition from this to that future and better world, all may be well.
Feb. 8, 1900   Amish, Iowa   S. D. Guengerich

Announcements of conferences:
Eastern Amish Mennonite Conference, Mattawana, Pa. May 31 - June 1
Ohio Mennonite Conference, Midway congregation, May 24, 25
Mennonite Church, Sterling, Ill., Science Ridge, May 30, 31
Indiana-Michigan Amish Mennonite, Clinton Brick, June 7, 8
Western Amish Mennonite Conference, Hubbard, Ore. June 8, 9
May 24, 1906

The Amish Mennonite Conference of Ohio and Pennsylvania, if the Lord will, shall be held in the Belleville Church, Mifflin Co., Pa., beginning on May 30th. All who are deeply interested in the salvation of souls and in promoting the cause of Christ are invited to attend.
May 16, 1901   Belleville, Pa.   Pre. Joseph Byler, contact person

We attended the A.M. Conference near Archbold last Wednesday and Thursday. Many good thoughts were presented out of God's Word. A large multitude of people were there, and it is said that 2,700 people took dinner there the first day.
June 11, 1925   Defiance, Ohio   Mrs. A. D. Miller

The Amish Mennonites had their counsel meeting at the Forks church on the 26th inst., and had a very good sermon by Daniel Johns.
Nov. 1, 1900   Middlebury, Ind.   Andrew E. Kauffman

The sewing circle of the Amish Church was held at the Central Church and was well attended, some 50 sisters were present.
Oct. 15, 1919   Archbold, Ohio   Anna Ma Short

44

Amish and Mennonite: The Amish and Mennonites until the year 1696 were one and the same church and both adhere to the same creed or confession of faith, differing only in a few minor points; the former maintaining a more strict discipline in regard to simplicity of dress and a few other minor points. [This statement appeared along with an explanation of Articles 13 and 14 in the Dortrecht Confession of Faith. It had first appeared in the *Holmes County Farmer* in May 1862.]

Aug. 29, 1917   Article submitted by Benjamin Weaver, Trail, Ohio

Amish in Europe: The consistent record of the Amish people as a stable religious group not given to much change has made them widely known, and probably more favorably respected in this country than they ever were in Europe. Over 200 years ago many of them came to America. But not all of them crossed the mighty ocean to come to this country. What happened to those Amish people who stayed in the Fatherland? Did they keep their distinctive life and principles? If not, why not? [This was the first paragraph of an article by John A. Hostetler entitled "The Last Amish Church in Deutschland." In column length it occupied about 57 inches.]

July 22, 1954   John A. Hostetler

He might be interested to know there was no such group in Europe known by this name at any time according to my observation. It is known that those who came over the ocean had no relations with any group left in Europe. [Miller took issue with Hostetler's article and called it a "perverted view of the Amish."]

Dec. 9, 1954   Millersburg, Ohio   C. S. Miller

[Two letters in German, apparently from Amish ministers of the Alsace, appeared in THE BUDGET in 1905. A letter from John Petersmitt was included in the issue of May 11, 1905, and one from Johann Gingerich in June 15, 1905.]

Amish way of life: Prof. Schreiber says the Amish are the only cultural group in America which has maintained its old world traditions in every phase of living. He recognizes that the economic and social forces engulfing them in present-day America are probably stronger than anything they have had to contend with in the past, but he believes there will always be Old Order Amish. [These were part of the comments by the Editor on the book, *Our Amish*

Neighbors by William I. Schreiber, Professor of German, College of Wooster.]
Dec. 13, 1962   Editor's Corner

There is much made of the Amish in our day, but when I was a boy the Amish were looked down upon and unpopular with the public as a whole. Now, much is written about the Amish, much ado is made about the Amish and Pennsylvania Dutch cooking, etc., which is nauseating to most of us and we certainly would not be making a Directory for the purpose of publicity or men's curiosity's sake.

However the Directory has a wide variety of uses. The 1970 Directory was made by the request and financial help of the Johns Hopkins Hospital at Baltimore for study of Genetics in hereditary diseases and tendencies that asked, "Why choose the Amish to study?" The answer was that no wide group of people have so complete and adequate genealogy information among themselves so suitable for study as the Amish have.

Then of course, the name and address and map information have a wide variety of uses. We realize, also, like anything else it could be used for evil purposes. Some fear the communists might use the information to find us out. Anyone knows, however, that when someone meets us on the street they can tell we are Amish. Also, the same way with our homes.

Feb. 6, 1980   Middlebury, Ind.   Eli Gingerich

The Amish pattern of life (where it is conscientiously lived) is hard to beat when it comes to holding a family together and keeping them on the farm. The advocates of the modern way of life have good sounding theories of how to make more money with less work. But first let them prove, not by theories, but by results, that they have something better as measured in terms of old-fashioned satisfaction from family living.

Mar. 2, 1961   Aylmers, Ont.   David Wagler

The old coach shop at Gap was sold some time ago and is being dismantled. This carriage shop was owned and operated by Miller and Simmons for 50 years or more, and now they are both old and decided to sell out. They were reliable and dependable, and had much respect for our people, and we regret their retirement. Listen folks, can you tell me of very many business men that worked

together as partners for 50 years? I don't think a pair of
Amishmen could!

> Jan. 23, 1964   Gap, Pa.   John F. Glick

Ammann-Reist controversy: I think there is far too much mis-
representation in the remarks made about these two men.
Why do we do these things? We have the history of both
these men, plain and clear, and available to all, so why cut
our own throats by making remarks that misrepresent?
Many insults and much bitterness could be avoided by
simply encouraging everyone to read the original, or by
quoting directly and fairly.

> Jan. 13, 1955   Dover, Dela.   Amos J. Gingerich

Boundaries: We hear through some of our English friends that
there may be other Amish people interested in our area,
perhaps only 6 to 8 miles away from us, although perhaps
not interested in communion with us. We hope this is not
true as it would be too close for expansion for either group
and this is one thing we tried to avoid when we picked this
area is getting into other church areas interfering with
their intended boundaries, etc. We feel it would be a
better light to our neighboring friends around us to all
commune together who live in one area. No harm meant
whatsoever, but written to avoid hard feelings later on.

> Oct. 12, 1977   Andover, Ohio   Levi L. Hershberger

"High" Mennonite: . . . left our church years ago for a "high"
Mennonite Church.

> Jan. 21, 1987   Waterloo, Ont.   Aaron & Barbara Weber

Mobility: This brings to five the number of Amish settlements
which have been made in Southern Ontario since 1953, and
indications are that there will be more before long. This
seems to be caused by a growing dissatisfaction among our
people in the States because of certain conditions such as
social security, draft, unfavorable school laws, and conditions in the world in general and in the churches.

> Sept. 8, 1955   Aylmer, Ont.   David Wagler

Names: Now, if he had tried in the name of Jacob Aman it would
have been a failure; if he tried in the name of Menno
Simons it would have been a failure; if he had tried in the
name of Martin Luther it would have been a failure, but in
the name of Jesus Christ there was power. [Mast was
referring to the healing of the crippled man; Acts 3:6.]

> May 27, 1909   Hutchinson, Kans.   D. E. Mast

47

Now in that great day, do we suppose that the door to the fold is going to open to any flock belonging to Menno and the other belonging to Ammon? (and how many more names could be added to denominational sects?) I say no, in the presence of that great Door all these names will have to flee.

July 19, 1900   Middlebury, Ind.   J. W. Bontrager

If I could I would change it! [Responding to the name Beachy Amish Mennonites, coming from the names of three men. Moses Beachy, Jacob Ammann and Menno Simons. Jacob was a Beachy Amish Mennonite minister.]

June 28, 1962   Lynnhaven, Va.   Jacob J. Hershberger

New Mennonites: The New Mennonites are holding a series of meetings at present.

Oct. 19, 1899   Logan, Mich.   SPORT

The New Mennonites closed their meetings last Wednesday evening.

Jan. 21, 1904   Jet, Okla.   Mamie and Maude Troyer

Stuckey Amish: The Stuckey Amish Church building was dedicated last Sunday; quite a large number were present.

Sept. 25, 1902   Hopedale, Ill.   J. C. S.

THE BUDGET: According to our judgment, the majority of the Budget subscribers are from the Amish Mennonite congregations; therefore the Budget may be termed an Amish paper, or at least supported in its circulation and correspondence mostly by the Amish. Therefore the Budget should be a model little family paper....

Feb. 8, 1900   Amish, Iowa   S. D. Guengerich

"Amish Pike" was a name used informally in some communities, but Madison County, Ohio, has a road officially so named.

Animals were a vital part of the life of the agriculturally based readers of THE BUDGET. For the Amish, farming operations and community transportation were based on animals for the full century. Wild animals served as a supplement to the diet and even income. Throughout the century, hunting, fishing and trapping were forms of recreation. The heavy dependence of the readers upon domestic animals and their practical views of wildlife led to some interesting experiences and expressions.

Attitudes and values expressed: The birds are very happy these days.

Oct. 9, 1958   Fairfax, S.C.   Mrs. Alvin Kropf

The driving horse of Bishop and Mrs. Sam Graber decided the town of Grabill needed a little sweetening up as she started out running while they were loading a chair. . . . [Scattered 100 pounds of sugar on the streets of Grabill.]

Oct. 15, 1953   New Haven, Ind.   Anna Kauffman

Some women around here have incubators and hens setting. We are hoping that the weather will be warmer before they hatch, else it will keep us busy knitting stockings for them.

Mar. 29, 1916   Garden City, Mo.   Mamie Pearl Schrock

A yearly steer committed suicide for N. J. Schlabach Saturday night.

Mar. 18, 1914   Brush Run, Ohio   Local news item

Jonas Beechy has two Parrots and one of them calls the dog.

Aug. 9, 1911   Millersburg, Ohio   Noah S. Yoder

I sold our family cow yesterday to the butcher and took her to town today, then went and bought another one and took her along home, so we haint out of milk after all.

April 27, 1922   Middlefield, Ohio   E. M. Hochstetler

The mule sale was quite large this year; over 800 head of

the long-eared things, plus some horses. Top price paid was about $5600.00 for a team of mules.

Jan. 21, 1987   Nunnelly, Tenn.   Lester Graber

A neighbor complained of three of her big fat chickens dying and she can't tell why, as there is no disease among them. Now my poultry book says that whenever an old chicken gets overly fat, it will die. I have seen so much of this that I believe it to be correct. It is always the big fat one that dies, unless disease gets among them.

June 16, 1904   Smithville, Ohio   Dr. J. L. Miller

A lot of young girls of upper Pequea -- 6 in number went to the husking at Henry Lapps of Centerville, Tuesday, on a spring wagon, with only one horse. I suppose the girls had a better time than the horse.

Nov. 16, 1899   Ronks, Pa.   A Subscriber

I wish I would have taken note of the cars of hunters that passed the last few minutes as I am jotting these lines. I am sure there were 25 or 30 at least - 6 at a time. I do not pity the innocent deer, just so no one gets hurt or lost.

Nov. 21, 1929   Mio, Mich.   Mrs. E. S. Troyer

If we kill snakes they will not die until sun down. I rather think it was the black snake that talked to Eve, but she ought to listen to what God had told her. Many people throw their snakes on a brush pile when it is in flame, but I could not do that, it reminds me of hell on this earth.

Mar. 20, 1918   Meyersdale, Pa.   S. S. Summy

Health and care: All dogs in Mifflin Co. are under quarantine. Those not muzzled or tied will be shot. These precautions have been taken to prevent the spread of hydrophobia, as quite a number of wild dogs have been at large, biting everything they came in contact with.

Sept. 23, 1910   Belleville, Pa.   Cor.

Daniel Esh Jr. had an exciting experience at his home on Sunday morning. He was in the horse stable when a mad dog fell through the strawhole into the stable. There was a mare with a small colt in the stable and the dog tried to bite them but it is not known if it succeeded or not. Dan called to his wife to ring the bell, which she did, and soon a half a dozen neighbors arrived upon the scene, and after procuring a gun the dog was shot in the stable. The colt has since died, and the mare is kept securely tied.

April 25, 1901   Gordonville, Pa.   John H. Kauffman

The recent mad dog scare has caused a law to be passed, that every dog in Ontario must be chained or safely muzzled for a period of eleven months.

Feb. 25, 1910   Brunner, Ont.   Ezra Nafziger and Elia Roes

Some people are losing horses by the blind staggers. Eli M. Yoder lost a double team this week; L. W. Yoder lost one, and M. E. Yoder also lost one.

Sept. 21, 1922   Princess Anne, Va.   Mary Miller

There are still some horses dying of fodder poisoning.

Mar. 20, 1912   Latour, Mo.   Sarah E. Hershberger

Last week we received a request from a reader for a remedy for moon-blindness in horses.

Mar. 2, 1961   Aylmer, Ont.   David Wagler

Horse stories: I recently had occasion to have a ride with one of our young people who is said to have the fastest driving horse of any of our people in this county. We traveled at the rate of approximately a mile in 2:40. I do not wish to give the name of the driver and owner, other than to say his parent's initials are "A.E." . . . . The animal is a handsome young bay mare with flowing jet black mane and tail. That kind is not to be found just every day.

April 29, 1948   Lancaster County Briefs   Jonathan B. Fisher

[The *Middlefield News*, in speaking of the races at Burton on June 25th, has the following about a horse owned by D. M. Miller of Troy:] "One of the races was greatly enlivened by the appearance of a mare driven by an Amishman, which apparently could not go very fast, but soon demonstrated that she was the fastest in the bunch - - Belle, owned by D. M. Miller of Troy, and this was her first race. She has never been trained and has been used about the ordinary work on the farm. The few who knew her were aware that she has great natural speed and as a three-year old stepped a quarter in 35 seconds. She came to town Saturday night hitched to a milk wagon, and appeared in the race in an old high-wheel cart and heavy farm harness and was baited between heats on grass by the trackside. (Reprinted from *Middlefield News* under the heading "Amish Dark Horse is a Fast One.")

July 12, 1910

Bro. Hershberger stayed but one week, while Bro. Yoder and I stayed three weeks, and took a general view of the country. As we had a mule team for two days whose rate of traveling was two miles per hour we therefore had plenty of time to size up that part of the country. [Bender was describing a visit to Bay Minette, Ala.]

Mar. 20, 1912   ElkLick, Pa.   Valentine Bender

Horse buyers are getting quite plentiful but only such that will come up to a certain standard which of course means horses for war.

Oct. 20, 1915   Tuleta, Tex.   C. C. Schrock

An advice of fifty years ago as to how to choose a good horse stated: "A horse that is wide between the eyes, honest and true; narrow and full between them, tricky; a hump between the ears on top of head, if it extends high on its sides next to the ears, shows activity, if low, the other way." Some phrenology to live by! Years ago a well-known horseman would go along a line of horses in a sale barn (Blue Ball) and raise each horse's tail. If stiff it denoted toughness. If limber, easily fatigued. A slogan gives it: "One white foot, buy him. Two white feet, try him."

Aug. 19, 1948   Lancaster County Briefs   Jonathan B. Fisher

Unbelievable things do happen sometimes, for instance, driving a different horse home from church than you drive to it, and not knowing it until after arriving home.

Nov. 24, 1976   Burton, Ohio   Mrs. Olin A. Yoder

After church when Eli J. Miller wanted to go home, he couldn't find his horse and so he decided to stay overnight, but when most of the people had gone one horse remained, which proved to be Eli's.

Dec. 14, 1922   Brush Run, Ohio   Local item.

Names of animals: [The names of animals finding their way into THE BUDGET were not as many as might be expected. The ones found are summarized below:]

A driving horse: Old Bill   Jacob S. Yoder, Charm, Oh 1913
Twin colts: Dewey and Lady   Elma Mast, Altus, Okla. 1913
Horses: Snap   Daniel Girod, Canaan, Ind. 1987
      Napolean   Mrs. Edwin Miller, Minier, Ill. 1900
      Alice   Uria Byler, Huntsburg, Ohio 1980
      Theodore   Ray Weaver, Mifflintown, Pa. 1954
      Robert   Ray Weaver, Mifflintown, Pa. 1955
      Old Banner   Jacob Eicher, Camden, Mich. 1977
      Jeanie   Cephas Kauffman, Aylmer, Ont. 1977
      Four Winds

Bull: Jasper	Mrs. John Ressler, Elkton, Minn. 1980
Dogs: Ginger	Steven Nissley, Fishersville, Va. 1980
Shep	1960
Max	Uria R. Byler, Huntsburg, Ohio 1980
Pet wolf: Billikens	Elma Mast, Altus, Okla. 1913

Rodents and pests: A neighbor who partitioned off part of his old straw shed for poultry noticed holes in the partition and his water fountains and feed hoppers being drained through the night so he made slides so he could close the holes from the outside. One evening after putting out the lights, they went in with several dogs, and killed 100 of the rodents, the bunch weighed 75 lbs. Who can beat it?

Feb. 4, 1943   Wilmot, Ohio   E. J. Miller

The biggest pests we are having now are rats and rabbits. I wish some of you Ohio hunters were here a while, I would pay you to shoot the rabbits and just let them lay. I never saw the like. I guess we should get up a rat hunt like they have there in Ohio.

Mar. 21, 1940   Kalona, Ia.   Daniel J. Glick

If anybody would like to be entertained in a social way, just come in our Progressive Valley where the 17 year locusts give their daily concerts.

June 18, 1931   Fresno, Ohio   Local news

In regard to the question whether there are any mosquitos here, will say, they are not bad, and I would not want to live where there is not enough moisture that some mosquitos could live.

July 5, 1910   Ordway, Colo.   Amos Stutzman

The pocket gophers are getting to be a detriment to the alfalfa in this country and the farmers are getting rid of them pretty fast. The writer's father, V.D. is busy trapping, and he has now caught 146 gophers in a little less than three weeks.

April 14, 1904   Haven, Kans.   D. M. Yoder

Unusual: The writer's pet cat caught a little chipmunk or grinny, as they are called, this morning and it was almost white all over.

Oct. 30, 1912   Bunker Hill, Ohio   Mrs. Daniel Middaugh

The latest pet around here is a white mouse with pink eyes, which the boys found under a corn shock while husking.

Feb. 14, 1963   Ashland, Ohio   No name

Wild animals: Last week one night Levi heard a noise in the basement as tho something was romping across the cellar floor. On investigation, he discovered that several muskrats had entered the cellar thru the drain tile and were busy helping themselves to the celery which had been stored there. They escaped down the tile, but later, he managed to take them by surprise and captured two.

Feb. 21, 1957   Aylmer, Ont.   David Wagler

Quite a few snakes have been seen (and killed) this Spring. Am not sure if they're just coming out to sun themselves or to test the newcomer's courage.

Oct. 20, 1976   Caaguazu, Paraguay   Mrs. Paul Eichorn

Mrs. Willard Shellhorn . . . saw a rattlesnake close to the house. She got a hoe and chopped off the rattler's head. Next she cut off the rattles and picked up the body and tossed it away. Forgetting an old-timers tale that rattlesnakes heads live long after they are dead, she picked up the head, which promptly bit her thumb.

July 6, 1977   Garnett, Kans.   Susie Beachy

[Urie Byler approached some crippled buzzards. To protect themselves several flew towards him about twenty feet above ground level.] . . . and throwing up as they came. I ran to escape that white stream of stink, but some hit me anyway . . . never in all my born days did I ever smell anything like that.

April 30, 1980   Huntsburg, Ohio   Urie Byler

Last evening son Menno's were here for supper, and at 10:30 we were hitching up for them to go home. The train went by and the sound of the whistle went far out in the country. After it was silent we heard a few coyotes howl about 80 rods off. It was enough to make the shivers go down your back. A train whistle at night is apt to make them howl.

Feb. 16, 1950   Haven, Kans.   Leander S. Keim

The writer received a live alligator from William J. Overholt in Florida. He is just doing fine and people have been here from all directions to see it, and those who haven't seen him yet are welcome to come and take a look as long as I have possession of him. He is a curiosity for this part of the continent.

Mar. 25, 1926   Montgomery, Ind.   Harvey Wagler

54

It seems that the wolves are getting to be quite tame as they can be seen playing in the fields in the daytime. Yesterday morning they were seen playing between Emery Yoders and Dave Millers.

Jan. 10, 1912   Latour, Mo.   Susan Hershberger

Last week one morning Grandma saw our whole herd of calves jump over the fence. She told Grandpa that our calves had just jumped over the fence. The "calves" turned out to be 10 deer. It was just at dawn so it was very easy to mistake them for calves.

Mar. 11, 1987   Jay County, Ind.   Fannie Schwartz

Mel Weavers who live in the woods back at our place, are enjoying an interesting visitor at their squirrel feeder the past week. A large black bear is coming down from the mountain every night and helps himself to the corn which is placed right outside the house for the squirrels. Now when it comes to eating corn on the cob, Mr. Bear is the undisputed champion in this neighborhood. The other night he ate 22 ears of corn and topped this off with a generous helping of table scraps. The bears in this area are usually very shy, but this one doesn't seem to mind when Mel shines on him with a spotlight.

April 8, 1987   Beaver Springs, Pa.   Mrs. Emery Weaver

Unclassified: Recently an unusual thing happened. Four cows in pasture found their way into a small furnished house, that was only used part time to live in. They bumped the furniture around in such a way that it closed the door and they couldn't get out again. Were in for awhile, nobody knows how long, I guess. But they were almost starved when discovered of their plight by a neighbor man while mowing hay (Joe E. Miller). They had chewed up the mattress and bedding and what not. You can imagine how the house looked and when removed the cows were offered some hay and two of them just stared at it and would not eat anymore and died.

June 27. 1963   Topeka, Ind.   Mrs. Jerome Hochstetler

Abe Weaver has a cow that sucks herself. He tried to wean her and finally gave up. The other morning Tab looked out the window and there was Robert, the horse, sucking his cow. Tab says, "Anyhow we get enough milk to use." Tab you must give the horse and cow credit for having good common sense for not drinking all the milk."

July 14, 1955   Mifflintown, Pa.   Ray Weaver

Bro. Noah had the fortune of catching a jack rabbit in his hands, which was running at high speed through his corn field while he was husking.

Dec. 14, 1922   Hutchinson, Kans.   Mrs. Susan Yutzy

John S. Yoder has the best cow in the state of Michigan. She gave birth to three calves.

Mar. 18, 1914   Mio, Mich.   Mrs. M. S. Zook

Mahlon Yoders have a mama cat that is nursing 2 little wild rabbits along with her kittens.

April 1, 1987   Dixon, Mo.   Monroe D. Miller

The most remarkable freak ever born in Howard Co. was reported by Dr. J. O. Greeson, the local veterinarian. On the C. C. Willits farm a Durham cow gave birth to a calf that had a double complement of heads, forelegs, and bodies back to the hips. At the pelvic arch the two bodies became one. There was but one pair of hips and only two hind legs, though there were two tails the termini of two spinal columns. There was also a double complement of internal organs, and Dr. Greeson is of the opinion that they would have performed their functions normally could the creature have been born alive.

June 2, 1904   Greentown, Ind.   T. L. Miller

Moses Weaver has a calf a few weeks old which has five legs. Much attention is given to it and many people come to see it. The extra leg is on top of the neck or rather between the shoulders and hangs down on the side of the shoulder and can be placed from one side to the other. It is limp where it joins the body, but the rest of the limb is stiff, with a bone in it and has the shape of a hind leg. He has been offered two hundred dollars for it.

April 7, 1904   Davidsville, Pa.   Levi J. Kauffman

This scribe was seeding down some wheat with grass seed yesterday morning, when a sight behind our barn caught his attention. A 13-year old boy was making a B-line through the pasture field, with our year-old ram close to his heels. He made it on top of a fence post before he got hit.

Mar. 25, 1987   Andover, Ohio   Levi Hershberger

M. J. Yoder lost two of his blood hounds last week. He keeps them on his farm most of the time. Last Thursday one of the old hounds got out and was going towards Oyster Point, where she was found dead beside the road, and it is supposed she was struck by an automobile.

Feb. 5, 1925   Oyster Point, Va.   Mrs. S. H. Glick

We had some hungry dogs on our porch on Sunday night. We had some covered dishes with meat, etc. on the porch to keep cool. When my wife came to pack my lunch the meat was all gone including some of the dishes were dragged away and haven't found them yet.

Nov. 30, 1977   Mifflintown, Pa.   Floyd Yoder

Heavy work horses are central to farm work and highly prized. Sometimes they got out of pasture such as these in Lancaster County, Pennsylvania.

Births and Baptisms 6

The announcement of births took some unusual forms prior to 1950, judged from current standards. For one thing, it was customary to mention only the father by name, with the mother and child unnamed. The announcement below by Mrs. John D. Yoder was the first one found which included the name of the child. It took another decade or two before the name of the mother became prominent in birth announcements.

The descriptions of the father's response or reaction to the birth appear most unusual, especially in view of the fact that the mother was not named. Little information was given about the mother's response. Some of the things ascribed to the fathers are humorous and hilarious. It was one way of expressing self-satisfaction or perhaps of being acceptably proud.

Adult baptism has been one of the foundational beliefs and practices of the Amish and Mennonite Churches. Baptism in the Amish Church was a rite usually requested by the young people in their late teen-age years. In the Mennonite Church in the twentieth century the age was lowered to ages ten to fourteen.

A period of instruction class preceded baptism. Attending these classes with the intention of being baptized was called in Pennsylvania German, "Die Gma noch gay." The Anglicization of that led to "following the church." The origin of the expression is not clear, but it has been used widely in Amish circles as the following excerpts will show. Since the Amish meet in homes and the services are rotated among the members, the term might well have had its origin in the change of location of the services. Sometimes the phrase "joining the church" was used to mean the same thing. The latter was more likely to be used among Amish Mennonites and Mennonites than among the Amish.

The articles in the Dortrecht Confession of Faith were the basis for instruction prior to 1950, and even yet among the Amish. The young people were instructed in the basis beliefs of the church and the ordnung, or regulations of the congregation. By the time of baptism, the young people were expected to be in conformity with the ordnung.

Baptism and church membership went hand-in-hand. It was not a matter of being baptized and then after a period of decision becoming a member of the congregation.

Announcements of births: Born to Menno Yoder and wife a son named Samuel.

July 7, 1920   Elk Lick, Pa.   Mrs. John D. Yoder

Peter J. Kramer is sitting on the south side of his house on the fence, telling the people it is a boy.

Oct. 17, 1901   Plain City, Ohio   TWO BOYS

Joseph Yoder walks on top-toe and says, it's a girl.

Nov. 9, 1899   Yoder, Kans.   It Was Us

V. D. Miller is all smiles and says it is a cook in the "shanty".

Aug. 2, 1906   Mantua, Ohio   Joe J. Yoder

The county is increasing fast in population. A little dishwasher was added to the family of D. D. Schlabach, one to the family of S. K. Detweiler and a little cornhusker to the family of Joseph Schlabach....

May 19, 1892   Partridge, Kans.   Noah Helmuth

The other morning V. S. Hostetler stuck his head in the rain barrel and hollered "pap" uncommonly loud. We boys were brightly astonished at the idea, but with a little further information we learned it was on account of that little boy that came to stay with him.

Aug. 14, 1902   Mt. Ayr, Ind.   Willie D. & Phineas Miller

The stork visited at Abe Millers and left a baby girl to stay with them last week. Sometime earlier he brought a barefooted woodcutter to Joe Millers.

Dec. 1, 1921   Lizzie Boley

Andy Miller doesn't know on which side to wear his hat, for it is a 10 lb. boy.

Oct. 26, 1899   Smithville, Ohio   T. L. Miller

Three young hay makers arrived in this vicinity lately, one stopped at Jacob Roggies, one at Solomon Widricks and the other at Joseph J. Zehrs.

Aug. 3, 1905   Croghan, N.Y.   Lena R. Moser

We recently noticed a two by four smile on the face of S. G. Shetler since the arrival of a young son at his place.

July 3, 1912   Hollsopple, Pa.   Cor.

J. I. Miller is an inch taller since that little plowboy came to his home.

June 29, 1899   Corn, Okla.   Miss Lydia Yoder

Often, when a new-born babe is reported, it is said: Mr. and Mrs. so-and-so are the "proud" parents of a little son, or daughter, as the case may be. I have been made to wonder whether we really know, or understand the meaning of the word "proud"? Webster defines the word as having an inordinate self-esteem, possessing a high or unreasonable consent (sic) of one's own excellence, either of body or mind: haughty, etc. The translation in German is "stoltz".

April 8, 1937   Fairbank, Iowa   Joe Borntrager

An unusual midwife: For the past 28 years, Barbara Hostetler's neat, comfortable and modest Amish farm home at 8154 S. Apple Creek Rd., Fredericksburg, has been the birthplace of an estimated 7,000 infants with many of them now mothers and fathers.

The home has been a birthing center for many Amish women from Wayne and Holmes counties and beyond to have their babies delivered by a doctor in a home-like atmosphere and then received necessary rest and relaxation under Hostetler's expert care.

The unique home occupation for Bill Barb, as she is known throughout the community, began 40 years ago when she started to help prospective mothers during natural childbirth, a traditional way of life for Amish women. After 12 years of assisting with births, Bill Barb found it more convenient to bring soon-to-be mothers to her house instead of going to theirs.

Doctors who treat the Amish found themselves called more and more often to the home and it soon became a birthing center. "It just grew more and more," said Bill Barb, who has become somewhat of a legend among the Amish and Mennonites. Without Bill Barb, some not using hospital facilities would choose unattended home deliveries.

Aug. 14, 1985   Marcia Troyer

[Barbara's announcement of her "retirement" led to the formulation of plans for some suitable alternative. With Amish and community help the new non-profit Mt. Eaton Care Center was constructed. It is located just south of Mt. Eaton on Winesburg Rd. It is an 8-room clinic providing the services similar to those which were provided at the Hostetler home, but in modern facilities. Two Mennonite doctors serve the care center, which may see as many as 300 births annually.

Barbara was not a licensed midwife, but she had received plenty of instructions from doctors who came to her house. The patients had great faith in her judgment and were well-pleased with the arrangements.]

Baptism: Thirty six converts were baptized last Sunday at South
Union. There are yet eight who will be baptized at the
stream as soon as weather permits.

April 19, 1906   Round Prairie, Ohio   Ellen King

There are eleven young boys and girls joining church this summer in the North District.

June 4, 1925   Plain City, Ohio   Two Readers

The young folks who are following the King Church will be baptized. . . .

Sept. 27, 1923   Hartville, Ohio

Sunday, Jan. 31, 1932, 37 young people were baptized at the Central A.M. Church and three taken in the church again.

Feb. 4, 1932   Archbold, Ohio   Mrs. Jos. S. Short

Our people gathered at Dea. D. J. Millers on the 10th, where we worshipped together, and where eight children made the wise choice to accept Christ as their personal Saviour.

May 14, 1936   Hutchinson, Kans.   N. D. Mast

Thirty-three souls were baptized into church fellowship last Sunday by water baptism at the Sycamore church.

Dec. 10, 1908   Garden City, Mo.   Nettie Miller

A series of meetings were held last week and part of this, in the Stahl M.H. by Pre. S. F. Coffman of Elkhart, Ind. 11 young souls became willing to renounce the world and its allurements and join the army of God. They will be baptized today. (Thursday)

Jan. 18, 1900   Davidsville, Pa.   Levi J. Kauffman

Last Friday night, after communion service was dismissed, one of our sisters expressed her desire of being re-baptized, as she had backslidden after she was baptized at the age of 11 years, and was taken into our church by confession of faith, without baptism. She had convictions that she needs to be baptized after repenting, according to Acts 2:38, 39. So before the group went home we had a short baptismal service. She says she is much happier now, and that she had longed to be baptized before, but was afraid of what people might say, but the convictions wouldn't leave her.

Feb. 23, 1950   Calico Rock, Ark.   Mrs. M. E. Bontrager

I received a most unexpected Christmas present this year but one that was most welcome. One of my sisters, just younger than I , has accepted the Lord as her personal Saviour and was baptized. Of course, having been a Catholic, she had been baptized as a baby but she too was dissatisfied with the teachings of that church and is trying to learn more of the real teachings of Christ as found in the Bible.

Jan. 9, 1964   Hicksville, Ohio   Mrs. Eli E. Mullet

Yesterday there were 60 young people baptized at Central church in forenoon; 29 at the Lockport church in the afternoon, and 25 at the Clinton in the evening. There were also 10 reinstated that had drifted away. May they remain steadfast and true to their vows and be faithful to the end. [Mrs. Joseph Short, a scribe of Archbold, Ohio, gave the numbers as follows: Central 61, Lockport 32, Clinton 26, and nine reinstated.]

April 20, 1933   Prattville, Mich.   Mrs. A D. Miller

Blunders and Misprints 7

Misprints and blunders are sometimes collectively called bloopers. Since the word "blooper" is still classified as slang it will be avoided. These misprints and blunders are divided into three categories in this chapter. The first and most obvious group are the apparent misprints, caused by one or more of the following: insufficient or incorrect information supplied by the scribe, a mistake by the type setter, or a failure of the proof reader to spot the inaccuracy.

The reader must remind himself of the fact that even in the 1980's the number of scribes submitting letters in typewritten form is a minority. Before 1950 there would have been few, if any, who used the typewriter. Many of the hand-written letters were prepared with pencil. Currently the scribes are urged to use lined paper of a standard size, which helps reduce the number of blunders.

The first selection in this collection of excerpts resulted in a profuse apology the following week. The scribe was writing about butchering chickens, as most readers would suspect. In some cases the word which the scribe apparently wanted to use is placed in [brackets] by the author.

> Last Wed. forenoon some of us women and Menno Erb butchered 145 children in Menno Erb's butcher house. [chickens]
>
> October 22, 1986   Sugarcreek, OH   Mrs. Emma A. Yoder

> Bun butchered 3 more guilts today with the help of his neighbors. [gilts]
>
> Feb. 6, 1980   Hartville, MO   J. T. Wickey

> Most cotton growers have finished their first picking and have begun on the second. I noticed by official report that nearly 3,000 males have been shipped out of Allendale Co. [bales]
>
> Sept. 22, 1955   Fairfax, SC   Mrs. Alvin Kropf

...the broiler section near Gainsville. Some time ago that city passed an ordinance that whoever eats fried chicken with knife and work is subject to a fine, as the fingers are to be used. [fork]

July 13, 1961   Montezuma, GA   Mrs. Enos W. Yoder

A dog rain in front of them, throwing both boys. (The boys were riding bicycles.) [ran]

Nov. 1, 1962   Uniontown, OH   Savilla Lapp

If only there could be some kind of a low passed to outlaw this awful drinking. [law]

Jan. 9, 1964   Phoenix, AZ   Tom Byler, Jr.

A misprint in my last letter - - there were 54 present, instead of 544, when my wife's side of the house were together the other Saturday.

Aug. 29, 1963   Belleville, PA   Ezra Kanagy

A number of young people attended the drunkard meeting at Baumtown, on Sunday. [Dunkard]

July 27, 1922   Elverson, PA   Lena Stoltzfus

All these cholls are having two weeks vacation. [schools]

Jan. 10, 1924   Chappell, NE   Mrs. C. S. Yoder

There was a bad mistake in my last letter in May 28 issue. I wrote today 52 years ago, Daniel Johns was ordained a minister, and it was printed, Doctor Johns. I think it must have been the printer's mistake.

June 22, 1933   Topeka, IN   Mrs. Polly King

I had a big mistake in my letter last week, about my nephew, John H. Miller, that had a fall. I had in my letter that he was 19 years old, but he is 91 years old.

Feb. 9, 1933   Topeka, IN   Mrs. Polly King

I want to correct the mistake I made in my last letter. They have 25,000 ducks now for layers and between 40,000 and 45,000 that they butcher instead of 4,500. [She had given the number as 2,500 ducks. This was following a visit to the "duck farm" near Lancaster, PA.]

Feb. 17, 1938   Monroe, IN   Sarah Schwartz

Herman Eichorn, who had be redivering milk, for the last year, quit now. [delivering]

April 13, 1944   Clarence, NY   Mrs. Susie Weirich

Visitors were the Edgar Helmuths from Costa Rica. They are spending some time here white washing at the carpenter trade.

Sept. 7, 1977   Whiteville, Tenn.   E. Lloyd Mast

64

The second group involves confusion resulting from the failure to write clearly, which includes both penmanship and grammar. Penmanship is included because the letters were handwritten in most cases.

> I think N. Helmuth of Hutchinson, is mistaken about Lawrence Sweitzer, that he died of smallpox, if you learn the true story you will know that he did not have the smallpox, and he is living, and has about recovered from his illness.
>
> Mar. 22, 1901   Yoder, KS   D. M. Yoder

> Name of man with runaway should have been given as Yost J. Byler instead of Yost K. Byler
>
> June 6, 1907   Middlefield, OH   E. M. Hochstetler

> Simon J. Millers now have twelve goats including the twin kids - - not "twin babies" like the editor had stated in one of my letters. But mistakes are no haystacks, or it would have been a big one.
>
> July 2, 1930   Glen Flora, MI   Barbara Borntrager

> In an article of my last letter, it was stated that I wanted to talk to George Maggert's over the 'phone but they had no 'phone, like old mother Hubbard's dog. This should have read, that I wanted to talk to George Maggerts over the 'phone, but they had no 'phone, so I had to do without, like old Mother Hubbard's dog.
>
> Mar. 16, 1905   Seville, OH   T. L. Miller

The third group gives examples of unintentionally passing on information that is incorrect.

> News was spread last week that Harley Coblentz was married, but found today it was gossip.
>
> Nov. 2, 1933   Mylo, ND   Gladys & Viola Borntrager
> Freeda Schwiertert

> In regard to the "Joseph Armstrong" in "Light from Heaven", I wish to correct a report that is prevalent here and likely in other places as well, that he is considered as being a Mennonite preacher living in Knoxville, Tennessee, by the name of _____. I have been kindly informed by a relative that the above is incorrect and that _____ originated from the Catholics, which is in contrast to the facts in the serial.
>
> Feb. 19, 1948   Lynnhaven, VA   Mrs. Enos W. Yoder

65

Booming and Blowing 8

A first glance at the chapter title might cause raised eyebrows for some readers. Booming and blowing, however, were terms used frequently prior to 1910 on the pages of THE BUDGET. Before 1910 there was still land to be claimed for settling on it or for a very reasonable cash price. The search for cheap land and good locations led to the establishment of numerous Amish and Mennonite communites between the Mississippi River and the Rocky Mountains, as well as a few along the west coast.

In order to attract additional settlers the scribes resorted to bragging about their region, embellishing the good points, and in many cases neglecting to mention the disadvantages. This exaggeration of good points and the intentional omission of the unfavorable ones was referred to as "booming one's country" or "blowing", the latter of which is closely related to the figure of speech, "hot air". Whether the ethics of booming and blowing were addressed on the congregational level was not detectable from the letters of the scribes.

THE BUDGET was the one medium by which these people could communicate with other communities in their appeal for additional settlers to join them and strengthen their struggling settlements. The value of THE BUDGET in this type of communication has not been fully appreciated or assessed.

This section will be introduced with some examples of the ways in which the terms were used. These will be followed by some excerpts illustrating the booming of particular communities.

Usage of terms: The letters of the Budget are written from a great many states, but I think Kansas is making the biggest blows of all. And it needs it too.
>   Mar. 23, 1893   Milford, Neb.   Lettmer G. Galager

It is amusing to hear a certain class of people blow about their countries. If a person was ignorant of the fact that the "Garden of Eden" was closed long ago, they would have people believe it was still accessible. We have heard all you have got, now let us hear what you haven't got.

June 27, 1895   East Brook, Pa.   BOWSER

We are well satisfied with our locality, although we have a few that are inclined to find fault with this country; such is the case in all new countries. I put the question to all the readers of the Budget, where is the country that no men are finding fault to the country they are located in? God made the whole world and called it good; I have no right to condemn what God made. If we do our duty God will add his blessing.

Aug. 6, 1896   Corn, Okla.   M. K. Yoder

I agree with Mr. D. K. Byler of Belleville, I believe our country is as good as any, and a little better than some of those brag countries, I believe in letting a country brag for itself, and not the inhabitants.

Aug. 13, 1896   Keim, Pa.   Joel J. Yoder

In a former issue of the Budget we noticed a request from Brownstown, Ill. for some news from this place. We don't know much to write now; if we were in some new Western state we might blow about the country.

Aug. 13, 1896   Goshen, Ind.   E. S. Troyer

Since our correspondents occasionally indulge in a good deal of blowing and bragging about their respective countries, telling what good crops they can raise, what a good stock country it is, etc. etc. When we receive such a letter we turn to our subscription book and see whether the subscribers in that particular good country have all paid their subscriptions in advance. If this is the case we conclude that the correspondent has not exaggerated things very much. But on the other hand, if the subscribers are nearly all in arrears we conclude that it must not be quite as good as reported, or the subscribers do not care to pay up; there's a screw loose somewhere. Some months ago we received such a letter and on looking over our list we found that every one of the 6 subscribers of that particular locality was in arrears, the six together owing us for over 15 years.

Dec. 31, 1896   From the "Editor's Corner"

I noticed in last week's Budget that B. Wierich, of Needy, Oregon, was running a little on Kansas, but we do as the fellow who got kicked of the mule; consider where it came from.

Jan. 7, 1897   Haven, Kans.   C. V. Yoder

67

Nearly every correspondent of the Budget seems to think his country is the best, but we all know that every place has some drawbacks. Now would it not be a little more honest and interesting if we would sometimes tell some of the drawbacks of the country where he lives.
May 13, 1897   Garden City, Mo.   Eli Hostetler

... But here is the point I wanted to get at, the correspondents should always be very careful and not praise one state or country too much, for it always creates a feeling that isn't any too good.
Dec. 26, 1901   Milford, Neb.   H. H. Miller

Anyone wanting to buy land anywhere should investigate same, but it seems to me, the worse the graft, the better people like it. It is very easy to find out the true conditions of a country.
July 19, 1911   Chappell, Neb.   N. E. Zehr

I had a letter from a friend one time, who stated that his country was as near heaven as any place he ever knew. I went to see it and decided that "great minds differ", which is a very good thing. I have learned this, that the best place to live is where you are contented, and one will never gather figs from thistles in any old place. The splendid places are mostly in the fertile minds of land agents, and their best crop is a lot of unsophisticated land buyers.
Mar. 18, 1910   Quincy, Mich.   Amos J. Yoder

I have been in 26 of the states in the union and must say that the two states bordering the ocean, Oregon on the west and Virginia on the east are my favorites as to the climate and the lay of the land.
Mar. 11, 1914   Kokomo, Ind.   J. S. Yoder

Alabama: The Amish colony here has increased very much the last six weeks - - from seven families to eighteen. There are at present thirty-nine grown persons and fifty children here, and a few more families are expected in the near future.
Jan. 15, 1913   Bay Minette, Ala.   John E. Bontrager

California: [J. A. Gingerich wrote a letter covering two columns in which he praised Portersville, Cal., in Tulare County about half-way between Los Angeles and San Francisco.]
July 23, 1908   Portersville, Calif.   J. A. Gingerich

Colorado: The three-year Homestead Law is now a sure thing.

Each homestead holder will be notified what the law will be, and that twenty acres must be broke and farmed on each one-hundred and sixty acre farm. The time will be counted from the time you have filed.

June 26, 1912   Brandon, Colo.   Mrs. Ella Yoder

Wonder if those Colorado people got the blues that they don't write more for the Budget.

July 12, 1911   Topeka, Ind.   Lizzie Frey & Susan S. Miller

Florida: I am here 8 years and like it better every year. I am satisfied that Florida is the best state in the Union to get a home with little money and grow in wealth.

June 28, 1894   Hawthorne, Fla.   Jno. Yoder

I never saw a place where a poor man can make a living as easy as here in Florida. The natives say that nobody can be starved or frozen out here, but I am sure they would go hungry if they were in Indiana and were as careless as they are here.

Jan. 4, 1900   Grandin, Fla.   H. C. Lehman

Georgia: I was very glad for Bro. Keim's letter in the Budget, in regard to the south; I had the Georgia fever pretty bad. I suppose I am one of the 3 out of 1000 that the *Herald of Truth* mentioned that wanted to tell that Bro. Keim is no land agent. That makes it so much better for me, as sometimes land agents only tell the good points. Last fall I wanted to go to Georgia, so I wrote to a certain person who lived there, and he would not answer all the questions I asked him; that somewhat checked my fever, and the dose I got from Bro. Keim's letter broke the fever all up.

Feb. 15, 1900   Monitor, Kans.   H. E. Hostetler

Illinois: In nearly every issue of the Budget we read letters from all parts of the U.S. and each one is bragging and blowing on their country but we do not read much of that kind from Ill., as it always stands up to the head and speaks for itself.

May 16, 1895   Arthur, Ill.   Jay Sei Miller

Idaho: We like Idaho, and think it is a good country. It beats Indiana all to pieces.

Jan. 4, 1900   Nampa, Ida.   Cora Hostetler, Wilma Mishler
Edna Miller

I will say to cousin W. L. Shrock of Nampa, Idaho, I understand that you say you have no use for an undertaker out there. I am no undertaker, but if that is the case, I'll never come out there, for I want to die sometime and go to a better place than Idaho.

> Mar. 1, 1900   Smithville, Ohio   T. L. Miller

Does the sage brush produce honey in Idaho? Will the scribe from Idaho name us some of the drawbacks of the country?

> Apr. 24, 1902   Seldon, Kans.   A. E. Stoltzfus

Kansas: If any of you folks in the east want to come to Kansas, just come, and don't be bluffed by them men that put Kansas down below zero. I lived in Ohio 18 years, in Indiana for 20 years and in Kansas for over seven years, and I like Kansas by far the best.

> Feb. 16, 1893   Haven, Kans.   J. J. Miller

A few lines from this place may be interesting to some of them Budget readers that would like to have some Kansas boomers to boom their country. We don't need anybody else to boom our country, and we can boom our country without condemning other countries, because Kansas was made when all the rest of the world was made, and was pronounced good. So I don't think it is right for some people to appraise a country too high, nor to condemn it. So I think right is right.

> April 6, 1893   Hutchinson, Kans.   DUTCHY

Michigan: I will not blow about this country, but to those who have any desire to know anything about it I would advise them to come and see for themselves, as there is a vacancy for many more.

> June 19, 1902   Fairview, Mich.   L. L. Yoder

We like our homes well, but would still be better if there were more of our people here, and I hope there will be more here this fall.

> June 14, 1900   Fairview, Mich.   Lizzie J. Troyer

Montana: The homesteads are nearly all taken up in this part of the country. Of course further west there are thousands of them yet.

> March 11, 1910   Bloomfield, Mont.   Daniel F. Miller

New York: [Western] I think N.Y. is an ideal place to live. We have very good fertile land and can grow anything that is grown in any middle northern states . . . . The climate is hard to beat . . . . Taxes are lower than in most states . . . . This is an ideal place for a renter to get a start . . . . We have three churches here, the Mennonite, the Advanced Conference Conservatives, and the plain German Conservatives.

July 14, 1938   A Budget Reader

Mississippi: You might think it is pretty far south, especially to take a trip like that in the summer, but I wish I could convince some of you northern people that this is an ideal place to live. I call it little California. But that's right for if there is any place in the U.S.A. building up faster than it is here I certainly would like to see it. Tourists are coming in from all directions.

July 2, 1936   Pass Christian, Miss.   Chriss J. Glick

Minnesota: [Isaac Slabaugh praised the land of southern Minn.]

July 5, 1894   Arthur, Ill.   Isaac Slabaugh

North Dakota: John A. Yoder of N.D. is visiting friends in this locality, and booming up N.D. Max Bass, Rev. L. E. Miller and John A. Yoder gave our town folks and citizens quite a N. D. blow on the 22nd. I suppose the Dakota thermometer must be made in the sunny south, as they say when the thermometer is down to 48 below zero, the people go rabbit hunting and hauling hay, and don't think it is very cold then.

Feb. 7, 1895   Shipshewana, Ind.   HUSTLER

After a poor man is located here for a few years with the right kind of stuff he will have his feed, water and fuel handy and in fine weather he will be doing his necessary outdoor work and in rough days he sits by the stove, enjoying his pipe and reads newspapers and private letters, and grins at the remarks the eastern homeless makes at the N.D. climate, while at work every day in order to make a scanty living as a tenant for some land owner, or trying to pay a high priced farm.

Mar. 4, 1897   Grass Lakes, N.D.   John A. Yoder

North Carolina: Has the N.C. boom struck a snag that they are already moving back? [Washington, NC]

Aug. 20, 1896   Partridge, Kans.   N. Helmuth

There are some more people having North Carolina fever. Some more expect to go down to see the land next week.

Feb. 8, 1923   Hartville, Ohio   A Stark Kid

Ohio: Perhaps I would better call a halt, or some one might say I was blowing. [Describing Atwater, Ohio]

April 5, 1916   Atwater, Ohio   Leah J. Harris

I am not going to blow much on Madison Co., merely give
my opinion.

Mar. 11, 1897   Sullivan, Ohio   B. F. Gerber

We arrived here all O.K. and have met a clever and accom-
modating set of people. We like it tolerably well here. I do
not want to boom on this country as some people do in
other countries, because this country is good enough without booming it, nor do I want to condemn old Holmes,
because God made all the lands and called them good, but I
will say that we don't need to crawl around the hills down
here as we did in old Holmes. I can't give much information
on the country yet, because I am here only a few days but if
I would write all that I know then you would think it's only
a little gas.

Sept. 10, 1896   Sullivan, Ohio   E. N. Beachy

Oregon: This is the most lovely part of the United States. If our
people of Pennsylvania, Ohio, Indiana, Michigan, Illinois,
Iowa, Nebraska, Kansas, Missouri, etc., would know how
beautiful it is here, this country would be one great Amish
settlement.

Apr. 5, 1900   Needy, Ore.   Moses Yoder

What's Wrong With Oregon?
'Tis from the west with irrigation
　'Tis from the south with suffocation,
'Tis from the north with its freezation;
　Yes, everywhere, there is stagnation,
We plainly hear the declaration:
　"Get thee behind me such ruination.
I'm going back to my wife's relation."
　"Oregon is now my salvation."
For there we need no irrigation,
　With best of climate in creation,
Under the present administration,
　The Watchword there is "Purification."
With just a little education
　A man can there, by speculation,
Support himself and wife's relation,
　And with no danger of starvation.
Can have good times and jubilation.
　Now this is worth consideration,
In Real Estate and speculation.

Sept. 1, 1938   No location or name of scribe.

72

Oklahoma: All ye renters, come to Oklahoma, the land of prosperity.

June 28, 1900   Cora, Okla.   B. B. Miller

We like this place. If you want to raise cattle; if you want to raise corn and hogs; if you want to go someplace for good health; if you want to find easy farming; if you want a cheap home, come to the "Strip".

Nov. 1, 1900   Milon, Okla.   J. M. Troyer

I would like to see some of our friends come here on or before Aug. 6th . . . . [the day when the new territory was to be opened for settlement]

July 18, 1901   Cora, Okla.   M. K. Yoder

Oklahoma is the booming country; people from all directions are here, looking for town and country locations.

Dec. 25, 1902   Cora, Okla.   Enos I. Bontrager

Ontario: We read in this paper that the Sunny South had over 50 kinds of flowers. Over here the most families have over 60 kinds some have 70 or more.

May 13, 1914   Brunner, Ont.   Cor.

Pennsylvania: We read many letters in the Budget from Minnesota, North Dakota and Arkansas, about the good countries they have. Now, we do not mean to boom old Lawrence county, but we do believe if the people knew the good points of our country more people would come here to locate.

Jan. 24, 1895   East Brooke, Pa.   Cor.

I read a good deal about North Dakota in the papers, but you might as well talk about going to Rome or some other worn out country; people stick to this valley like flies to flypaper.

Aug. 6, 1896   Belleville, Pa.   D. K. Byler

Lancaster Co. is a very productive country by some called the Garden Spot of the world, perhaps they have seen the whole world is a question, nevertheless a fine place to live and visit among its pleasant and hospitable people, whose women folks are splendid cooks and know how to entertain strangers also how to raise fine gardens and beautiful, yes, very many beautiful flowers.

June 30, 1915   Gordonville, Pa.   D. K. Beiler

Prairie Provinces, Canada: According to reports we read in the papers, Western Canada will have a great boom this spring by new settlers going in.

April 25, 1907 Milford, Neb. D. Bender

Tennessee: The people of Holmes Co. may think that Tennessee is about dead, but it is not. We are well satisfied with our new houses and have met with a clever set of people.

June 2, 1892 Hazelridge, Tenn. P. V. Yoder

Texas: As this is Christmas and my northern friends are sitting by their stoves and we people down here can sit on the porch in our shirt sleeves, looking over the yard and watching the young chickens hunting something to eat.

Jan. 5, 1911 Alice, Tex. L. J. Miller

Amish church services are frequently held in barns during summer, such as on this Holmes County farm.

Church Life and Practice 9

This is a chapter dealing with rather broad issues. Some persons will not find in it all they are looking for. The persons seeking information and causes of congregational divisions, for instance, will find very little. The reason is that the pages of THE BUDGET contain very little information about such matters. Proper decorum and modesty among the Amish and Amish Mennonites would look with strong disfavor to the publishing of such information. The author knew personally of numerous cases of congregational difficulties and even divisions of congregations, and carefully checked the pages of THE BUDGET during the time periods of change in question without finding anything other than perhaps indirect remarks made about the situation.

Most of the information about church life deals with the range of activities and services. Deliberate evaluations of congregational life are next to impossible to find. Record-keeping by means of written records is minimal, and what does exist would not immediately become public, especially by way of a newspaper. The scribes reflected these same attitudes and values. The sampling given in this chapter reflects the best of what was found in the research.

The names used of church services deserves some explanation. Some interesting names were found. For regular services the two most common were "church services" and "Gma". The special service normally held twice annually and focusing on matters of discipline and Ordnung (regulations) was most frequently called council meeting. This special attention on regulations and discipline led to names such as "rule church", "order meeting", and "Sol Gma". Sol is a a Pennsylvania German word meaning "must" and gives some insight in the scribe's understanding of the service. This examination service probably should be referred to in English as counsel meeting rather than council, but the latter spelling prevailed in THE BUDGET.

Communion services followed a successfully concluded Counsel Meeting. It was a service in which all members were expected to attend. In Pennsylvania German it is frequently referred to as "Gros Gma". A literal translation would be "big church". Perhaps two factors led to the usage. One is the fact that all members were expected to participate, which meant that the number in attendance was probably higher than normal. Another is the fact that communion services were usually all-day meetings, and the name seems to have had something to do with the length of the services. It should be stated that the ministers in their formal announcements used the terms such as Abendmahl or Nachtmahl, meaning the Lord's Supper.

Church attendance: Perhaps some of my friends would like to know what I have done the past year. I wove 2700 yds. of carpet and rugs, and done lots of other work; attended church services 88 times, funerals 21 times, and was at 8 Sunday school convention sessions; at 8 lectures and at 18 Young People's Meetings.

Jan. 11, 1900   Smithville, Ohio   T. L. Miller

Church services, in honor of: I have noticed that some writers sometimes make the statement that church was held in honor of a certain minister. I wonder if it were not just as good if this were worded differently. Although we believe much honor is due to the ministers, yet I think we could all agree that the reason for having church services is for the benefit of the hearers. Probably the best way to honor them would be to give our full attention to the sermon and then live up to what they teach us.

July 29, 1954   Aylmer, Ont.   David Wagler

Yesterday during church services (we have services on Christmas) a car with four men in it crashed in front of our church house - needless to say, some seemed to be more interested in the accident than in the sermon, at least for a time. (When folks lose interest, the first thing to do is to wake up the preacher.)

Dec. 31, 1959   Lynnhaven, Va.   J. J. Hershberger

Church difficulties: I think churches of today have one bad habit. Nearly every member sees something of his brother's or sister's that is against the rule of the church, but if each one would turn around and look back over his own life and his own heart and over his own home, I think we would all say that we are not living quite up to the laws of God. I think we make it worse instead of better, so let us try to correct our own mistakes.

Sept. 17, 1903   Topeka, Ind.   From a reader

There is a program out for a Sunday School meeting at the Oak Grove Church on Oct. 6, judging from the number of meetings of this kind held all over the United States and Canada the spiritual dynamo of the Mennonite Church should be in first class running order.

Sept. 27, 1906   Smithville, Ohio   A. K. Kurtz

Owing to disputes, the Poole A. M. Church has been locked till some better settlement is arrived at. Oh, Brethren could we not put aside selfishness on both sides and come to some better understanding and go hand in hand in the work of the Lord.

June 18, 1903   Milverton, Ont.   David Schwartzentruber

I have been informed that they have trouble in the Church in Champaign Co., Ohio. That old satan is very busy sowing tares among the wheat. There are also some tares sown here among us.

Nov. 6, 1902   Gridley, Ill.   Joseph Yoder

I was told that some people moved away from here, on account of church matters.

Jan. 2, 1902   Hartford, Kans.   Samuel S. Eigsti

We wish those who were here at the Conference would not publish that there were all kinds of style and fashions of dress and fixing of the hair at the Conference; we hope they saw and learned of things more spiritual than those that belong to the world.

Nov. 5, 1903   Wayland, Iowa   Two Budget Readers

Church services, conduct: I also agree with that article in the Budget sometime ago, about chewing gum in church. Chewing gum may be healthy, or good for a person, but DON'T chew while in Church, or at singings.

Nov. 13, 1953   Thomas, Okla.   J. B.

Much has been written the past summer on sleeping in church, which is a bad habit and ought to be condemned, but what about going out while the preacher is trying his best to admonish his hearers and perhaps staying out till at least one chew of tobacco is gone, think it over brethren, is it not worse than falling asleep in church.

Aug. 29, 1917   Burton, Ohio   L E. Miller

Church services, names: We had our counsel meeting yesterday; it passed off in love and union.

Mar. 27, 1902   Elmdale, Mich.   Mrs. Emanuel Kime

77

South ordnung gma was held at Bud Schmuckers . . . .
>   Apr. 5, 1989   Quincey, Mich.   Mrs. LaVern Steury Sr.

We had ordnings gmay Sun. and are planning to have gros gmay this coming Sunday.
>   Nov. 2, 1977   Franklin, Ky.   Mrs. Jake Stutzman

Rule church was held at Michael W. D's on Sunday.
>   Mar. 29, 1989   Homer, Mich.   Mrs. John W. Delagrange

Order meeting is to be held at Moses Reihl's in two weeks.
>   Apr. 18, 1907   Gap, Pa.   Cor.

The "Sol Gma" was at Allen Yoders today.
>   Sept. 3, 1942   Benton, Ohio   No name

Our side is to have rule church at Chris W. Schwartzes. . . .
>   Apr. 1, 1987   Seymour, Mo.   Mahlon N. Schwartz

Southeast ordnungs gamein was held at Andy Yoders. . . .
>   Apr. 8, 1987   Bowling Green, Mo.   Mrs. A. E. Yoder

Council meeting was held at R. A. Yoders' last Sunday. Large meeting will be held at D. D. Bontregers in two weeks.
>   Oct. 21, 1909   Bucklin, Kans.   A reader

Church services, place: Some families here are slipping out of their turn to take church, just because they think they are too hardup, and some a little out of the neighborhood. This makes it worse for those that take church. I think nobody ought to back out, (because of hard times) as I believe we are all about in the same "boat." We ought to all be willing to give room to hold Christ's meetings.
>   June 23, 1932   Centerville, Mich.   Mrs. Joseph Stauffer

Last Sabbath day church services on the West side were held at the home of Joseph R. Hostetler.
>   Aug. 12, 1926   New Wilmington, Pa.   Y. D. Mast

Our Amish people don't have a house large enough to hold all the Amish people here now, so our Amish Church services were held with a full house attendance in the Pinecraft Church last Sunday.
>   Jan. 24, 1946   Sarasota, Fla.   E. N. Beachy

In a former issue of the Budget I noticed the correspondent of Vogansville had wrote that C. J. Miller of Kalona, Iowa, preached at Millcreek Meetinghouse, which is a mistake, the services were held in the barn at Moses Stoltzfus. [An important correction - - preaching in a meetinghouse rather than a house or a barn would create difficulties for the minister.]

Nov. 12, 1896   Ronks, Pa.   John L. Fisher

A division was formed in our church sometime ago, on account of the houses being too small for so many people. The division was made straight east and west between C. C. Millers and Daniel J. Bontragers, making about an equal number on each side.

June 22, 1899   Yoder, Kans.   D. M. Yoder

Communion services: Prospects are that half of our Lancaster Co. churches will have communion on Easter and the other half the week following. No doubt some will need to have it through the week due to the Bishop "bench" being so small.

Mar. 10, 1955   Gap, Pa.   John F. Glick

The last sacramental meeting to be held this spring will be at the Weaver M.H. Sunday May 24th.

May 21, 1903   Dale Enterprise, Va.   Annie L. Heatwole

The adjoining Amish congregation in Penn. is somewhat in dissension and no communion is hoped for this spring.

June 14, 1900   Tub, Pa.   N. N. Miller

N. W. GrosGma was held today at Mrs. Dena Gingerichs where a minister was ordained out of a lot of 8 men....

Apr. 13, 1961   Fairbank, Iowa   A. B. Miller

Communion services were held at J. J. Marner's last Tuesday, by Revs. Wagler, Troyer, Coblentz and Wittmer, of Indiana and Ohio, who were summoned here to rectify certain so-called church difficulties. They, however, adjusted the controversy.

June 21, 1900   Kalona, Iowa   A. D. Zook

Congregational size and boundaries: Church line has been changed between South Middle and Southwest districts, which gives us five more families.

Sept. 22, 1976   Fairbanks, Iowa   David A. Yoder

We realize our group is small for a building of that size, but we're "hoping forward" to an increase in membership, as the Lord sees fit.

May 16, 1957   Fairfax, S. C.   Mrs. Alvin Kropf

Amish church was again overflowing today.

Mar. 4, 1987   Pinecraft, Fla.   Mattie Miller

In larger settlements many Amish do not know each other. Last Sunday at church services . . . we had a visiting minister. I suppose at least half of the people in our district did not know who he was. In smaller settlements this fact is not recognized.

June 11, 1980   Lagrange, Ind.   John L. Lambrights

Conversion and membership: Six young souls started to serve the Lord.

June 15, 1899   Archbold, Ohio   A. A. Yoder

Jerry Yoder, who became a Christian just a year ago, is 89 years old.

June 3, 1948   Hutchinson, Kans.   Mrs. Dan Headings

We have nine converts in our church, who have confessed Christ and wish to forsake the world, with all its vanities. I do hope they may realize the change and become followers of Jesus, as there are so many professors, but so few true followers of Christ.

Mar. 1, 1900   Flanigan, Ill.   Joseph Yoder

Several young people came out for Jesus, at the Zion Church, and made a good start to forsake the world. Hope more will follow.

July 8, 1910   Woodburn, Ore.   S. E. Roth

Dedication of meetinghouses: The writer would like to ask a question and would like to have a reasonable, biblical answer. Why are dedication services for church houses necessary? The writer believes they are not necessary and the fruits of the churches that practice this have not been too good. [The scribe had discussed the dedication of three buildings near Goshen - - East Goshen, Clinton Amish, and Clinton Brick. The fourth, Pleasant Grove, was completed at about the same time, but no dedication services were held, "because it is not deemed necessary by the ministry."]

Nov. 18, 1948   Goshen, Ind.   Jonas Christner

Language: We have a prosperous church, with nine converts, and a good Sunday school but a few members do not take part, but stay outside or go home, because there is too much English. It is sad to think of the superstition in some Christians that they think they cannot serve the Lord in English. Is it superstition or selfishness?

June 23, 1908   Volant, Pa.   Jacob Moose

Meals after services: . . . we attended church services at the

home of Bro. Jonas Yoder, in what is called the Peachey
congregation, where services are held in dwellings, and
heard a good sermon by Christian Yoder and Samuel
Peachey. After preaching, dinner was served for all who
wished to stay.
       Jan. 3, 1901   Tub, Pa.   E. S. Miller and wife

We hear some reports being circulated in Geauga Co., Ohio
about our people or denomination, which are untrue; those
so believing can come and see for themselves. We
organized a small church here last summer, and have services every two weeks. We all know that a church organization must have its rules and regulations but do not
believe in publishing them to the world, through the Budget or any other paper, but will say we do not have the
rushing and crushing to the lunch table after services as
they have in some of the congregations in the East.
       Jan. 17, 1907   MicMinnville, Ore.   A. M. Beachy

Our east district will again be at Joe Chupps, May 28.
Church will furnish dinner.
       May 25, 1972   Nappanee, Ind.   Mrs. Mose W. Yoder

Meidung: The writer of the article also refers to a case of
"miteing" meaning of course *Meidung*. During the past
years there has been a tendency for newspapers to use the
improper, derogatory, and disrespectful word "miteing."
It is nothing more than an attempt to Englishize the Pennsylvania Dutch word *meide* which comes from the German
word *Meidung*. It is likely that most people know nothing
of its real meaning, and of course they know much less
when the word is corrupted in this manner.
       Feb. 9, 1950   From the Book Review Column   John Hostetler

We received a flood of letters about the Wooster "Miting"
Case this week. So many that we can't possibly publish all
of them in their entirety. We are publishing below comments taken from some of the letters and will probably
publish additional comments later.
       Jan. 8, 1948   Comments by the Editor

[No attempt will be made to give a sampling of the dozens
of letters and articles resulting from the Wooster case.
The case in question was Yoder v. Helmuth in 1947. The
persons responding were most polarized, either strongly
defending *Meidung* or attempting to show that it should
not be used in the way it was.]

Meetings: The announcement has been made to hold a real old time revival at the Albany Mennonite Church....

> May 13, 1910   Albany, Ore.   S. D. Yoder

Protracted meeting has been going on at Maple Grove Church the past week.

> Aug. 17, 1899   Centralia, Mo.   Mrs. El J. Guengerich

Our meetings are over with 13 converts, and seems rather lonesome.

> Feb. 17, 1927   Greenwood, Dela.   Val Bender

During our past few meetings 10 young souls have made a start to forsake the world and live for the Lord.

> July 2, 1896   Walnut Creek, Ohio   E. N. Beachy

Sunday observance: The annual coon chase south of Kenton is under way. On our way to Church Sunday the woodland area seemed filled with pleasure seeking people. No doubt many seats in Church houses were empty. It appeared that thousands had gone to the dogs.

> Sept. 5, 1963   Mt. Victory, Ohio   F. E. Troyer

Recently a load of young folks arrived in time for our singing on Sunday evening. If I am correctly informed they had spent Sat. night in Detroit, at the zoo, and other places of interest. Not that we disapprove of seeing a zoo, but the question that comes to my mind is whether we are justified in spending the Sunday, a day set aside for rest and worship, in sightseeing.

> Sept. 14, 1961   Aylmer, Ont.   David Wagler

Reminds me, years ago when Yoder Dairies was started (our Amish-owned milk plant) it was decided that there would be no Sunday deliveries. For over 25 years that has been the rule - - and it is possible that this way of doing has had its effect on others - - at least we know of no dairies making retail deliveries on Sunday, in the Norfolk area. Moral: Don't be afraid to stand for the right, eventually it may have its influence.

> Sept. 21, 1961   Lynnhaven, Va.   J. J. Hershberger

Spiritual condition: Is not the falling away of the latter days at hand, with so many leaving the church of their youth? Some ten years ago a Mennonite heard two Englishmen talking. One said he believed the end of the world is near, as the Amish are starting to use tractors to farm. This tickled the Mennonite. But to me it is a sad thing to see so many so-called Christians laughing and mocking at the humble ways of those who wish to stay humble. What would that Englishman say were he living today?

Ma 28, 1959   Plain City, Ohio   Allen E. Yoder

Visitation: Visiting the sick is Biblical but over-visiting is not. I often recall as a boy in Daviess Co., Ind., one Sunday afternoon after a baby had come to stay at our home, the house was full of relatives and friends. My father said to me, "I love to have visitors, but not when mother is so very weak."

Mar. 21, 1963   Hartville, Ohio   Gideon Stoll

I would say to those ministers that are well gifted and filled by the Holy Spirit, do your duty and visit other churches, as strange voices make more impression on the minds of the people, and I think it is very necessary as pride, vanity and fashions of the world are running away with Christianity.

Aug. 13, 1903   Gridley, Ill.   Joseph Yoder

Yesterday, church was at Menno Schrocks where we heard very interesting sermons preached by Joe Schrock and Bishop Samuel N. Beachy. Council meeting is to be held at Joe L. Schrocks in two weeks. We would be very glad to have more visits from some of our distant friends and ministers of our faith. I can't remember the time that we had less company from our friends and ministers of the surrounding churches than in the last few years but we can imagine that the depression is the cause.

Mar. 23, 1933   Jessup, Iowa   Mrs. Gideon N. Kaufman

We would kindly ask our ministering brethren to come to this place whenever they can. There are between 25 and 30 members of the Mennonite faith here, but have had no preaching here for nearly five months. We would be glad for the "crumbs that fall from the Master's table." Come along, brethren, and give us some refreshing food.

Apr. 12, 1900   White Cloud, Mich.   J. P. and Fannie Miller

I can't express in word how I appreciated what people did for me. Forty-two different persons visited me while in the hospital.

July 1, 1937   Norfolk, Va.   Jemimia Yoder

In the Old Order house we were privileged to have Abe Yoder of Stark County, Ohio and Cousin Enos Miller of Middlefield, Ohio, deal out the way of salvation.

Feb. 20, 1958   Sarasota, Fla.   John J. Miller

Church and Outreach   10

Outreach is a term used for efforts and activities that extend beyond the confines of the local congregation/s. It includes, but is not limited to, what are commonly called missions and evangelistic efforts. Also included is assistance given to alleviate hardship and suffering, whether due to natural disaster or war. In addition, it includes the influence and witness of a quiet way of life upon the society at large, a life that is consistent and faithful.

Evangelism: It is sad to see so many sinking in these days of prosperity in all parts of the world. And that is the reason why our dear missionaries in India hardly know where the next meal is coming from, sometimes.

    Apr. 30, 1903   Nampa, Idaho   David Garber

We should also help to support missionary work. Christ taught his disciples, "Go ye into all the world and preach the Gospel to every creature and baptize them in the name of the Father and of the Son and of the Holy Spirit." Truly there is a blessing to open-hearted souls who contribute to the cause of Christ. I believe the heathen are as dear to Christ as any other nation, if they obey his commandments.

    Oct. 31, 1901   Middlefield, Ohio   NIX FER UNGUTE

Dear Christian friends and readers, do not let satan bring to your hearts that there is no need of the mission; it is the most necessary thing that the Mennonites ever established. We can build the Church without a college better than with it, but the Mission is one of the great helps to make true Christians.

    Jan. 30, 1902   May City, Iowa   A. S. Bauman

The tent meeting is going on and another opportunity is being given the unsaved to "flee the wrath to come", but it appears that they care less about their eternal interests then in the things of this life, and so they neglect the most needful.

    July 6, 1905   Smithville, Ohio   A. K. Kurtz

84

Our people help along in missionary work but we want our heavenly Father and Son to have the honor for it. That is the reason we don't want to advertise it in the papers.

Mar. 9, 1961   Oelwein, Iowa   Ab M. Kauffman

The young people held cottage meetings yesterday, visiting a family, with singing, and a short devotion.

Sept. 29, 1976   Arenal De Tilaran, Costa Rica   Mrs. Gerald Yoder

Quite often I am asked what I think would happen to those scattered tribes if they are never reached with God's word. Has God got a plan to save them with out his word? Quite frankly, I don't know what God has planned for those who never have the opportunity to hear His word. All I know is, that He instructed his followers to go and teach all nations.

Apr. 9, 1980   Gambier, Ohio   Melvin L. Yoder

I believe it would be well to keep stirring in the Budget for help, as this paper reaches many of us (Old Amish) who did not have any organized efforts to help along missionary work, many of whom I believe feel it their duty to give of their abundance entrusted to them, to the needy and oppressed. In these modern times it is as easy to know the conditions and needs of people across the sea as our own countrymen, and as easy to help them in distress if we desire.

Mar. 15, 1910   Belleville, Pa.   ALMS IN SECRET

Many Mennonite and Amish churches are contributing to this cause and are sending donations regularly to the Northern Bible Society.

Dec. 16, 1937   Shipshewana, Ind.   Eli J. Bontreger

If people can be saved from the bondage of sin and superstition and from heathenish practices and suffering, here in this life, and from hell and damnation in eternity, if we bring them the light of the Gospel, how can we be justified to stand back and not help to make it possible for someone to go and preach to them the Gospel of Christ. . . .

Nov. 25, 1948   Scottdale, Pa.   Elias Schlabach

[A Bible Conference was held at the Bethel Church, West Liberty, Ohio, January 24-31, 1906. Speakers were J. B. Smith, D. D. Kaufman, and A. D. Wenger. There were 75 responses to accept Jesus as Saviour.]

Feb. 22, 1906

Giving, cautiously but liberally: We do indeed wish that it were possible to send God's Word to the Russian people, and appreciate the efforts put forth by our people in that line. Certainly however, the Russian Bible Society should present us with a statement showing what is being done with funds received before we support them further.

Jan. 8, 1953   Lynnhaven, Va.   J. J. Hershberger

By letter from the Christenpflicht where I had suggested investigating a certain person who appealed for aid, they found evidence that there was no dire need for a donation. The individual had written an appealing letter to us. It of course touched one's heart strings.

Jan. 15, 1948   Lancaster County Briefs   Jonathan B. Fisher

We hereby desire to make mention to the public that about March 1st we were visited by two men from Persia giving their names as Alexander Molick, aged 35, and B. Khosbaba, aged 65, who claim to be charity mission workers and had gained the confidence of the people in big valley to such an extent that they took quite a bit of money with them and above all a letter of recommendation as being honest Christian men of the truth signed by Abraham S. Yoder, Bishop John P. Zook and John E. Yoder which we beg to have considered void. As we have since by the best of evidence become very doubtful as to their honesty.

Mar. 25, 1914   Belleville, Pa.   A. S. Yoder

Not long ago a man in a pickup came into the Charm area soliciting funds for "Abe Yoder" of Sugarcreek whose barn supposedly had burned down with great loss. His story was convincing enough to deceive a few. Some people realized it was a scheme, knowing we do not collect money in this manner for such purposes. Anyway, the story wasn't true.

June 18, 1980   Wilmot, Ohio   Sarah M. Weaver

A number of weeks ago I wrote concerning the organization in Missouri that swindled people by pretending to support an orphanage in Jerusalem. The name of this is the Christian Approach Mission.

Jan. 30, 1964   Sarasota, Fla.   Sarah Weaver

Mission awakening: There are also many who know that Russell Maniaci from Elkhart, Ind. is responsible for the organization of our Mission Conference from the very beginning, and has helped along with it up to the present time, and

has been Editor of "Amish Mission Endeavor" also. . . .
[Reference was to the Amish Mission Endeavor, of the late
1940's and early 1950's.]
　　　　　April 9, 1950　　Kalona, Iowa

Relief and service:　Some of the Budget scribes are doing fine
work in advising and helping the readers along to send to
the unfortunate in Europe, in a way that we shall find out
where it went and how much it was appreciated.　So let us
be liberal and share some of our surplus that the good Lord
has again blessed us with the past season.　What has happened to others may also some time come over our country.
Our saved up wealth may be of little or no value to some of
us then.
　　　　　Jan. 9, 1947　　Elverson, Pa.　　B. F. Stoltzfus

We were very glad for the relief notes in *Gospel Herald* of
May 18.　For a long time we have been giving liberally
every 3rd Sunday in the month to relieve starving in
Russia and elsewhere.　Now come two expressions of
gratitude - - one from 120 men and the other from family
groups which both were being cared for by American
donations.
　　　　　June 1, 1922　　Latour, Mo.　　Sarah E. Hershberger

Oh! What a great work might be done with the surplus of
our Conservative Amish Mennonites if it were used or
handed over to those poor and greatly distressed creatures
instead of using it for our carnal desires.　Oh! that we
might give ourselves a living sacrifice, holy acceptable
unto God, especially our reasonable service. [Response to
Armenian relief efforts.]
　　　　　July 1, 1910　　Oakland, Md.　　L. J. Swartzentruber

Today over 50 Amish women sewed coats at the clothing
center all day.
　　　　　Aug. 15, 1946　　Akron, Pa.　　Levi L. Hershberger

Alfred Brenneman left last Monday for France to do recon-
struction work.
　　　　　Feb. 5, 1919　　Denbeigh, Va.　　Mrs. S. H. Glick

John Bender, Old Order Amishman of Kalona, Iowa, is the
leading plumber and "jack of all trades."　It is the third
time he is rendering his services to the Gulfport projects.
　　　　　Feb. 23, 1950　　Lancaster County Briefs　　Jonathan B. Fisher

Risks in outreach:　Eddie Collins, alias William J. Souza, a young

criminal from a Rhode Island prison, was apprehended in Elkhart County, Ind. where he resided with an Amish family as a farm hand for five weeks without suspicion. [Elam Hochstetler, Bishop of Woodlawn Beachy Amish Mennonite Church, was teaching and counseling Collins in preparation for baptism. Collins wrote a letter for the July 20 issue. Elam Hochstetler visited Collins in prison, which visit was reported in THE BUDGET of Sept. 28, 1961.]
> July 13, 1961   News item

Sunday School: Sunday school at the Amish church every Sunday. Bible reading at the Mennonite Church every Sunday evening. Let the good work go on.
> Feb. 25, 1897   Tub, Pa.   Joel J. Yoder

Sunday School was reorganized at the Amish Mennonite Church last Sunday.
> Jan. 7, 1897   Waupecong, Ind.   Farmers Boy

Some churches are too apt to let the Sunday School take the place of the church services, in the lives of the children, and this is a deplorable mistake; let the church take precedence always, and the habit of church attendance should be deeply implanted in earliest youth, in order that good fruits may be born in later days.
> July 23, 1899   Daytonville, Iowa   Mrs. N. D. Yoder

A German Sunday School was organized last Sunday by the Old Order Amish at the Gusler schoolhouse with Dan Gingerich as superintendent.
> May 6, 1909   Fairview, Mo.   Mrs. M. S. Zook

Witness, faithful: One day in the hospital another patient gave me the Canton daily newspaper and on the front page was a picture of Amish brethren in a horse race at the Stark Co. fair. I was shocked to see it. Christians are to be a light to the world, to bring the lost sinners to a better life in Christ, and not to furnish entertainment to the public. It stated that this was the first time in the history of the fair (110 years) that anything like this occurred. I was made to think of the time when Nero was emperor of Rome. He burned Christians in his garden. What a contrast in these two entertainments!
> Oct. 1, 1959   Hartville, Ohio   Abe J. Yoder

Church Polity and Preachers 11

The preaching of the Word of God was a central part of the Amish and Mennonite services. Among the Amish there are usually two sermons, one of which is called the "Aufang", or beginning sermon. The second is the longer one, and called the main sermon, or "Schwah Dale", meaning "heavy part." Calling on fellow ministers, and sometimes lay persons, for testimonies following the main sermon is the general practice.

The term "Bench" refers to the ordained ministers of a congregation. A full bench means having the full complement of ministers of the various offices for a particular congregation. The Amish were accustomed to use the term "Fulla Zall" rather then bench. The latter meant having ministers filling all three offices - - deacon, ministers, and bishop.

In most cases it was merely reported who preached and the date or place. In some cases a word or term was used to describe the sermon. The term used more than any other was "interesting." Other terms appearing occasionally were touching, instructive, impressive, beneficial and able. On rare occasions double adjectives were used such as interesting and touching, or very able and interesting.

Bench: The Amish had a hymn singing at Felty Yoders Sunday afternoon. There are a lot Amish here but we are lacking on the minister's bench.
Feb. 4, 1987   Phoenix, Ariz.   John J. Raber

In our community there are 2 districts with "full Zall" in the ministry.
Feb. 18, 1987   Aylmer, Ont.   Mrs. Polly Anna Stoll

Communion services were held by the Amish, on Sunday, October 16th, at the home of D. I. Miller. Attendance was large and the services were such that should not soon be forgotten. Services were conducted by Rev. Christian Beachy, John Beachy and John Yoder of Pennsylvania. 24 ministers were present.
Oct. 24, 1892   Mt. Hope, Ohio   E. D. M.

We have eight ministers and deacons in our church and
there were only three present at church the last two Sundays.
Feb. 2, 1928   Brunner, Ont.   Cor.

Diener-Versammlungen: The twice yearly ministers meeting for
north side was held at Dan L. Stoltzfuses near Honey
Brook on Oct. 12 and today for south side near Strasburg.
Oct. 20, 1976   New Holland, Pa.   Lizzie E. Lapp

Fall "Diener Ver sammlung" in Lancaster County was held
for the north side on Tuesday at Pre. Daniel L. Stoltzfuses
of Honeybrook. The south side meeting is scheduled for
today at Bishop Amos S. Lapps of Strasburg.
Oct. 20, 1976   Ronks, Pa.   Levi A. Esh

Some time ago a question was brought before conference
by a Bishop, "What could be done that more spiritual life
could be brought into our churches." This was very
necessary to talk about and not only then but now also I
think if the ministers and a conference give their consent
by a rising vote to something that they call unscriptural it
should be carried out and not allowed in any of the churches. The good Lord could and would bless the fruit and
the good tree would bring forth good fruit.
Sept. 27, 1906   Milford, Neb.   D. Bender

Yesterday, Tues., March 28 our annual diener versamm-
lung was held at Bish. Abe W. Bontreger's in West Yoder.
79 bishops, ministers and deacons were present.
Apr. 5, 1989   Middlebury, Ind.   Eli Gingerich

Today the respective bishops, ministers and deacons of our
districts who are at all able to do so, convene at Pre. Chris
Fishers in the Upper Pequea district. Here in the east the
event always takes place the first Monday previous to
communion.
Oct. 12, 1939   Lancaster County Briefs   Jonathan B. Fisher

Ordination and service: On account of a very sore arm the
former "Fisher" was unable to attend communion and out of
a group of 12 in the lot the book remained for him. Rather
an unusual event in this section.
May 15, 1941   Gap, Pa.   John F. Glick

A Deacon was ordained in the Mennonite Church at Fentress last Sunday and the lot fell upon Roy Wengerd.
July 7, 1936   Lynnhaven, Va.   Jemimia Yoder

90

The Lebold Church intends to ordain ministers on White Sunday and in the Nafziger Church ordination of ministers is set for Whit Monday.

June 9, 1938   Milverton, Ont.   No name

The two recent ordinations, that of Jacob L. Stoltzfus for W. Conestoga district and John E. Stoltzfus for S. Pequea district, are both descendants of the widely known Pre. Dan Esh of our county. Of the some 80 ministers, bishops and deacons here, more than a third are of the afore mentioned family.

Oct. 23, 1947   Lancaster County Briefs   Jonathan B. Fisher

We now have two Amish bishops besides our regular preacher, Enos D. Yoder, and three deacons, so none of the unordained men need to be afraid that they will be called on for remarks. [Beachy refers to testimony following the sermon.]

Jan. 23, 1947   Sarasota, Fla.   E. N. Beachy

Bishop Eli, at nearly 82 (Jan. 19), is presumed to be the oldest active bishop among our people. There are others who are older but are more or less retired. His father "Hansey" was a bishop before him. Had attained some ninety years. [He had reference to Eli Bontreger, who had arrived in Lancaster to officiate at a wedding.]

Nov. 24, 1949   Lancaster County Briefs   Jonathan B. Fisher

Ordnung: Regarding the proper length of hair, I do not wish to start a controversy on this subject as there are different opinions. But at the same time, I feel that what Paul wrote about it being a shame for a man to have long hair (I Cor. 11:14) does not apply to the Amish as I have not yet seen any men with long hair like a woman's. That is what Paul was talking about. Now if our wives and mothers were to cut their hair to the length that our men do among the Amish, we would no doubt call it short, and rightly so. Just because there are women in the world who cut their hair the length our men do, does not change that I think it is still short hair. At the time Paul wrote bobbed hair was unknown among the civilized world.

Aug. 11, 1955   Aylmer, Ont.   David Wagler

To some of the inquiries we have had concerning the prospect of work here, I'm writing this on my own, but know the others feel the same. Yes, we could use more and are more than glad to know others are interested to find out a few facts and get acquainted. However, we have some rules and restrictions. We cannot allow worldly fashions such as smoking, drinking, fancy clothes, etc. so if you cannot give up your smoking or whatever there is, there's little use of inquiring any further. Some might say, let them come, they can be changed after a while. That might have its merits, but if enough of that class come, that could be taken over, then what would be left?

Sept. 29, 1976   Rexford, Mont.   Ora N. Miller

The automobile in our section is used freely by the Amish people, but ownership and driving one is considered wrong. They are used freely by the older folks in day time. What do we expect from the young people after dark. The telephone is not to be used in an Amish home, but it is not considered wrong if we bother our neighbors from all directions any hour, day or night. This is not written to hurt anyone's feelings, but let us stop and think what causes some of the trouble that we are in.

July 16, 1953   Narvon, Pa.   No name

Polity: Much of the apostasy in today's church in America, stems from a lack of counsel with the church body. Church doctrine is dictated by a church board composed of a few powerful church leaders. Young men going into the ministry are educated in seminaries where the curriculum again is dictated by a few select individuals and completely without counsel of the church body.

April 30, 1980   Gambier, Ohio   Melvin L. Yoder

This brings us to the question asked by J. H. Miller of why we have bishops? I don't know as I can say where that originated.

April 23, 1980   McVeytown, Pa.   Eli Renno

They do not have a resident pastor as yet, and for a layman who is not ordained to speak, among his own people, is just about unknown among the Amish. Some of them can speak well enough when in an informal gathering; but to speak as a Divine mouthpiece without formal authority from your religious superiors, in a religious meeting is not done. They only gather for public worship once every two weeks, and have practically no other religious services, it is not much clerical work for a man to be a preacher, but he must have formal authority, and this takes time to delegate such an one, he must first be approved, by living in the community, and be fairly well settled, and all this takes time.

Sept. 17, 1980   Danville, Pa.   John Renno

Preaching: The funeral of Danie Z. Fisher was held today. A large concourse of friends and relatives attended. The chief sermon was by Pre. Chris U. Fisher. The forepare by Pre. John K. Fisher. The hymn was read by Dea. Dan U. Stoltzfus.

Sept. 16, 1948   Lancaster County Briefs   Jonathan B. Fisher

Last Sunday counsel meeting was held at Summit Mills Amish Church. Moses Beachy, of this place and Daniel D. Yoder, of Norfolk, Va. preached very interesting sermons and made everything plain so that the listener could understand it.

Oct. 22, 1913   Meyersdale, Pa.   S. Summny

Bro. Roth preached two very interesting sermons, one in German and one in German and English.

Jan. 16, 1902   Thurman, Colo.   Bella Schrock

Pre. David Miller of Oklahoma is spending some time visiting with friends here in Lancaster-co. He was in Conestoga district yesterday at the home of Steven Stoltzfus, and today on the Honeybrook side, and understand tomorrow in Lower Pequea district.

Aug. 7, 1952   Bareville, Pa.   Mrs. Mattie S. Stoltzfus

Church and Sunday school here has not been so well attended for sometime. Let us come out and show our colors and stay for services. Plain gospel preaching shall not hurt anyone; if it does, it fits us, and we should accept it and better ourselves thereby.

Dec. 18, 1902   Iowa, La.   Le. E. Liechty

Bishop Moses P. Miller of Geistown, gave us an instructive sermon on Sunday a week ago, although he is bearing the frost of eighty two winters, his familiar voice is still distinctive, his mind bright and he is enjoying good health.

Dec. 26, 1901   Davidsville, Pa.   Levi J. Kauffman

Now then; whenever I hear a Shepherd (minister) complain and lament about the unruly behaviour or dissatisfaction of his sheep (church members) the question that comes first in my mind is this: What do you feed your sheep? Is it green lush pastures? (the pure unadulterated Word of God) or is it brambles and thorns? (ordinances of men). That faith is preached as fervently and with power today as it was in the days of our forefathers, it just must draw the people to the invisible and living God, and give them a new spiritual taste, and not for that which is earthly.

July 24, 1954   Belleveille, Pa.   Ezra Kanagy

This custom of reading another man's sermons to the congregation, we understand, was also at one time a common practice among the Amish. [This in response to visiting the Russian Mennonites who had recently come from Mexico.]

July 24, 1958   Aylmer, Ont.   Joseph Stoll

Titles: It is interesting to read the Lancaster Co. Briefs, but I am surprised that Jonathan B. F. calls a Preacher Reverend.

Sept. 12, 1940   Ligonier, Ind.   Mrs. David D. Zehr

Why is it that our people use the word Reverend so much among themselves? I believe that is meant for the dear Lord only, as it appears only once in the Bible. . . .

Apr. 19, 1906   Centralia, Mo.   Mrs. Shem Swartzendruber

There was a banana supper at Rev. Joseph Byler's,. Tue. evening.

June 15, 1899   Belleville, Pa.   Miss Nancy Byler

We seem to be a very "peculiar people" in the estimation of the "Higher Class". Ideal "God's People" are a "Peculiar People", not only in dress but in their conduct in general. However, some people wish to honor us preachers, and give us flattering titles, such as Rev., etc. I advise that these flattering titles be avoided, even by those who write for the Budget. Why? Because it's the right way to avoid them. The Psalmist, in speaking of God, says: "Reverend is His Name." Psa. 111:9. Elisha thought it much out of place, (Job 32:21, 22) and so do I. "Brother", "Preacher", or "Minister" is sufficient.

Feb. 22, 1900   Nampa, Idaho   David Garber

Trance preachers; also called sleeping preachers: We had a visit from the trance preacher; he preached three nights - - one night at Bro. Jonathan Schrocks; one at Oak Grove and one at N. S. Burkholder's. There are some things hard to explain about this strange occurrence. Perhaps to be candid, we might as well admit that we don't know.

Jun 16, 1904   Smithville, Ohio   A. K. Kurtz

If A. K. Kurtz . . . will read the first three verses of John 4, he will have an unfailing test-stone to try such as the so-called trance preachers.

June 30, 1904   Garden City, Mo.   Eli Hostetler

[John D. Kauffman, of Shelbyville, Ill., the well-known . . .] "sleeping pracher", was in our midst recently and preached three very earnest and impresseive sermons. When at home he still preaches twice a week, but while away from home every evening, except while on the way.

July 1, 1910   East Lynne, Mo.   Eli Hostetler

It may not be generally known to the present readers of the Budget that for several years before Bro. Kauffman began to speak in this way there was another man, in the person of Noah Troyer, of Johnson Co., Iowa, who might be considered as the predecessor of Bro. Kauffman. Bro. Troyer, during the year 1879, preached about 250 sermons, of from one to three hours in length.

July 12, 1910   No location given   Scribe's name not given

I heard him (John D. Kauffman) two times. In Feb. 1888 we moved from Holmes-co. O., to LaGrange-co., Ind., and the next year in April my folks and Uncle Jacob Miller and wife came out to visit us. After being around there about a week they continued their trip to Howard-co., Ind. I was to take them to Goshen for the train, so we went one Wednesday afternoon and went to Abe Troyers for the night. After supper Abe told us about this preacher and decided to hear him. As we approached his house he was standing and preaching, and before he closed his sermon he said, "There are folks in my presence that expect to be on a trip tomorrow. Let's pray for them." And he went on his knees and prayed. I only remember of hearing him preach three times and that was in my boyhood days. He preached every Sunday and Wednesday evening, and it was said he was not conscious when preaching, and I was told the next day he did not know what he preached. The beginning of it was he would lay on the lounge and soon fall into an unconscious condition. When preaching time came, he gave signs to raise up and by the aid of other people he got to his feet and had to be steadied some until he was able to stand by himself. He had to be guarded from a hot stove. He always preached German first. When he was through he conversed in English in a very perfect form. He and his wife dressed in the Amish form but never attended the Amish Church that I can remember. He later moved to

Shelby Co....
Jan. 17, 1946   Haven, Kans.   Leander S. Keim

Unclassified: In a former issue of the Budget we noticed that a certain preacher introduced Texas; why not introduce the New Testament instead?
Mar. 8, 1894   Goshen, Ind.   E. S. Troyer

Immediately after services were over and before the congregation arose, I was asked to make a few remarks. With some urging and excusing myself in being rather too timid to arise before a concourse of people, I at least consented. I was surprised with myself in the courageous way I could express myself to the whole congregation and must say it greatly helped to bind me with them in both friendship and spirit. [Jonathan was describing his experience in attending the Mennonite Church in the Colmar District, in Alsace, then part of Germany.]
Dec. 3, 1908   Written in Alsace   Jonathan B. Fisher

A color photograph would show simple and modest clothing of solid colors on the porch of this Amish home.

Clothing and Attire 12

Clothing and items of attire have been among the most noticeable external features of Amish/Mennonite life during the past century. In spite of that, there is less discussion of the issue of attire on the pages of THE BUDGET than one might expect. Probably one of the reasons is the reluctance to comment on such a sensitive matter, compounded by the many local differences, however slight they may seem to be.

Samples of advertising: [Geo. Gohn Y. Sons advertised Amish clothing. One advertisment included the following:] "We make all kinds of Amish clothing, suits, overcoats, corduroy suits and coats. We make them for less money than you can buy the cloth and make them yourself.
    Nov. 5, 1908

I have a suspender machine and I am making plain suspenders for the Amish people. I get the leather trimmings and elastic and make them myself.
    Mar. 10, 1938   Meyersdale, Pa.   Ada N. Kinsinger

Spector Stores Cater to Amish needs, plain yard goods, hats, shawls, black stockings, coating, and suiting. [This was part of a Spector ad on page one. All shades of blue were advertised with the statement that blue is the favorite color.]
    Dec. 2, 1954

Men's hats: [A news item on page one included the following statement about men's hats.] Men's hats are an article which indicate the differences in dress of many of the sects. Each church prescribes the type of hat the men wear. They differ on the width of the brim, height of the crown and width of the band.
    Dec. 2, 1954

[John F. Glick accompanied a group to Ohio from Lancaster County to learn some Ohio songs and language. On one

occasion he had difficulty keeping his hat on his head. The wind blew it off his head and he gave it a hearty chase before retrieving it. The Editor's Corner included some advice to Mr. Glick on how to keep a broad brimmed hat on; advice included in correspondence to the Editor. Someone suggested use of a leather chin strap, but admitted it would give him a Mexican appearance. Others advised equipping his hat with a baler twine chin band, or perhaps carrying an extra hat.]
Sept. 23, 1954

Some row they had about my old hat. I didn't think my "skypiece" would cause so much disturbance.
Sept. 30, 1954   Gap, Pa.   John F. Glick

Sometime ago on one of our windy days husband Olin lost his hat while in Burton on the street and chased after it and fell, which left him with a sore knee....
Jan. 9, 1980   Burton, Ohio   Mrs. Olin A. Yoder

Facial hair: (I Cor. 6:9-10) Be not deceived ... shall not inherit .... Effeminate means womanish on face like beardless. Notice how it says "be not deceived." It means to be much feared if one doesn't want to wear a beard, thinking it is harmless or too ashamed to wear it. God made it so to be different from women and it keeps man's chin warm in very cold weather like God created hair on animals to protect them from cold. It also keeps the man humble and separate from the world.
Sept. 13, 1956   Shelbyville, Ill.   Mrs. Grace Toll

An Amish youth has been dismissed from his position as I-W worker in a hospital in an Eastern state because of the fact that he insisted on growing a beard in accordance with his religious conviction.
Sept. 23, 1954   News item, p. 1.

A dear brother has written us a letter of encouragement, and among other things asked a timely question. "I wonder whether you have any tract or literature on the beard. It seems that people find it hard if not impossible to give any reason for the beard. Some even seem offended if asked about it. Some seem to feel that we've always had the beard and should therefore keep it. Some say we should go very slow in demanding anyone to keep a beard who didn't understand it that way. I would appreciate any help or light that you can give me on this subject."

In seeking through the old writings there is very little explanation to be found on this subject. However all historians give it that the Mennonites as well as the Amish wore full beards in the old country, before coming to America. In the Ausbund Liederbuch, the 102nd song, 10th verse it says that the Anti-Christ shore bald spots on their heads and cut their beards, which they found contrary to the Scriptures.

Sept. 1956   John W. Martin

The beard is a perfect setup by God, and not man. Shaving is a tradition set up by man, and not by GOD. . . . Another point that is often overlooked about the beard. Nowhere in the Scriptures can a person find that a difference was made of the beard, whether the hair grew on the chin or lips or below the ears, all was included in the word beard. If anybody wants to say that there is no mention made in the New Testament requiring the beard, I answer that nowhere in the entire Bible is mention made allowing shaving or trimming of the full beard.

Sept. 1956   John W. Martin

Tobias Eash trimmed his mustache on account of that little boy that came to stay with them.

April 25, 1907   Holsopple, Pa.   Twin Sisters

Coats, shawls: Someone took the wrong mutza at the wedding. . . .

Jan. 23, 1980   New Wilmington, Pa.   Martha E. Mast

I was asked to mention that a boy's serge coat was left in church at Abe A. Troyers the second time when having church there. It may fit an 8 yr. old.

Oct. 20, 1976   Baltic, Ohio   Mrs. John J. Miller

When church was at Min. Al Burkholders the last time a ladies' bonnet was left there.

Sept. 29, 1976   Nappanee, Ind.   Mrs. Mose W. Yoder

When we came to Norfolk it was so warm it was uncomfortable to wear a shawl.

March 11, 1910   Norfolk, Va.   Misses Savilla & Sadie Beachy

Someone got the wrong shawl at church at Eli Helmuths, Sunday, Sept. 12. The shawl that was taken belongs to Mrs. (Min) Eli Mast. It has two small safety pins on the inside, one on each side, and she had 2 large safety pins on the outside.

Sept. 29, 1976   Nappanee, Ind.   Mrs. Mose W. Yoder

Stockings: It has been rumored that in some localities the Amish are wearing nylon stockings. I happen to know that this is true but it happens to be work socks, not the transparent ladies' hose. These work socks look much like ordinary every-day cotton socks, but are made of 100% nylon. They outlast anything I have ever seen. Early last fall I got two pairs and they have lasted me till now, worn every day, oftentimes in rubber boots without boot socks, and are still in perfect condition. They are fully as warm as heavy cotton socks and do not cost much more to start with. Nylon is made of synthetic material.

> Mar. 28, 1957   Aylmer, Ont.   David Wagler

Veiling: [Several paragraphs of a letter were devoted to arguing for the veiling, using Isa. 3:16-17 and I Cor. 11.] . . . as if she were shaven . . . bald women.

> Oct. 18, 1956   Berlin, Ohio   Sarah Weaver

Unclassified: The season for very thin summer attire is again at hand and you are liable to have your modesty shocked any day by persons appearing in transparent clothing, who you thought would have common sense enough not to wear such clothing.

> May 27, 1914   West Liberty, Ohio   Chris L. Miller

Let us be careful not to abuse our plain clothing, out of the abundance of the heart the mouth speaketh. I heard a story about an old man, he threw off his coat to fight a man and he said to his coat, you lay there religion till I fight this man. You see the religion was in the coat, but not in the man.

> Aug. 27, 1919   Bunker Hill, Ohio   Mrs. Daniel Middaugh

M. Swartzentruber and Menno Miller dressed some roosters Tuesday and when they got to town with them Wednesday morning the Canton women said their bare feet were hanging out of a little hole in the curtain of their wagon.

> Dec. 1, 1921   Hartville, Ohio   Naomi Miller & Lizzie A. Boley

Slacks poorly fitted to figures and figures poorly fitted to slacks are combinations that lend little grace to any public occasion or building.

> Dec. 7, 1961   Phoenix, Ariz.   Tom Byler

Is it any wonder many of you advanced Mennonites have said I have spoken too plain these last few weeks. . . .

> June 7, 1962   Johnsville, Ohio   Reuben I. Harvey

100

It was interesting to the writer to learn that people yet dress in plain clothes in Europe, which has been settled by the White Man for more than 6000 years. America has been known only since 1492, less than 500 years, and many have lost the desire to dress plain.

Oct. 5, 1961   Mt. Victory, Ohio   F. E. Troyer

Might mention that there were 4 pairs of rubbers, 1 hat and 2 bonnets left here over pinsksta. Still have 2 pairs of rubbers left and also one pair of rubbers left from several weeks ago that we do not know who left them.

June 21, 1962   Topeka, Ind.   Mrs. Jerome Hochstetler

About 8 men were minus hats when they wanted to go home from the Fair Haven Church Sunday evening two weeks ago. The guilty ones have been caught now and the hats will be returned except 2 which they had burned. Those will be replaced.

Feb. 6, 1964   Goshen, Ind.   A. H.

Levi Z. Stoltzfus had an unusual experience a few weeks ago when he was hauling a load of household goods for Samuel Fisher. He was driving along and was smoking a cigar, and it seems a spark set fire to some of the goods. He happened to be near the home of Elias Stoltzfus when he first noticed the smoke. Mrs. Stoltzfus also saw the smoke issuing from the wagon, and quickly provided a few pails of water to quench the flames. Not very much damage was done, although the cape on his overcoat was pretty badly burned.

April 22, 1909   Gordonville, Pa.   John H. Kauffman

We did exchange rings in front of the church. The rings have a special meaning to us and a lot of other young people feel the same. It is a symbol of a promise we made before the people and God. A lot of Mennonite young people have exchanged the rings behind the people's backs. We did not feel this was right, because that would be trying to do something we were ashamed of, and we are not.

May 11, 1961   Ironwood, Mich.   A. J. Miller

Courtship and Marriage 13

The length of time considered appropriate for two young people to court before marriage, and the frequency with which they might see each other are not mentioned by any of the scribes. Comments on couples who were published to be married and weddings themselves occupy considerable space. One of the excerpts includes the Pennsylvania German word "steala". A "steala" is a small chair or stool, and is a symbol of a place at the wedding, meaning an invitation. The following is presented as a sampling of what appeared in the pages of THE BUDGET on courtship and marriage.

Dating and publishing: Abner Nissly and Barbara Beachy were published to be married last Sunday.
> Feb. 18, 1926   Baltic, Ohio   Abraham Shetler

With Leap Year coming up and the girls outnumbering the boys in this vicinity, we expect several weddings in the coming year.
> Jan. 9, 1964   Clark, Mo.   E. J. Miller

To John A. Yoder of Dover, Delaware I wonder if you think of the bachelor buttons and whisker crackers yet when you were in Mifflin.
> April 24, 1930   Belleville, Pa.   A Reader

Cupid has been making terrible inroads upon the young people of this neighborhood.
> Feb. 9, 1905   Noble, Iowa   J. W. A.

It is reported that David B. Schrock, formerly of this place, has captured a dear in Lancaster Co....
> Dec. 6, 1906   Arthur, Ill.   William L. Mast

Those girls who were out scouting some time ago put me in mind of some starving cows, which hunger forces to break their lines to seek some green pastures.
> June 4, 1896   Nappanee, Ind.   A Reader

We have no weddings to report, probably because we have

no one here to tie the "Knot".
Dec. 28, 1899   Grasslake, N. D.   S. Y. Yoder

At one school, known as the Little Red Schoolhouse, all the pupils attending were cousins . . . (Conestoga-Stoltz-fuses). For a number of years the young folks of marriageable age were obliged to seek their life mates in the Pequea-Mill Creek or other still more distant districts. . . . Some had a distance of 22 miles to travel to do their courting. One of them remarked, "Wass die liebe triebt is kenn wek zu weit". . . . By now there are nearly half a dozen other names brought into the Conestoga district by later marriages. (Translation: For that which love drives, no distance is too far.)
Dec. 23, 1948   Lancaster County Briefs   Jonathan B. Fisher

Invitations: I read in the Budget that Lovina Ryler is to be married. I think she might have sent a steala, but I guess she lost all her writing paper, when she was in Rag Hollow.
Dec. 3, 1903   Belleville, Pa.   Miss Amelia C. Kurtz

. . . they were just announced yesterday to join in the holy bonds of wedlock. We wish them much joy and happiness. I hope they will call on me to kill the chickens for the wedding.
Jan. 11, 1900   Waupecong, Ind.   A. King

Ceremonies: If properly observed, a wedding should be a time of rejoicing. (See Matt. 9:15). If kept in the fear of the Lord, it should remind us of that great spiritual wedding which is fast approaching when Christ will come to claim His Bride, the Church.
April 11, 1957   Aylmer, Ont.   David Wagler

Yesterday a double wedding took place at the Maple Glen meeting house near Grantsville, Md., where Annie E. Yoder of Grantsville Md. and Menno Yoder of Va., and Fred S. Yoder of Va. and Sara E. Yoder were married. They were attended by Jerry S. Yoder and Thelma S. Yoder of Va., and Chriss Yoder and Rhoda Shrock of Grantsville.
Dec. 26, 1940   Springs, Pa.   No name

Yesterday a double wedding was solemnized, something the writer never saw before. The 1st couple, Joel Yoder and Lydia Yoder, were married within the last five minutes before 12 oclock noon; the other couple Eli Stutzman and Fannie Yoder, were married within the first 5

103

minutes after 12 o'clock noon, or both couples within 10 minutes. . . . These were the first marriages that were solemnized in Oklahoma by the old orthodox Amish denomination; but others may follow soon. Bishop David Kauffman of Langrange, Ind. officiated at the above marriages.

Jan. 3, 1901   Cora, Okla.   B. B. Miller

Noah Kinsinger and Sarah J. Yoder were married last Sunday. Es war zimlich kalt and stermisch, aber ich denk net das sie so stermisch leben dun. (Translation: It was quite cold and stormy, but I do not think they will have such a stormy life.)

Dec. 26, 1901   Meyersdale, Pa.   Elias Kanagy

Both of the contracting parties are both quite well known in this vicinity. [A description of two couples in a double wedding.]

April 7, 1904   Walkerton, Ind.   E. Knepp

Church is now bestellt on Sunday the 27th as Sam L. Swartzentruber is around here yet over Sunday. The young couple getting married yesterday were also given together by Sam.

Jan. 30, 1980   Heuvelton, N.Y.   Rudy S. Yoder

In regard to what I had reference to about having made our trip, part with pleasure and joy, and in part with sorrow and grief, will say that it was a great pleasure to meet so many friendly and smiling people, and former acquaintances, some that I hadn't met for forty years. By the attendance of three weddings in three different states. I discovered a great difference in conduct of our Amish people at such occasions during the afternoons and evenings, it being the custom and practice in the three states to sing spiritual songs, both in the afternoon and evenings, and can say it was indeed a delight to see how nice, quiet and respectful both old and young have been in one state, while they were engaged in singing. At most all such occasions there are some that do not take part in singing, but in this instance, those that didn't take part in the singing kept quiet and orderly, and showed respect to those that took interest in singing. But at a wedding in another state, it was different, especially in the evening, when the young folks were at the table. Those that didn't take part in the singing, instead of keeping quiet and respectful, got so loud and disorderly that the others could not go ahead with their singing.

Jan. 13, 1938   Springs, Pa.   Eli N. Beachy

Some descriptions: A very pretty and quiet wedding service.

Jan. 14, 1932   West Liberty, Ohio   Maude E. Peachey

A sly little wedding occurred at the home of the bride Mrs. Mary Mast and Levi Hartzler on Tuesday evenng.

Feb. 23, 1916   Topeka, Ind.   W. W. Hartzler

A very pretty and sociable wedding occurred....

Jan. 1, 1913   Allensville, Pa.   S. L. Byler

Bridal parties and dinners: Thursday was the well attended wedding of Nicholas and Ida Graber. The "nava huckers" were Henry Graber and Mary Lengacher and Nicholas Wagler and Anna Graber. The table waiters and waitresses were....

Dec. 31, 1931   Montgomery, Ind.   Mabel & Rachel Wagler

Edna Miller and Bill Slabaugh were married last Thusday. The table waiters were Joe E. J. K., Fannie Bontrager, Andy S., Ora Mae Mullet, John Hochstetler and Alma Miller. The "side-kickers" were....

Nov. 3, 1932   Nappanee, Ind.   Nora Nisley

We had a very nice wedding on Thursday at David P. Spicher known as Fog Hollow. This is not a very large place, two farmers live in its territory. One is a minister. There were about 175 people at the wedding. 136 chickens were killed and 4 ducks.

Dec. 24, 1931   Belleville, Pa.   S. D. Peachey

On the wedding day the immediate family will not need to do any of the arranging and supervision of the affair. The outside chores, too, will usually be done by some of the neighboring young folks, which of course includes the milking.... In former years turkey was used for the noon roasts. Now it is chiefly Muscovy duck. Boiled chicken with plenty of gravy and dressing is prepared for supper. It costs considerable now-a-days for an Amish maiden's wedding.

Nov. 14, 1946   Lancaster County Briefs   Jonathan B. Fisher

It has been suggested by our leaders to have them more limited. Formerly was nothing unusual to have 300 invitations extended. Now 200 seems to be more general size.... The restrictions are to be recommended, especially con-

sidering the present situation. The events began to be somewhat "overdone" as most everyone agreed, yet they kept on as before.
　　　　Nov. 12, 1942　　Lancaster County Briefs　　Jonathan B. Fisher

Weddings are on the program again and much is the time and money that is spent in the preparation and attendance of these ceremonies and the question often comes to my mind if we are doing according to I Cor. 10:31.
　　　　Dec. 15, 1921　　Bird-in-Hand, Pa.　　John H. Kauffman

Numbers and seasons:　Wedding bells are ringing again in Lancaster Co. as Nov. is the marrying season here.
　　　　Nov. 10, 1976　　Ninepoints, Pa.　　Hannah L. Stoltzfus

The weddings are on the list again, and quite plenciful. They already started on Tuesday, Nov. 1.
　　　　Nov. 10, 1955　　Bareville, Pa.　　Mattie S. Stoltzfus

The weddings are on the go already. There were only seven couples published last Sunday. Too many to give the names.
　　　　Nov. 14, 1929　　Leola, Pa.　　Mrs. M. P. Stoltzfus

Former week 8 weddings were held, four each Tuesday and Thursday respectively. Certain ones of the older folks had an invitation for "four" while some of the young folks had more. They usually manage to attend 3 in one day, viz; morning, afternoon and evening.
　　　　Nov. 14, 1940　　Lancaster County Briefs　　Jonathan B. Fisher

It seems if the wedding season was closed for this season. There were 56 weddings in our Amish territory and it seems as if the moving season was over too.
　　　　April 14, 1920　　Charm, Ohio　　Jacob S. Yoder

There seems to be no end to weddings this winter.
　　　　Mar. 1, 1900　　Baden, Ont.　　Jacob Iutzi

Spring or summer is less justifying than winter for weddings.
　　　　May 30, 1895　　Limpytown, Ohio　　Conrad Schultz

As the wedding season is again at hand it would be well for us to read what Christ tells us we should do upon such occasions, as it is written in St. Luke 14:7 to 14.
　　　　Nov. 25, 1910　　Ronks, Pa.　　John H. Kauffman

Wedding trips:　Mr. and Mrs. Abe Keim made a honey-moon trip around here last week.
　　　　Jan. 14, 1932　　Millersburg, Ohio　　Two Girls

Mrs. and Mrs. Wilbur Yoder have gone to Midland on their wedding trip and expect to return about Tuesday.

Feb. 1, 1934   Prattville, Mich.   Mrs. A. D. Miller

Unclassified: J. Tice, who was visiting around here for some time, leaves for Indiana one of these days; he is interested in the poultry line, but we would be sorry if he would take one of our chicks along.

Sept. 7, 1899   Wellesley, Ont.   COLD CANADA

An Amish hearse near Sugarcreek, Ohio.   The only professional service required by the Amish for a funeral is that of a mortician, to embalm the body.

Deaths and Funerals

14

Death is one of the life experiences included in the rites of passage. These rites are pivotal and transitional experiences common to all persons. Death is referred to in a variety of ways, both in spoken word and in print. This diversity can be observed in comparing references to death in the 1890's and early 1900's and in the 1980's. The first group of excerpts are a sampling of the descriptions of death.

Descriptions: Another loud call of death....
Aug. 1, 1901   Amish, Iowa   L. S. Yoder

... we have the hope that the angels carried him to that heavenly kingdom in Glory with his Saviour. Let us be ready for the day will come that we will have to go.
Jan. 9, 1902   Bertrand, Neb.   Jno. S. Yoder

I learn through the Budget that my old friend, Christian Gingerich, has gone to the spirit land.
Aug. 9, 1900   Flanigan, Ill.   Joseph Yoder

Franklin Wells is no more; died at about 2:30 o'clock, Friday morning....
July 16, 1903   Mottville, Mich.   Grandpa

Old Daniel D. Otto, after being helpless for the last three years, was called to rest by the death angel last Sunday morning....
April 2, 1908   Arthur, Ill.   Lewis D. Yutzy

The death messenger has been very busy in our community the past week taking away both Mr. and Mrs. Evans....
May 30, 1907   Pulaski, Pa.   Mrs. J. L. Kauffman

The death reaper has again been in our midst and called away Abe C. Miller....
March 18, 1914   Middlefield, Ohio   A Reader

The heavenly reaper again entered our midst to bear away the golden grain....
April 19, 1911   Hartville, Ohio   Viola F. Miller

108

The tireless reaper death has been at work in our community again.

Oct. 20, 1915   Smithville, Ohio   A. K. Kurtz

The Lord has again needed another jewel and has called away the dear little baby of Will Headings and wife.

Aug. 28, 1918   Hutchinson, Kans.   Miss Susan Mast

A young wife and mother was called to the Great Beyond last week. . . .

Nov. 1, 1956   Bareville, Pa.   Dorothy S.

Discussions of: To G. S. of Hartville, O., your statement that old people must die and young people can die, reminds me of what a dear friend told me about this statement, which often is quoted. He felt that in some cases old people must die, while others (for those who are waiting on their Master's Call) it is not a must, but a joyous release from the physical to the spiritual realm, from the mortal to immortality. This same person had, a short time before death, the beauty of heaven revealed to him in a trance and he spoke to those present, of what he saw as it was revealed to him as he came out of the trance. His questions were, "How did I come back, why could I not stay there?"

July 11, 1963   Plain City, Ohio   Jonas E. Beachy

Speaking of translating Pennsylvania Dutch words into English, I was asked to inquire if any of the Budget readers know how to show the difference between a person dying or an animal. When a person dies we say "schtorva" which is a form of "Gestorben" in German, but when an animal dies we say "dote ganga." You never hear the word "schtorva" referring to an animal. The only thing I could think of right now which would correspond to the other would be "went dead."

April 19, 1956   Aylmer, Ont.   D. L. W.

Funerals and burials: Sometimes some things look a little strange, and here is one that has just come to the writer, which has been a very sad one. In looking over the news of our old home papers of Indiana, we noticed the death and burial of my father-in-law, H. C. Yoder of Lagrange Co., Ind., and we do feel very sorry indeed to think that there were not friends or relatives enough left to give notice to his children of his death or even of his illness; or are the statements of the papers not true.

Feb. 20, 1902   Iowa, La.   C. C. Schrock

Emanuel E. Bontrager's baby died Saturday morning, and was buried Sunday afternoon, aged 1 year.

Mar. 26, 1903   Cora, Okla.   Enos I. Bontrager

Mrs. Susan Heading's children have black diphtheria. . . . On Monday morning her daughter, Esther, aged 10 years, died and was buried on Tuesday. No funeral services could be held on account of the contagious disease.

Mar. 16, 1905   Round Prairie, Ohio   Ellen King

The 3rd the angel of death claimed as its victim Annie Hostetler, nee Renno, aged 35 years, 6 mo., 2 d, the following day her husband, Samuel D. Hostetler followed, aged 34 yr., 4 m., 1 d. They were both buried in one grave the funeral of which was postponed the second time it being impossible to convey the bodies to the cemetery, the roads being totally blocked by snow.

Mar. 24, 1920   Belleville, Pa.   Rudy J. Kanagy

My parents, John and Mary Headings, who were killed almost instantly in a pickup truck collision, on Nov. 26, 1946, near Joliet, Ill,, were buried in the same grave in the Fairfield A. M. cemetery near Tampico, Illinois.

May 4, 1961   Fairfax, S. C.   Mrs. Alvin Kropf

Yesterday I went to the cemetery to see whether it was true what we hear and I seen fourteen men digging graves and they said it was all they can do. They said a mile from here they have a steam shovel to dig graves and would put 2 or 3 bodies of poor people in one grave, and would lay them on straw. [This was the time of the flu epidemic.]

Oct. 30, 1918   Marcus Hook, Pa.   Mrs. C. J. Schlabach

It was a large funeral, had preaching in 3 different places, 4 bench wagons and then some standing. Many out of state. . . .

Aug. 3, 1977   Arthur, Ill.   Ida M. Schrock

A lot of people were there for a "vochen" that night and a funeral was held Thursday morning. (Her way of saying there was a "wake".)

Sept. 19, 1946   Iowa City, Iowa   Mrs. Lena F. Mast

I heard tonight that they will start a cemetery on Jake's farm, and will bury a young man almost three years ago for the first time. His death was due to measles and lung fever.

Feb. 29, 1940   Topeka, Ind.   Elmer K. Miller

110

Gravemarkers: In our Amish graveyard we have one grave only marked with an 8-inch tall hedgepost, a Magdalena Miller, who died in 1904. She requested that no stone marker with name on it be placed on her grave.

Oct. 25, 1989   Hutchinson, Kans.   John & Anna Headings

[The above letter was part of the letter in the Editor's Corner.]

Suicides: I was shocked to see the statement that one of the correspondents from Mo. made about suicides among the Amish. I would be afraid to make such a statement for fear that I would be guilty of slandering (after-reden) and propagating a falsehood. We hear lots of rumors and it is almost impossible to always know what is true and what is a lie. It might be wise to apply the age-old three-fold test before saying or writing something which could injure another; First, it is true, second it is needful? Third, is it kind?

Any case of suicide is to be regretted. There are too many cases among the Amish, that is true, as well as among any other group. But to say that the suicide rate among the Amish is higher than the average of the population is grossly distorting the facts. Nearly all suicides among the Amish are listed as suicides whereas this is not true of the population as a whole. Several years ago, I read in an authentic sourcebook that only a fraction of the suicides in the world today are listed as suicides. It went on to say that in the United States, suicides have a high rating as the most frequent cause of death. It think it was either fourth or fifth place.

Feb. 27, 1980   Bloomfield, Iowa   David Wagler

[Wagler gave considerable detail about a young woman who killed her two children, one and seven years old, then tried to hang herself. Both she and her husband were members of the Mennonite Church but traced their roots to the Amish. He describes the motivation as "Not out of hate but of pity because she was afraid they would be unable to go thru the troubles of life." The young couple was described as "very religious, highly respected and of good reputation."]

Is it possible that a change from the simplicity of a rural way of life to the worldly environment of the city was too great? This should be something to think about for those who look down upon the simple way of life.

April 11, 1957   Aylmer, Ont.   David Wagler

111

Drugs, Alcohol and Tobacco   15

Alcohol and tobacco were frequently discussed during THE BUDGET'S one-hundred years of publication. The introduction of either of the subjects by a scribe usually led to a flurry of responses, and no subject polarized readers as did these. The Editor stated the case clearly in the March 11, 1954 issue in "The Editor's Corner." He stated unquestionably that "There is no way you can start trouble quicker than to print something about tobacco."

During the late 1950's and early 1960's a spirited discussion of alcohol and tobacco ensued. This was during the time that Jacob J. Hershberger, Beachy Amish minister of Lynnhaven, Virginia was writing the weekly column, "Lynnhaven Gleanings" for THE BUDGET. His column consisted of two parts; one of news and one dealing with religious matters. Jacob was also Secretary of Amish Mennonite Aid. He received many private letters in response to his column. Jacob often responded to these letters via the religious part of "Lynnhaven Gleanings." There were scribes who openly agreed with him and there were others who took issue with him in their letters to THE BUDGET. Part of that exchange on tobacco and alcohol is included in this chapter.

Alcohol: I fully agree with John Christner of Wilmot, Minn., so far that it is very wrong to indulge in the habit of going to saloons.
> Aug. 6, 1903   St. Agatha, Ont.   Jacob Iutzi

This is a prohibition state, and it seems odd for an eastern man to go through a city without a saloon in it. I understand however, that liquor is something sold here, but not publicly.
> Mar. 3, 1904   Conway, Kans.   Niles M. Slabaugh

Mrs. Lydia Brenneman of Smithville, Ohio in answer to your question, "Are we as Christians praying enough to get this evil-rum out of the land?" If it could be done by prayers alone, I believe it would have been done long ago.

It seems to me that the drunkards wives, and mothers alone must have prayed enough, if that was all that is required. But what do our prayers avail so long as many of those who have the power in their hands to help vote this evil out, will not do their duty. It is a mystery to me, how a Christian can pray for the destruction of the liquor traffic, and then at the first opportunity go to the election and vote for its continuance, or think himself too good a Christian to vote at all.

Mar. 24, 1904   Calhan, Colo.   Mrs. A. F. Yoder

To S.S., total abstinence from the use of intoxicating liquors for over seven years allowed my system to cast off the ailment. I have no faith whatever in your hard cider cure for rheumatism.

Jan. 23, 1908   Yoder, Colo.   Abner F. Yoder

[Lester Hostetler wrote an appeal to vote for Prohibition. It covered 1¼ columns.]

Oct. 30, 1918   Holmes, Co.   Lester Hostetler

John Barleycorn is dead, and since it is a fact that no "drunkard shall inherit eternal life" it is positively the greatest blessing that has ever come to this land.

Jan. 22, 1919   Smithville, Ohio   A. K. Kurtz

Some people in our church are quite often having company from Fort Wayne, Ind., who bring along beer and "stuff" with which to have a good time, making them unable to go to church. Is it not as bad to not go to "Christ's meetings" as it is to not have them in your own home? I believe some people do not think quite far enough.

June 30, 1932   Centerville, Mich.   A Budget Reader

There must be quite a sporting place up in Centerville, Mich., as we read again in the last Budget, of those that were there from Fort Wayne with some beer and "stuff" and had to stay out of church. Would it not seem better if they spent their time in such a way as we read in Col. 3:16 and 17?

July 14, 1932   Middlebury, Ind.   Enos J. Bontrager

Drugs: The Mervin Hight family had quite an experience last week when Mervin was out in the corn field cutting the outer rows getting ready for silo filling. He took notice of something else growing in the corn rows. Neatly spaced, was almost as tall as the corn stalks the stems were as thick as a lead pencil the leaves started out with 3 fingers the next lower leaves had 5 like fingers the next lower had 7 on, always having an uneven numbers.

We suspected some one had planted marijuana because the lower leaves were already harvested. Because this illegal weed had already grown very near the Lancaster and Berks County line, both counties got involved with their police officers, after it was identified to be marijuana. We do hope and pray for the Mennonite and Amish people as well as others. They might never learn to use this illegal weed.

Sept. 22, 1976   Laurel Hill, Pa.   A. M. Shirk

Tobacco: I noticed an article in the Budget stating that tobacco is a filth. When God created the earth and what is in it ꜱe called it good. Why should we now say it is filthy?

Mar. 5, 1908   Kalona, Iowa   A Subscriber

During the year ending June 3, 1917, 30,529,193,538 cigarettes were made and taxed or three hundred and five for every man, woman and child in the United States. It is estimated that 1200 American boys begin the tobacco habit everyday. One who has given up the habit speaks this: I am cleaner; my breath is not revolting' I am not a public nuisance, I am not an offense to my wife and children or brothers and sisters or parents or unto the Lord. My house is fresh and clean. I can work harder, walk farther, climb higher, have a better heart; I have a better conscience; I am not a stumbling block to the boys.

June 15, 1922   Bird-in-Hand, Pa.   Simon Troyer

In regards to what the Mendon, Mich. correspondent says that he has been reading so much in the Budget lately about the dirty habit of smoking. I just don't think we all understand just what Christ meant in Matt. 15-11 and other scripture, or it wouldn't be that so many of our people were so different minded about the tobacco habit.

Jan. 1, 1942   Wilmot, Ohio   E. J. Miller

[N. Yoder submitted a one-column article exposing the evils of tobacco. He also suggested that the high price received for tobacco in 1945 might be shared with war sufferers. He quoted a conference statement appearing in *Gospel Herald.*]

April 11, 1946   Dover, Dela.   Noah Yoder

As far as I can see, we could do without tobacco but I do not approve of anyone using the whip just because he has hold of the handle and the lash can swing on whoever it reaches, as there is a wrong way of doing a right thing and also a wrong time of doing it. Read the 4th book of Moses, 14th chapter, the last six verses.

May 23, 1946   Belleville, Pa.   No name

If tobacco is wrong as some of our Budget friends think, we are in bad shape in Lancaster-co. I think we have plenty to think of in church matters, just as bad and maybe worse than the use of tobacco.

June 13, 1946   Narvon, Pa.   Amos Ebersole

While I do not want to uphold or condemn the use of tobacco, I fully agree with an old bishop. He said in His opinion the man who doesn't use it and leaves the man alone who does use it, is the best off. I also heard a preacher, who was himself opposed to the use of tobacco, make the remark that in his opinion those who talked so radically against it were just as far out of place as those who used it.

Aug. 20, 1953   Centerville, Mich.   John M. Bontrager

We saw by the Budget of last week's issue that a correspondent writes about what he thinks about an old-fashioned Amishman using tobacco. We all KNOW, and not just THINK, that this unnecessary use of tobacco in its various forms is one of the most highly esteemed worldling habits or practices; it belongs and goes with the world' we all know that.

Aug. 6, 1953   Thomas, Okla.   J. B.

[Jacob Hershberger was the recipient of many letters during the more than ten years that he was a BUDGET scribe, but the shortest one was the following:]
Dear Tobacco:
"Tobacco is so sweet and so good. Dumb people don't use me."

April 6, 1961   Lynnhaven, Va.   Jacob Hershberger

Tobacco is the main crop for the natives. But don't move here to raise tobacco and expect to join with the Mennonites, or you will be left. Most of us are dairy farmers.

May 25, 1961   Rustburg, Va.   Willis C. Glick

I would advise all such folks to try to tell God once, that since He had called everything good, He had no "business" in making toadstools and chokeberrys and cocklebur seeds poisonous - - they were "good".

Jan. 25, 1962   Lynnhaven, Va.   J. J. Hershberger

[A scribe posed the following five questions and the answers for a few, and follows it with some comments.]
Who makes tobacco grow?

> The Almighty God.

Why does it grow?

> To see if we are foolish enough to quarrel over it.

Who has the right to condemn the work of God?
Where in the scriptures do you find tobacco forbidden?

> Let me remind you when I say scripture, I do not mean pamphlets or other misprinted books, I mean the Holy Bible, or the NT.

But don't misunderstand me, I am not saying tobacco cannot be misused, the same as many other things, and I am not advertising tobacco.

Now if anyone can answer those questions I have asked, let me know I promise you I will quit using tobacco if and when it is proven forbidden.

Mar. 7, 1963   Apple Creek, Ohio   Emanual Y. Hostetler

Well, I don't have all the answers - - but I do recall that years ago father brought home what he thought were mushrooms (God had made them) and that father tried to eat them - - with almost fatal results. I also recall that in some places they have to watch their cattle lest they eat a certain kind of week (loco weed - - which God also made) or their cattle will act like crazy, and even die. So I'm not quite ready to "eat" everything that God made, even if He called it all good. [This was a response to the Mar. 7, 1963 letter above.]

Mar. 21, 1963   Lynnhaven, Va.   J. J. Hershberger

About tobacco. One thing we liked about it was the way it killed all the cecal worms in blackhead and intestinal worms in turkeys.

Mar. 21, 1963   Shelbyville, Ill.   Mrs. Sam Toll

It has been for some time my humble opinion that the apostle would class tobacco as lawful, but not expedient. (I Cor. 6,12) Food is lawful too, but somehow I sometimes wonder if a table set with all the goodies and dainties which so many of us are accustomed to is expedient.

Mar. 21, 1963   St. Joe, Ark.   R. Wickey [Editor's Corner]

More interest is being shown in the booklet, "Tobacco, a Burning Issue" than in any other material we have ever offered thru the columns of the Budget.

Jan. 9, 1964   Aylmer, Ont.   David Wagler

116

J. J. Troyer and Levi Gingerich have both quit chewing tobacco for a wager of 5 lbs. of tobacco, and by all appearances Mr. G. is the loser.

Sept. 28, 1899   Hutchinson, Kans.   N. Helmuth

I am glad that the Editor will stop the publication of opinion in regards to the subjects formerly given, as it was a very neat way to throw slurs against one another. One slur from Goshen, Ind. was surely meant for Lanc. Co. It mentioned tobacco and beer. Surely us Lancaster countians were brought up with tobacco farming and paid many an honest debt with it. As for drinking beer and other alcoholics, that is very strictly forbidden and if it's done it is behind the backs of parents or preachers.

Mar. 30, 1950   Gap, Pa.   John F. Glick

Economics and Ethics 16

Economics deals with the material welfare of mankind and the problems related to it such as capital, labor, wages, prices, tariffs, taxes, etc. Ethics deals with the rightness and wrongness of attitudes and actions.

One of the purposes of this book is to serve as a sampler. That is all that this chapter can be. Economics and ethics are two broad topics, worthy of an entire volume each. This chapter merely opens some windows and gives the perspective and thoughts of the scribes.

The reader should be reminded that two of the advantages of THE BUDGET were to share information on the making of a livelihood, and also to inform fellow-readers of impostors, swindlers and high-pressure salesmen traveling from community to community.

Chain stores: [The growth of chain stores raised some discussion (April 24, 1930) and opposition, with some feeling that the government should give relief to the small independent retailers.]

Credit/cash: . . . but I surely think we should adopt the cash system or do without which we certainly can do to a great extend.
Jan. 26, 1928   Arthur, Ill.   David S. Beachy

Depression: I have to think of what Bishop Leander Keim of Haven, Kansas stated in the Budget last summer, that he didn't think times are as hard as they are going to get even if they tell you prosperity is just around the corner.
Feb. 11, 1932   Ligonier, Ind.   M. D. Glick

I don't believe we mind the depression as much as the southern and central states.
Mar. 3, 1932   West Branch, Mich.   C. S. Bender

[The following was an ad by Garver Bros. Co. and was the first appearance of the word "depression" found in THE

BUDGET.] To Help You Through This Depression We are Offering the Most Dramatic Values in a Decade.
July 9, 1931

[News item in THE BUDGET; referring to October 1931.]
Articles which farmers bought declined 19%.
Articles which farmers sold dropped 51%.
Retail prices dropped 26%.
Farm prices dropped 51%.

We are not living on fried mush, ground wheat, rivel soup and bread and milk. Traffic is as heavy on the road as ever, and our children don't sit alone in school so that others can't see their cold sausage and applebutter sandwiches. Wages are up there yet, and Spectors of Middlefield are busy. People weren't using taxis for short trips for they cost too much. Patched up pants are practically a bygone thing, doctors now charge $20.00 for office calls where they used to come to your house for five to ten dollars. Ah! for the good old depression. Oh, yes, baling wire was truly a "farmer's friend."
Sept. 17, 1980   Huntsburg, Ohio   Uria Byler

Varied economic activities: Wish some more businessmen would come and locate here, such as merchants, etc. Would also like to have one here that is experienced in undertaking and embalming, as we know that we must all die sooner or later, and most of the people living here have many of their relatives living in other states, and very inconvenient to get here, with no way to keep a corpse until they can get here, especially in warm weather. It seems sad when we think about it.
Jan. 14, 1909   Fairview, Mich.   Mrs. M. S. Zook

Auctioneer Elliot says, at A.D. Miller's sale everything sold the highest of any sale he cried this winter.
Mar. 3, 1903   Plain City, Ohio   A. J. Kramer

I am informed that Pigeon will have a new buggy factory to be in running order by September. There were about 85 lots sold in Pigeon in one day on the strength of the location of the factory.
July 4, 1901   Baden, Ont.   Jacob Iutzi

Our little town is on a boom, on account of finding oil. This is the fourth well that has been drilled in about a year.
Oct. 19, 1899   Loogootee, Ind.   Joseph S. Overholt

About all the Amish are tending market day at Norfolk, Va.
Jan. 8, 1925   Norfolk, Va.   No name

Seven car loads of maple syrup was shipped from Croghan lately, in one day, amounting to about $20,000, that being about half the out-put of this vicinity; the rest was sold to local dealers.
May 30, 1907   Croghan, N.Y.   Joseph J. Zehr

Nearly all the Amish there raise rabbits on a commercial basis. [Writing about St. Joe, Ark.]
Mar. 28, 1963   Vilonia, Ark.   Adin Yutzy

Years ago I advertised my rat-killing recipe and received over $600 for it. Now I wish to let it appear in the Budget free to anyone.
Feb. 16, 1950   Dundee, Ohio   Jacob M. Yoder

Fraud: There is a man by the name of Bitschy selling plum trees by the thousands to some of the farmers. Mr. Bitschy keeps the plums and the man that buys keeps the trees. Readers, which is the luckiest man?
Feb. 27, 1902   Baden, Ont.   Uncle Dan

[The following comment is a response to the above named "salesman."] Dear readers of the Budget, such a man should be watched by a big dog. Uncle King [Canada] and Uncle Sam together ought to bring him to a place where flies and mosquitos would not bother him for the next 20 years.
Oct. 16, 1902   Baden, Ont.   Daniel Jantzie

[In the Editor's Corner appeared a quotation from a private letter by Joseph J. Miller of Orrville, Ohio.] "Recently we noticed more of these high-powered salesmen on the road again. Why is it that they so often follow our Amish people?" [The response of the Editor was, "The sooner we quit playing suckers to these so-called high-powered salesmen, the sooner we will be rid of them."]
Feb. 12, 1953

I wish to give a word of warning to our people in general, concerning a certain "seller of dry goods," who has been through this section of the country. He is a base swindler and deceiver and ought not to be patronized.
June 13, 1901   Carmel, W. Va.   BROTHERHOOD

Up to the recent past we used to hear quite a bit about Jeremiah 33:3 and the inventor Arnold Burke, and his wonderful machine that was supposed to operate anti the laws of physics. Or that falling water could produce electricity for a household, plus pumping the water back to recycle and reuse it, continually with only minimal cost. This would have been a boon to mankind. We had asked for a dealership and someone else had made a prior application for this area. [The Jeremiah 33:3 machine was a fraud. The money sunk into it by Amish and Amish Mennonites probably ran into the hundreds of thousands of dollars.]

Jan. 9, 1980   Virginia Beach, Va.   John H. Miller

Insurance: [The house of Michael Kauffman of Chester Co. burned.] It was insured in the Amish Mutual Insurance Co., for $1200.

Oct. 8, 1903   Gordonville, Pa.   John H. Kauffman

[The following comments were responses to a suggestion to form an insurance association. One scribe even suggested appointing the Editor as the chairman.] I agree with A. B. Miller of Weatherford, Oklahoma; an insurance association, I think would be all right in case of fire; if the readers of the Budget would stick together and give but a small sum it would amount to a good bit.

July 11, 1901   Whiteson, Ore.   Joel J. Yoder

I will let you know what I think about the proposal made by Abe Miller, of Oklahoma, about organizing an insurance company of all Budget readers. I for my part do not trust in man. The Lord is my refuge, in Him will I trust. Anyone that takes out an insurance policy departs from the Lord. See Jeremiah 17:15; Isa. 31:3.

July 11, 1901   Goshen, Ind.   POOR PEOPLE'S FRIEND

In the Budget of July 11th we noticed a letter written from this place, dated July 8th, signed, "Poor People's Friend". In my opinion the person who takes up an argument and hides his name "under a bushel" has a small influence, whether his opinion is right or wrong.

July 25, 1901   Goshen, Ind.   E. S. Troyer

I agree with the Bro. in the west; an insurance association, I think, would be all right in case of fire. Our house and most of the household goods burned up. The people in surrounding sections helped us a great deal. If the Budget readers would feel to help a little, a few cents of each one would help a good deal.

July 25, 1901   Middlebury, Ind.   Elizabeth Stutzman

Language: Well, they say good times are just around the corner. Have been saying it for a couple of years, but we don't know which corner.

April 11, 1935   Topeka, Ind.   Perry B. Miller

Lewis Troyer and John Baliard traded properties; Baliard pays $2000 boot money.

Jan. 16, 1902   Middlebury, Ind.   Moses E. Bontrager

Rudy Yoder sold his farm to Shem Schlabach. Rudy thought he knew where he was going, but it seems that it "fizzled" out in a "sizzle" to know where to. He would have better "left well enough alone".

Jan. 21, 1910   Thomas, Okla.   B. B. Miller

Moving/renting: It looks as though there will be a good deal of moving around next spring.

Jan. 16, 1902   West Liberty, Ohio   C. K. Y.

There are now 43 Amish families that bought farms, and 34 renters; so you see they are not all renters anymore in "Yankeedom".

Aug. 16, 1900   Burton, Ohio   Eli J. Slabaugh

You renters come and get homes and work for yourselves and not for the other fellow all your lives.

May 23, 1907   Fairview, Mich.   Mrs. M. S. Zook

Guess moving will soon be on the go again, as quite a few intend to move next week.

Feb. 29, 1940   Sugarcreek, Ohio   Mrs. Olen J. Miller

N. E. Miller traded his farm to W. J. Warnock, for 240 acres near the Centennial school house, about 8 miles west of this place. Mr. Miller is making more land deals than all the rest of the dutch people combined.

Sept. 7, 1898   Hutchinson, Kans.   N. Helmuth

D. K. Beiler has returned from Douglas County, where he rented a farm. "Douglas or bust". That rolling stone has not yet gathered any moss.

Jan. 18, 1900   Vandalia, Ill.   I. K. Beiler

Prices: Abraham D. Miller bought a second-handed bicycle for 20 cents.

Sept. 24, 1896   Mt. Hope, Ohio   A Reader

Milch cows sold high this past winter, according to price received of milk and butter. Price for cows; $ 30 to $62.

Mar. 25, 1897   Ronks, Pa.   Ben H. Fisher

David Jantzi shipped a car load of number one hay to

Chicago and realized $11.00 out of his carload; not enough to pay for the baling.

Mar. 18, 1897   Fulda, Minn.   M. J. Slabaugh

Our factory at Kirschnerville has started making cheese; one sale has been made at 12 cents per pound. It frightens some of the farmers to think their cows give so much milk.

May 21, 1903   Lowville, N.Y.   Mr. & Mrs. Daniel Steria

Our market prices are as follows: Wheat, good, 44 cts; corn 26 to 30 cts; oats 22 to 25 cts; butter 20 to 25 cts; eggs 20 cts; hogs $4.85 per cwt.. Railroads still claim to be blockaded with wheat. Which pays best; big crops and low price, or hi price and not much to sell. Mr. "Spy" of Mt. Ayr, Ind. please answer.

Nov. 17, 1892   Partridge, Kans.   Noah Helmuth

In reply to Mr. Helmuth of Kansas, would say, that we would rather have big prices, and not much to sell than to have such enormous crops, and low prices. As we cannot afford to raise and reap such crops for almost nothing. All that is missing here, is a few Kansas boomers to boom up our country, then we would be allright.

Dec. 22, 1892   Mt. Ayr, Ind.   SPY

Strip mining of coal: It would take hundreds of years, to say the least, before there would ever be productive forests on it again. And as for farming or pasture lands, a person would have to be rather optimistic to ever expect to farm it again without spending a huge sum for leveling, mulching and fertilizer. There are other ways of mining coal. Can we believe that God intended for men to use the big machines to turn the earth upside down? Your fathers worked hard to make those hills green. Let's hope you can keep them so. I would agree that it is better to do so than to wish you had.

Apr. 2, 1959   Aylmer, Ont.   David Wagler

[Rev. William Stauffer also joined the opposition of strip mining of coal. He supplied several articles for THE BUDGET on the subject.] How does Mr. Stauffer get his authority to say something is a sin against God. I certainly respect his right to feel strongly for or against something and tell others of his views, but claiming one's own views to be God's way and all others to be sinful is one of the ills of this world. I imagine the Indian felt that cutting down the forests, plowing up the prairie and driving out the buffalo was also a sin. ... I think he has the cart before the horse.

> Apr. 2, 1959   Navarre, Ohio   E. W. Miller

Taxes: M.S. and son are working out their road tax today and tomorrow over on this side of Neeland....

> Aug. 30, 1906   Fairview, Mich.   Mrs. M. S. Zook

Many farms can be rented for the paying of taxes, and bought at from $12 to $20 per acre. Most of the farms have good maple timber to run a sugar-bush if desired.

> Mar. 8, 1934   Columbus, Pa.   David D. Miller

One sees the assessor coming; reminds one of his yearly taxes. Some people can so easily pay them. For others the efforts are almost futile.

> Feb. 15, 1940   Fairbank, Iowa   Emanuel Miller

January is the month the farmers report their income to the Bureau of Internal Revenue. We should all report it correctly and it is sometimes a real headacle even if we do not need to pay tax.

> Jan. 13, 1955   Bird-in-Hand, Pa.   Paul Stoltzfus

Wages: Threshers are paying $1 a day for hands, and they are pretty scarce, wages are $1.50 through harvest.

> July 6, 1899   Yoder, Kans.   D. M. Yoder

Hired hands are very scarce at present; it is almost impossible for farmers to get help at any price. They offer $25 a month, and some even more, for good hands.

> July 6, 1899   Welshfield, Ohio   N. J. Hershberger

Yes, Menno says it pays to raise girls when they get just about as much wages as the boys, and that is what they do for working in town, and the work is not as hard as it is at home on the farm.

> July 24, 1902   Wilmot, Minn.   * *

There are about twenty boys and girls here from Holmes Co. to husk corn. The boys get 3 cents per bu. and the girls get about 75 cents per day.

> Dec. 11, 1902   Plain City, Ohio   Mrs. Anna K. Yoder

[The following comment was made in response to quilting a quilt, the pattern of which was called Watergate.] If a person would charge what they really should the price would be fantastic so I guess will just donate a lot of our time. It seems I have a knack of always getting into things I really don't want and I don't have the heart to say no.

> Oct. 6, 1976   Seymour, Mo.   Mrs. Mose Mishler

Wealth/ethics: I will say this country looks to me as if it surely was the country for a poor man, and much better for a man with plenty of money.

April 29, 1897   Island Lake, N.D.   Eli Hochstetler

I think this is a good place for the poor, they can get a cheap home.

Feb. 20, 1896   Milan, Okla.   J. C. Bontrager

Joe Bontrager has now two windmills up, and is feeding about sixty head of steers. He is considered the richest man in this part of the country. He also contemplates getting a new threshing outfit this fall, which is much needed here.

April 26, 1900   Weatherford, Okla.   A. B. Miller

Mr. Christner has rented another farm. Wonder if he intends to farm the whole county.

Jan. 10, 1895   Arlington, Kans.   Young Sunflower

Last week was one of the record breakers for corn pickers. When the sound of the "bang" boards is heard in the land, then rejoice ye, for the country is growing rich.

Jan. 3, 1901   Worthington, Minn.   Cor.

Many of our church districts are very much blessed financially. Last week I received a letter from a brother who said the district where he lives has a valuation of nearly a million dollars.

Feb. 14, 1963   Aylmer, Ont.   David Wagler

We use the German "vieh" when referring to cattle. My stepfather said at one time the Amish church members in Holmes County were warned against becoming too "money-minded" and the ministers thought it best not to have too many "Fettah-vieh". [Fat cattle] What would our forefathers have thought of the large caged chicken houses such as are common today?

June 4, 1980   Wilmot, Ohio   Sarah M. Weaver

There is one subject I feel to express myself on. We lost most of our property on account of the depression. Cause of the depression: Nobody to eat up the billionaire. The billionaire is eating up the millionaire and the millionaire is eating up the rich man. The rich man is eating up the common farmer and the common farmer is eating up the poor farmer. Now it has come to the point that money is piling up only at one end and obstructing the circulation of money. To get out of this serious position is to limit the wealth. Whatever money goes over the limit should be transferred to the U.S. Treasury.

Aug. 15, 1935   Sugarcreek, Ohio   Jacob M. Yoder

Threshing is in full blast. A thresherman can charge almost any reasonable price this year and get a good run, if he charges his neighbor one cent a bushel more than others that are blessed with more of this world's goods. This may seem all right before men, but how will it hold out at the judgment bar of God?

Aug. 31, 1905   Shipshewana, Ind.   B. E. Miller

Unclassified: . . . recently one of our boys decided to go to the sale to buy a few calves and they had one here that they decided to sell at the same time. Somehow the first calf he bought was the same one he had taken to the sale. I'm not sure whether he made any money on this deal or not.

Nov. 16, 1977   Abbeville, S.C.   Mrs. Wm. Stoll

John and Jake Miller have sold their threshing outfit. This is the third time in a little over a year, but they say she is gone this time, as they have the cash for it.

Nov. 23, 1899   Weatherford, Neb.   A. B. Miller

It is amazing to see the exorbitant prices some people will pay for antiques.

Sept. 19, 1946   Meyersdale, Pa.   Mrs. Enos J. Maust

The writers, through complications and erroneous survey, was notified by the land office the first of March that he could not hold three forties of land he had filed on, and that should relinquish same and use his rights somewhere else; so to-morrow he makes final proof on the remaining forty, and files for three forties, four miles distant.

May 15, 1902   Lakeside, Wash.   Mr. & Mrs. J. J. Zook

Our newly organized milk Association of this place which consists of fifteen members of the Amish church of the Kempsville district, have just completed our first month of operation.

According to our stenographer this was done quite successfully, altho it may become necessary to change some of our bylaws which were framed before we had any experience along this line, as well as a few more of our old established church rules. The church is co-operating with the organization.

Nov. 19, 1931   Kempsville District, Va.   No name

126

The editor of THE BUDGET during the first three decades did not have an easy task. "Budget John" had a difficult pioneering task. He faced several formidable problems. For one thing, the division of the Amish Church was unfolding in 1890 when Miller embarked upon this venture. A second matter was how to handle delinquent subscriptions among his fellow church people. A third area was developing and applying a suitable policy for dealing with highly opinionated scribes and readers. A fourth was the ongoing debate of whether it shall be a newspaper or viewspaper. And finally, was English to be used exclusively or should part of THE BUDGET be devoted to letters and articles written in German.

The Amish division led to new viewpoints. It was now no longer Amish and Mennonite; a third element, Amish Mennonite, was to become more and more prominent and vocal. It is the position of the author, based on his reading of the letters, that some subscribers took advantage of Miller's position as Amish Mennonite. They knew it was against church regulations to go to law and use legal means for collection of delinquent accounts.

It seems that until the Smiths gained control of the paper that a small number of scribes believed they should be able to state their personal opinions emphatically and that the editor was bound to print it. The newspaper vs. viewspaper debate continued for many decades, with the newspaper concept prevailing. In spite of pressure to use German, it was never used except for an occasional letter. The editor used the added cost factor as an argument against the use of German. He at times resorted to the argument that with so many subscriptions in arrears, it was not financially possible to also include German "pieces."

Editorial policies and practices: [One of the Budget writers once stated that to give the text the minister had for his sermon was more newsworthy than to give the place he ate his

Sunday dinner.] I quite agreed with him. But each time that I include the text of the Sunday sermon or a scripture verse, when my letter is put into print that part is always omitted. Now, Mr. Editor, I know that's your privilege, but I have wondered why you do so.

May 16, 1957   Modesto, Calif.   Sarah Yoder

[Editorial response:] We know of no good reason why we should take the time and space to give sermon texts.

May 16, 1957

Also wish to commend the Budget editor for the way he handles things in general. He may censor the news letters if he wishes and omit arguments if he considers them harmful. As far as I am concerned, let them blow off steam. If one reads a newspaper, a book, or hears a sermon, he can do as the apostle says, "Prove everything and hold fast to that which is good."

April 11, 1957   Bird-in-Hand, Pa.   Paul Stoltzfus

The editor will not publish anymore letters on Menno Simons v Jacob Ammann. If it continues it may approach the controversy on shunning of a few years ago.

Jan. 13, 1955   Editor's Corner

Some [letters] will not be printed because the writer's asked us to withhold their names. We do not think highly of anyone who makes nasty remarks about another correspondent and then asks us to print them without using their name. If you are ashamed of what you write, don't ask us to print it. [By 1940 it was a strict policy - - no name, no letter printed.]

Feb. 13, 1958   Editor's Corner

Eli L. Hershberger and family, John H. Hershberger and family, Allen L. Hershberger and family, Levi L. Hershbergers and three daughters spent Epiphany day at Jake L. Hershbergers. [How would you use your editorial pen on this paragraph?]

Jan. 16, 1958   Middlefield, Ohio   Mamie E. Hershberger

[The Editor shortened a North Dakota letter stating that "the remainder of the above letter was a weather report for Dec. which we cannot publish for lack of space." He did give a summary of the letter.]

Jan. 17, 1895   Island Lake, N.D.   Moses H. Hostetler

We omitted one letter this week because the writer

referred to practically everyone mentioned by their nicknames only. We have no objections to having nicknames of persons mentioned as it sometimes helps to identify them, but be sure to give the real name also.

Oct. 8, 1942   Editor's Corner

Had we thought that the article written by Bro. Kurtz would lead to so much commotion about this matter, upon which there are so many and varied opinions, it would never have found its way into print.

July 19, 1900   Editor's Corner

Can the editor give me the address of Mrs. Anna (Schrock) Hazen? She lives somewhere in Kansas. [The editor was asked numerous such favors. He provided the address in a footnote.]

Aug. 9, 1906   Atwater, Ohio   Leah J. Harris

[There was a big splurge of poems in 1893. Some scribes attempted to write their letters in poetry. The following question was asked:]
Say, Mr. Editor, will you endeavor to ascertain for us whether those poetical contributors of yours were born that way or whether they accidentally became so.

May 15, 1893

[Editorial response to above.] We cannot give a positive answer to your question, but venture to say that it appears to us as though they accidently became so. If they had been born that way, then great talent would not have remained hidden so long, but would have come forth in all its glory, long before it has.

May 5, 1893

Criticism and debate: Last week we omitted four letters - - two because they were not signed and two because they contained items which apparently were intended to embarrass someone.

July 22, 1943   Editor's Corner

This will positively close this subject, and not another article will be published for either party on this subject. We now have four lengthly articles and we doubt whether a majority of our readers are any wiser for it. It is a needless waste of space. [This closed a spirited debate between John Horsch and S. F. Gingerich as to whether the University of Chicago was a rationalistic school.]

Aug. 28, 1902

We receive many articles on religious subjects for publication in The Budget. Most of them are exceedingly dull and repetitious. Nearly all of them are too lengthly. A few of the articles show deep thinking on the matters discussed, but to the average reader they are more confusing than enlightening.
> Nov. 13, 1958

Now please make your Budget a paper that is satisfactory OR ELSE! [An excerpt from a threatening and slanderous letter which the Editor received, having been mailed in Apple Creek, Ohio.]
> Feb. 21, 1957   Editor's Corner

Two weeks ago I received a letter from Nappanee, Ind. signed "An Undecided Amish Boy," who writes sarcastically about members of his faith who travel to Florida and other parts of the U.S. [In a note to the editor he says,] "I have heard some people say that you won't publish anything without the writer's name but I hope you will make an exception. [No exception was made.]
> Feb. 9, 1950   Editor's Corner

[The Editor was accused in a letter from Holt County, Nebraska, that] "it is very seldom one of our letters is seen in print, as the editor takes care of them when he fires them in the waste basket and that is all.
> Dec. 11, 1902   O'Neil, Neb.   Katie Erb and Annie Kennel

You are talking through your hats, girls; there are no more Holt Co. letters going to the waste basket than from any other place. [Editorial response to the O'Neil, Neb. letter.]

Letter writing - - need of: Is it that people are too busy to write or does the Ed. intend to make a story paper out of the Budget? Think most people like news better than stories.
> Sept. 15, 1915   Ronks, Pa.   K. B. L.

I don't think the people had ought to chew the rag so much about the advs in the Budget as the ed. can't print no letters if he don't receive them, we would feel a little funny if we would get the Budget and half of it would have nothing in it.
> Mar. 8, 1916   Fair Oaks, Mich.   A Reader

Again I think the editor knows that it is more profitable to print a few well paid ads than to print a paper for a lot of delinquents.
> Feb. 16, 1916   Shipshewana, Ind.   M. S.

130

Yes, we have thus far printed all the letters we received, and will stand by our promise to print supplements as soon as we have an oversupply of letters. [In response to a scribe expressing confidence that all letters had been printed, and were not crowded out by advertising.]

Feb. 9, 1916   Editor

Two weeks ago my husband and I really played a joke on each other. On Sunday we had been to church and then the children and I spent Sunday night and Monday with my parents and my husband went home to do the chores and go to work Monday morning from there. So each of us decided to write a letter for the Budget, having no idea the other one had the same idea. It sure was disgusting for both of us.

Jan. 6, 1955   Garnett, Kans.   Mrs. W. I. Yoder

Special rates: Preachers, Bishops, and deacons have always been permitted to subscribe at one-half the regular price.

Jan. 14, 1937   The Editor's Corner

If you write for the Budget at least twice a month you are entitled to receive it without charge. If you do not receive it free, enclose a note with your next letter and I will see to it that you do.

Jan. 7, 1937   Editor's Corner

Effective Oct. 1, will offer a free 6 mo. subscription to each newly married couple. A current subscriber must submit the names, date of marriage, and correct address.

Sept. 28, 1939   Editor's Corner

Subscriptions: A western publisher runs his paper on this plan: When a subscriber fails to pay up in one year the publisher sends him a statement of account at the end of the year. If he does not answer the statement by remittance the publisher continues to send the paper for another year; at the end of the second year he sends him another statement and requests him to remit at once. If however, he does not hear from him in a short time he proceeds to publish an obituary notice in the paper and drops him from the list, thinking that a man must certainly be dead if he does not pay his paper for two years. We had been thinking of adopting this plan but are afraid it would take up too much space to print the obituaries, as we have so many that owe for two years or more.

June 11, 1896   Editor

A word to the subscribers of the Budget; How could we bring it about that the editor would report a broad smile through the paper. Now let's all "get up and dust", and pay our subscriptions up to date, and if it will not produce the above results I will say no more about it.

      Jan. 21, 1897   Grantsville, Md.   Emanuel Hershsberger

How is this county for paid up subscriptions? Can we boast about it? [Lancaster and Mifflin Counties are among our best, was the Editor's response.]

      Feb. 11, 1897   Ronks, Pa.   B. H. Fisher

I was horrified when I read in last week's paper that a very large number of subscribers are still in arrears.

      Aug. 24, 1899   Baden, Ont.   Jacob Iutzi

There was much said about the delinquents; I would advise the Ed. to send them blank papers until they do pay up.

      May 10, 1900   Shipshewana, Ind.   Mona Hochstetler

As I am a member of the delinquent family since the first day of this century I feel it my duty to have a little silent chat with my delinquent brothers. [He follows this with 48 lines urging the paying of bills in arrears.]

      Mar. 14, 1901   Kempsville, Va.   D. D. Hershberger

It seems that one of the difficulties in the way is a lack of funds, caused by delinquent subscribers not meeting their obligations. This is strange, as the great majority of subscribers belong to the different branches of the Mennonite Church, which class of people formerly were noted for their promptness in paying their honest debts; but it seems some of them have lost their peculiarities in this respect.

      Feb. 20, 1902   Smithville, Ohio   A. K. Kurtz

WE'RE NOT "FOOLING" when we say that all subscriptions will be discontinued promptly at their expiration.

      Dec. 17, 1936   Editor

Editor and Scribes   18

The scribes were ordinary people from the widely scattered communities. Some were ministers; most were not. Some were encouraged and prodded by friends or community people to begin writing letters for THE BUDGET. Others overcame shyness and modesty sufficiently to begin volunteer writing.

The first letter appearing in THE BUDGET was one written by Absolom King of Stuttgart, Arkansas. It was written in June of 1890. The number increased rapidly. Mrs. P.P. Miller was the first woman scribe, with a letter in the Nov. 7, 1895 issue. For information on the sources of letters see Chapter 25.

By 1980 a total of 324 correspondents were scattered in thirty-three states and Canada and eight foreign countries. Some wrote every week; others were much more irregular. More than 300 persons attended the 1980 Correspondent's Get-Together. Some were spouses or friends of scribes, which means that the number of scribes in attendance was considerably less than 300. Mrs. Enos W. Yoder of Montezuma, Georgia, had the longest period of service. She was given a plaque for sixty years. She began writing under her maiden name, Mary Miller, before she was married. About half of the years were in the Lynnhaven [Norfolk], Virginia community and the other half at Montezuma. At the same meeting, Steven Nissley of Fishersville, Virginia was recognized as the youngest scribe. He was eighteen years of age.

During 1912 and 1913 opportunity was given for youngsters to write letters. These were grouped together in each issue. There was a spurt of letters for several months, but did not last more than two years. One excerpt below is from a ten-year old.

First woman scribes: [Mrs. P.P. Miller described her trip from Ohio to Iowa, but did not give her home address. She appears to have been the first woman scribe.]
Nov. 7, 1895

[The second was one who simply signed her first name.]
Jan. 9, 1896   Baltic, Ohio   Ruth

133

[The third was Mrs. Noah Kauffman.]
Jan. 9, 1896   Davidsville, Pa.

Identification: I think it would be well for all the scribes to give the middle initials when giving names in their write-ups, so that the readers may know to whom they are referring. There are quite a few having the same names, especially in our parts. If the writer does not know the middle initial they could give the church district to which they belong, or the location.
July 7, 1949   Lancaster County Briefs   Jonathan B. Fisher

Some will not be printed because the writers asked us to withhold their names. We do not think highly of anyone who makes nasty remarks about another correspondent and then asks us to print them without using their name. If you are ashamed of what you write, don't ask us to print it.
Feb. 13, 1958   Editor's Corner

Include a German part? In regard to printing part of the paper in German, I wish to say that the editor does not need to go to any extra trouble or expense on my account. I think he is doing his duty right along, by enlarging the paper and giving us more news; but if he decides to do so I will not kick. It may be a good plan though to hold back until his tardy delinquents pay their honest dues.
July 13, 1899   Millersburg, Ohio   Y. P. Byler

A few words about a German paper. If there would be an extra sheet printed in German, I honestly believe that half the German people (who are Budget readers) would take an interest in it. I had an inquiry lately whether the Editor would accept a German letter and print it in English.
Mar. 21, 1901   Shipshewana, Ind.   E. M. Hochstetler

[Editor's response to Hochstetler's letter.] We have refused a number of such letters, for the reason that it would make us much extra work to print them. We thought the "German paper" problem had died out, but it seems that there is still some life left in it and with the approach of spring is reviving.
Mar. 21, 1901

[The Editor responded to an inquiry about a German part.] There would not be enough to make it pay to print the Budget in German, neither have we any German type.
Sept. 4, 1902

Editor, in regard to enlarging the Budget, I will tell you what Grandfather Christian Stahly thinks about it. He thinks the Budget is good enough the way it is, and if the readers wish to read more they should read the Bible. Grandpa Stahly is now nearly 82 years old. . . .
> May 15, 1902   Nappanee, Ind.   Yost I. Yoder

Pencil or ink?   As the Editor advises all correspondents to use pen and ink instead of pencils. I will gladly do so but kindly ask in return to also use a little more ink in printing as several papers came to this office recently that a good part of the print could not be read at all.
> June 2, 1915   Belleville, Pa.   Rudy J. Kanagy

I wouldn't blame the fellow that sets the type if he would kick all letters written with lead pencils.
> July 10, 1918   Elk Lick, Pa.   Mrs. John D. Yoder

There were a few mistakes in my letter in the Budget, but mistakes are no hay stacks or the writer would have hay stacks to sell.
> Oct. 6, 1915   Meyersdale, Pa.   S. S. Summy

Quotations: [Quoted material was used at times by scribes without giving credit to the source. One example was "The Destruction of St. Pierre" which was sandwiched between several opening and concluding paragraphs, with the quotation occupying the equivalent of a full column. The author has a copy of it as it appeared in *Reader's Digest*, November, 1961. It also appeared in some other national magazines earlier. The article describes the eruption of La Montagne, a volcano near the city of St. Pierre on the island of Martinique.   The city was destroyed in "60 seconds." No credit was given whatsoever to any source.]
> June 22, 1972   Kutztown, Pa.   Esra Burkholder

Task of writing: As my mind runs every where writing goes hard as there is so much work that ought to be done at this time.
> June 2, 1915   Mio, Mich.   Mrs. M. S. Zook

The Budget, in a great measure will be what its correspondents make it. So let us all try our best to make it a neat, clean and instructive family newspaper. It can be the messenger of news and events from far and near. Let it also be an exhorter and admonisher.
> Apr. 26, 1900   Amish, Iowa   A Friend

As the editor allowed space in the Budget for little folks to write letters. I will now try and do my best as long as the Lord will help me. [Age 10.]

Aug. 14, 1912   Walford, N.D.   Katie Gingerich

Now, Ezra, don't get peeved when your letter gets de-horned; the Editor is trying to teach you what he wants and doesn't want in his paper.

April 25, 1963   Belleville, Pa.   Ezra Kanagy

Please don't mind the chaff in this letter, as we just can't raise wheat without any chaff here in this backwoods country.

Oct. 11, 1962   Mifflintown, Pa.   D. Y. Renno

We notice it is customary with the Budget scribes to start letters by giving weather reports and crop conditions, etc. This being my first letter to the Budget you can expect some things hind foremost, as I did not start this letter that way, and am not sure I will keep this job or not, as I am a poor writer.

Sept. 23, 1954   Lewisburg, Pa.   C. D. Sharp

The Budget is a paper dedicated mostly to bring us news of the Amish and Mennonites over most of the United States and Canada. Why not use it for that purpose. There are some religious articles in it that are good and offend no body. Let's keep it that way. If each and everyone of us would work on the beam in our own eye instead of picking at the splinter in our brother's eye we would all be a lot better off and I think a lot of strife and contention would not be in our churches like it is today.

Aug. 20, 1953   Centerville, Mich.   John Bontreger

I know just what David Wagler meant when he wrote about people stopping in to see the Budget scribe. I'm always glad to know that there are people who read my letters, but on the other hand, I'm almost ashamed to be called a scribe, as I can think of so few things to write about.

June 13, 1963   Montgomery, Ind.   Jerome Raber

I do not want anybody to find fault with my writing, there-fore will ask the Editor to cull out every article that is not fit for publication. [From the last paragraph of a letter one and one-half columns long.]

May 28, 1980   Bay Minette, Ala.   E. N. Beachy

When and what to write: A writer from Hutchinson, Kans.

stated last week that there is too much written where people visit and that is not of interest to strangers. Well I don't think a letter for the Budget can please everybody, and I wonder if it is any harm in writing such things as long as it is true.

April 11, 1940   Monroe, Ind.   Sarah Schwartz

Maybe I better quit now as a friend met me on the street last week and gave me a "talking to" about my last letter in the Budget.

July 22, 1954   Belleville, Pa.   Ezra Y. Peachey

Usually in most businesses it's the middleman that is the big fellow but in this business of writing for the Budget the middlemen (correspondents) are the little people, getting the squeeze from the publishers and reading public.

May 2, 1963   Dover, Dela.   Mrs. Alfred Troyer

I have noticed that the Budget is being dominated by certain writings which from time to time seem to condemn, criticize and ridicule certain faiths. I can't help but believe that this is brought on by one's conscience, which keeps gnawing at its owner, reminding him of some wrong which he had done. So he has to find fault with some one else in order to keep himself thinking he is right.

Sept. 21, 1961   Grabill, Ind.   William Zehr

Some people would better attend to their own business and quit writing for the Budget, if they can't write the truth. Saying that others are happy or feel big when they know there is not the least bit of truth in it, and remember that not only the community reads your letter but thousands of people all over the world, who read them and perhaps believed it not knowing any better. It seems as though some people can't write for the Budget unless they can throw a slurr at some one.

June 16, 1904   Arthur, Ill.   A Budget Reader

This is only one subscriber's opinion on this ridiculous idea of these self-appointed apostles efforts to single-handedly reform this country and abolish sin. Sometimes it has been the characteristic of a contest, with each one of them trying to outdo his fellow-scribes in preaching the loudest and longest. I believe in the Bible, but I somehow fail to see where we have a right to indulge in a fault-finding contest. Does that make me an unbeliever, or a sinner, or just a plain dummy?

Feb. 18, 1960   Quotation from a letter in Editor's Corner.

Some people think the Budget should be only a newspaper, others prefer a views-paper.

Mar. 2, 1961 .Aylmer, Ont. David Wagler

I was censured by some because I did not send the news to our home paper, the Budget. I says, says I, as soon as the Dog Days are past you will see me in the limelight again.

Sept. 3, 1931 Fresno, Ohio No name

Some of the Budget readers seem to think that the reading matter of this paper is changing too much from a "News" paper or original reading matter of a farm paper, or agricultural news borrowed from other papers. It may be there is a lack of correspondence through the busy season that has compelled the Editor to fill the paper with general reading, which is all right, if there is nothing better at hand.

Aug. 9, 1911 Centralia, Mo. J. D. Guengerich

Writing on Sunday: This is written on the sabbath. I noticed something in the Budget about not being quite in its place to write on the sabbath for the Budget. If so, let me know. We should always be careful what we write on week days or on the Sabbath, for the Budget or private letters.

Feb. 28, 1901 Daytonville, Iowa Mrs. N. D. Yoder

[Editor's response to Mrs. N. D. Yoder.]
We do not wish to encourage anyone to write letters for the Budget on Sunday, and have made mention of this in the past, but would say we do not think it more out of place to write a respectable letter to the Budget than to spend that time on the Sabbath in idle gossip (as no doubt is frequently done). Nevertheless, we think in most cases it can be arranged that such letters can be written during the week, and there is no doubt a great diversity of opinion as to what may with propriety be done on the Sabbath day, so we will say, "Remember the Sabbath Day, to keep it holy."

Feb. 28, 1901

Education has been an important element in Amish and Mennonite life during the past century, even though the Amish do not look with favor on high school or higher education. The value of literacy in the vocation of farming has always been recognized, but even more so the importance of literacy in understanding the Scriptures. The following will give a sampling of the comments which appeared in THE BUDGET since 1890.

Amish schools; value of: Our school closed on Tuesday of the past week and we feel that the effort and expense put forth in the interest of our children's education has been a decided success so far, inasmuch as religious education is being eradicated from our public schools, even having been ruled out by the court in one of the large cities of our so-called Christian United States.
> June 10, 1948   Lynnhaven, Va.   Mrs. Enos W. Yoder

Amish school problems: [Describing Amish school problems would be a volume in itself. The following headlines of news items which appeared in THE BUDGET will help to give some idea of the scope of the problems. The observant reader will notice how they cluster in the late 1950's and early 1960's.]
PA Eases School Attendance Laws for Amish
> Oct. 13, 1955

Wayne County Amish Face School Trial
> Feb. 20, 1958

Jail Amish Parents in School Case
> Mar. 13, 1958

State Inspectors Visit Amish Parochial School in Prairie Twp. (Ohio)
> Dec. 25, 1958

Kansas Bill, Opposed by Amish, Defeated
> April 2, 1959

Amish Schools in Hardin Co. Enjoined from Operating (Ohio)
> April 9, 1959

Indiana Amish Seek Own Schools
> May 21, 1959

Amish Pay Fines But School Boycott is Continued (Pa.)
> Mar. 17, 1960

Catholic Bishop Voices Sympathy for Amish Plight
    April 7, 1960
Amish School Problem Will be Studied by Ohio Legislature
    May 19, 1960
Plans of Wisconsin Amish to Establish Own School Advance
    [This article states that eight Amish students were expelled and two
    others suspended from a school where 23 Amish pupils refused to watch
    classroom films.]
        Sept. 8, 1960
Amish Teacher is Jailed   Homerville Twp. (Ohio)
        Sept. 29, 1960
6 Amish Jailed in Iowa School Fuss
        Nov. 29, 1962
Bill to Upgrade Amish School Defeated
        June 20, 1963

Amish J. Yoder, Menno G. Brenneman, Jonas Petersheim
and Enos Mast returned home Friday from the county jail
at Somerset, where they were committed to jail for not
sending their 15 year old children, who have passed the 8th
grade, to school.
        Oct. 14, 1948   Springs, Pa.   Nettie M. Yoder

[Three Amish fathers fined $5 for each day children miss
school. They have been placed on probation. William H.
Yoder, Lester B. Miller and Jonas J. Miller]
        May 1, 1952   Summarized from a news item

Attendance: Children should be taught to believe that it is a
wrong thing to miss school, even for a single day. Parents
make a mistake in allowing children to miss school when it
is not absolutely needful. Some parents are very careless
in this respect. The result is, their children fall behind in
their school work and they fail to take a proper interest in
their studies.
        Jan. 9, 1902   Charm, Ohio   Benj. D. Miller

We owe 100 percent attendance whenever possible, and
much more, for all the benefits we enjoy and the wonderful
blessings of having our children taught by our own teachers who have a grave responsibility on their shoulders.
        Sept. 17, 1980   Andover, Ohio   Levi Hershberger

If the truant officers keep on getting the children to school
under the age of 16 they will probably have to build an
addition to some of the school houses.
        Oct. 3, 1913   Middlefield, Ohio   E. M. Hochstetler

Adult education: The spelling and ciphering school of this vicinity
is generally well attended which is held once a week.
        Dec. 24, 1908   Adams, Mont.   Enos D. Yoder

140

Jonas Miller is teaching German school and has 25 pupils enrolled. This school will close this week, and will have a spelling....

Mar. 20, 1912   Nappanee, Ind.   Aaron L. Beiler

An old fashioned spelling school was held at Pleasant Valley....

April 5, 1916   Harper, Kans.   Gladys Hostetler

A spelling took place Thursday evening with Abe Kauffman standing last.

Feb. 7, 1935   Kalona, Iowa   No name

The German Spelling at J. N. Mullets was fairly well attended. Crist Miller got the floor.

Feb. 8, 1934   Conway Springs, Kans.   Anna Mae Yoder

Beginning and close of school year: When 5 years old, my mother took me to my first school at Weiler's school house, where James Haggerty held forth as my first teacher.

May 12, 1904   Pawnee Rock, Kans.   Joel Miller

When I think back to my school days, I think it was my happiest time. I can feel the pleasure when I see my pupils leave for school with their dinner pails.

Sept. 3, 1953   Medford, Wisc.   Mrs. W. M. Schrock

It seems when the first of September rolls around there is always something that touches a former teacher's heart. The smell of new denim pants and new books. Then usually comes the new bat and ball, and the most touching thing of all those little first graders entering the school house the first morning. Always very shy, but seem to take things more seriously than the older ones.

This is always the most important step for the teacher. It sure is surprising what a friendly smile and a few suckers will do to make these beginners feel wanted. A teacher's attitude is like a mirror. It reflects right back into the schoolroom.

July 27, 1977   Spartensburg, Pa.   John W. Miller

School will begin next Tuesday. I think I am going if nothing will happen. I will be in the 6th grade.

Sept. 13, 1916   Hartville, Ohio   Eli A. Hostetler

Dutch school started Dec. 27, with Mary Bender as teacher. There are fourteen scholars. They had twenty visitors the 6th.

Jan. 13, 1921   Kalona, Iowa   Miss Ida Miller

My school closed yesterday. The children and patrons took me on a surprise by having a big dinner. In the morning the children came in with their empty dinner pails, but by eleven o'clock the patrons came with large baskets filled to the brim. We then spent the afternoon by singing songs and speaking pieces.

Mar. 19, 1903   Greentown, Ind.   J. F. Slabaugh

It seems real nice not to have to pack school lunches this morning, instead some are doing dishes, some are doing laundry, and some are hauling manure and plowing. Education hasn't stopped just because school is out. Instead of learning from books, they are now learning by experience.

May 7, 1980   Linneus, Mo.   Mrs. William Hershberger

Chris Miller will close his school at the Dumbhundred school house. . . .

June 21, 1900   Kalona, Iowa   Jacob Shetler

Director's Meetings: Lots of strangers here at present due to the parochial teachers get-together which was held at the Bish. Neil Hershberger home on August 1st. If I recall right, they said there were some in the 60 teachers there, with some committee men and board members coming too, then also others came along to fill up the loads. The next day teachers and some board members enjoyed the day together at Nelson Ledges. Also a singing on Thur. eve. at Neil Hershbergers.

Aug. 8, 1963   Burton, Ohio   Mrs. Roman Schmucker

Saturday was the annual meeting for our Parochial School board members and teachers, also quite a few ministers attended. (Fox Run School) It is a very interesting and worthwhile day, to listen, and see the effort of the teachers and our county superintendent and his helpers.

Nov. 16, 1977   Middlefield, Ohio   John E. Mullet

Perhaps the major interest to the directors of Lancaster Co. is to hire more than 30 teachers for the '80 fall term. Only those involved in this took (sic) task to find new ones, knows what it is. Only the teachers know the full meaning of teaching school. So in hiring it would mean, have the teachers feel it is a needed position that must be filled by someone, that is an interesting profession and has satisfying rewards of parents cooperate and have their children know you go to school to learn and improve your mind. They are

142

of their best years to cultivate and stimulate mind growth and ability to learn.

In time many of those new students will also be teachers, ministers, farmers, carpenters, in all kinds of places, where they will be glad, if they did not just squander time away. Also fairness in payment must be considered for even at the highest wages this is an ever-demanding, most endless task and is many a day a sacrifice on the teacher's part as much else in activities that other folks attend or do, must all be laid aside.

School comes first, so unless some of this recognized and teachers given fair wages, due cooperation it is possible that the quota of Amish teachers in Lancaster will prove an endless hunt all summer to fill.

All 14 year old's should not be put into the eight grade school. The teacher already has her share and in the beginning when it was organized, was not meant to be so. The 3 hour class was to be held separately and does not belong to these already busy school rooms. [The description was about the annual June Director's meeting of Amish schools in Penna., held on June 6, 1980.]

June 25, 1980   New Holland, Pa.   Mrs. Amos Huyard

Handicapped: It may sound like bragging to keep writing what our children can do, but my goal is to somehow encourage any parents with deaf children to relax, count your children as normal and help them along the best you can. It's so hard to explain to others without experience that few deaf children are retarded. Most of them can live normal lives if given a chance to be and act normal.

Feb. 20, 1980   Smoketown, Pa.   Mrs. Christ Glick

Higher eduation: A young man left his home church and went to another. He also went to a religious institution to study and came home with a "swollen" head and knew everything. As a result his character and habits were not as he was taught in the days of his early youth.

July 9, 1942   Gap, Pa.   John F. Glick

It may be of interest to those of you who formerly regularly attended the school meets in protests to higher education, that John Seizet, plain German-speaking Mennonite, who also attended the meetings, now has a family of twenty children. Five are married. The youngest is three.

Nov. 18, 1948   Lancaster County Briefs   Jonathan B. Fisher

143

Marie Hartman, who is studying for a trained nurse at the Chrisfield hospital spent New Years at the home of her parents.

Jan. 10, 1924   Westover, Md.   Mrs. Ira M. Zook

A number of Chapel talks on Bible Study recently given at the Institute, by Daniel Kauffman, have aroused a deeper interest on the part of the students in the study of the Bible. God's truth as unveiled in the "Book of Books" is the basis of all true education. [S. F. G. reported numerous events of the Elkhart Institute during 1899 and 1900. He reported 20 new students enrolled on Nov. 23, 1899.]

Feb. 15, 1900   Elkhart, Ind.   S. F. G.

Our Mennonite college, which is situated at Newton, has for this school year enrolled 103 students; five of these have already gone out to teach. Five eights of the students are Russians, two eights are Germans and one eights Americans.

Feb. 12, 1903   Partridge, Kans.   W. J. Dellanback

The Mennonites have bought a schoolbuilding with 30 acres of ground in Rockingham county for fourteen thousand dollars. . . .

Aug. 23, 1916   Fentress, Va.   Sol King

Public schools: In the school here in Blountstown, they have a period of worship each morning. It is quite formal though and followed by a flag salute.

Aug. 31, 1961   Blountstown, Fla.   Edw. Yoder

Our public schools were all closed during the week, with the exception of one which was only closed on Christmas.

Jan. 9, 1902   Allensville, Pa.   Rudy J. Kanagy

Religious Freedom: [John A. Hostetler submitted an article "The Meaning of Religious Freedom - - The Supreme Court Decision." Spacewise it covered 1¼ columns. It was both an explanation and a clarification of two installments by a Washington correspondent, Glenn D. Everett. The court decision referred to was the nationally important Wisconsin v. Yoder, handed down by the U. S. Supreme Court on May 15, 1972. In spite of its importance, the author did not find any references to it in the regular letters of the correspondents.]

June 15, 1972   p. 12

Teachers: The bell ringers at Sandy Ridge School are Lena Miller and Martha Sue Helmuth, at Burkholder school, Martha Raber.

Aug. 24, 1977   Nappanee, Ind.   Mrs. Daniel J. Miller

Have you considered teaching in an Amish School? Previously about 80% of the teachers have been unmarried women. With such a large percentage of single girls teaching, it is no small wonder that teaching ranks are constantly being thinned by that hallowed institution, marriage. Some say young girls make the best teachers. We will leave that up to the school boards to decide. We do believe, though, that there is a real opening for men . . . experience.

Aug. 1, 1963   Aylmer, Ont.   Joseph Stoll

[The following is a summary of a Midwestern Teachers Meeting held at Ward Burkholders. It was the Annual Teachers Meeting in northern Ind.] Church services Fri. A.M. while teachers went to the different schools to be "taught" by a more experienced teacher." 107 teachers present on Thur. and 5 or 6 more on Friday. 450 were present for dinner and supper on Thur. and 500 on Friday. The teachers came from 8 states.

Aug. 20, 1980   Nappanee, Ind.   Fannie Burkholder

Textbooks: The free textbook system was adopted at the annual school meeting . . . . What a help it would be to the schools if all the schools had free textbooks. It is as worthless for a child to go to school with just half enough books as it is for a farmer to try to farm with just half enough tools; and if anything, it is more worthless.

Dec. 19, 1901   Fairview, Mich.   L. J. Troyer

[An article from the *Cleveland Plain Dealer* describing an Amish author and a book he wrote appeared in THE BUDGET. It stated that 70 Amish schools were in operation in Ohio.] *Our Better Country* is the first book ever written by an Amishman as a textbook for Amish children. As you would expect of an Amish text on history, there is more of peace than war, more of love than hate, more of God in man than of the devil in him.

May 30, 1963

Vocational schools: "Vocational Plan" gains favor, whereby 14 year-old Amish and Mennonite would be allowed to stay at home and work under supervision . . . . The Lancaster Co. Amish School Community has again planned to meet and

discuss school problems . . . at Johnny Lapps.
Oct. 1, 1953   News item

Aaron E. Beiler of Lancaster says a group of Amish parents which he heads is working on a plan to permit plain sect children to continue school studies, after 14, in their homes under the supervision of state authorities.
Jan. 20, 1955   News item

Amish ninth grade students in Holmes County arc now pretty well following a regular attendance to either a parochial school or separate ninth grade class within the present county system.
Jan. 27, 1955   News item

Unclassified: In a certain school several mischievous boys, intent on getting one over on their college professor, carefully glued together parts of different kinds of bugs until they came up with something quite extraordinary. Carefully laying their prize before their teacher they asked, "Teacher, what kind of bug is this?"

The professor, a student of biology, carefully examined the boy's prize, and then said, "Boys, this is a humbug!"
Aug. 15, 1963   Lynnhaven, Va.   J. J. Hershberger

A Holmes County private Amish school.

146

Everyday Life   20

The excerpts in this chapter under the title "Everyday Life" could very well be included in other chapters. But grouping a sampling of excerpts under this heading was considered one of the additional windows by which to gain a glimpse into the day to day activities and affairs of THE BUDGET scribes and readers.

Accidents: Jonas Hershberger had a run away the other day, while cleaning the stable. He had almost a full load when the bronchos scared at the dog. The dog was away, and came home with a tin can tied to his tail and frightened the team. They landed at Isaac Millers, with everything all right.
Jan. 24, 1901   Grass Lake, N. D.   G. D. Chupp

I would like to explain thru this letter about the accident involving my horse and buggy. Some folks get wild ideas just as soon as they hear something. I just can't understand how people come to such conclusions with so little knowledge of a certain instance. Gossip certainly doesn't belong to Christian people. [Dannie S. Yoder used his "team" with permission. A car ran into the horse and buggy, but no one was seriously injured. The accident gave rise to a flurry of speculation and gossip.]
Feb. 28, 1963   Richland Co., Ohio   Warren L. Fusner

Animals: I must come to a close with my letter, for the gnats are tormenting me fearfully and are bolder than Absolom King's potato bugs.
Aug. 29, 1901   Davidsville, Pa.   Levi J. Kauffman

The mosquitos are quite bad nowadays; now is the time we need Nathan Yoder. Come around, Nate, and bring your pipe along, we will furnish the tobacco.
June 2, 1904   White Cloud, Mich.   Michigan Chums

Last week one day I and my neighbor went to the woods and cut three trees and took out ten pails of honey. How is that for Geauga Co.?
Jan. 17, 1907   Chesterland, Ohio   J. W. Spensinger

147

Sheep dogs better steer clear of Levi Yoder's premises, as he sometimes takes two on one shot.

> Feb. 22, 1900   Hubbard, Ore.   A. Yoder

Bees and frolics: The women had a pop-corn shelling at Ralph Kauffmans Monday evening.

> Jan. 16, 1930   Sikeston, Mo.   Budget Readers

The young folks had a nut picking at Edward Schmuckers.

> Dec. 22, 1976   Bronson, Mich.   Mrs. Reuben E. Hershberger

There was a popcorn shelling at Frances Millers on Thursday evening to shell the popcorn the young folks raised on their project this summer.

> Nov. 15, 1945   Greenwich, Va.   Mrs. Ira M. Zook

The "Friendship" quilt from the church and close relatives for Eli C. Millers, who plan to move to Lawrence Co., Ind. soon was quilted on Thurs. and Fri....

> Mar. 1, 1962   Burton, Ohio   Mrs. Roman J. Schmucker

John S. Weaver had a bee this week to haul gravel to make a wall under the barn on the farm which he has bought some time ago, and tore down part of the wall to repair it this fall if it don't get too cold.

> Nov. 25, 1926   Middlefield, Ohio   E. M. Hochstetler

The wood bee at Chris. Widricks was well attended; about 35 cords were cut, and a nice time was enjoyed by all.

> Mar. 20, 1902   Croghan, N.Y.   J. J. Zehr

... today was a chicken butchering at Romans. Tomorrow will be a day of noodle making again.

> Nov. 16, 1977   Dover, Dela.   Mrs. Alfred Troyer

Chicken butchering is in full swing. Over 1,500 have been done so far. We discovered that it goes much faster when the menfolk help! On Sat. forenoon we did 320 at Vernon Nissley's. Now we've been doing 280 evenings too. [A heavy snow caused many roofs to cave in because of the weight.]

> Apr. 5, 1989   Fairview, Mo.   Allan Millers

Burglary, thievery & vandalism: Chicken thieves are playing their trade again. Several weeks ago they paid a visit to E. L. Kauffman's henroost and took over the half of their fowls in one house, and lately they came back and took the balance. They don't seem to have much sympathy for a person.

> Jan. 6, 1915   Ronks, Pa.   John H. Kauffman

Recently, Joe Miller, having placed his stove poker for a burglar alarm, it mysteriously disappeared; no clue to its whereabouts. It is supposed to be lost in darkness.

Dec. 21, 1899   Mt. Hope, Ohio   POKER

On Nov. 1, the buggies along the Amish pike were very hard to find but was all found in twenty-four hours time.

Nov. 8, 1906   London, Ohio   Abner W. Miller & Jno. K. Miller

Last evening some reckless youths in an old car were roaming the countryside, annoying the Amish young folks as they were on their way to the singing. They threw stones and branches of trees at the horses.

Oct. 22, 1953   Kalona, Iowa   M. E. G.

I know that the Bible says to love your enemies. This would be a lot easier if they quit taking our buggies for joy rides. Last Feb. and again in Nov. they took one of the boy's buggies out of the shed and took it down the road at a high speed. Then let go of the shafts and when the shafts would dig into the ground the buggies would flip several times and by then the buggy would be about half the size it was before. The shed is fairly close to the road but was there when we moved here. I guess we will need to fix the doors to lock.

Jan. 7, 1987   Milroy, Ind.   Andy C. Hershberger

["Amish Youth Beaten by Gang" was the title of the article about the attack on three Amish youths, including Lester Miller, 20, who underwent surgery at Cleveland Clinic. The three youths were attacked in Holmesville. They said they were warned by the attackers, "We've warned you Amish to stay out of Holmesville." No charges were filed at the time when the article was written.]

May 16, 1957   News item   p. 3.

Communication: The majority of the farmers around here now have phones and can now enjoy a little chat with their neighbors after supper, then feel refreshed after a hard day's work.

May 4, 1905   Stuttgart, Ark.   Two Little Girls

Mr. Beachy was called to the bed-side of his mother, but I am sorry to say she was buried before he got there.

Mar. 6, 1902   Topping, Ont.   Peter Boshart

To those wanting to give death messages to this Mercer community, you can call the Sawmill No. in 5 Points . . . .

Call at noon if possible and let ring for awhile as it's a pay phone. You can try between 6:30 and 7 in morning and around 4 p.m.

March 11, 1987   Jackson Center, Pa.   Mrs. David Coblentz Jr.

Florida activity: What do the people in Pinecraft do? The women do a lot of quilting, some do housework. The men play checkers, marbles, shuffleboard, etc. Others work with carpenter gangs, some go fishing.

Jan. 2, 1964   Sarasota, Fla.   Stephen E. Stoltzfus

I am living here in a small tent 9½ by 12 and enjoy this sort of life and cook for myself. [He was located 150 miles south of Jacksonville and worked in a sawmill and crate factory, making orange crates.]

April 23, 1925   Apopka, Fla.   Menno F. Kauffman

There are a couple of washing machines here in Pinecraft, but most of us do our washing by hand. A few have sewing machines, too, so others that have sewing to do go in and use them.

Dec. 28, 1944   Sarasota, Fla.   Sarah and Susie Hostetler

Household matters: The women are all wearing broad smiles in this neck o' the woods since Milo Hamsher went thru here sharpening knives and scissors.

Feb. 21, 1917   Shanesville, Ohio   Two Buds

The other day while out calling at some of our neighbors we saw a strange sight, and what do you think it was. They were cooking dinner without a stove pipe, und es war gespas fur uns. (... and it was great sport for us.)

Aug. 21, 1902   Milford, Neb.   Cor.

The writer's father bought 40 acres of pasture land, with some timber on. I like to cut cedar for firewood, especially when it comes to splitting, as it splits like glass.

Jan. 1, 1903   Cora, Okla.   Lorenzo S. Schlabach

Joe Sr. and Jacob Yoder buzzed their next winters wood the other week about 160 cord and that certainly makes nice wood and clean firing through the winter instead of burning coal and the wood here is plenty and easy to make. They go out, and cut the poles down from 4 to 8 inches think and 30 to 60 feet long and they are as straight as a candle.

May 9, 1935   Fairview, Mich.   M. J. J. Yoder

Coal oil is very hard to get at present. I suppose we will have to begin making candles.

Feb. 15, 1910   Fairview, Mich.   Mrs. M. S. Zook

This is a time of great hurry, in which everything is to be done in short time, and Sam Jones is keeping well up with the time. Two weeks ago he had a frolic to haul lumber for his house, the next day he commenced to build, and on last Tuesday he moved with his family in the new house, all merry and well satisfied with their new house.

Sept. 26, 1901   Davidsville, Pa.   Levi J. Kauffman

A housewarming was held for Harold Bontrager and wife who moved into their new house just recently. Each one present brought some groceries.

Nov. 21, 1940   Midland, Mich.   Mrs. A D. Miller

Humor: Several weeks ago some people were out late at night and were quite amazed about some "spooks" or "jack-o-lanterns" they saw in Seth Hershberger's orchard. They were seen every night; but after investigation they were found to be torches that were set in large basins half full of water, to catch insects instead spraying the fruit trees. We believe this is a good thing; if it does scare the people who are out late at night.

May 22, 1902   Greentown, Ind.   A. and B.

Henry Stutzman was cutting wheat by moonlight the other night. Someone put a few of his wheat shocks up that he can't understand how it happened; but he ought to have looked on the other side of the road, then he would have caught the fellow.

July 3, 1902   Milford, Neb.   H. H. Miller

. . . if he is getting so posted that he can wash the dishes with a handful of grease instead of soft soap. [This was done by accident.]

Nov. 16, 1899   Monitor, Kans.   B. A. King

J. J. Miller got 52 gallons of apple butter and 27 gallons of jelly from Emanuel Troyer of Goshen, Ind. I guess Mona thought the Minnesota people may earn their jelly to get it out of the barrel; it is just like taffy; we could take a pitch fork and stick it in the jelly and lift the whole barrel. That is all right, we will get it out just the same.

Dec. 28, 1899   Worthington, Minn.   J. J. Yoder

I would like to give the difference in some things to some that some of the ways or work is just the reverse here to what it is in Ohio. If a man sows wheat he has four horses and drills from 16 to 20 acres in a day, while in Ohio they use two horses and sow from 6 to 10 acres. If you meet a farmer driving out of Shanesville or Sugarcreek with a load of manure you ask him how much he has to pay for a load of manure, and he will tell you 50 to 75 cents a load. If you meet a teamster here with a load of manure he tells you he is getting 25 cents a load for taking it away, and another man is paying him 10 cents a load to fill up a mud hole in his stockyard; so that he will make 35 cents a load for hauling it. In Ohio they don't put their hogs in the smokehouse until after they are killed; here they fatten them in the smokehouse, for I bought some right out of the smokehouse yesterday.

> Oct. 10, 1901   Milford, Neb.   H. H. Miller

I had to laugh at him (Edward S. Schrock) Friday night. He stopped in here on the way home from work to see if my oldest daughter is over the mumps as they wanted her to work for them while he is in the hospital (operation on rupture). My wife and the girls were out in the barn doing chores and I didn't realize there was anyone around till he came into the house and started talking. He didn't have the mumps yet either so he asked, "Is Ada all right again?" I said, "Yes, she is, but I have the mumps now." "Oh," he said, and turned around and went for the door, and ran for the road as if the mumps were after him.

> Mar. 18, 1954   Shipshewana, Ind.   Chris L. Miller

Recreation and social matters: Sam Yoder made the writer a call Saturday evening.

> Aug. 6, 1925   Alto, Mich.   No name

A little crowd of young folks spent the evening here at the writer's home. The evening was very much enjoyed by all of us.

> July 10, 1918   Bird-in-Hand, Pa.   Annie K. Beiler

A number of young people went out sailing yesterday, and caught forty fish and 5 eels.

> May 22, 1902   Denbeigh, Va.   Mamma and Emery Glick

Last Friday evening four gallant young men took the same number of ladies out rowing; of course the young ladies placed implicit confidence in these very kind young men, for well they might, knowing the dexterity with which the oars, etc. were being handled, and all things may have went well, had it not been that the boat was rather crowded and one unfortunate individual had the misfortune to dip the boat, when much to the dismay of the gentler sex, the young men (having inherited no little curiosity from their mother Eve) all with one accord looked for the place that had been leaking, and the result - - - well this would fill volumes.

July 16, 1903   Denbigh, Va.   FOUR FRIENDS

A load of wild horses was shipped here from the west. The boys evening sport is to break them.

June 20, 1901   Topeka, Ind.   Miss Mattie J. Hershberger

It's so good to sit on the wood pile and let the world roar by in the distance, for in quietness and confidence shall be your strength.

Feb. 8, 1962   Stillwater, Pa.   John Renno

Sleighing parties are all the rage.

Feb. 27, 1902   Topeka, Ind.   Alvin E. Yoder

The young folks plan to have a pound supper at Levi Knepps this evening in honor of Marie Yoder and Rully Miller of Ind.

Sept. 29, 1976   Haven, Kans.   Eli W. Miller

Rumors: I have not yet noticed anything in the Budget about the wonder or miracle in Kansas, about the child that talked when it was only five weeks old. Every day at the hours of 9 a.m. and 3 p.m. it raises its right hand and with a loud and clear voice says: "A six year famine in Kansas." Hundreds of people are visiting the scene everyday. If you want more information write to John Hershberger or John Miller of Arthur, Ill., who were eye witnesses.

Apr. 17, 1902   Gridley, Ill.   Joseph Yoder

If any of the Budget readers have seen the child and heard it speak, as described by Joseph Yoder . . . in last week's Budget, we would like to hear more about it.

May 1, 1902   East Lewiston, Ohio   THREE SISTERS

Ed. Budget, saw a wonder in the Budget about a child in Kansas that talks. It was stated in the Budget that I and John Hershberger were eyewitnesses, and that was the first that we heard anything about it. I have not been to Kansas for 13 years and Hershberger said he had not been there for 16 years, and we never saw that child and never heard anything like that till we saw it in the Budget. Yesterday I got 13 letters from all parts of the United States, asking about the child, and I thought I would better state in the Budget that we do not know anything about the child,

153

and do not think there is a child in Kansas that talks like that.
May 1, 1902   Arthur, Ill.   John J. Miller

To Joe Yoder . . . in regard to that child, which made those wonderful expressions about this famine stricken country, I will say, we did not know anything about that child until we seen your letter in the Budget. We should be careful not to have such trash published which are told by tramps, who try and make a living by telling lies. I hope all Budget readers have read the letter in last week's issue, written by John J. Miller, of Arthur, Ill, which will show that this was a fraud.
May 15, 1902   Yoder, Kansas   D. M. Yoder

The story is a bare-faced lie from beginning to end. [A traveling salesman, supposedly from Ohio, told the story.]
May 8, 1902   Gridley, Ill.   Joseph Yoder

Between three and four hundred letters were received at the post office, inquiring about the child, but nobody knew anything about the child.
May 22, 1902   Hutchinson, Kans.   Eli Helmuth

Superstitions: Seems more and more is read and heard of hypnotism these days and like the Ouija board and the "laying of hands on the table" of the past, it seems to be growing in popularity. How far is this removed from witchcraft, for it is believed to stem from the 6th and 7th book of Moses.
Sept. 6, 1956   Berlin, Ohio   Sarah Weaver

Some people consider water-witching as either ridiculous or as superstitious or like the forbidden arts mentioned in the Bible. Personally, I do not consider it anything to laugh at because I have seen too often where it worked. Nor do I think it is anything superstitious or the like because we have seen too many honest people who are not in the least superstitious, who could do it.
Nov. 10, 1955   Aylmer, Ont.   D. L. W.

Visiting: Joe Millers had lots of visitors on Easter Monday; there were 51 in all, and the afternoon was spent in singing spiritual hymns and in social conversation.
Apr. 18, 1907   Dodge City, Kans.   Annie C. & Katie C. Troyer

There was quite a scare in the neighborhood yesterday. Mr. D. C. Borntrager spent the day talking with church brethren and when he came to John Planks he scared Mrs. John Plank and the baby terribly.
Dec. 12, 1929   Garnett, Kans.   Chums

Work: Women folks are busy sewing and quilting while the men are hustling around in order to attend the Farm Show in Harrisburg this week.

Jan. 23, 1941   Belleville, Pa.   Jonathan R. Byler

Work among the men folks is cooking cane syrup and planting fall crops. The women are quilting, sewing and some are taking care of baby chicks.

Nov. 15, 1934   Lumberton, Miss.   Lovina Yoder

Today I am going to can sweet corn. I have so much to do.

Sept. 10, 1925   Harrisburg, Ore.   Mrs. Andrew Yoder

Canning beans and black-eyed peas and black berries is the order of the day among the women folks.

July 14, 1949   Calico Rock, Ark.   Mrs. M E. Bontrager

Unclassified: Yesterday we had the pleasure of satisfying our hunger for the old-fashioned maple "spotze".

Mar. 20, 1902   Keim, Pa.   E. S. Beachy

The latest novelty is a ring with a chain and a heart attached to it; some are already in use.

Feb. 13, 1902   Croghan, N. Y.   J. J. Zehr

One of our well-known farmers made a 400 mile round trip to attend an auction sale yesterday. Everything went fine, except that he happened to be a week ahead of the sale. Seems he got his Fridays mixed up. To save embarrassment it would be better not to mention any names.

Apr. 16, 1959   Lynnhaven, Va.   J. J. Hershberger

A Chinese proverb says "Who takes revenge in less than twenty years, does so in haste." Reminds me of a distant relative, now deceased who was naturally slow motioned, but a kindly sort of a fellow, who once said, he seldom gets mad, because by the time he gets around to that point, it's too late.

Nov. 2, 1977   Montezuma, Ga.   Mrs. Enos W. Yoder

Mr. Peele operated one of the fast disappearing old-time country stores which were not complete unless they contained a pot-bellied stove, cuspidor, nail kegs and of course a cat, whose duty it was to keep the mice under control but seemed more efficient in keeping the meat block clean.

Feb. 19, 1953   Lynnhaven, Va.   J. J. Hershberger

There was some excitement the other eve., when a man drove in at John Yoder's about 9:00 and told them to call the law, as a Negro boy was hanging on the steel truss river bridge (close by), rope and all. James and Paula heard it too, so they went back with the man right away. James quickly climbed up the truss and cut the rope. What a surprise when it hit the floor and went all to pieces. It was only a dummy made out of clothes and newspapers.

Feb. 25, 1987   Gonzales, Tex.   Mrs. Ervin Yoder

I had a rather unpleasant experience last Friday while helping an English neighbor cementing his cattle yard, as I had been going barcfooted most of the time since around the first of June, I didn't realize any danger in wading around in the fresh ready mix cement, but by noon my left food had a raw spot on the inside just below the ankle joint. It is about 2 inches in diameter and it is hard for me to get around to do anything. . . . It must have been ammonia or lye that was in the cement.

Aug. 13, 1980   Cashton, Wisc.   Joe C. Borntrager

Do these Amish farmers Joe Bontrager was telling about also get up with the sun? We farmers wouldn't get much done if we waited on that.

Mar. 4, 1943   Centerville, Mich.   Mrs. P. D. Miller

[John A. Byler of Lawrence County visited in the "Big Valley". One of the results was a poem, of which the two following lines were a part.]

Joe Zooks had some grown up girls,
I'll bet the boys do love their curls.

Sept. 30, 1940   Reedsville, Pa.   Rebecca Yoder

An Amish farm in southern Holmes County.

Farmstead and Fields

The farmstead was the center of activity in the rural communities. The centerpieces of the farmsteads were the house and the barn. There were many auxiliary buildings. The more diversified the farm, the more kinds of buildings were needed. Most of the Amish and Mennonite farmers were engaged in diversified farming, very few specializing in a single crop or kind of livestock. The excerpts given in this chapter provide a sampling of what was written about the farm-stead, but should be supplemented by the chapters on agriculture and on everyday life in order to get the fullest benefit.

Animals: I was requested by some people to put in the Budget how many "beabelin" [chicks] we've got. I don't know exactly, but there is some over 300. How is that for a frigid country?

May 9, 1900   Worthington, Minn.   J. J. Yoder

I wonder if anyone would be interested in banties? When we moved, nearly three years ago, we brought along one rooster and two hens. This fall our girls said the banty population was close to seventy! That's too many banties for one farm, we think! We've sold some, butchered some, given them away, and still have some left. Debra came in yesterday and said she found a hen setting eighteen eggs again!

Jan. 30, 1980   Whiteville, Tenn.   The Lloyd Troyers

[A horse was hitched 15' from a beehive. The bees attacked and in the flurry the horse kicked over the hive; the whole swarm attacked the horse as well as Ray Nisly and wife. They were rushed to the hospital where 43 "stingers" were removed from Ray. He was in intensive care. One-half hour after the attack the horse got up, walked a short distance, but fell to the ground, dead.]

Aug. 1, 1963   Goshen, Ind.   A. H.

Jasper our crippled bull had to be finally shot. It seems

one becomes attached to animals so easily. No one watched the event.

Aug. 27, 1980   Elkton, Minn.   Mrs. John Ressler

However, all good things come to an end. Max got older and like humans, more grouchy and crabby with older age. One day in a fit of anger he bit Crist, one of our boys, for no reason so sadly, I took the rifle and Max and went back into the woods. We came back without him, but it was a long heart-breaking trip. Max's life was over and dogs of his kind are few and far between.

Aug. 20, 1980   Huntsburg, Ohio   Uria R. Byler

John Kanagy and my brother Dan were supposed to go get the other two hogs and bring them over to the scalding barrel. They brought back the hogs alright, but they got two young brood sows instead of the two they were supposed to get, which were out in the barnyard.

Dec. 31, 1959   Stillwater, Pa.   John R. Renno

Levi got a little goat this week, which caused some commotion around here already. The cows had never seen a goat before, and wouldn't do it to go in the barn if the goat was near. The first morning one of them jumped over a board fence to get away. The next morning she didn't come in at all. But they're getting used to it. We want the goat to keep weeds down along fences, etc.

May 21, 1980   Fredericksburg, Ohio   Mrs. Levi S Miller

Having purchased two cute little goats at the Mt. Hope sale last week, within two days they had themselves on "death row" already by munching some of our azaleas, so they are on good behavior which is not too easy for these little fellows, but I think I might win the case because I've got the little girls on my side and some good leather collars around their necks.

June 11, 1980   Millersburg, Ohio   Andrew Miller

We have 400 little chickens two weeks old. Some people have as high as 1500.

Mar. 11, 1926   Norfolk, Va.   I. K. Fisher

There were some dogs after Milton E. Bender's sheep, Friday morning. Sam U. Yoder came along and was fortunate enough to catch one of the dogs and killed him with a stick.

May 7, 1931   Salisbury, Pa.   Nettie M. Yoder

The mice crop in this community is abundant. Everybody

158

seems to think we could get along with less mice. They did very much damage to little orchard trees such as apple, plum, June berries, raspberries, etc. They are all pealed from the ground up. I've seen it peeled as high as three feet from the ground.
May 14, 1936   Owen, Wisc.   J. C. S. Chupp

One of the main advantages in raising geese is to get the feathers. Nothing can equal a feather-bed or pillow.
Dec. 26, 1963   Aylmer, Ont.   David Wagler

Beautification: Whitewashing fences, etc. is next on the program which adds greatly to the appearance of our pleasant homes.
May 4, 1905   Willow Run, Pa.   Cor.

Old Daniel D. Miller is still improving his place by planting more trees. His hired hands planted over 4,000 trees this spring and Daniel talks of planting more next spring.
April 30, 1908   Hydro, Okla.   E. E. Bontrager

It is quite evident that people are investing more in shrubbery and flowers about their dwellings than in former years.
May 15, 1956   Princess Anne, Va.   J. Elmer Yoder

Buildings: Quite a few of our farmers are putting up silos and putting basements under their Yankee barns.
July 23, 1903   Middlefield, Ohio   Y. K. Byler

For the benefit of those who do not know what a silo is, I will say, it is a large air tight vat or tank for preserving green corn, oats and other fodders, which is an excellent feed for stock of all kinds, and especially dairy cows. [The information given was timely. Silos were developed during the 1890's.]
Sept. 14, 1899   East Lynne, Mo.   Eli Hostetler

Percy Miller and David Reber are digging a cistern for R. C. Yoder. The cistern is to be 16 ft. deep and 7 ft. in diameter.
May 21, 1903   Windom, Kans.   Viola B. Yoder

Norman S. Yoder moved into the springhouse at the residence of his father, S. D. Yoder.
April 10, 1902   Grantsville, Md.   Emanuel Hershberger

C. S. Beachy is preparing to build a new spring and washhouse, combined.
July 20, 1899   Midland, Va.   Mrs. S. S. Beachy

David S. Beachy's bake oven, wash house and smoke house burned down....
Dec. 21, 1899   Arthur, Ill.   Levi J. Lee

159

Levi Zook is making some necessary improvements about his home by having a new furnace and wash house put up. Levi is an up-to-date farmer, and he will no longer be kept behind in the way for improvements with his neighbors.

Nov. 2, 1899   Allensville, Pa.   B. Y. Zook

There were four bank barns built in our neighborhood this spring.

Aug. 2, 1900   Gortner, Md.   D. C. S.

C. B. Lapp recently made a manure carrier installed in his stables.

April 19, 1906   Gordonville, Pa.   John H. Kauffman

We are living on our place now. A dug out is all right. We have built a barn and are building a house....

Jan. 25, 1906   Hydro, Okla.   Mrs. Fannie E. Miller

Henry Briskey and force finished Jonas J. Kauffman's straw barn....

June 7, 1900   Arthur, Ill.   Levi J. Lee

Tobe Weaver is building a two story hog stable.

June 9, 1915   Trail, Ohio   A Reader

The dooryard is a part of the home - - why not keep it clean and pretty as you like to have the inside of the house?

Aug. 11, 1920   Filler material

Levi Beiler is putting an ornamental fence around the yard. It is built upon a concrete foundation.

Aug. 10, 1922   Elverson, Pa.   Lena Stoltzfus

The plain people have always been noted for being practical and accepting anything that makes sense, regardless of what the style or fashions are in the world. That's why many of our people are beginning to use metal roofing for houses even though it is not the style in the world. We're sold on metal roofing for any building (maybe because we sell it), for what could be better or worth more in the long run. The baked on enamel kind is used as it is a lifetime job. [Wagler remarks in the letter that the patter of rain-drops on a metal roof was music to his ears, as a boy, especially if it happened in the morning. Did an early rain mean getting out of some chores or work?]

Aug. 13, 1980   Bloomfield, Iowa   David Wagler

When my cousin Levi was here a few days ago, he called my attention to some happenings of bygone days when I was a boy at home in Cheyenne Co. Colorado, about 1911 and 1912 when we used to have some of those western blizzards. We had sod houses built but no barns for our cows. When a real blizzard came, our cows went with the storm. After the worst of the blizzard subsided we set out to find our cows and we finally got all of them back. The ones that were giving milk suffered the most.

On another occasion after we had our barn built which was also built of sod, we had another severe blizzard. This time it was so bad that it was impossible to get to the feed which was north of the barn and the wind and snow blew so hard that it would have just blowed away if we would have tried to move any into the barn. I don't recall getting any water to our cows and horses, but I do remember that we managed to get a straw tick from the house to the barn, so we divided the contents of that straw tick to all the stock that one day. It also blew in one of the doors and door frame of our sod house. I haven't forgotten what kind of fuel we used while on those lone prairies; "prairie chip".

Sept. 5, 1946   Hutchinson, Kans.   D. A. Hostetler

Chores: I overheard a couple men discussing the subject of choring in wintertime. The one expressed himself in such a way, which gave me something to think about. He said people who don't live where it gets cold may not believe it, but he feels they are missing out. To him it gave him such a good feeling to enter the house where it's nice and warm, if all goes well at the barn with the chores. It made me realize what an influence our "houses" can make. Are the men glad to come in or would they rather stay in the barn?

Feb. 20, 1980   Hale, Mich.   Mary Miller

Dairy: Summer is coming on and flies are bad on cows that it is unpleasant to milk. A good many farmers buy expensive spray to spray flies, but I have used coal oil now for two years and find it just as good as the prepared spray. Try it and be convinced.

June 16, 1915   McMinnville, Ore.   A. M. Beachy

... W. E. Miller, manager of the ranch was living and who only milked one side of two cows while the calves were milking the other side and they were no dairy cows and butter was very scarce....

June 23, 1915   Tuleta, Tex.   C. C. Schrock

The dairy barn inspector is making his daily rounds. Quite a lot of people stopped selling milk till they get their barns

161

clean. Then they can sell it again. There are a lot of barns being made sanitary this summer.

June 23, 1921   Uniontown, Ohio   Pete

In regard to the dead line placed by Milk Co. officials to refuse farmers milk unless there was a partition between horses and cows, nothing has been done. The deadline passed three days back and farmers are waiting to see what action the officials take and how soon they take it. It is not known of many partitions installed on the route.

May 1, 1941   Apple Creek, Ohio   Daniel J. Miller

Equipment and power: Moses Yoder bought a new twenty-five horsepower gasoline traction engine this spring. He expects to do most of his farm work with it.

Mar. 15, 1910   Mylo, N. D.   Cor.

The well drillers at Homer Grabers have found water and a windmill has been erected on the site. A number of used windmills have been purchased recently by our people, as they furnish cheaper, and in some ways handier power for the pump than gasoline engines.

June 9, 1955   Aylmer, Ont.   Joseph Stoll

The sheep shearing machines are on the go these days.

May 2, 1935   Harrisburg, Ore.   Mrs. Alvin Kropf

The toot of the thresher can now be heard.

Aug. 9, 1906   Belleville, Pa.   M. P. Zook

John D. Miller and Andy Gingerich sold out all their machinery, consisting of engine, thresher, water tank, buzz saw and feed mill, to N. O. and J. I. Hershberger, for $800.

July 4, 1901   Welshfield, Ohio   Jonas C. Miller

Harvest: The hum of the ensilage cutters can again be heard in almost every direction.

Sept. 18, 1918   Elverson, Pa.   Elsie Stoltzfus

... while C. B. Lapp was threshing, he had two horses in his straw shed to help pack the straw, when all at once the floor gave way and they dropped to the ground a distance of about ten or twelve feet. One of the horses escaped serious injury, but the other one had his leg broken and had to be killed. Crist was leading the horses and went down with them but escaped injury.

Aug. 29, 1901   Gordonville, Pa.   John H. Kauffman

Benjamin Beechy fell from a load of hay when the grapple let loose, while pulling up hay. Nothing serious resulted.

July 4, 1963   Hazelton, Iowa   Mr. J. M. S.

162

Security: Some rogues entered our poultry house last week and got away with about twenty or thirty chickens.

July 24, 1902   Grantsville, Md.   Emanuel Hershberger

A burglar tried to get into J. J. Yoder's house Monday night, but was discovered before he had gained an entrance. J. J. Y. got up and awakened Henry . . . ; he took the shotgun and went out after the burglar. Finally he thought he saw him going along the picket fence, and Henry gave him the load. The next day he found out that he shot an old sow in the back.

June 22, 1899   Charm, Ohio   S. J. Miller

It seems that some people are getting very bold through Howard and Miami counties. Last week one night someone entered the smoke house of Jacob J. Troyer and took every piece of smoked meat they had - - 7 or 8 pieces; on last Monday in day time, Harvey Troyers chickens were nearly all taken. Such fellows may get to the wrong smoke house some night.

June 8, 1899   Kokomo, Ind.   G. W. North

Soil care: Several limestacks have been burned this fall and some more are to be put up in the spring.

Jan. 14, 1909   Reedsville, Pa.   S. H. Byler

The latter part of Oct. and forepart of Nov. when we were out plowing we could easily hear the shrill whistles of the seed bed steamers, as a lot of that was done this fall. [Used to prepare seed beds for plants, destroying weed seeds and insects.]

Jan. 12, 1961   Gap, Pa.   John F. Glick

Communication: There are a few men working on our telephone line, which had been out of commission for 2 months. . . .

May 4, 1922   Midland, Mich.   Mrs. A. D. Miller

The men are going to Jessup this morning. We don't get our mail except when somebody goes to town.

Feb. 20, 1936   Jessup, Iowa   Mrs. Ida Gingerich

Food and Diet   22

It seems that eating good food was one of the most enjoyed activities mentioned in THE BUDGET. Among others were visiting and traveling, both local and beyond the immediate community. These are very closely related and blend very well. The enjoyment of one would likely bring one or both of the others into play. No evidence was found that food and diet were included in the church regulations. Overeating and gluttony were rarely mentioned in THE BUDGET. Among the readers of THE BUDGET gluttony was reserved to describe the extravagant meals of the "wealthy outsiders" rather than overeating at their own tables.

Reference to a seasonal food or the main staple of diet brought into play a phrase appearing many times - - "bill of fare." For farm and related work the phrase was "order of the day."

The reader should make an effort to distinguish between the serious and humorous in these excerpts, especially in the several under the heading "Mistakes".

Bill of fare: Mushrooms are on the bill of fare at present.
    May 20, 1914   Mio, Mich.   Mrs. M. S. Zook

Pumpkin pie are on the bill of fare.
    Sept. 20, 1920   Latour, Mo.   Sarah E. Hershberger

Dandelion and cress greens are on the bill of fare.
    April 2, 1919   Westover, Md.   Mrs. Ira M. Zook

Melons are on the bill of fare and are quite plentiful.
    Aug. 20, 1925   Westover, Md.   Mrs. Ira M. Zook

Peas, lettuce, radishes and rhubarb pies are on the bill of fare, and baby chickens seem very plentiful.
    April 14, 1927   Harrisonville, Mo.   Sarah E. Hershberger

Butchering is about over. Eating brode wurst and killing rabbits is the order of the day.
    Jan. 2, 1908   Arnold, Kans.   J. C. S. Chupp

Spoken of favorably: People have commenced making brotewarst.
    Nov. 29, 1901   Middlebury, Ind.   Laura E. Kauffman

164

The farmers are apparently thinking how good ice cream will taste on the long hot summer afternoons this summer, as most of them are putting up ice.

Mar. 4, 1914   Trail, Ohio   Three Readers

I am looking forward to a shipment of Trail Bologna coming in sometime this week. This delicious meat is processed mostly among the Amish. This, with Swiss cheese, is strictly on the menu in Ohio, and oh, so good.

Dec. 17, 1959   Lagrange, Ind.   Em. B. Miller

The chicken roast, the other evening, was simply delicious.

Nov. 5, 1931   Berne, Ind.   Margaret Girod

Read a formula in the Budget how to make good corn mush. Will say take out a dishful and pour hot butter over it. This will make fine eating.

Jan. 7, 1909   Central Lake, Mich.   Mrs. Susan Weirich

Butchering is about all past and the brode worst seem to be plenty.

Jan. 2, 1918   Lagrange, Ind.   No name

Women are mostly baking their own bread, making crackers and cereals, of which is much cheaper than store price. Many households are building up their own supply and are learning to be more economical.

Mar. 23, 1933   Elverson, Pa.   Amos J. Stoltzfus

Fish and oysters fresh from the bay almost every day in the week if you want them now.

April 7, 1921   Westover, Md.   Mrs. I. M. Zook

Mistakes: Marvin Rhodes and family had a taste of toadstools by mistake, thinking they were mushrooms. One of the girls did not vomit so she was taken to the hospital to get her stomach pumped empty.

Sept. 5, 1963   Millmont, Pa.   N. Z.

They tried to raise a pig at Poplar Hill by feeding it lots of fresh northern pike and finished him off the last 6 weeks, before butchering time with corn. But it wasn't very successful as the bacon tasted somewhat like sardines.

Dec. 1, 1959   Red Lake, Ont.   No name

Cornelius Miller, who is here from Ohio, to visit his father and sister, seems to enjoy himself, and the country seems to agree with him, as he is gaining one pound a day. I don't know whether he smokes too much, or eats too much mush and milk, his pants got so small that he had to borrow a

pair from his father to go home.
Jan. 25, 100   Waupecong, Ind.   Amanda Hostetler

Pastries: Jacob Hershberger's for their family use, through the year 1899, baked 1550 pies and 380 loaves of bread. This is a land for pie, as well as for noodle soup.
Jan. 18, 1900   Davidsville, Pa.   Levi Kauffman

Unusual/new/different: Jacob Zook's greatly enjoyed a feast of sparrows, sometime ago. A number of the birds roosted in a tree in front of the house; during a storm one evening they were driven on the porch by the wind and the rain, where forty-two of them were caught by the family. The next morning they killed and cleaned them all and cooked them for dinner.
Sept. 7, 1897   Ronks, Pa.   PANSY

Those Geauga Co. people that don't like fried corn mush, would better not come here, as people here make that too, because they like it, or be satisfied with what they get. I have traveled some in my life and that was one of the best meals I got.
March 2, 1905   Nappanee, Ind.   J. J. Borkholder

Aaron Masts cooked some pear butter yesterday.
Oct. 26, 1922   Westover, Md.   Mrs. Ira M. Zook

We couldn't help but laugh when we heard that they had sourkraut and pig tails on the wedding table.
Mar. 3, 1932   Spartensburg, Pa.   Elsie Mast

I mentioned in a former letter that the men around here went smelt fishing. Well, after the people had eaten a lot of them they found out that they were grubby so the rest of the smelt went to the dogs.
May 1, 1941   Midland, Mich.   Mrs. A. D. Miller

If earthworms are so bad consider this: John the Baptist ate locusts, John Kanagy ate knats, and John H. Miller ate "chitterlings", the modern word, I believe, is tripe. We will let readers "gag" this week on the earthworm, but, next week we will let them sit up and take notice (Lord willing) what science and research has found out about this silent worker created by God. The Japanese dry them and grind them up some way and sprinkle them over their food for more protein. They are practically all meat, and like spaghetti, they have no bones. "Could you pass that worm a la casserole again, Mom?"
Oct. 12, 1977   Blackville, S.C.   John Kanagy

166

An interesting feature to us, related by them (V.D. Millers of Va.) was the method they used in "putting up" the "skins" (intestines) and stomachs of the porkers for their market trade in Norfolk. Both are well washed and rinsed, not scraped, thoroughly boiled with one another, and the entire mixture is sold as "chitlins" at 35 cents a pound. What a smell! They themselves do not eat them. Was informed everything of the hog permissible was made into sausage, even the hams.

Feb. 6, 1941   Lancaster County Briefs   Jonathan B. Fisher

Europeans are accustomed to eating horse meat. This is true mostly among the laboring classes. Again reminds me of a certain nice red elegant sausage I began to like so well on one of my tours overseas. It was outstandingly delicious and tender. After learning it was made of horse meat, pooh! No more for me! But why not?

Nov. 25, 1948   Lancaster County Briefs   Jonathan B. Fisher

We had bear meat given again and if you have never tasted it then you are missing a treat. Some people can't seem to bring themselves to eating it but it isn't the taste, it is more just the thoughts of what they are eating.

Sept. 29, 1976   Bancroft, Ont.   The Stoners

A thing that I thought was odd when we first came to Virginia was that robins were shot for table use during their spring migration. I am glad to say that is no longer the case, but not many years ago a man still came out from Norfolk to shoot blackbirds. To him the "four and twenty black birds baked in a pie" was no idle table talk.

Mar. 1, 1962   Fentress, Va.   Ira E. Miller

Back to that hungry old possum at the feeder, as we were watching it I mentioned something about having it for dinner. Mom wasted few words in vetoing that idea, and probably 90 per cent of the Budget readers would be on her side there. However, regardless how homely they are, and what their food is, they are good eating. Back in the Durkee Farm days, Dad had quite often wanted Mother to prepare the carcass of possum we used to catch in our traps, but no way, she just couldn't eat those ugly things. One day Dad was hunting rabbits and shot one, then on the way home he tracked a possum into a hollow log, and got him out. He was nice and fat, so a bright idea entered Dad's mind. Right there he dressed both rabbit and possum, and

167

took them home without saying a word to anyone about what we all thought were two rabbits. He could tell the difference in the legs and other parts, and when we started eating, Mother happened to get a possum leg. She ate it, and remarked how good it tasted, and said it must have been a young one. Dad kept a straight face and didn't say much. Sure enough, Mother's second piece was also possum, and she thought that was just about the best rabbit she ever ate.

When all was done and the last of the two "rabbits" cleaned up, Dad told us his secret. Mother was rather flabbergasted at first, but from then on whenever we caught a possum she wanted us to save the carcass, and never again said that they were not fit to eat. A possum hide was $1.00. There were many around, and we ate possum.

    Feb. 16, 1977   Huntsburg, Ohio   Uria R. Byler

Possum and sweet potatoes is no strange dish in this part of the country and if properly prepared is just as appetizing as any other meat.

    Jan. 3, 1963   Fentress, Va.   Ira Miller

Opinions expressed: Have we not drifted from nature, from the way our forefathers live? What is it that leads us that way, is it not the lust of the flesh? Why could we not form the habit of eating plain, wholesome food instead of the spiced and sweetened mixtures that so often are put upon the table? Then we would not be so liable to overeat.

    Jan. 18, 1906   Gordonville, Pa.   John H. Kauffman

As we are health minded, and believe in the organic method of producing food be it in the field or garden, some find delight when we have a siege of sickness. We have been reminded that this or that which we may eat isn't Organic. Well, we take all such as gracefully as we can, and don't let it bother us.

    Jan. 23, 1980   Virginia Beach, Va.   John H. Miller

Our health department advised people of Mansfield, Ohio, not to buy meat from farm peddlers, as it was not state inspected. Isn't it a wonder we farmers don't all die from eating rotten food?

    Dec. 8, 1932   Shiloh, Ohio   Rudy Rader

The 20 gallons of ice cream which were mentioned in a recent Budget which were consumed at a birthday party, was interesting reading, providing it was done to the glory of God (I Cor. 10:31) and an asset to Christian living.

Aug. 27, 1959   Kempsville, Va.   Levi Bontrager

As the food we eat has a great influence on our health it is well to give some thought to the matter, and in this article we shall see what the Bible teaches on the subject. [Kauffman follows the above with nine paragraphs of explanation, in which he praises the herb bearing seed; he deplores the removal of the outer coating of grain; notes that meat is not regarded highly, after Noah, and that Christ served bread, fish and honeycomb. Then he concludes with the following paragraph.]

But now at our weddings the setting of tables is carried to extremes, serving such a great variety of dishes, of highly seasoned and sweetened viands as to induce one to eat so as to overburden the body instead of strengthening it. Well might we ask ourselves if such practices are pleasing to the eyes of God. (I Cor. 10:31).

Dec. 5, 1910   Ronks, Pa.   John H. Kauffman

Recipes: I am doing some modern cooking. Got a new Crock Pot and want to start it tonight for tomorrow noon. Maybe next week I will tell how it turned out. Unless it was a flop.

Oct. 20, 1976   Pinecraft, Fla.   Mose B.

Mrs. Joe Weirich found this unusual recipe in one of her cookbooks while paging through the casserole section. She was looking for a recipe to take to a potluck Sunday dinner. She wrote that she hardly had time to make it by the time of the dinner, but wanted to share it with Budget readers anyway. It appeared in the section called "Cookin' with Maudie".

Elephant Stew

1 elephant, medium size

2 rabbits, optional

Cut elephant into bite-size pieces. Takes about 2 months. Add water to make a brown gravy. Cook over a kerosene fire for 4 weeks. Serve 3800 people. If more are expected add the 2 rabbits, but do this only if needed. Most people don't like hare in their stew.

Feb. 18, 1987   Summersville, Mo.   Mrs. Joe Weirich

Greetings and Closings 23

During the early decades most letters contained some type of greeting to the editor and readers. This apparently was a carry-over from the style used in personal letters. These were, after all, at first looked upon as personal letters to a large family scattered in several states. Editorial policy gradually eliminated the greetings, some of which were quite extensive.

During the 1890's the customary salutation was "Editor Budget". In 1892 a scribe from Mt. Hope, Ohio and one from Bear Creek, Wyo. used "Enitor Budget." In the January issues of 1901 the following salutations appeared:

> Greetings to the editor and all Budget readers.
> A greeting to all readers.
> A friendly greeting to editor and Budget readers.
> Editor Budget and readers, greeting.
> A friendly greeting to all readers of the Budget in the 20th century.

> Ein gluckliches und segenbringendes Neues Yahr sei dem editor und Budget leser gewunscht.
> Jan. 9, 1902   Albany, Ore.   You and I

> A kind greeting to the editor and Budget readers, wishing all good health and God's richest blessings and prosperity, in everything most needful to us as pilgrims to the celestial Jerusalem.
> April 9, 1903   Amish, Iowa   S. D. Geungerich

> We notice that some of the correspondents greet "the editor and wife". Now perhaps many of the Budget readers would like to know if he has a wife.
> Jan. 2, 1902   Olivet, S.D.   JOE BUTTERMAKER

In the event a scribe launched immediately into a discussion of an issue, the usual greeting was replaced with something similar to "I thought I would write about the subject of . . . ." or "Now, let us consider . . . ."

Due to editorial counsel and practice the greetings were used less and less. To use the January 4, 1962 issue to illustrate, the first sentences in the letters dealt with the following subjects: weather (51 letters), church (10 letters), travel (2 letters), writing (4 letters), social events (13 letters), and death (1 letter).

The conclusions or closings of letters also showed great variety. Just a few examples will be given. The final group of short ones concluded discussion letters, rather than the general informational letters. Only the date will be given with them.

> Not wishing to detain you too long, or become too familiar at once, I will close.
>> Dec. 26, 1901   Larned, Kans.   D

> As I am getting my epistle rather long, I will close by sending my love and best wishes to the editor and all God fearing people.
>> Oct. 22, 1903   Gridley, Ill.   Joseph Yoder

> Since our Lord and Savior Chirst Jesus did not please everyone, I well know it to be impossible, and am aware that I will be held accountable for what I write, say and do, so I never intentionally write anything to harm anyone, but admit that I have faults and make mistakes, and will gladly apologize to any faultless person who can prove any of my writings to be untruthful. Otherwise your objections will be in vain, as far as I am concerned. Wishing you all, objectors included, God's blessings, I remain your humble scribe.
>> July 29, 1954   Enon Valley, Pa.   Jacob Z. Yoder

> Aus lieve.   Sept. 3, 1980
> Submitted by an unprejudiced Old Order Amishman.
>> Mar. 17, 1955
> One of the least of you.   April 9, 1953
> "Priefet alles und behaltet das gute."
> From a consecrated Christian.   Jan. 9, 1920
> Old Order   Jan. 6, 1944
> A Saint of God.   Jan. 13, 1944

Nom de plumes: Pen names were very common during the first two decades. Some of these were occasional names, meaning that they were used only several times by the writer. Others were used over a period of months. There was a running debate about the use of the nom de plumes vs the real names of the writers. Even though J. D. Guengerich in the quotation below calls them nom de plumes, or pen names, some of those used in THE BUDGET were more on the order of presenting an image, and even playing a kind of "guess who" game with Budget readers. It was not on the level of Samuel L. Clemens who used "Mark Twain" as his nom de plume.

> I know of no other paper that gives so much local news from so many places, as does the *Budget;* it is almost like reading so many personal letters. Still I believe there is place for improvement. Personal matters, which are liable to give offense, should be avoided. Fictitious names, especially of the slang and vulgar sort, are not in keeping with Christian love, and should be avoided. As the editor can only furnish such news as is sent in for publication, let every correspondent be very careful about what he writes and think of what Jesus says, that we must give an account of every idle word that we have spoken in this life: Matt. 12:36. We can hide for a time here from the eyes of the public, behind a nom de plume, but at that last day everything will be an open book....
> Amish, Iowa   J. D. Guengerich   July 20, 1899

The debate: The debate about the use of nom de plumes continued for two decades. It seemed to be effective because after 1910 the use of such names was virtually nil. There were still, however, some writers who signed off as "A Budget Reader" or some similar term.

> There are so many letters in the BUDGET with bogus names. Why not sign your right name? If there is anything to write that people are not to know where it comes from let it go. The best is not to write such items.
> Beemer, Nebraska   L. H. Lantz   Nov. 5, 1903

> I have noticed several times in the Budget that there are quite a few that want correspondents to sign their full names. I don't think it is necessary at all; it does not matter who writes the items, just so I get to read them. The news is what we want, not names.
> Hopedale, Ill.   A Budget Reader   May 10, 1900

> In a recent issue I noticed some of our Canadian correspondents had the misfortune of forgetting the name their parents gave them and had to substitute some other to sign their letters.
> Bealton, Va.   M. Wagler   August 31, 1899

Did the readers of the Budget notice that there was one issue of the Budget, a few weeks ago, that had all the letters signed with the name of the writer. The sentiment in favor of correspondents of the Budget signing their correct names to their letters appears to be growing.

East Lynne, Mo.　　Eli Hostetler　　Oct. 11, 1900

Exposing the writers: By way of the community "grapevine" network most people in the communities directly affected knew who the writers were. There were some open threats to expose those hiding behind the nom de plumes.

The last issue of the Budget was more interesting than usual, because the correspondents signed their names except two; hope the next time they will all sign. Mr. BOWSER of Pa. would better sign his name the next time, because we know who he is anyhow.

Walnut Creek, Oh.　　E. N. Beachy　　Feb. 28, 1895

We wonder how the two "Blue Bells" are getting along. They would better be careful who they are giving away so much, because the "Twin Sisters" will give them away. Annie is all right; she is a good cook.

Eureka, Ill.　　Twin Sisters　　July 31, 1902

In the issue of April 4th I noticed a letter, signed "Shoo Fly", asking what became of "Uncle John Yoder" of Florida, and that he would like to hear from "Uncle." If your real name is "Shoo Fly" then you are not related to me whatever. If it is not your real name then give it the next time and be honest about. It would be much more satisfaction to the readers if all the correspondents would sign their real names.

Hawthorn, Fl.　　John Yoder　　April 25, 1895

I do not know who that correspondent is who calls himself Dutchy but a fatherless letter is worth about as much as a fatherless note - - no good.

Troyer Valley Items　　A. M. Miller　　July 7, 1892

Examples: More than three-hundred nom de plumes were discovered. Some were used by more than a single writer. They provide an interesting study in psychology. What may have been the underlying reasons for the use of each of the following by these widely scattered individuals?

Some seem to indicate the austere sense of humility verbalized in the Amish and Amish Mennonite community then and is still

173

heard among some of their offspring. Examples are Zero, Waste Basket, and Nobody. Others seem to show a sense of vulnerability, such as A Sucker. Some seem to be used as an acceptable way of "bragging" about one's status or achievements, such as Sweet Honey, VISEKOP, or Clover Blossoms. Some have their origin in geographic location, such as Western Boy, Ranch Girl and Sage Brush. Probably most were part of the social bantering and extensive use of nicknames common at their time. The following are presented for your interest and study. Some were used by more than one correspondent/s. An attempt was made to list only the first usage of these pen names, but without any calculations about frequency of usage.

Origin of letter	Date of letter	Name used by Scribe
Deutchland, Ind.	Dec. 8, 1890	Schnickkelfritz
Orrville, Ohio	July 22, 1890	Scribler
Eureka, Mich.	March 12, 1891	Who Is It?
East Brook, Pa. Lawrence Co.	May 18, 1891	Guess Who
Arthur, Ill	June 1, 1891	Reporter
Welshfield, Ohio	June 22, 1891	Who Do You Think?
Mount Ayr, Ind.	July 1, 1891	Bee Jay Em
Middlefield, Ohio	Sept. 28, 1891	So Sauged De Marrie
Waupecong, Ind.	Nov. 10, 1891	ICH UND MY PARTNER
Berlin, Ohio	Nov. 26, 1891	Jupiter
Hazelredge, Tenn.	Nov. 16, 1891	Nix Kum Rouse
Eureka, Mich.	Dec. 19, 1891	O.K.
Trail, Ohio	Dec. 31, 1891	Trailer
Mt. Hope, Ohio	Dec. 31, 1891	Buckeye
Under Possum Valley Items	Dec. 28, 1891	Ich Vase Ned Var
Shanesville, Ohio	Jan. 14, 1892	BAY PARTNER
Shanesville, Ohio	Feb. 1892	Pacific
Emma, Ind.	Feb. 1892	Ich Vase Var
Burton, Ohio	April 1892	Nix Fer Ungute
Welshfield, Ohio	May 2, 1892	Tom, Dick & Harry
East Brooke, Pa. (Lawrence Co.)	May 19, 1892	PINKEY
Charm New Items	June 9, 1892	DANDEY SAMMY
Welshfield, Ohio	June 27, 1892	JINGO
Charm, Ohio	July, 1892	Charmer
Mt. Ayr, Ind.	July 11, 1892	SPY
Sage Creek, Wyo.	July 7, 1892	Sage Brush
North Bunker Hill, Ohio	July 23, 1892	WASTE BASKET
Geauga County Items	July 30, 1892	Kentucky Lawyer
Charm News Item	Aug. 11, 1892	Democrat
North Bunker Hill, Ohio	July 30, 1892	All Right
Welshfield, Ohio	May 25, 1893	Sometimes
Hutchinson, Kan.	May 25, 1893	BOOMER
Burton, Ohio	Feb. 11, 1892	Young Reporters Dog
Amish College Items	Feb. 22, 1892	Net Schlecht
Burton Station, Ohio	Mar. 1892	D. X. Gingersnap
Middlefield, Ohio	May 12, 1892	J. I. Case
Hutchinson, Kans.	July 21, 1892	DUTCHY
Cherry Ridge, Ohio	May 5, 1892	Arctic
Germantown, Ind.	Feb. 4, 1892	The Budgets Friend

Arthur, Ill.	Jan. 14, 1892	Vor Net Mich
Possum Valley Items	Jan. 14, 1892	Daddy's Boy
East Brook, Pa.	Jan. 4, 1892	One Who Was There
Cherry Ridge, Ohio	Jan. 14, 1892	Dixie
Walnut Creek	May 13, 1892	Straight Goods
Charm	May 16, 1892	Sweet Anna
Hutchinson, Kan.	May 12, 1892	Sel Dutes
East Brook, Pa.	Jan. 4, 1893	BOWSER
Walnut Creek	Jan. 16, 1893	Nichodamus
Garden City, Mo.	Feb. 1, 1893	DOYOUKETCHON?
Cherry Ridge, Ohio	Feb. 6, 1893	Mayflower
Needy, Ore.	Jan. 27, 1893	Who Do You Think?
Needy, Ore.	Feb. 13, 1893	I AM NEEDY
Dickson, Tenn.	Mar. 29, 1893	SWEET HONEY
Welshfield, Ohio	April 8, 1893	So Sagt Der Sam
Monitor, Kans.	Mar. 27, 1893	Shoofly
Needy, Ore.	April 19, 1893	HAPPY VALLEY
Peach Orchard, Ark.	May 1, 1893	ARKANSAS PLUG
Waupecong, Ind.	May 10, 1893	It Was I
Monitor, Kans.	June 1, 1893	Poetically Inclined
LaGrange, Ind.	June 23, 1893	Correspondent
Emma, Ind.	June 16, 1893	A Reader
Nappanee, Ind.	July 3, 1893	Somebody
Needy, Ore.	July 26, 1893	Contributor No. 2
Welshfield, Ohio	July 29, 1893	I and My Pa
Hutchinson, Kans.	Aug. 7, 1893	CRICKET
Troyer Valley, Ohio	Aug. 24, 1893	GERMAN T-P
Arthur, Ill.	Aug. 24, 1893	NONE OF MY BUSINESS
Inman, Kans.	Sept. 8, 1893	Young Sunflower
Arthur, Ill.	Sept. 8, 1893	Don't Blame Me
Yoder, Kans.	Sept. 6, 1893	NOBODY
North Bunker Hill, Ohio	Sept. 21, 1893	IT WASN'T ABE
Mt. Ayr, Ind.	Sept. 18, 1893	STRAIGHT GOODS
Needy, Ore.	Sept. 20, 1893	HOP POLE
Shipshewana, Ind.	Sept. 25, 1893	HUSTLER
Needy, Ore.	Sept. 20, 1893	MR. SOMEBODY
Woodburn, Ore.	Oct. 13, 1893	WEBFOOT
Charm, Ohio	Oct. 23, 1893	PETE PATCH
Middlefield, Ohio	Oct. 28, 1893	BLAME ME
Trail, Ohio	Oct. 30, 1893	RAMBLER
Emma, Ind.	Nov. 8, 1893	BOYS DON'T BLAME ME
Middlebury, Ind.	Nov. 15, 1893	U. R. RIGHT
Yoder, Kan.	Nov. 16, 1893	JAY HAWKER
Nappanee, Ind.	Nov. 23, 1893	THEY BLAME ME
Chesterville, Ind.	Nov. 17, 1893	ZIP
Middlefield, Ohio	Nov. 25, 1893	NIXIE
Mt. Ayr, Ind.	Nov. 27, 1893	BLAME THE BOYS
Welshfield, Ohio	Dec. 5, 1893	L. A. GRIPPE
Hubbard, Ore.	Dec. 6, 1893	Don't Tell
Charm, Ohio	Jan. 15, 1894	LITTLE JOKER
Barr, Pa.	Jan. 15, 1894	SAMBO
Hubbard, Ore.	Jan. 10, 1894	HELLO! WHAT'S THAT?
Mt. Hope, Ohio	Jan. 20, 1894	ASE WAR NED MICH
Hutchinson, Kans.	Jan. 24, 1894	Z. Y. X.
Nappanee, Ind.	Jan. 26, 1894	HARD TIMES
Kalona, Iowa	Jan. 22, 1894	WESTERN BOY
Hubbard, Ore.	Feb. 5, 1894	TA-RA-RA-BOOM

Middlebury, Ind.	Feb. 5, 1894	O. B. CAREFUL
Pashan, Ind.	Feb. 7, 1894	HOOSIER
Nappanee, Ind.	Feb. 12, 1894	HOONOS SHEASER
Emma, Ind.	Feb. 17, 1894	J. J. WHITE HANDS
Needy, Ore.	Feb. 19, 1894	BEE STING
Berlinton, Ind.	Feb. 26, 1894	HARD TACK
Goshen, Ind.	Mar. 8, 1894	Daddy's Son
Kalona, Iowa	Mar. 15, 1894	WE, HIS & CO
Inman, Kans.	Mar. 24, 1894	O. I. C.
Yoder, Kans.	Mar. 23, 1894	OH PSHAW
Welshfield, Ohio	April 9, 1894	SEE O DOUBLEYOU
Emma, Ind.	May 8, 1894	CORN DROPPER
Needy, Ore.	May 2, 1894	FUGATIVE
Arthur, Ill.	June 28, 1894	YOU KNOW IT
Mt. Hope, Ohio	May 19, 1894	TOUGH WHEELING
Mt. Ayr, Ind.	May 24, 1894	U. R. WRIGHT
Woodburn, Ore.	Feb. 12, 1895	WEBFOOT
Glasco, Kans.	Feb. 3, 1895	CRICKET
Nappanee, Ind.	Jan. 14, 1895	SNOWMAN
Charm	Oct. 28, 1895	JUDGE
Dickson, Tenn.	Dec. 23, 1895	PAP'S BOY
Plevna, Ind.	Feb. 4, 1896	BIBLE READER
Arthur, Ill.	May 4, 1896	PEQUEA CHUMS
Belleville, Pa.	June 6, 1896	NOVICE
Peach Orchard, Ark.	June 6, 1896	THE HACKER
Arthur, Ill.	June 13, 1896	HIDY
East Claridon, OH	June 15, 1896	STRICTLY IN IT
Charm, OH	June 15, 1896	JAVA
Farmerstown, Ohio	June 29, 1896	IKE, THE DAUBER
Charm, Ohio	July 24, 1896	GUY
Belleville, Pa.	Aug. 14, 1896	GOOSE QUILL
Waupecong, Ind.	Sept. 7, 1896	B. 4 U, WHO?
Plevna, Ind.	Nov. 17, 1896	UP-TO-DATE
Island Lake, ND	Nov. 23, 1896	BILLY THE KID
Gibson, Miss.	Dec. 15, 1896	HOW IS ALL?
Welshfield, Ohio	Dec. 28, 1896	CUP AND SAUCER
Belleville, Pa.	Mar. 5, 1897	Supplement
Menno, Pa.	May 5, 1897	I C ALL
Lowell, Mich.	Dec. 31, 1899	BEAUTY
Shipshewana, Ind.	June 2, 1899	DAD'S GIRLS
Intercourse, PA.	June 4, 1899	GUESS MY NAME
Baden, Ont.	June 23, 1899	A Baden BOY
Yoder, Kans.	June 3, 1899	HUTTLER
Baden, Ont.	July 7, 1899	YOU KNOW
Bedford, Ohio	July 10, 1899	BELLE OF THE VALLEY
Logan, Mich.	July 9, 1899	LOG SKITTER
Browne, Mich.	July 27, 1899	PRODIGAL SON
Menno, Pa.	Aug. 12, 1899	SUNFLOWER
Logan, Mich.	Aug. 13, 1899	SPORT
Benton, Ohio	Aug. 7, 1899	THREE BOYS
Belleville, Ohio	Aug. 11, 1899	COLD WATER
Mascot, Pa.	Aug. 27, 1899	MOTHER'S DAUGHTER
Ronks, Pa.	Aug. 28, 1899	PANSY
Wellesley, Ont.	Sept. 1, 1899	COLD CANADA
Albany, Ore.	Oct. 6, 1899	MAMMA'S GIRL
Yoder, Kans.	Oct. 31, 1899	IT WAS US
Hutchinson, Kans.	Nov. 20, 1899	CITY LAD

Arthur, Ill.	Nov. 25, 1899	SOMEBODY'S GIRL
Amish, Iowa	Nov. 26, 1899	SOLLY AND POLLY
Loweil, Mich.	Nov. 30, 1899	CHATTERBOX
Belleville, Pa.	Dec. 7, 1899	An Old Scribe
Mt. Hope, Ohio	Dec. 9, 1899	ANONYMOUS
Elmdale, Mich.	Dec. 9, 1899	VISE KOP
Dewey, Ill.	Dec. 11, 1899	Little Willie
Amish, Iowa	Dec. 12, 1899	Fairy Belle
Mt. Hope, Ohio	Dec. 14, 1899	POKER
Pleasant Valley, Ohio	Dec. 28, 1899	X-RAYS
Baden, Ont.	Jan. 26, 1900	* *
Elmdale, Mich.	Jan. 24, 1900	TWO CHUMS
Belleville, Pa.	Jan. 30, 1900	I AND MYSELF
Pleasant Valley, Ohio	Jan. 29, 1900	PANSY
Emma, Ind.	Jan. 12, 1900	PIE
ibson, Miss.	Jan. 13, 1900	BLAME US
Grand Rapids, Mich.	Feb. 8, 1900	You all Know
Pleasant Valley, Ohio	Mar. 19, 1900	U - NO
Lowell, Mich.	Mar. 22, 1900	SUNBEAM
Kempsville, Va.	Mar. 18, 1900	A CHURCH LOVER
Logan, Mich.	Mar. 25, 1900	TOWN TALK
Nampa, Ida.	April 23, 1900	DON'T U KNOW
Tavistock, Ont.	June 2, 1900	DICTATED
Tavistock, Ont.	June 5, 1900	GOOSE QUILL
Cora, Okla.	June 3, 1900	WHITTLER
Daughtery, Mo.	July 1, 1900	THE LONELY SISTER
Tavistock, Ont.	July 17, 1900	COLD WATER
Logan, Mich.	July 13, 1900	OLD SPORT
Fentress, Va.	July 28, 1900	A TWIN SISTER
Grantsville, Md.	Sept. 28, 1900	JUSTICE
Pleasant Valley, Oh.	Dec. 17, 1900	SNOWFLAKE
Island Lake, N.D.	Jan. 16, 1901	SNOWDRIFT
McKinley, Mich.	Jan. 24, 1901	BLAME ME
Wilmot, Minn.	Feb. 5, 1901	NEVER MIND
Mt. Tabor, Ohio	Feb. 28, 1901	TWIN SISTERS
Needy, Ore.	April 4, 1901	MOSSBACK
Welshfield, Ohio	April 19, 1901	THE SALT AGENTS
Fairview, Mich.	May 18, 1901	MICHIGAN
Carmel, W. Va.	June 3, 1901	BROTHERHOOD
Cora, Okla.	May 27, 1901	TRIBLETS
Orrville, Ohio	June 24, 1901	LILACS
Clarion, Iowa	June 25, 1901	TOPSY
White Cloud, Mich.	June 27, 1901	PERCH
Hubbard, Ore.	July 18, 1901	ORANGE BLOSSOM
Fairview, Mich.	Aug. 25, 1901	FISHERMAN
Shipshewana, Ind.	Oct. 13, 1901	TIGER LILY
Needy, Ore.	Nov. 20, 1901	PANSY BLOSSOM
Middlefield, Ohio	Dec. 5, 1901	AN EYE WITNESS
Vandalia, Ill.	Dec. 1, 1901	LITTLE GIRL
Cora, Okla.	Dec. 1, 1901	BEE BEE EM
Charm, Ohio	Dec. 15, 1901	THE MERRY CIRCLE
Stuttgart, Ark.	Dec. 9, 1901	JOLLY JAY
Fairview, Mich.	Jan. 1, 1902	HAY
Olivet, S.D.	Dec. 30, 1901	JOE BUTTERMAKER
Albany, Ore.	Jan. 9, 1902	You and I
Jerden Falls, N.Y.	Jan. 27, 1902	A SILENT READER
Belleville, Pa.	Jan. 27, 1902	PANSY BLOSSOM

Allensville, Pa.	Jan. 28, 1902	JUNK'S PARTNER
Middlebury, Ind.	Jan. 24, 1902	A Tribe of 12
Middlefield, Ohio	Jan. 31, 1902	WINKEY
Albany, Ore.	Mar. 3, 1902	TWO WEBFOOTS
Middlefield, Ohio	May 22, 1902	TWO LADIES
Bowne, Mich.	May 22, 1902	BLACKJACK
Lowville, N.Y.	June 5, 1902	THREE SPORTS
Warren, Ohio	June 7, 1902	LONELY SISTER
New Wilmington, Pa.	June 14, 1902	JOLLY LAD
Thurman, Colo.	July 3, 1902	RANCH GIRL
Flanigan, Ill.	July 10, 1902	TWO BLUE BELLS
Pontiac, Ill.	July 25, 1902	TOPSY AND BETSY
Welshfield, Ohio	July 28, 1902	A SUCKER
Berlin, Ohio	Aug. 1, 1902	KITTIE
Mt. Eaton, Ohio	Aug. 4, 1902	SUNSHINE
Cleona, Ind.	Aug. 4, 1902	BROWNIE
Diamond Loch, Colo.	Aug. 15, 1902	TRIPPY AND TRIMMY
Lowville, N.Y.	Aug. 17, 1902	TALLY HO
Concord, Tenn.	Aug. 26, 1902	KATY-DID
Pocahontas, Iowa	Sept. 8, 1902	HOW I WONDER
Panola, Ill.	Sept. 15, 1902	TWO WHITE LILIES
Haven, Kans.	Oct. 21, 1902	CATCH ME
Pleasant Valley, Ohio	Nov. 17, 1902	DO FUNNY
Bristol, Ind.	Nov. 15, 1902	US TWO
Whiteson, Ore.	Dec. 18, 1902	PETE WHISKERS
Charm, Ohio	Feb. 14, 1903	GUY SON
Pleasant Valley, Ohio	Mar. 1, 1903	DO FUNNY
Wooster, Ohio	Feb. 28, 1903	PEACH AND STRAWBERRY
Walnut Creek, Ohio	Mar. 9, 1903	LILY OF THE VALLEY
Burton, Ohio	April 8, 1903	MAYFLOWER SONS
Diamond Loch, Mich.	April 15, 1903	CITY GIRLS
Hutchinson, Kans.	April 19, 1903	JAYHAWKER
Croghan, N.Y.	June 14, 1903	LITTLE CLARENCE
Denbeigh, Va.	July 10, 1903	FOUR FRIENDS
Nampa, Ida.	July 12, 1903	FIND ME OUT
Loogootee, Ind.	Aug. 19, 1903	DOCKIE
Mt. Ayr, Ind.	Sept. 6, 1903	MIDNIGHT AND MORNING
Middlebury, Ind.	Aug. 30, 1903	PENCIL PUSHER
Hampton, Okla.	Sept. 24, 1903	THURSDAY EVE
Hopewell, Ill.	Nov. 1, 1903	HAPPY HOOLIGAN
Kalispell, Mont.	Nov. 7, 1903	MIS SNOWBALL
Lake Odessa, Mich.	Nov. 22, 1903	DUTCH
Arthur, Ill.	Nov. 28, 1903	JAY KAY BEE
Lagrange, Ind.	Dec. 4, 1903	KITTY
Island Lake, N.D.	Nov. 30, 1903	GID JUB
Goshen, Ind.	Jan. 14, 1904	TWO ROSES
Shrock, Ind.	Mar. 3, 1904	IT WAS I
Grass Lakes, N.D.	May 4, 1904	ZERO
Millersburg, Ohio	June 16, 1904	SHE AND I
Loogootee, Ind.	June 15, 1904	ONLY A GIRL
Garnett, Kans.	July 14, 1904	SUMMER
Middlefield, Ohio	August 7, 1904	MAMMA'S DAUGHTERS
Bowne, Mich.	Sept. 28, 1904	WHO KNOWS
Mt. Ayr, Ind.	October 21, 1904	OCTOBER BUD
Hearing, Va.	Nov. 19, 1904	SUNNY SOUTH

178

Mt. Ayr, Ind.	Jan. 7, 1905	TWO GOOD GIRLS
Stuttgart, Ark.	April 23, 1905	TWO LITTLE GIRLS
Nappanee, Ind.	May 6, 1905	A BALL PLAYER
Middlefield, Ohio	July 7, 1905	CLOVER BLOSSOMS
Fairview, Mich.	July 23, 1905	THE OTHER ONE
Topeka, Ind.	Aug. 17, 1905	THE OTHER FELLOW
Greentown, Ind.	May 10, 1906	MAYFLOWER
Grabill, Ind.	July 28, 1906	TWINS
Fairview, Mich.	Aug. 1, 1906	SAFY
Denbeigh, Va.	Nov. 9, 1906	SUBSTITUTES OF TWO SISTERS
Charm, Ohio	Nov. 11, 1906	TWO COUSINS
Mylo, N.D.	Apr. 17, 1907	BUSY BEE
Fairview, Mich.	Apr. 19, 1907	N.I.X.
Goshen, Ind.	May 26, 1907	APPLE BLOSSOM
Louisville, Ohio	Dec. 22, 1907	DEW DROP
Fentress, Va.	Jan. 15, 1909	SUBSTITUTE FOR SUNNY SOUTH
Iowa City, Iowa	Dec. 23, 1909	X.Y.Z.
Belleville, PA.	Feb. 10, 1910	ALMS IN SECRET
Plainview, Tex.	April 19, 1910	LONE STAR
Reinert, Kans.	Jan. 26, 1913	FOUR FRIENDS
Ordway, Colo.	June 19, 1913	TWO OF A KIND
Trail, Ohio	Mar. 4, 1914	Three Readers
Brunner, Ont.	Mar. 6, 1914	SOLITARY
Burr Oak, Mich.	April 15, 1914	TWIN SISTERS
Greenwood, Del.	Aug. 4, 1915	Factory Girls
Lancaster, Pa.	April 25, 1920	A Lover of the Truth
Hartville, Ohio	July 20, 1921	A Cheerful gal
McMinnville, Ore.	Sept. 24, 1922	A.B.C. and X.Y.Z.
Lancaster, Pa.	Dec. 29, 1922	A Jolly Bunch Traveling East
Sugarcreek, Ohio	Jan. 4, 1923	Z.Y.X.
Hartville, Ohio	Feb. 3, 1923	A Stark Kid
Hope, Mich.	July 4, 1923	A Jolly Bunch
Uniontown, Ohio	July 7, 1930	"Just Us"
Nappanee, Ind.	May 3, 1931	The Happy Trio
Arthur, Ill.	Feb. 28, 1932	"A Friendly Bunch"
Shipshewana, Ind.	Mar. 27, 1932	Just Me
Dover, Dela.	Mar. 28, 1932	The Kansas Bunch
Plain City, Ohio	Mar. 31, 1932	Madison Bums
Fountain Hook, Ohio	May 27, 1934	Mutt and Jeff
Conway Springs, Kans.	May 31, 1934	From a Dry Sunflower
Sugarcreek, Ohio	Sept. 27, 1943	"Puttle"
Kemp, Texas	Mar. 19, 1989	Tolosa Girls

Health and Hygiene   24

Health was one of the most frequently discussed topics, probably because it affects everyone in some manner. Partly as a result of this, it was also one of the topics that could lead to sharp differences of opinion. These differences surfaced particularly when remedies were discussed. One of the most controversial matters was the practice of "Brauching", called powwowing by some scribes. The letters abound with accounts of persons traveling to a wide variety of places and to a wide variety of "doctors" to seek relief and/or cure.

AIDS: It seems the rumor mills are going again. Nobody among the Amish here has AIDS that we know of and nobody takes a blood test to get a marriage license in Ia. anymore.

Oct. 25, 1989 Bloomfield, Iowa David Yutzy

Braucha: [The Editor quoted from a letter to him by an unnamed party in Oakland, Md., Editor's Corner.] Many years ago I was loaned a book on powwow based on the 6th and 7th books of Moses. At that time I was single and worked at the carpenter trade. I read the book until late at night but when I went to bed I could not sleep. This happened each night so I returned the book. Then I could sleep, but the things the book contained I wish I could forget.

July 17, 1952

A reader requests an article on Pow-Wowing (Braucha) and wonders if this practice is Scriptural or not? Answer: No, this practice is not scriptural.

Now, please, before you condemn the writer for the above statement, will you at least agree with him that the Word of God is the final authority, and that practices are right only when they are in agreement with the Word of God? Is it not true that which the Word of God commands is right, and that which the Word of God forbids, is forever wrong, though practiced by generation after generation?

A practice is never made right by long use - - God's Word
is unchangeable.

Sept. 14, 1962   Lynnhaven Gleanings   Jacob J. Hershberger

To those who object to taking children to have "brauched"
for them when all doctor's medicine has failed to help
them, would you refrain from taking your sick child to a
medical doctor just because a neighbor or friend or relative
was opposed to an M.D., believing only in Divine Healing?
I have heard of parents refusing to take their children to a
chiropractor even after a medical doctor was unable to
give them relief. To my way of thinking we need both the
M.D.'s and chiropractors and yes, those who "brauch" too.
How could anyone give themselves so completely in the
devil's power as to be able to "brauch" only thru his power
but otherwise live such a christian life as puts to shame
some who "profess" to be christians. No, I do not believe in
witchcraft, nor do I believe there is any connection
between witchcraft and "brauching."

Sept. 14, 1961   Dover, Dela.   Effie Troyer

As for "Pow-wowing" and "braucha" not being the same
thing - - it is a fact that our dictionaries do not list the word
"Braucha". It is simply a Pa. Dutch expression. But the
fact remains that the nearest English word thereto is
"Pow-wowing", which has several meanings. One of these
at least is the same as "Braucha".

At least one party wrote to me that "Braucha" was scriptural - - he claimed he had studied it in the 6th and 7th
books of Moses. (???) Others wrote of cures they had witnessed, etc. - - "and therefore it can't be wrong." On the
other side was a brother who personally told me he
believed many of the things done by those who "Brauch"
had crept in "in order to rob God of the honor and glory."
This one said he believed "Braucha" was originally simply
the gift of healing - - as God gave it, and man had added
these mystical rites himself - - for the above purpose.

Oct. 5, 1961   Lynnhaven Gleanings   Jacob J. Hershberger

Recently there has been some "Pow Wowing" and
"Braucha" going on through the Budget. Do not know if it
cured anyone or not. I believe I agree pretty well with
Mrs. Effie Troyer, if I understand her right. I believe fur-
ther than some would-be authority (?) gave the name
Braucha, "Pow wow", and that wrongfully, but now it

181

finally goes by that name.
Sept. 21, 1961   Shipshewana, Ind.   Joe B.

This issue of "Brauching" seems to have caused a lot of comment. Some of these old ideas I will let as they are, but as for actual "brauching" which is done by repeating a paragraph or two out of the Bible, it is hard for me to believe that those words put the spirits to work.
Sept. 21, 1961   Grabill, Ind.   William Zehr

40 years ago a certain Braucher (a minister) told me that I could learn to Brauch. I did not see anything wrong about it, until he told me a man must learn the trade from a woman and a woman from a man. That was sufficient for me. I never learned it.

Some persons are apparently gifted with the power of healing. About 30 years ago my wife had a severe dose of erysipelas in her face, and the doctor's preparation seemed fruitless. We called for a godly gifted brother, old Daniel D. Miller of Ohio, who happened to be in Virginia at the time. He laid his gifted hands on, and as a miracle she almost immediately got better and soon was cured.
Oct. 26, 1961   Princess Anne, Va.   Levi Bontrager

If "Braucha" would work only for those who claim to be Christians it might also change the picture, but one of the persons that I have known with the widest reputation for doing it successfully was by no means what the average person would call a Christian.
Oct. 26, 1961   Lakeside, Ont.   Samuel Hertzler

Reading the pros and cons of "braucha" or pow wow healing, in my opinion there is a vast difference between these and the gift of healing as referred to in . . . . [Five Scriptures given.]
Oct. 5, 1961   Plain City, Ohio   Jonas E. Beachy

I had not intended mentioning about this "Braucha" deal but I do think it is coming to the point where some are taking the Scriptures to argue with, which I think is far more wrong than "braucha" itself if done in the right. I'm afraid we will keep on till our kind Editor will again have to ask us to stop - - and we pretend to be so-called Christians.
Nov. 2, 1961   Medford, Wisc.   E. B.

Contagion and quarantine: There is quite a smallpox scare; there are 16 cases reported among the Amish people.
Jan. 8, 1903   Goshen, Ind.   Noah S. Yoder

There has been a smallpox scare in our town recently, but we are glad to note that it turned out to be chickenpox.

June 22, 1899   Shipshewana, Ind.   Mona Hochstetler

We had no church and Sunday school on Sunday, on account of scarlet fever. The children in this neighborhood are having whooping cough.

Feb. 18, 1910   Greentown, Ind.   Mrs. Emma J. Miller

The measles, chicken pox and whooping cough are prevailing around here among the children.

Mar. 24, 1904   Conway, Kans.   Lizzie Mast

Eli Yoder's family is having quite a siege of that dreadful disease, diphtheria, since week before last. There were six down with it last week at one time. Their baby died Dec. 9th and was buried that night.

Dec. 28, 1899   Topeka, Ind.   J. E. K.

Isaac Plank who was quite low with diphtheria is up and around again. There house was fumigated today. Quite a few children have spinal meningitis around here.

April 9, 1913   Pigeon, Mich.   Alma G. Zehr

Public meetings are forbidden at present; we had no Sunday school and church last Sunday, and do not expect to have next Sunday. This makes a person feel somewhat lost. [Smallpox epidemic]

Feb. 15, 1910   Fairview, Mich.   Mrs. M. S. Zook

Weddings everywhere are postponed on account of the flu.

Dec. 25, 1910   Ronks, Pa.   Gideon B. Fisher

People don't come in your house to see you when you are sick with the flu and I don't blame anyone to stay away from it.

Dec. 4, 1918   Plain City, Ohio   M. M. Kauffman

The dreadful disease flu is spreading thru out our locality. . . . Had no church for four weeks which seems lonesome, schools are also closed.

Nov. 13, 1918   Topeka, Ind.   Miss Katie & Emma Lehman

At the Mennonite Orphan's Home of this place, where superintendent John Hilty and assistants have about 70 children to care for, there has been something like 55 cases of influenza but no deaths.

Nov. 6, 1918   West Liberty, Ohio   Maude Peachey

Pink-eye is making its rounds in the Troy School.

Mar. 1, 1918   Burton, Ohio   Cora V. Miller

The Board of Health ordered all schools and churches closed for the present time.
Oct. 23, 1918   Elverson, Pa.   Elsie Stoltzfus

I think a person exposed to any contagious disease should not be allowed to send items to the editor of any paper.
Mar. 22, 1900   Vandalia, Ill.   J. D. Yoder

[Editorial response to the J.D. Yoder comment above.] A person exposed to smallpox should not only be prohibited from writing to the editors, but to anyone else; neither should they be allowed to write to anyone for several weeks after they have had the disease. Instances are not rare where contagious diseases have been carried through the mail.
Mar. 22, 1900

We had no church services here in the east congregation since Sunday eight weeks ago we had council meeting at Aaron Beachys and within the next three weeks there were five funerals in this church.
Dec. 4, 1918   Topeka, Ind.   Mrs. Harvey N. Glick

Cures and clinics: Mrs. . . . is not so good at this time and they were along to Holmes to consult with John Yoder, Holmes County's Amish doctor. Mostly self-taught, I understand, but I have no qualms with that for I always contended that a willing mind could absorb as much from good books as could be taught in school or should I say college. For to my way of thinking a teacher's job is to instill the desire to learn in the pupil and then point them in the direction of where to find the answers, not to tell them.
Feb. 25, 1987   West Union, Ohio   Atlee J. Hochstetler

A load left early this morning for Berne, Indiana to doctor at Sol Wickey's.
March 18, 1987   Ashland, Ohio   Mrs. Henry S. Miller

We are farther west here than the railroad goes. This place is situated 26 miles from the R.R. Some people may be interested about the price of the baths. $2.60 per bath is charged and the Kelp ore he sells at $2.50 per lb. One pound is sufficient to make several gallons of drinking water, which is then a mineral water.
Aug. 20, 1925   Cloverdale, Ore.   E. M. Hochstetler

The doctor treats his patients by scientific fasting, spinal adjustments and diet. No drugs or medicine are used at

184

all. [This was a description of Dr. Dahl's 4 week treatment at Henderson, NC; taken by numerous Amish people.]
Oct. 12, 1939   Lynnhaven, Va.   Mrs. Enos W. Yoder

[Many pages could be filled with letters describing a wide variety of treatments and so-called "cures" sought and the many places visited in the interests of health. Because of space limitations, only the following summaries will be given.]

This Dr. doesn't take care of anything else but Epileptic fits. He doesn't say that he can cure it, but he sent us a lot of testimonials that we could see what he had done for hundreds of others.

We have never seen the Dr. You can do everything in writing just as good as if you would go direct to him.
April 20, 1939   Plain City, Ohio   Mrs. Roy E. Yutzy

I received a lot of help by going to Mineral Wells, Texas, but should have stayed a few weeks longer, and I do wish some of those poor sufferers could also receive help there as I did. They doctor for nervousness, rheumatism, and just about everything else, but they don't recommend it much for cancer.
July 29, 1939   Conway Springs, Kans.   Susie Miller

We have been here nearly one month. Our husbands have made a marked improvement from the Hot Springs baths.
Sept. 30, 1943   Hot Springs, Ark.   Mrs. Ira Zook

We are bathing in the Lamar bath house. Some may wonder what we are all here for, and I hardly know myself, as some of us are practically sound, (that is bodily) but prevention is easier than cure.
Oct. 4, 1945   Hot Springs, Ark.   Joe l. Hershberger

Quite a few of our people from here and Pinecraft go to Salt Springs to bathe in the warm salt water which comes out of the earth.
Feb. 17, 1949   Sarasota, Fla.   E. J. Miller

I came to Dr. Nichols Sanitorium May 3 and started treatment May 4, for a tumor on my face....
May 20, 1948   Savannah, Mo.   Mrs. Eliza J. Yoder

I am getting quite a number of letters from cancer patients since I had a letter in the Budget from this place. The doctor here is very busy. It seems the medical men are fighting him very hard and he doesn't know how long he can stay in business. It doesn't seem as if this is a free

185

country anymore.
Nov. 27, 1947   Chattanooga, Tenn.   Stephen J. Hostetler

For more than 20 yr. treated people with a serum which he said would cure cancer, arthritis, diabetes, and peptic ulcer. [The Helt Clinic of Windsor, Ont. His name had been removed from the medical profession list in 1952.]
Oct. 4, 1956   Aylmer, Ont.   David Wagler

[A public warning against the Hoxsey Cancer Treatment Clinic of Dallas, Texas was included in THE BUDGET. The Editor received some indignant responses from readers.]
May 31, 1956

Dr. Yergin was reported giving "health instructions to live the natural way according to the Bible, called the Harmony System, the drugless and surgeonless method."
Oct. 22, 1953   Kidder, Mo.   Tillie M. Beachy

Eli J. Bontrager described the Ortman Clinic of Canistoto, South Carolina, saying it "is now world renowned, and has a very large patronage, it would no doubt be of interest to many to know more about these noted doctors." [Bontrager used more than a full column for his account.]
May 5, 1949   No address given   Eli J. Bontrager

He calls his way of treating the Hygienic System. Specializes in proper rest, exercise, sunbathing, rational fasting, corrective diet and mental poise - - the rules of nature. [Dr. Shelton, San Antonia, Tex.]
May 10, 1951   Milford, Neb.   Susie and Emma Yoder

[Some went to the Excelsior Springs Clinic in Missouri.]
July 2, 1953   Hartville, Ohio   Nancy Coblentz

[A full column news item "State Nabs Quack Doctor in Pa." led to some strong responses favoring Henry E. Wolford, the man in question.]
April 30, 1950

Healing: About the Divine Healer. Some people have very much faith in them and some do not believe in them at all. I am better in some ways. I could walk better that evening, but since my walking is just about the same as it was before. They want to be in Detroit through the month of July but they have no meetings on Mondays. [The "healer" was not identified.]
July 14, 1949   Shipshewana, Ind.   Mrs. Anna Knepp

A little girl of Mahlon Otto choked to death on a grain of

coffee. They used the "Christian Science" faith cure, but could not save the child.

Dec. 28, 1899   Aurora, Neb.   John H. Smucker

One of our acquaintance in Norfolk said they almost cried when we consulted a doctor and trusted in the arm of flesh, but lying in the recovery room my heart went up in praise to Christ for the provisions made through the hands and feet of doctors and friends in caring one for another.

Nov. 1, 1962   Princess Anne, Va.   John Kanagy

Hospital Aid Plan: There was a Amish Hospital Aid meeting held last Thurs. evening, with some present from Garnett, Haven and Partridge Kansas Churches and Mayer Co. Okla. So far we've only had volunteer donations, but need something more with the high cost of hospital care.

May 7, 1980   Haven, Kans.   Mrs. Eli W. Miller

It was interesting to read in the Budget, that the Oklahoma and Kansas Amish Churches are planning to start a Hospital Aid Plan, which from experience, I can hearty recommend, as many Ohio churches have had this service for many years. It also has spread to some Pennsylvania Churches.

May 14, 1980   Plain City, Ohio   Jonas E. Beachy

Mental health: A daughter of Daniel D. Yoder, who has been afflicted, physically and mentally for many years, is very much improved and is doing some work around the house. If I am not mistaken, all this change has been brought about without any medicine, evidently through the will of God alone.

Aug. 3, 1905   Grantsville, Md.   Emanuel Hershberger

On the health side there is a report that . . . is in the hospital with an "emotional upset" something which always brings sorrow and heartaches to the family and friends. Just why one person out of ten (so say statistics) must endure such an experience sometime in his life is something we must leave with "Higher Powers," though we accept and know that such disturbances may come from various causes.

May 4, 1961   Lynnhaven, Va.   Jacob J. Hershberger

Polio: There are seven cases (Infantile Paralysis) in and north of Kalona. [21 day quarantine during which no public meetings were to be held.]

Oct. 2, 1912   Kalona, Iowa   Miss Maggie Miller

187

By order of the county health officer . . . all schools have
been closed on account of the prevalence of infantile paralysis.
> Sept. 12, 1940   Garnett, Kans.   Miss Minnie Beachy

Donald, two year old son of Lester Hershberger of Hartville, died Tuesday at Aultman Hospital, Canton, of polio.
His one year-old sister, Dawn, is also a polio patient.
> July 24, 1952   News item placed in a Hartville, Ohio letter
> by Mrs. Elam Stoltzfus.

The recent outbreak of the dreaded polio in Amish sectors
has caused considerable questions as to why these out-
breaks occurred mostly among Amish farm children in the
communities of Holmes, Tuscarawas, and Wayne Counties.
County officials and doctors say they cannot give any reason why these cases are more numerous among Amish
residents.
> July 17, 1952   News item, "Polio Among the Amish"

God is chastening us with a plague; by this we know that
God still loves us, for whom the Lord loveth He chasteneth.
(Heb. 12:6)
> July 17, 1952   Fredericksburg, Ohio   Editor's Corner

Remedies: A few weeks ago I was to Newton, Co., selling patent
medicines. I left some at nearly every house that I came to,
and feel thankful to the people for their kindness.
> Dec. 25, 1902   Goshen, Ind.   D. D. Chupp

I saw in the Budget that Emanuel Hershberger has the
rheumatism. Father says; Tell him to grease mit bis-katza
fet. He says his father used to have it for years, and it
cured him.
> April 5, 1906   Gap, Pa.   Annie Stoltzfus

It is easy to prevent malaria if attended to in time, but if it
gets chronic it is a bad thing. Drink a cup of hot water
every morning 30 minutes before breakfast and you will
have no malaria.
> Sept. 20, 1916   Fentress, Va.   Sol King

We have just heard of a cure for consumption or tuber-
culosis, this is coal smoke. . . . It is said that blacksmiths
never have lung trouble.
> April 7, 1920   Smithville, Ohio   A. K. Kurtz

I read in the Budget that someone had an attack of Asthma.
I wonder if you know of that simple remedy that has
brought such great relief to my husband. Simply soak

ordinary ink blotters in a strong solution of Saltpeter then let them dry. When a spell of asthma strikes, just tear off strips and burn them and inhale the fumes.

Oct. 8, 1942   Kingston, Md.   Mrs. Clarence E. Miller

Recently I read about a simple remedy for troublesome eczema, even for long standing cases. Two teaspoons Black Strap Molasses in a glass of milk twice a day.

Oct. 19, 1977   Hazelton, Iowa   Mrs. Felty Yoder

I guess I am too old fashioned but I do have to wonder if some of those old remedies wouldn't do better for babies and small children than these many shots they get.

Nov. 2, 1961   Sarasota, Fla.   Mrs. S. M. Miller

We'll say to all the Budget readers, if there is anyone having a rupture, inquire of Joseph S. Yoder of this place. He has been cured for only eight or ten dollars and will gladly help anyone who is troubled with a rupture.

April 27, 1914   Burr Oak, Mich.   TWIN SISTERS

[Beet remedy recipe for gall bladder.] Boil 5 medium size red beets in a quart of water. When beets are tender, add enough water to make a quart. Yes, I drank the juice all in one day, also ate the beets.

July 24, 1958   New Wilmington, Pa.   C. H. Byler

The black pearl pills were in the public news last week with the Federal Drug people investigating. Test show the black pearl pills contain drugs that are illegal. The drug has to be purchased by prescription only or administered by a doctor.

30,000 pills were turned over to the authorities by the unnamed Ohio distributor. The distributors won't be prosecuted because they were unaware of the contents.

A local man sold two million pills called black pearls. They are supposedly some kind of cure-all. The label on the bottles suggested taking six pills in the morning and six at night to relieve pain of arthritis, sore joints and muscles, and many other ailments. It has now been discovered that the pills contain valium. The dosage was potent enough to cause drowsiness and even addiction.

Oct. 25, 1989   New Bedford, Ohio   Melvin E. Hershberger

Teeth and dentists: Ab King, the poultry man had his teeth pulled by a Kokomo dentist, at 50 cents each.

Oct. 26, 1899   Plevna, Ind.   C. A. L. M.

A good cure for toothache. Wet a cloth with vinegar and rap around the face.

Jan. 7, 1909   Central Lake, Mich.   Mrs. Susan Weirich

A load left for Kentucky, Sunday night to be fitted with false teeth.

Feb. 6, 1964   Apple Creek, Ohio   Lovina Miller

Visiting the sick: Pre. Abe J. Yoder is getting weaker and can hardly be understood when he talks. Also is failing to recognize the people who come to visit him. Over 1000 different people have come to visit him since the first week in July.

Aug. 25, 1960   Hartville, Ohio   Nancy Coblentz

It would be nice if Jacob S. Peachey's relatives and friends would write him a few lines instead of visiting him. It would be a visit without excitement.

Sept. 3, 1953   Selinsgrove, Pa.   Mrs. Noah J. Yoder

Two or more women went to visit an old couple, because they heard that the man had been sick. They found him able to sit up. Their daughter, who was their mainstay, so far as doing their housework was concerned, had gone to her brother's house a short distance away. So when company came they sent for her. My informant said, when she came home she looked cross and didn't talk much.

After dinner one of the visitors washed the dishes, and when they were done, the daughter said, "We always have so much company on Sunday, and I get tired of it." This proved a sort of eye opener to the visitor.

Nov. 12, 1953   No address or name given

Vocabulary: Three-day measles are sneaking around.

June 16, 1949   Meyersdale, Pa.   Vernie M. Maust

The measles are making their rounds again. They are in several schools. The chicken pox have not all died as yet.

Jan. 17, 1924   Latour, Mo.   Sarah E. Hershberger

Health is not the best at present, as measles are on the program.

Jan. 9, 1930   Independence, Iowa   Mrs. Ida Gingerich

Mumps is still in the neighborhood, and quite a few youngsters are making crooked faces.

April 2, 1917   Midland, Mich.   Mrs. A. D. Miller

The measles and the mumps are making their rounds stopping at nearly every family, some people had quite a tussle with the mumps.

Feb. 17, 1921   Allensville, Pa.   M. P. Zook

The whooping cough is making a raid through here at present.

Nov. 20, 1912   Hartville, Ohio   Viola F. Miller

Some people through here are having a swell time as they are having the mumps.

Feb. 20, 1918   Sugarcreek, Ohio   Mrs. B. E. Beachy

A number of schools have been vaccinated on account of the smallpox scare.

Feb. 5, 1913   Oakland, Md.   A Reader

Unclassified: When I was a boy about one out of twelve complained of not being well, and how is it today. Everything must be clean and sanitary and how many are complaining of not being well. About eleven out of twelve. Sixty years ago little was known about hospitals and now they are overloaded.

Feb. 20, 1936   Middlefield, Ohio   J. S. Smucker

Another, eat an apple in the morning is the doctors warning. Eat an apple thru the day, you need not care if the doctor is away, eat an apple when you go to bed you need not care if all the doctors are dead.

Oct. 16, 1918   Pasadena, Calif.   Sarah Gnagy

We heard there are four polio cases around here. I think there has always and always will be a sickness or disease that medical science will know no cause or cure.

Aug. 7, 1952   Middlefield, Ohio   Esther J. Miller

I wish to hear how that wife is getting along near Meyersdale, Pa., who was reported last summer to have a rattle snake in her stomach.

Jan. 26, 1922   Charm, Ohio   Jacob J. Yoder

I have not heard of any new cases of smallpox this week; they are about over; it is more scare than smallpox.

Mar. 27, 1902   Smithville, Ohio   T. L. Miller

This chapter will focus on some of the highlights of THE BUDGET itself as a newspaper. Some aspects of its importance have been woven into the Author's Preface. The significance of the newspaper from the view-point of the scribes is dealt with in the following chapter, "Historical Significance." This chapter is a "sampling" of the newspaper's history and is consistent with the major purpose of the book.

Landmark events:

1890	May 15	First issue printed. It was a bi-weekly paper.
		J. M. Richardson served as the first Editor.
		John C. Miller, Proprietor. Also called "Budget John".
		It was called THE SUGAR CREEK BUDGET.
	Oct.	J. C. Miller became the Editor, following Richardson's acceptance of Superintendent of Mineral City Schools.
1890	Nov.	Changed from a bi-weekly paper to a weekly.
1910		For part of this year it was published as a semi-weekly, called THE SEMI-WEEKLY BUDGET. Within the same year it was placed back on a weekly publication basis, and was called THE WEEKLY BUDGET.
1912	Apr.	Mr. Miller sold the operation to his nephew, A. A. Middaugh.
		Following this purchase, the status of the paper was a bit uncertain. It was printed for a short time at Mennonite Publishing House of Scottdale, Pa.
1913		Purchased by Samuel H. Miller, a minister of the Walnut Creek Amish Mennonite Church. Miller edited and managed the affairs of the paper.
1916		Purchase of a linotype.
1920		Samuel H. Miller sold the operation to S. A. Smith.

1928	Sept.	The name was changed to what it is now, **THE BUDGET.**
1936		George R. Smith, son of S. A. Smith, became manager of operation, and served as the Editor.
1940		Celebration of the 50th Anniversary and publication of a special issue commemorating the event.
1956		Sixty-five BUDGET scribes attended a gathering planned for them.
1961		Introduction of the Home and the National Editions.
1969		George R. Smith sold the business, but returned as Associate Editor. Mr. Sylvester R. Miller was Editor.
1969		65 scribes attended a correspondent's gathering.
1980		More than 300 attend THE BUDGET correspondents "Get Together."
1985		The business was purchased by Mr. Spector, a Wooster, Ohio dry goods retailer.
1990	May	One-Hundredth Anniversary

The first issue:

The official name on the paper was THE SUGAR CREEK BUDGET.

The subscription price was given as 50 cents per year in advance.

Editor: J. M. Richardson; Proprietor: J. C. Miller

Date of publication: May 15, 1890

Four pages in length.

A circulation sampler:

1890	430 copies	
1892	1,020 copies	
1900	2,850 copies	
1904	4,806 copies	
1907	5,117 copies	
1912	3,405 copies	The years 1910-1913 were a period of transition and
1924	3,500 copies	restructuring.
1933	2,800 copies	The 1933 circulation was probably the result of the
1944	5,500 copies	Great Depression.
1952	7,304 copies	
1961	10,200 copies	
1979	+ 17,000 copies	
1989	+ 16,400 copies	

Circulation by states and number of post offices it was sent to in each state at the close of 1899. TB Jan. 4, 1900

State	Post Offices	Copies	State	Post Offices	Copies
Ohio	112	944	Idaho	2	6
Indiana	53	592	W. Virginia	4	5
Pennsylvania	67	370	Tennesee	3	3
Iowa	19	166	Washington D.C.	1	2
Illinois	27	143	Colorado	2	2
Kansas	22	133	Wyoming	1	1
Michigan	31	93	Louisiana	1	1
Nebraska	21	68	Texas	1	1
Canada	13	59	Florida	1	1
North Dakota	10	38	Massachusetts	1	1
Oregon	12	33	Wisconsin	1	1
Maryland	6	31	Georgia	1	1
Oklahoma	7	19	California	1	1
Mississippi	2	17	Washington	1	1
Virginia	3	15	Utah	1	1
Arkansas	4	14	India	1	1
Minnesota	6	13	Germany	1	1
New York	7	12	England	1	1
			Totals	463	2,841

Correspondents:

1980   There were 324 correspondents in 33 states and Canada and eight foreign countries.

1890   First out of state letter was from Stuttgart, Ark. June 29, by Absolom King, appearing in the fifth issue of the paper.

1890   Second letter outside of Holmes County was from Orrville, Ohio, appearing in the sixth issue and signed, Scribler.

1890   Third letter outside of Holmes County was by Moses I. Hochstetler from Magnetic Springs, Ohio, and appeared in the seventh issue of THE BUDGET.

Sources of letters through the year 1895: (by post office)

Arizona
Glendale

Arkansas
Almyra
Stuttgart

Indiana
Germantown
Emma
Mt. Ayr
Waupecong
Shrock
Nappanee
Berlinton

Illinois
Arthur

Kansas
Hutchinson
Partridge

Maryland
Keyser

Michigan
Redman
Eureka

Nebraska
Milford
Chappell

Ohio
Charm
Walnut Creek

Ohio (continued)
Mt. Hope
Smithville
Berlin
Troyer Valley
Trail
Mud Valley
Cherry Ridge
Shanesville
Amish College
Saratoga
Magnetic Springs
Streetsborough
Welshfield
Middlefield
Burton
Farmerstown
Possum Valley

Ohio (continued)
Bunker Hill

Oregon
Woodburn
Williamette Valley

Pennsylvania
East Brooke
Lancaster

Tennessee
Hazelridge

Wyoming
Bear Creek
Philips
Sage Creek

Comments and descriptions:

Here it is that the Sugarcreek Budget, a seven-column quarto is published weekly, sending out a circulation - - it is said - - of more than 4,000. Its editor is an Amishman, and the Amish regard it as their organ. Housed in its own two-story quarters on the very tip-top of the hill, the Budget comes mighty near being "monarch of all it surveys."

A quotation from the *Newcomerstown Index* and appearing in THE BUDGET Aug. 6, 1908.

With this issue of the Budget we enter upon the 23rd year of the existence of the paper. Little did the people think when the Budget was at its infancy, (a wee little thing no larger than a sheet of foolscap, and printed on one side only) that it would grow until it attained its present size.

May 15, 1912   From an Editorial

Fifty one year Honor Roll of subscribers: 1890 - 1941

John A. Miller, Kalona, Ia.	J. J. Miller, Milford, Ind.
Moses M. Beachy, Farmerstown, Oh.	Yost K. Byler, Middlefield, Oh.
Mrs. E. S. Troyer, Mio, Mich.	Noah J. Schlabach, Sugarcreek, Oh.
Mrs. S. S. Beachy, Hutchinson, Kan.	William Koch, Stuttgart, Ark.
J. E. Hochstetler, Hartville, Oh.	S. V. Yoder, Middlefield, Oh.
Henry Smith, Sugarcreek, Oh.	Seth Erb, Millersburg, Oh.
J. H. Stutzman, Hartville, Oh.	D. Z. Byler, Middlefield, Oh.
Jacob F. Yoder, Dover, Dela.	Joe C. Miller, Haven, Kans.
E. M. Hochstetler, Middlefield, Oh.	Wm. Slife, Bedford, Oh.
E. N. Beachy, Springs, Pa.	S. J. Farmwald, New Holland, Pa.
May 8, 1941	

What was included? Some of the things included in the paper at some time during the century?

Advertising

Some poems and humorous items

Syndicated stories and columns [from various sources]

Letters from missionaries to India, J. A. Ressler & W. P. Page.

Announcements and summaries of church conferences

"Es Pennsilfaanisch Deitsch Eck"

Mennonite Central Committee news

Especially as it relates to relief work.

Reports from Mennonite Board of Missions [Elkhart]

Opening of Mennonite Sanitarium in LaJunta, Colorado and many other news items about mission work.

Notes from Meadowbrook Farm [syndicated column]

International Sunday School Lesson commentary

Chronology of the Year [Most important events of year; 1920's]
Travelogues
"The Window Seat" [syndicated column]
Jonathan Fisher's "Lancaster County Briefs".
Jacob J. Hershberger's "Lynnhaven Gleanings."
"Think on These Things" by Minister Edward Miller
"Japan Witness" by Lee Kanagy
"Mountaineer Commentary" by William McGrath
Letters from the many correspondents
A Children's Corner - - for several years beginning in 1921.
Our Little Folks - - a section for letters from children.

Crop report of 1901:

The Editor prepared a condensed crop report for the year 1901. About eighty responses appeared in THE BUDGET. The report is included primarily to show the sources of the letters and the names of the persons responding. The names appeared in two issues. They should give the readers of this volume a better understanding of the scattered readership of THE BUDGET.

Postal address	State	County (if given)	Correspondent
August 22, 1901			
East Lynne	Mo.	Cass Co.	Eli Hostetler
Arthur	Ill.	Moultrie	Levi J. Lee
Kempsville	Va.	Princess Anne	D. D. Hershberger
Geddes	S. D.		W. V. Stahl
Nampa	Ida.	Canyon	David Garber
Mt. Ayr	Ind.	Newton	D. Helmuth
Chesterville	Ill.	Douglas	I. A. Miller
McVeytown	Pa.	Mifflin	Emanuel Byler
Belleville	Pa.	Mifflin	M. P. Zook
Concord	Tenn.	Knox	T. Newhauser
Davidsville	Pa.	Somerset	Levi J. Kauffman
Grass Lake	N. D.		Eli Bontrager
Hutchinson	Kans.	Reno	Eli Helmuth
Chehalis	Wash.	Lewis	Moses Yoder
Thurman	Colo.	Arapohoe	Joseph Schrock
Grantsville	Md.	Garrett	Emanuel Hershberger
Lowville	N. Y.	Lewis	John K. Schwartzentruber
Flanigan	Ill.	Livingston	Daniel Orendorf
Auroar	Ore.	Marion	J. C. Hostetler
Weatherford	Okla.		A. B. Miller
Berne	Ind.	Adams	Jacob J. Schwartz
Smithville	Ohio	Wayne	T. L. Miller
Shipshewana	Ind.	Lagrange	E. M. Hochstetler
White Cloud	Mich.	Newaygo	S. S. Miller
Timberlake	Okla.	Woods	Tobias Hershberger

Menno	S. D.	Hutchinson	Joseph U. Jantzi
Topeka	Ind.	Lagrange	Jacob T. Miller
Jet	Okla.	Woods	J. C. Bontrager
Monitor	Kans.	McPherson	C. Summy
Elmdale	Mich.	Ionia	Mrs. Emanuel Kime
Yoder	Kans.	Reno	D. M. Yoder
Vandalia	Ill.	Fayette	J. D. Yoder
Maxwell	Iowa	Story	John H. Hochstetler
Shickley	Neb.	Filmore	P. P. Hershberger
Fairbanks	Tex.	Harris	L. B. Rohrer
Loogootee	Ind.	Martin	John A. Miller
Centralia	Mo.	Boone	J. D. Guengerich
Worthington	Minn.	Nobles	J. J. Yoder
McEwen	Tenn.	Humphreys	J. F. Keim
Geistown	Pa.	Cambria	Moses B. Miller
Little River	Kans.		J. D. Kauffman
Peach Orchard	Ark.	Clay	John Schmucker
Kenmare	N. D.	Ward	D. M. Troyer
Gibson	Miss.	Monroe	J. C. Miller
Iowa	Louisiana		C. C. Shrock
Stuttgart	Ark.	Arkansas	P. C. Stahly
Cleona	Ind.	Brown	David E. Kauffman
Kokomo	Ind.	Howard	G. W. North
Canton	Ohio	Stark	Adam Dietz
Garden City	Mo.	Cass	N. Shepp

August 29, 1901

West Liberty	Ohio	Logan	M. S. Yoder
Ligonier	Ind.	Nobles	J. Kurtz
Middlefield	Ohio	Geauga	A. A. Coblentz
Dalton	Ohio	Wayne	L. J. Buckwalter
Manson	Iowa	Calhoun	Barbara Zehr
Millersburg	Ohio	Holmes	J. H. Stutzman
Tiskilwa	Ill.	Bureau	Frank I. Smucker
Midland	Va.	Faquier	L. J. Swartzentruber
Archbold	Ohio	Fulton	A. A. Yoder
East Lewistown	Ohio	Mahoning	S. P. Yoder
Hubbard	Ore.	Marion	Levi Erb
Kalona	Iowa	Washington	Jos. S. Yoder
Hopedale	Ill.	Tazewell	J. C. Springer
Wayland	Iowa	Henry	Luvina Gerig
West Jefferson	Ohio	Madison	J. J. Miller
New Wilmington	Pa.	Lawrence	John W. Cox
Lagrange	Colo.	Laramie	Alvin Yoder
Woolstock	Iowa	Wright	J. C. Gingerich
Fairview	Mich.	Oscoda	S. W. Weaver
Waupecong	Ind.	Miami	Noah W. King
Chappell	Neb.	Deuel	J. J. Roth
Mantua	Ohio	Geauga	M. D. Miller
Charm	Ohio	Holmes	J. J. Yoder
Maximo	Ohio	Stark	Jos. Knopf
Nappanee	Ind.		Y. I. Yoder
Needy	Ore.	Clackawas	Joseph S. Yoder
Gortner	Md.	Garrett	Daniel Schlabach
Rolf	Iowa	Pocahontas	Daniel Schantz
Aurora	Neb.	Hamilton	J. S. Stutzman
Gordonville	Pa.	Lancaster	John H. Kauffman

Historical Significance of   26
THE BUDGET

Far too few people comprehend the importance of THE BUDGET. Many look upon it primarily as a paper dealing with insignificant topics such as weather, visiting, etc. There were many scribes and readers, however, who perceived the importance of THE BUDGET to be far beyond the news printed on its pages. They recognized that THE BUDGET was creating an invisible bond among the family of readers in spite of their great diversity.

It is probably safe to say that the transfer of persons to groups other than Amish or Mennonite would have been greater without a newspaper such as THE BUDGET. This is not documented, but it is the impression of the author of this book after scanning most of the issues during the one-hundred year period of its publication.

Some scribes speak out: I hear some folks have queer ideas about the Budget. They would not subscribe for it, but still they are anxious to read it. For my part, if I would not like it I would not spend much time in reading it. I never look it over but what I could find some interesting letters or items about relatives and friends, and what is not interesting to me is to somebody else. I would rather read the Budget than worldly papers.
     Aug. 22, 1901   Amish, Iowa   Mrs. N. D. Yoder

May the Budget live long and grow in the esteem of its patrons. May it find its way into many more isolated homes like mine, where I am a stranger in a strange land, among a strange people. You do not know how it cheers one to get news and see familiar names to one who has been away from home for forty years. It is impossible for you to know how much comfort it gives us who away from the Brotherhood and kin-folks when we get the little paper, and how we appreciate the correspondence. I sometimes get very lonesome here by myself; but then again the thought comes that it will be but a short time and we shall go home no more to roam, but be at home forever with God and those who are worthy to be there. Let me exhort you who knew me personally when I was a young man, a boy, to meet me there, with God is my prayer.

Dec. 19, 1901 Toddspoint, Ill. E. D. Mast

The Budget is very handy; through its columns one can get news from almost every settlement of Amish people; only some localities must be very scarcely supplied with news, or nobody sends them in to the Budget.

July 9, 1903 Wayland, Iowa S. E. Roth

A few words for the Budget. Perhaps many of its readers can not fully appreciate the value of such a paper, as it is a visitor nearly over the whole United States, and while friends oft times live hundreds and even thousands of miles apart, can occasionally hear from them and the happenings amongst them, and especially in former old communities; therefore we make a plea that we open our hearts towards each other, and think of our loved ones, and keep the columns of the Budget filled with such news that may be of interest to the readers.

April 5, 1916 Tuleta, Texas C. C. Schrock

I wrote my first letter to the Budget in May 1900, nearly 40 years ago. Was a regular correspondent with the exception of a few years till in 1936 when I just failed in writing as I had lost my health, lost courage and was so discouraged I could not do much. But must say, the Bible and the Budget are my pastime in lonely hours. I can read the Budget every week. Always news and nearly every letter in the Budget I can read of some I know and had lost track of them. You find your old friends through the Budget.

Jan. 11, 1940 Middlefield, Ohio Mrs. Lizzie E. Frey

I agree with the different correspondents who say, "Read what interests you and be satisfied," for what doesn't interest you may be an item of great interest to someone else. I think there must be very few Amish people in the United States that are not known to quite a few others in other states who are glad to see their names in the Budget.

Aug. 26, 1948 Dover, Dela. Mrs. Alfred D. Troyer

The reason I like the Budget is because I have relatives around Dover, Del., and west across the Rockies, in California and Oregon. And as I was born in LaGrange Co., Indiana, I usually look for the Middlebury and Topeka items. Also for the Midland, Mich. news, which my niece writes. I am now three score and 12 and am at the sunset of my time.

Feb. 23, 1950   Grabill, Ind.   Menno D. Miller

To Sarah Schwartz of Indiana: I agree with you. There are different states and many parents and younger people anxiously look through the Budget for news of a loved one, or nieces, nephews and cousins they do not hear from in any other way. Somebody, somewhere is interested in whether Joes were at Johns.

Feb. 9, 1961   Mechanicsville, Md.   Mary Byler

Editor's note: I hope that everyone who writes for the Budget will read and heed the following portion of David Wagler's letter. It expresses my thoughts on the matter much better than I have been able to do it.

Oct. 26, 1961

The Budget is surely an unusual paper which can be a help to our communities in general. It seems to me that not only has the size improved but also the quality of the material. A quarter of a century ago, when I contributed my first letter, the Budget was considered by many as merely social gossip, of who had been where, and of not too much actual value. While it still contains many strictly local items, there is a much larger percentage of general interest. This combination takes it into the homes of every class and group of Amish and related peoples.

Oct. 26, 1961   Aylmer, Ont.   David Wagler

All of us, "the Budget family" ....

Jan. 18, 1962   Hephzibah, Ga.   Thelma Yoder

Gradually it [The Budget] became the unofficial publication for the various Amish and Mennonite groups and since then it just grew ... and grew!

May 2, 1963   Editor's Corner

[The Budget served as an avenue to bring together Ira Hostetler and his daughter, Mrs. Irene Miller, of Houston, Tex. who had lost track of each other forty-two years earlier. He was in Berea, Ohio.]

Feb. 2, 1956   News item

I wonder if we really appreciate what the Budget means to

us, as it is probably circulated in every Amish and Mennonite community in the U.S. and Canada, with the many interesting letters from the various correspondents.

Jan. 20, 1938   Burton, Ohio   Levi Miller

The Budget is a unique paper. There is perhaps no other paper quite like it. Many of us are dependent upon it for news of our people throughout the greater part of the United States.

Sept. 9, 1948   Milverton, Ont.   Sarah Ebersol

Through it we get both rejoicing and sorrowful news so that we can rejoice with them that do rejoice, and sympathize with the sorrowful and afflicted. Through it we are being reminded of the uncertainty of humanity, as almost every issue informs us of the pasing away of a friend or former acquaintance. To the bereaved, sorrowful and afflicted I extend my sympathy. To the rejoicing will say, above all let us rejoice in the Lord, and not in worldly pleasures and amusements. Through the Budget we every now and then get the opportunity of helping to cheer up some poor or afflicted person by taking a part in the showers that are announced for such.

Apr. 14, 1938   Springs, Pa.   Eli N. Beachy

Do we readers of the Budget really realize and appreciate the good the Budget is doing for us. Through it Mrs. Andy D. Kurtz of Alburquerque, N. Mexico recognized Leander Keim's quack, the minute he started his deceiving story. Andy is my wife's brother. Was sorry to hear that the same party talked Bishop Sam Bender of Okla. out of $30. But the Almighty God knows what spirit lead both him and Leander Keim of Kansas to give the money, and no doubt will reward them both for an act of kindness.

Mar. 11, 1937   Springs, Pa.   Eli N. Beachy

The grandparent house on the left gives evidence of the intergenerational life on this family farm in Holmes County, Ohio.

Intergenerational Viewpoints 27

The church community and the family are both fundamental to Amish and Amish Mennonite society. Keeping the relationships sound between the generations is essential for the continued strength of the community. In view of this it is in order to ponder what some scribes have said about children, young people, adults and the elderly.

Child rearing: We have been in many homes during the last few years, often staying overnight. We have been in homes where it could easily be seen that family devotions were a part of their lives, and that they were firm believers, "That man liveth not by bread alone, but by every word that proceedeth out of the mouth of God." We have been in other homes where it appeared that family devotions were something new to the children, but must be gone through with, "Because the preacher was here." And then again we have been in homes where not a word of Scripture was read or or any prayer spoken, and the Lord's name was not even mentioned.

    Aug. 20, 1953   Lynnhaven, Va.   Jacob J. Hershberger

It seems to me one of the most common mis-uses is the attempt to keep children quiet by giving them something to eat. If they are too young to understand what is being said, a small toy or pocket sized picture book helps to keep them occupied. Eating when not hungry makes children irritable and thirsty and hard to handle. Indeed it is a poor substitute for discipline. Fortunate the child who is taught to respect his parents and others by keeping quiet at public gatherings.

    Jan. 11, 1962   Aylmer, Ont.   David Wagler

Last night I heard a young mother back here debate something with her boy that he wanted (and got it too). After all was said and done I thought it sounded like there was more said than done. About like putting forth efforts to make

water run down hill.
July 4, 1963   Buck Hill Falls, Pa.   David W. Miller

[Use of the term "kids" for children.] Even the tenor of scriptures should teach us as very unwise and unnatural for parents to call children "kids".
Dec. 20, 1951   Atmore, Ala.   Levi Bontrager

Comments on young people: I wish some of our gifted writers could do some writing to help clear this subject, as I can't help but feel that the wrong generation gets the blame.
July 2, 1953   Narvon, Pa.   No name

I do have just a bit of fear for President Kennedy, especially as I consider the youthfulness of his chosen cabinet members. Not only is he the youngest president ever, but he has surrounded himself with youthful advisors. [He referred to King Rehoboam of ancient Israel and his appointment of youthful advisors.]
Jan. 26, 1961   Lynnhaven, Va.   Jacob J. Hershberger

A number of years ago a Catholic Chaplain noted that people don't believe what their grandfathers believed and have no reason to hope that their grandsons will believe what you do. No community or church can accept that proposition unless it is reconciled to passing away. (Now we have seen this come to pass in the Amish churches too.]
July 9, 1980   Bloomfield, Iowa   David Yutzy

I agree with the words by N. S. Beachy in the Budget of Sept. 10, regarding the enormous amount of energy wasted by the young folks of the Amish denomination, but not only the young folks but by many older folks as well. I think in this regard we may be compared with the prodigal son, who received from his father his portion of substance; then he went and spent it in riotous living, living according to the lust of the flesh as I understand it.
Sept. 24, 1908   Gordonville, Pa.   John H. Kauffman

I wish to say a few words to our young people, as a commandment rests upon you, to obey father and mother. Perhaps many of you break this commandment and take your own way. Many a night you are gone and your dear parents are passing a restless night, wondering where their dear children are. Then again many are heedless to the warnings and pleadings of the ministers. Remember what heavy responsibility the minister has upon himself, and that it is not him alone that is speaking, but the spirit of God

203

through him. We should all stand by the ministers to help build up the church to the honor and glory of God. The time will come in your older days when you will remember your disobedience with sorrow and tears.

Sept. 12, 1907   Arthur, Ill.   Lewis D. Yutzy

There have been quite a number of young folks from other places here to husk corn and some have conducted themselves in such a way that there is a good bit of complaint, which is a bad example to the world.

Dec. 9, 1910   Arthur, Ill.   Mr. and Mrs. Emanuel Hershberger

I am sure that many of our Old Order Amish people feel that we are *the* salt of the earth. [Under the title "Who Will Be Responsible for Sins of Our Young People?" The scribe asks the question, "If we are, then act like it."]

Sept. 18, 1952   Article without an address or name

Conditions among the youths may vary greatly, and we have, as I see it, some very respectful and conscientious young people, also some who are indifferent, impure, and may rightly be classed, "Billys". A few of these wild young people may represent a whole community in a very bad way, when in reality, many are innocent.

Sept. 2, 1954   From a letter sent to Jacob J. Hershberger
and quoted in Lynnhaven Gleanings.

Hochstetler book: I suppose many of the Budget readers in the Hochstetler generation have received letters from Rev. Harvey Hostetler of Council Bluffs, Iowa. Give him all the information about your family that you can and help him through so that he will get it completed sooner. He will get your family anyhow and when he is not certain of a thing you will get a black mark and he will term you as a "no answer" in the history.

Mar. 21, 1907   Meyersdale, Pa.   S. Summy

Homes: It afflicts our hearts at times, to hear how very light minded people are in this respect. Very much could be said on this subject, but I will simply refer you to the book, entitled "Glimpses of Amish and Mennonite Homes," which is advertised in the Budget. We are all aware that quite a few people are strictly opposed to that book, but Paul says, "Prove all things. Abstain from all appearance of evil." (I Thess. 5:20, 22)

Mar. 22, 1910   Cor.   No location given.

Extended family: Adam Borntrager, Medford, Wisc. died at age

96. He had 11 children; 115 greatgrandchildren; 529 great-greatgrandchildren; and 20 greatgreatgreatgrandchildren. A total of 675 descendants. David Coblentz Jr. Jackson Center, Pa. had 622 descendants. Mrs. Joni Miller (Lizzie) Wayne County, Ohio, died at age 100. She had 7 children, 54 grandchildren; 543 greatgrandchildren for a total of 604 descendants.
> Nov. 18, 1987   p. 2

John Eli Miller of Middlefield, Ohio died at age 95 years. Had 63 grandchildren, 61 of which were living when he died. He had 338 greatgrandchildren at time of death.
> Dec. 21, 1961   News item

Divorce: [Two cases of divorces were discovered. One was reported in the July 24, 1902 issue by the THREE SISTERS of East Lewistown, Ohio. The second reported in the April 25, 1907 issue by BUSY BEE of Mylo, N.D.]

Singles: Quite a number of our people attended the Old Maid's Club at Dundee on Saturday evening, they had a crowded house.
> Feb. 18, 1914   Barrs Mills, Ohio   A Reader

On Sunday the widows had a carry in dinner at Griner, around 70 were present.
> Sept. 22, 1976   Millersburg, Ind.   Mrs. Levi Burkholder

Elderly: At last we are mostly settled in the daudy end, after a lot of work and "shoofing" around. Son Amos and wife Miriam occupy the farm end, thus relieving us of farm duties after 39 years.
> April 1, 1987   New Holland, Pa.   Mrs. Amos Huyard

I was 9 years old when Lincoln was elected the first time. It was in 1860 and in 1861 the Civil War began. I have lived through several other wars but none with nearly as much controversy as the Civil War.
> Sept. 9, 1943   Burton, Ohio   D. D. Miller

H.C.H. and wife will have public sale next Tuesday, to sell what little they have yet and while there is no place to be had for them, and no one to be had to take care of them, they agreed to go to the poor house.
> April 24, 1902   Davidsville, Pa.   Levi J. Kauffman

Say if you want to see a happy pair of birds in an old nest look at D. D. Yoder and wife, there they are all by themselves just as they started out years ago. Their nest full has all flown to homes their own. . . . D.D.'s have a fine grandpa house built to the other house for several years.

April 29, 1914   Inman, Kans.   Viola Yoder Cooprider

Old grandpa King is eighty years old and took a contract for clearing;   also does some farming. He said he don't want to work too hard now, so he is able to do some work when he gets old.

Mar. 25, 1914   Tuleta, Tex.   A. C. Miller

Would also like to go and see him, but visiting does not seem to go very well since I am left alone. The hours are long, months very long, years hardly to be expressed. Abraham parted his life to the great beyond in 1913. I and my granddaughter are living in Honeyville.

Dec. 8, 1915   Topeka, Ind.   Mrs. Fanny Troyer

I am still able to farm 160 acres of land myself, but I am not doing it to gain more wealth, but to save a little for old age, that is if I ever get old. I am only 67 years old now and did like a good many did in 1918 when times were good, took a little too big a bite so we will have to stand the consequences as best we can. We had dry weather since 1918 and not much crops, but we have plenty of rain this spring so far so we expect to get a good crop.

June 18, 1925   Creston, Mont.   J. J. Kauffman

We have torn the old porch off our house and are about ready to start putting the new one back on. I am getting a little tired of work, so today I intend to take mommy out to son Menno's and go on to the lake for the day.

June 25, 1980   Heuvelton, N.Y.   Rudy S. Yoder

Joni Yoders and Pre. Benedict Yoders are both making preparations to build "Grandpa" houses.

April 11, 1946   Thomas, Okla.   Joe Bontrager

The Enos Yoders had their 62nd anniversary the 16th, so Enos has finally decided to retire from doing carpenter work. Susie will be 85 Thurs. and Enos in February.

Jan. 4, 1989   Dover, Dela.   Mrs. Alfred Troyer

Population profile: [An enlightening profile of the Amish churches of the Kalona, Iowa community was provided by a scribe identified only as M.E.G.]

        6 Amish churches
        6 bishops, 13 ministers, 1 deacon
        13 individuals   80 yr. and older   163 family heads

38 individuals	70 - 79 yr.	17 widows
39 individuals	60 - 69 yr.	4 widowers
62 individuals	50 - 59 yr.	26 different family
49 individuals	40 - 49 yr.	names
65 individuals	30 - 39 yr.	55 Millers
121 individuals	20 - 29 yr.	10 couples who have
133 individuals	1 - 19 yr.	been married 50
179 individuals	0 - 9 yr.	or more years.
699 individuals total		

For year 1963: 3 marriages; 5 deaths; and 17 births.

Jan. 30, 1964

An intergenerational farmstead in Lancaster County, Pennsylvania.

Language and Vocabulary   28

The Amish and Amish Mennonites found themselves in a somewhat awkward position regarding language.   All Old Order Amish used German in church services and Pennsylvania Deitsch in conversation among themselves.   But in public it was necessary to use English, which meant that they were a bilingual people. Many of the Amish Mennonites made the transition from German to English in public services during the 1890's and the early 1900's. The use of Pennsylvania German in conversation and English for writing purposes led to some transfer of the German and Pennsylvania German into the written English. Some of the results have been the source of good humor and amusement. It must be said in their defense, however, that many of the scribes were excellent writers.

Attempts were made to teach the German to the next generation.   That German schools were conducted for this purpose can be detected from some of the excerpts.

Ascription of human characteristics to animals: A coyote has started the sinning business and is getting pretty bold. I saw him out here at the end of our walk that goes to the mail box last night. Some of these nights we'll be prepared to stop the foolishness.
> Sept. 29, 1976   Thomas, Okla.   David Miller

"Big words": Strong objection was raised by scribes when they perceived that some public speaker used "big words".   Their stress on simplicity clearly showed in their expressions.   The following excerpt was in response to listening to a speech at a public school meeting.

> ... I wish that speaker would have run his speech through a cream separator and take out the big words and maybe find a few facts.
> Dec. 1, 1976   Greenwich, Mich.   Mose Shetler

Bilingualism: Because of bilingualism there was pressure from the scribes and readers to have some German letters in THE BUDGET. Others were arguing that there should be a separate sheet or a supplement for the German. The following excerpts will be sufficient to show part of the struggle; a struggle with the Editor in the middle.

There have been many opinions and ideas about printing a space in German. It is disgusting to read that some of our "Dutch" are too "torry" to read their mother's language in print, and say they can't read it. I think the only way to make it interesting is to have a column in German. Let us follow the golden rule and not be selfish; not be ashamed with our good deeds.

Nov. 30, 1899 Belleville, PA L. S. Yoder

I noticed that some of the readers are not in favor for German, but some people said to me they don't want the Budget, because it is English. I think those that don't want German are selfish, and don't care for others. But I agree that it might be better to have an extra sheet by itself printed in German.

Oct. 26, 1899 Baden, Ontario Jacob Iutzi

I would say that I would not be in favor to have any German in the Budget, for the reason that a good many of the reader's can't read German, and they would give up the paper if part of it would be German; but if enough German people want the paper, you could print a German paper. I, for my part, can read German, as well as English, but I can't write it.

Oct. 26, 1899 Smithville, O T. L. Miller

Much has been said in regard of havng this paper printed in German. For my part I would say, no! This is a very cheap, interesting little paper the way it is and will be pleased to pay for the privilege to pay only 50 cents annually; but besides this paper, I would enjoy a German paper - - not to be printed with the same items as the Budget, altogether, as that would require very much in translating. But would enjoy more spiritual or religious writing, which I believe would be of more benefit than some arguing subjects.

Jan. 4, 1900 Middleburg, IN Joseph N. Bontrager

About printing part of the Budget in German, I say, we have a good paper, and why not let good-enough alone.

Dec. 7, 1899 Amish, IA J. F. Gingerich

In conclusion, I will yet call attention to an article in the Budget . . . by A.W.D., in which the writer portrayed in plain language the inconsistency of trying to do away with the German language by many; and asks the question, "Shall the German language be banished to the rear, into forgetfulness, by those who owe almost all that they are and have to their sturdy German speaking ancestors, and that, too, which some of the latter are still living in their midst?" I fully agree with the writer and endorse and sanction the sentiments therein expressed. I have observed very similar instances. I have also observed that it is not the spirit of meekness and humility that leads thereto, but haughtiness.

Aug. 31, 1905   Wellman, IA   S. D. Guengerich

Bungled modifiers: Some of the interesting and humorous outcomes were the result of misplaced modifiers. The literal meaning in the first excerpt is that he took the coffin to a corpse; the second that the showers were in THE BUDGET; and the final one indicates that there are Saturdays with guns.

Eli J. Miller, the undertaker, took a coffin to widow Stanton, on Thursday, who was to be buried on Friday....

Dec. 25, 1902   Elklick, PA   Martha L. Kinsinger

We appreciated everything we received in the showers that were in the Budget for me.

Dec. 13, 1962   Middlefield, OH   Mrs. Ervin A. Byler

Men and boys are having fox drives on Saturdays with guns.

Jan. 24, 1963   Montgomery, IN   Jerome Raber

Derivations and adaptations: Some words which have become a part of the Amish and Amish Mennonite vocabulary are derivations from the Pennsylvania German while others are English words but with shades of meaning which only the "inside" people understand. The following are some of the words which fall into this category, with the word in question *underlined*. At least one is an example of misuse.

A *crowd* of young people were visitors at J. B. Mullet's....

Aug. 16, 1906   London, OH   Abner W. Miller

As we do not all like the same reading, the Editor sometimes has a rather *ticklish* job....

Feb. 9, 1961   Centreville, MI   John M. Bontrager

Corn and tobacco is growing *wonderfully*.

July 24, 1952   Ronks, PA   Katie G. Stoltzfus

210

Labor Day is over and we are enjoying *fallish* weather....
Sept. 14, 1977   Uniontown, Ohio   Enos Miller

The sugar season has not been very *flush* yet by the way some of the farmers informed us.
Mar. 24, 1904   Topeka, Ind.   W.W.H. and A.E.Y.

Quite a few *strangers* are here visiting, from different places.
Mar. 3, 1904   Burton, Ohio   Miss Sarah M. Hershberger

Some people have *commenced* to cut tobacco while others have not *commence* yet.
Aug. 30, 1906   Groffs Store, Pa.   David B. Schrock

[Local news item describing how a suspect was *napped* by a policeman, rather than being nabbed.]
Sept. 12, 1901   Sugarcreek, Ohio

Valentine Schrock, of Idaho, is in the poultry business. He is a *hustler*.
Apr. 4, 1901   Whiteson, Ore.   D. J. Gingerich

Our Sunday School has *collapsed* for the present, on account of whooping cough.
June 28, 1900   Cora, Okla.   B. B. Miller

The Michigan Jack was here a week ago talking up North Dakota, some seem to *nipple* at the bait.
April 14, 1896   Welshfield, Ohio   JOKER

The name of the railroad station in Alton will be *"Infernal"*.
Nov. 23, 1899   Lowell, Mich.   Anna Wingeier

Hutchinson will have open saloons after May 1st, then we will have some *tangle footed* fellows on the streets.
Apr. 30, 1903   Hutchinson, Kans.   Jayhawker

The president of the bachelor's club in Wooster "has forsaken the club and joined the army *of benedicts.*"
Mar. 12, 1903   Wooster, Ohio   T. L. Miller

John Yutzy has *built up* a field on his farm with lime and fertilizer and raised on it a nice stand of alfalfa.
July 19, 1962   Vilonia, Ark.   Aden G. Yutzy

There was a "building bee" at Howard Kropfs on Wednesday.
Aug. 22, 1963   Fairfax, SC   Mrs. Alvin Kropf

A general house-cleaning *"frolic"* will be held....
Nov. 15, 1900   Goshen, IN   Goshen Scribe

There was a *frolic* for the raising of a straw shed....
June 7, 1923   Shipshewana, IN   Mrs. Harvey Glick

211

Today E. D. Smuckers had a *frolic* to cut wood and there was a lot to cut.
Nov. 3, 1915   Maryville, IN   J. E. Hershberger

Mose P. Miller expects to have a *frolic* to put up hay....
July 2, 1953   Apple Creek, OH   D. N. Petersheim

Humor: Several excerpts are added to show the choice of words and the style of writing. Those who write about Mennonite milk cans and Amish buggies probably mean milk cans and buggies owned by Mennonites and/or Amish. Suggesting that one can have an enjoyable time with an aching tooth must be an attempt at humor. The last two of the quotations seem to assume that everyone understands the details.

This morning before daybreak, I saw a truck go by on the highway, loaded with Mennonite milk cans. The truck was headed for the city of Cuauhtemoc.
Jan. 7, 1987   Cuauhtemoc, Mexico   P. & S. Hoover

Now and then a farmer has completed his haying.
Aug. 21, 1902   Croghan, NY   Joe J. Zehr

Abner J. Miller sticks to C. C. Schrock like a hot cake.
May 22, 1902   Iowa, La.   Levi D. Miller

Our fat, jolly old friend Levi Sommers moved to the village yesterday.
June 12, 1890   Sugarcreek, Ohio   Local news

Mrs. D. H. Miller had an enjoyable time with one of her teeth last Saturday night; it kept her awake until 1 oclock Sunday morning.
July 26, 1900   Minier, Ill.   Mrs. Edwin Miller

I presume you have all heard about the accident that happened to my husband about nine days ago.
July 31, 1902   Carlock, Ill.   Mrs. N. F. Holderly

Dodge City had a fire on Saturday night.
Apr. 3, 1912   Dodge City, Kans.   Lizzie Yoder & Lena Nisly

Things that may seem funny to a joker may be far from rumorous to persons involved in a untrue story.
July 22, 1943   Sugarcreek, Ohio   Editor's Corner

Identification: The large families and the increasing size of the Amish population coupled with the tendency to limit first names to a rather restricted list often called for methods to distinguish people with the same first names. One method resorted to was the use of "young" and "old". These terms were not used in a derogatory manner. Only one example is given.

> Old blind Lizzie Miller is about holding her own by last reports.
>
> Jan. 28, 1987   Cashton, Wisc.   Joe C. Borntreger

Language schools: The Stoll dutch institute opened on the 1st of this month. The Wagler dutch institute closed on the last of January.

Feb. 28, 1895   Trainer, Ind.   A Reader

> Jacob Schrock reports the attendance of 28 scholars in his German school, east of town.
>
> Jan. 9, 1902   Arthur, Ill.   TEDDY

> German school closed Friday where about 50 school children had been enrolled.
>
> July 25, 1963   Garnett, Kans.   Susie Beachy

Pennsylvania German adaptations: The following are some examples of words or phrases used in the letters. Some are clearly Pennsylvania German adaptations and others are forms of the English words rather widely used.

> On Saturday Jake E. Stoltzfus had an "infair" for Pre. Abe Beilers and family.
>
> Feb. 26, 1953   Ronks, Pa.   Barbara L. King

> Sat. our house was filled with guests at the "infair" or reception held for the Levi Zook and our family....
>
> Mar. 4, 1987   New Holland, Pa.   Mrs. Amos Huyard

> It seemed a little nippy yesterday on our 7 mile drive to church ... with reports from 14 to 40 below zero.
>
> Mar. 4, 1987   Rensselaer Falls, NY   E. Swartzentrubers

> The fremte at church Sunday were....
>
> Mar. 18, 1987   Wautoma, Wis.   Mrs. Chris Herschberger

> Harvey's moved into the "doddy haus" sometime ago.
>
> Feb. 20, 1964   Richland Co., Ohio   Warren L. Fusner

> But a Yankee man told them to get in his truck and he brought them home.
>
> Feb. 6, 1964   Parkman, Ohio   Noah J. Detweiler

> Incidentally, (English) ladies do not necessarily come from England, but is a word used by the Amish to describe anyone that is not Amish or Mennonite.
>
> Jan. 12, 1961   Stillwater, Pa.   John R. Renno

> The "youngie" of Nappanee and Topeka were at Jake E.

Schwartz's on New Year's day.
Jan. 9, 1964   Berne, Ind.   No name

We are having the first peas for dinner today, and, unexpectedly, a pheasant hen. Son Junior accidentally mowed off both hind legs while mowing hay this forenoon, so he quick "kepped" it. For you who don't know what "kepped" means it is probably about as confusing as the lady who wrote to mom praising her cookbook, "but just what the ... is a snitzed apple?"!! Yes, it is an Amish cookbook, so a bit of Dutch is bound to be found in it too.

July 2, 1980   Hazelton, Ia.   Mrs. Felty Yoder

Phrases and idioms: In addition to single words, some phrases and idioms stand out. Some were undoubtedly local and others universal to the Amish and Amish Mennonite community. Several examples will be given, with a few needing explanatory comment.

It *ripened up the butchering* for many. [Reference to 10 degree below zero temperature]
Dec. 20, 1962   Charlotte Hall, Md.   John F. Esh

... while a group of men were *making wood* ... timber ....
Dec. 21, 1961   Medford, Wisc.   E.B.

The *death angel claimed* two lives of the community ....
Oct. 24, 1963   Kokomo, Ind.   (No name)

[Following a description of the accident in which Daniel Eash was pulled into the corn shredder and his body mangled and injured fatally, the following sentence appeared.] This was not a corn husker, but a shredder, made out of an old threshing machine for the purpose. It was a *sad, shuddering and wonderful* accident. He was single, and about 28 years old.
Dec. 13, 1906   Millersburg, Ind.   David Yoder

[A scribe writes about *a miraculous accident*, meaning by this that no one was hurt - - which was the miracle.]
May 24, 1951   Fredericksburg, Ohio   Mose P. Miller

[The most common phrase used to describe accidents was *a very sad accident.*]

Weddings will soon be *on the go.* ...
Oct. 29, 1953   Elverson, Pa.   B. F. Stoltzfus

The weddings have *"run out"* for the season.
Jan. 2, 1980   Gap, Pa.   John F. Glick

Weddings are trump this week and next.
Jan. 21, 1897   Belleville, Pa.   Goose Quill

On Saturday a group of us Amish and English fellows got together and shocked up Jess S. Swartz's corn.
Oct. 27, 1955   Mifflintown, Pa.   (No name)

A good way to get rid of things you don't need. Mrs. Gary Schrock and Miss Sharon Schrock had a *buggy shed or a garage* sale the first of this week.
Oct. 6, 1976   Shipshewana, Ind.   A.M.Y.

We had an *evergreen Sunday School.* Good attendance....
Mar. 10, 1904   Cherry Box, Mo.   Ida Bissey & Loma Detw.

Margaret Weaver is still *hanging on,* going to the doctor....
Mar. 11, 1987   Narvon, Pa.   Amanda B. Shirk

Mom is somewhat *more agitated* the last several days.
Apr. 8, 1987   Garnett, Kans.   Susie Beachy

Sugaring is near at hand and many are making preparations to move *into their bushes.*
Mar. 12, 1903   Kirschnerville, N.Y.   J. Yousey

It is reported that 10 people were killed over the past week in Indiana. *Such a lot are getting killed.*
Oct. 16, 1958   Topeka, Ind.   Ida

Play with words: Some scribes liked to play with words, either in games or in cleverness of expression. The following was included in a letter, with the explanation near the end. The scribe seemed to be certain that the explanation was needed.

John, where James had had "had had", had had "had"; "had had" had had the publisher's approval.
Dec. 10, 1959   Aylmer, Ont.   David Wagler

Explanation: John and James wrote the same story and sent it to the publisher. At one particular place John had written the word "had" but James had used "had had" instead. Now the publisher had already approved "had had" for that place.

Sarcasm: The following excerpt is a response to a scribe bragging about a threshing machine outfitted with some new attachments. One was a straw carrier [before the day of blowers] and the other was a "packer" to compress the straw in the mow or stack, reducing the need for humans or horses to trample it. The reader will sense from the writing that the scribe was strongly opposed to the new technology.

The above straw carrier may be called the armstrong arrangement. Adam had part of it in the garden of Eden; likely used it to receive the forbidden fruit; and the packers are what Eve was to use on the serpent's head.
Aug. 31, 1899   Grantsville, Md.   Emanuel Hershberger

The Bible of Jacob Hertzler (1703-86), who may have been the first Amish bishop in America. It is now located in the Mennonite Heritage Center in Belleville, Pennsylvania.

That the Bible is the most important book for the Christian, and that it is fully God's authoritative Word is taken for granted by the Amish and Amish Mennonites. The certainty of and depth of this conviction was of such degree that it was not considered necessary to restate the position over and over in writing. Even ministers did not spend much time trying to "prove" that the Bible is the Word of God, it was taken for granted that it is, and, as such, reveals God's will for his followers today, who are duty bound to abide by its precepts.

The Amish consider the Bible the primary source from which to get guidance and direction for solution of current matters. In addition to the Bible, there have been several occasional publications. The past two decades, however, have witnessed much more activity in publication among the Amish. The Amish have never had a single publication as their official periodical or newspaper. Even the *Herold der Wahrheit*, first published in 1912 and still in circulation, has been read by only a minority of the Amish. Religious publications have apparently played a minor role in Amish life in the past century. The Bible, the bishop, and tradition have ranked higher in order of importance.

The reading fare generally was THE BUDGET and one or more farm magazines. What religious papers found their way into their homes depended largely on the interests of each individual family.

Bible study: ... the book of Revelations is very deep and hard to understand and I believe that some people have already spent too much time in Revelations. ... Don't misunderstand me that we should not read the book Rev. or another great Book in the Bible, but enough is enough.
     July 9, 1942   Gap, Pa.   John F. Glick

Continued stories: To give my views regarding the running of continued stories in the Budget, I would briefly say no.

Without doubt it would interest the young people, but that is not the kind of feed the dear young souls need to prepare them for that future life, or eternity. We have plenty of stories to be read, and are available to anyone, such as the story of the Bible, Pilgrim's Progress and many others that are essential for the years that are not far off, when again our young men may be called for the army. The conditions and circumstances in this nation are serious, whether you know it or not, so let us prepare for it.

June 9, 1938   Fairbanks, Iowa   Joe Bontrager, Sr.

[The Editor had raised the possibility of continued stories. By that he apparently meant up-to-date fiction, which was not to be used to replace letters from the scribes, but perhaps take the place of some other items in the paper. He received a number of responses, seven of which were in favor and twelve opposed. The Editor quoted the following excerpt from a letter sent him: "We all like the Budget as a newsgiver from Amish and Mennonite communities all over the U.S. and we don't want a story magazine made out of it."]

June 9, 1938   Editor's Corner

I must give the editor credit for not printing the love stories in our weekly paper. I think there are too many love stories in print already. Why not have the Bible for a story book which we can read as a true story.

June 16, 1938   Cochranton, Pa.   Mrs. E. E. Schrock

[The Editor reported an additional flurry of comments, with the overwhelming majority strongly disapproving of the proposition for continued stories.]

June 16, 1938   Editor's Corner

I agree with Joe Bontrager of Fairbanks, Iowa. There are plenty of good books available for our young people to read. I think most of the continued stories in newspapers and magazines are fiction, and Webster's dictionary defines fiction as something opposed to what is real. I feel that the Budget is a good clean, newspaper with clean, sane advertising with a few exceptions, such as a movie and night club advertisements as I believe most of the Budget readers do not want that kind of entertainment. I think the Editor's Corner is quite interesting and not harmful to anyone.

June 16, 1938   Burton, Ohio   Abe J. Yoder

May we suggest the reading of books such as Franklin's

Biography which has a tendency to promote an industrious and frugal life in our youths. [Jonathan Fisher discouraged consideration of reading fiction in magazines and newspapers.]

Aug. 18, 1938   Lancaster, Pa.   Jonathan B. Fisher

"Rosanna" is a true narrative, no fiction (Am myself greatly opposed to fiction.) Its reading helps to promote the frugal common living of our faith, relates incidents occurring in the "valley" years ago. But the Joas Yoder's here, who formerly came from that place, by marriage, are connected with the characters in the book. Joas O. Yoder, Bareville, had as his step-grandmother the Elizabeth who reared Rosanna and brought her to the Amish faith.

July 24, 1941   Lancaster County Briefs   Jonathan B. Fisher

The writing of the narrative of his book, "Rosanna", is not, as I first presumed, entirely non-fiction. It is fiction based on fact and may be accepted as such.

Aug. 7, 1941   Lancaster County Briefs   Jonathan B. Fisher

[A reader included several selections under the topic, *A Know so Salvation.*]

July 3, 1941   Hartville, Ohio   A Reader

Numerology: [D. J. Stutzman of Millersburg, Ohio submitted an article of more than one full column length on the significance of the number seven in the Bible.]

Mar. 19, 1936   Millersburg, Ohio   D. J. Stutzman

Pennsylvania German: . . . one of those columns of nonsense Pennsylvania Dutch articles.

July 25, 1940   Kalona, Iowa   Joe Bontrager

I might write a little about those so-called Pennsylvania Dutch letters. I was very much surprised to see that certain people would exercise themselves in such foolish stuff like that, which has no truth in it. And not that alone but they were so poorly spelled that a person could hardly read them.

Aug. 22, 1940   Belleville, Pa.   M. P. Zook

How many of our readers remember that some time ago the editor of the Budget put it up to vote whether or not he should print stories? The answer was "no," and are they not appearing already? I am not rebuking the editor, he prints what his readers want and so would I in his case. I do not think the fact that they are Pennsylvania Dutch exempts them from condemnation. If the editor does not understand that mixed language, he probably does not know what vulgar, insane words he has been printing. I feel sure he would not print them in English.

Aug. 22, 1940   Nappanee, Ind.   No name

Dear Readers, how far would these out-weigh the senseless Pa. Dutch articles which have appeared a few times, which to the writer's estimation belongs to the low immoral class. . . . [The scribe was referring to "Golden Gems', recommended by Noah D. Mast of Kans. THE BUDGET, August 15.] While one writer offered three cheers for more of Pa. Dutch articles, I give four cheers if they never appear again, while another remarked, we should have some "fun" once in a while.

Sept. 5, 1940   Lynnhaven, Va.   Levi Bontrager

Quite a few readers are making a lot of fuss about items in this weekly newspaper, I just thought it must be quite a problem for the Editor to print all these disagreeable letters. About the Pa. Dutch pieces - - I don't take much interest in them myself, but I don't think its any harm to anybody's soul to read them. I don't think they make more bad feelings than those that write so severely against them. It really hurts me to read of so many people disagreeing with each other. Its no wonder we hear of rumors of war.

Sept. 12, 1940   Sugarcreek, Ohio   A Reader

In the last week's Budget there was a letter in again about those Pa. Dutch pieces. Let's not be ashamed of our mother tongue. I for my part, can't even read them, but as this is only a newspaper, why should I tell the Editor what to print. I look at it this way - - - those that write them are paying just as much for this newspaper as the rest of us and maybe a little more than those that kick. We should be thankful to have a newspaper through which we can hear from our friends and relatives in different states. I don't think those "four cheers" fellows would be in favor of having our plain people preach over the radio. Why then, have it printed in the newspaper.

Oct. 3, 1940   Uniontown, Ohio   A. A. Coblentz

Periodicals, religious: I personally would suggest that any of the readers desiring an additional religious periodical, should subscribe to the Brethren periodical, *Gospel Messenger*,

220

Elgin, Illinois. I am getting six religious periodicals and no daily.

Sept. 18, 1947   Lancaster County Briefs   Jonathan B. Fisher

One man, of high church office, declined to subscribe to Herold der Wahrheit because "of a lack of funds." But he gave the solicitor, Pete Stoll, a tract "Madgebury Letter." [The scribe explains that the tract was supposedly delivered by an angel near a city in France. The tract declares that anyone who believes in and distributes this tract will be guaranteed not to be damaged by lightning, fire or flood.]

Dec. 10, 1959   Aylmer, Ont.   David Wagler

Quotations and sayings: Here is one, though simple, but which if heeded, will greatly better our surroundings:

There is so much good in the worst of us,
And so much bad in the best of us;
That it does not behoove any of us
To say evil about the rest of us.

Another Impressive one:

God said it, Jesus did it,
I believe it, that settles it.

Jan. 4, 1940   Lancaster County Briefs   Jonathan B. Fisher

While I was growing up and attending church services I used to hear the ministers quote a German verse in their sermons and I have often wondered in which song it is to be found. If any of the readers know it I wish they would report it to me. The verse is based on Matthew 25-41 and is well worthy of deep consideration to everyone. The verse is as follows:

In dem ganzen bibil buch,
Kommt mir nichts so schrekclick fahr,
Als die worten von dem spruch,
Ihr verfluchte weicht von mir.

Feb. 16, 1950   Haven, Kans.   Leander Keim

Gewohnheit hat gar grase kraft,
Viel gutes und beses sie schaft.

[The translation was given as "Custom has great power and works much good and evil."]

July 23, 1942   Haven, Kans.   Leander S. Keim

Is God Your Trust?
Said the Robin to the Sparrow,
"I should really like to know
Why these anxious human beings
Rush about and worry so?"

Said the Sparrow to the Robin,
"It is very plain to me
That they have no heavenly Father,
Such as cares for you and me."
April 21, 1949   Josiah L. Beiler   No address given

From the Matrimonial Primer:
Absence may make the heart grow fonder; presents
have been know to have the same effect.

Don't take all elasticity out of your husband's purse by
keeping your hand in it.
May 9, 1907

Science and the Bible: Evolutionists claim the earth is cooling off
over periods of billions of years but we will let them believe
as they wish about their wild conjectures. The Bible speaks
of a literal hell being in the middle of the earth, a place of
intense heat and indescribable horror. For my part, I prefer to believe the Bible even if I cannot understand it all,
and if we open our eyes to the happenings around us then
we have reason to believe that the Bible is, has been, and
always will be truth.
June 4, 1980   Bloomfield, Iowa   David Wagler

Versions of Bible; RSV: [According to the Editor's Corner, someone had sent in "quite a condemnation of the RSV."]
Nov. 13, 1952

[H. N. Troyer gave some clarification of the Revised Standard Version and a defense of its use for comparison.]
Nov. 27, 1952   Editor's Corner

I have been surprised of the approval that the Revised
Standard Version of the Bible has won among even some of
the so-called plain people.... This version has been stoutly
renounced by some of the so-called popular churches and is
looked upon with criticism by our people here.
May 7, 1953   Bayside, Va.   Mrs. Enos W. Yoder

We hear some good sermons on that this winter in Fla.,
then again there are other preachers who use the new
Bible to preach, but don't forget, Satan is as busy as ever.
May 7, 1953   Greenwood, Dela.   Mrs. S. M. Miller

Mail and Letters 30

Rural free delivery of mail in the United States had its beginnings in 1896. There was, however, mail service in the United States from its very beginning. Benjamin Franklin became the first American postmaster general in 1775. He made the postal system self-supporting and laid the basis for what became the Dead-Letter Office. But the mail service in its early stages was limited to that between post offices in the cities and towns.

Prior to 1896 the people who settled the rural areas in any part of the United States needed to go to the nearest post office to get the mail. You will be able to read some excerpts commenting on the introduction of rural free delivery in 1896. Free city delivery of mail was begun in 1863.

Rural free delivery: Arthur will soon have free rural delivery southeast of town, then the hired hands will have no excuse to go to town, Saturday nights, for the mail, and the tired horses will also have rest.

Nov. 26, 1901   Arthur, Ill.   Levi J. Lee

A petition is making its rounds among the farmers for rural free mail delivery. We hope it will be a success.

Jan. 23, 1902   Belleville, Pa.   M. P. Zook

Rural free delivery will make many changes here, and perhaps some confusion for a while, as the old East Lewiston post office will be discontinued on March 31st and the patrons at this office will get their mail from Columbiana and Calla.

Mar. 27, 1902   East Lewiston, Ohio   Three Sisters

We are expecting a free mail delivery through here by the 1st of April, which makes it quite handy for the people.

Mar. 31, 1904   Kempsville, Va.   Mrs. S. H. Glick

A thrice-a-week mail route was started out of Kingsdown, June 1st.

June 17, 1914   Bucklin, Kans.   SUNBEAM

Care of mail: Will the person who wrote for instructions to clean and repair a kerosene stove please write again? I don't remember the name and the letter has been misplaced. We have a few small helpers here who seem to think daddy's desk is a nice place to play school.

Oct. 20, 1976   Linwood, Ont.   Elmer Kuepfer

Chain letters: I read with interest Levi Borntrager's letter in the last issue of the Budget about the so-called "Good Luck Chain Letters." I have received three such letters but instead of sending them on I burned them and as yet have experienced no special bad luck by breaking the chain.

April 3, 1930   Hartly, Dela.   Effie Mast

I hope all Budget readers read in the last issue of the Budget that the so-called "Good Luck Chain Letters" are against the law. I have received five of them in the past eighteen months and think every one read different and instead of sending them on I burned everyone and have experienced no special bad luck by breaking the chain. The one I received last week was called "Good Luck flower," but was meant to be the same thing. I imagine there are thousands of these letters on the go.

April 17, 1930   Norfolk, Va.   Jemima Yoder

Received a "good Luck Chain" letter from an unknown Etna Green friend, in this past week. Am sure the person sent it in all kindness, as others did before to wish me good fortune, but am sorry to say that the letter found its way into the stove. . . . It is not my intention to hurt anyone's feelings, yet, I can't help but class the Good Luck, Luck of the Cards and the Madgeburg Letters as just another idol, "Abgetter," wherein people put their trust.

April 13, 1950   Berlin, Ohio   Sara Weaver

I received a chain letter which reads as follows: "This letter was sent to me asking help in prayer for peace so that this war might soon be over. It is not hard to pray the Lords' Prayer and read the 23rd Psalm for nine nights. We are passing this prayer around to go around the world four times and I hope you will not break it." [She was to make 4 copies and sent it on.]

July 17, 1952   Berne, Ind.   Sarah Schwartz

Frequency of delivery: This is the first year we are receiving mail three times a week, and already we are spoiled so that we complain when mail comes only twice a week.

Sept. 29, 1976   Guaimaca, F.M. Honduras   Joseph Stoll

224

Mobility and Travel

The scribes wrote about two principal kinds of traveling. One was the change of locations, including the search for land in suitable locations. The second was the traveling for purposes of visiting, as well as some domestic and foreign travel for pleasure. The travel for pleasure will be dealt with more at length in Chapters 39 and 42.

Agents, advertising and excursions: The real estate agent of Moyock, N. C. sold 18 farms to the Amish people.
Oct. 30, 1924   Norfolk, Va.   J. K. Fisher

I would advise any one to buy direct from the owners of land, and keep away from the land agents. I am no land agent, but will be glad to show any one wanting to buy farms that are for sale.
Dec. 30, 1910   Westover, Md.   D. P. Yoder

I would say in conclusion to every reader, never buy a "pig in a poke," but always see what you buy. This applies to everything. Western promoters are generally fakes and schemers to get your money. [Yoder had traveled 1700 miles to Texas and wrote a one and one-half column account of his travels.]
Sept. 23, 1910   Quincy, Mich.   Amos J. Yoder

If any Amish people come out here to buy land I would stay away from the land agents. I can take you to the owners of the land and you can buy it cheaper.
Nov. 23, 1905   Aberdeen, S. D.   Samuel J. Glick

The excursion last week brought 16 prospectors here from Ill. . . .
Nov. 8, 1900   Iowa, La.   C. C. Schrock

Several farms around here have been sold to Illinois farmers the past few months and we know of one good farm that was sold by land agents at $10 per acre more than the owner asked for his farm; the land agents of course got the extra $10 per acre, however they paid all expenses for the buyer to come and see the land, but when they come in that way a land agent comes along they are not allowed to gain any information, except what they can see with their eyes and what they get from the agent. Land agent's statements are not always the most exact and they are not apt to tell any of the unfavorable points of a country to prospective land buyers. We would advise people to come at their own expense and buy direct from the owner and save more than the expense of their trip.

Sept. 14, 1899   East Lynne, Mo.   Eli Hostetler

We expect quite a number of excursionists from the north this week; there is an excursion again on the 19th of this month and on the 2nd and 16th of Feb. I hope many will come and see us and the country during that time.

Jan. 14, 1897   Chesterville, Tex.   L. D. Troyer

In our last letter we did not say where those 40 cars of immigrants are coming from. They are from Illinois. The Illinois people are wise enough to buy land here, because they can get three acres here to one in Illinois.

Feb. 21, 1895   Brewster, Minn.   Isaac Slabaugh

James Shields, traveling land agent of Mich. was in our midst and made several interesting speeches and took a lot of our farmers along to show what a good country they have, and how people can buy farms there. Quite a number of land agents visited us the past few weeks. The people don't know where to go to get the best land.

Jan. 23, 1896   Charm, Ohio   J. E. Schlabach

There is an excursion going to Ohio on the 16th; also one going to Oscoda, Mich.

Oct. 23, 1902   Goshen, Ind.   Katie and Lizzie Miller

Land is booming here; 62 land seekers came to this place on the 22nd, mostly from Illinois. Every week they are coming and going. Mr. Sturgeon, the land agent, had nine livery rigs out one day last week, and the other land agents had about the same number. Land is selling at from $60 to $70 per acre; it raised about $10 per acre in the last three months.

Sept. 5, 1901   Clarion, Iowa   TOPSY

We are informed that the North Dakota land agent will be here in the near future.

May 24, 1894   Mt. Ayr, Ind.   U. R. WRIGHT

226

[The following are some examples of excursions that were advertised or reported in THE BUDGET.

1. Excursions to southern Minnesota. Aug. 16, 1894
2. Excursion from Shanesville, Ohio to eastern North Carolina, where 20,000 acres was available. June 20, 1895
3. Land excursion to Kissemee, Fla. from Shanesville, Ohio. Feb. 14, 1895
4. Jacks Land and Home Seekers Excursion sponsored one and sometimes two excursions each month to North Dakota, as well as others to Mich. Feb. 27, 1896
5. A. A. Jack of the above company closed a large advertisement with the following sentence: "Go with me and see the Amish Brethren now in their new homes and settled along the "Soo Line." Free government lands close to the railroad were featured.
6. Max Bass of Chicago promoted North Dakota land, and stated that a colony of Amish brethren has located on FREE Government land in the vicinity of Island Lake in Roulette County. July 23, 1896
7. A. R. Code of Au Sable, Mich. featured a full page advertising central Mich. Mar. 4, 1909]

Homesteading and Pioneering: The homestead land is all taken up in this locality, but relinquishments can be bought from $10 to $15 per acre.
>   Dec. 27, 1910   Limon, Colo.   Jacob M. Yoder

The writer was employed most of last week in locating settlers and surveying and finding the homesteads of those who had been located by an expert, at $15 each.
>   Sept. 26, 1907   Yoder, Colo.   A. F. Yoder

Six advance scouts of a party of five hundred from Missouri were here last week to pick out homesteads.
>   Feb. 14, 1907   Yoder, Colo.   A. F. Yoder

In regard to the opening of the country east of the writer's home. I will say it will come in for settlement on or before August 6th. If any of our German people wish to have information in regard to the new country, write me, and I shall answer promptly.
>   Jan. 27, 1901   Cora, Okla.   M. K. Yoder

Yesterday three passenger trains arrived from the east, loaded with people that are looking for locations; about 3,000 in all.
>   Apr. 12, 1900   Devil's Lake, N. D.   G. A. Yoder

The people here have Washington fever; we are informed that it is a good place for fruits, and many other crops.

Nov. 8, 1900   Grass Lakes, N.D.   David F. Chupp

There is no more Government land in this neighborhood, but still good chances to buy.

Jan. 24, 1901   Island Lake, N.D.   S. Y. Yoder

Land taken under the homestead law is free from taxation for seven years if desired, and there is no cost connected with the occupancy of 160 acres, except a small land office fee not exceeding sixteen dollars for the entire tract. [From an ad by Max Bass about North Dakota land.]

July 2, 1896

There are 416,000 acres of land west of town that will be opened to settlement. I was over this land last week and never saw a prettier country in my life; good soil, good water, nice level land. . . . We met many prairie schooners heading for there.

June 5, 1902   Bonesteel, S. D.   F. A. Stahl

By all reports, the Michigan fever with which some of our people have been afflicted, has some what abated. These fevers remind one of the quotation, "A sober second thought is always essential and seldom wrong." I hope no one will misunderstand this and be offended, as it is not meant that way.

Nov. 5, 1903   Kalona, Iowa   J. G. Gingerich

Mobility; examples of: [David Luthy, in *The Amish in America: Settlements that Failed 1840 - 1960* (Pathway Publishers), 1986, p. 390, described Jacob K. Miller as the "Movingest" Amishman. His information was culled from references in THE BUDGET. Jacob was born in Somerset Co. Pa., married at Arthur, Ill, moved to Oregon, east to Geauga, Co., Ohio, back to Oregon, south to Salinas, Calif., east to Norfolk, Va., north to Dover, Dela., west to Glendive, Mont. and farther west to Oregon, and then east again to Dover, Dela. Eight states and a distance of 15,600 miles. His travel was by train. It is no wonder that he was nicknamed "Oregon Jake."]

[Luthy in the same volume on page 384, tells of another Somerset Co. Pa. man, Daniel D. Miller who lived 20 years in Pa., 25 years in Ind., 4 years in Ill., 12 years in Ore., 4 years in Miss., 2 years in Tex., 1 year in Kans. and 3 years in Okla.]

[Another example is David D. Schlabach and his wife. Both were born in Holmes, Co. Ohio and lived at Hartville, Ohio for nearly a decade. David and Sarah were married in Hutchinson, Kans. where he was ordained. After 10 years they moved to Minn. (5 yr.) and from there to Fairview, Mich. where he was ordained to the office of Bishop; from there to McMinneville, Ore. (a trip that took from Monday to Saturday on the train); their next home was Kokomo, Ind.; then Hartville, Ohio, and finally to McGrawsville, Ind. in 1928. He died Dec. 2, 1935 at age 75 and was the father of 6 sons and 7 daughters.] [Son Levi lives near Hartville and described these travels to the author. Levi was born in 1900.]

[The final example is that of Joseph and Hannah Overholt. Four years after marriage they moved to Ford Co., Kans.; from there to Plainview, Tex.; next to Centralia, Mo.; then Hartville, Ohio; on to Norfolk, Va.; then to Buffalo, N.Y.; back to Hartville, Ohio; on to Moyock, N. C., and back to Norfolk, Va. where he died Nov. 24, 1937. Parts of this story are given in THE BUDGET. The full story was gleaned from local sources by the author.]

Mobility and community: Our church is about all gone to nothing. There are only eleven families here. Don't know how long they will stay. People say it won't be another year until the people will all be gone. It seems funny to think that just a few years ago there were something like forty families.

Sept. 2, 1937   Argonia, Kans.   Miss Fannie Mast

Farmers are hauling feed, husking corn, building, fencing and plowing. The next on the program will be unloading cars and taking care of emigrants. There will be seven to move in here within the next three weeks of our Amish denomination; two from Indiana, four from Reno, Co., this state, and one from Anderson, Co., this state.

Feb. 21, 1907   Dodge City, Kans.   Aaron A. Yoder

We count now about 40 people in our settlement; have preaching every two weeks, and Sunday School every alternate Sunday. We don't expect or wish for a great boom, but we would be glad to see this community increase with a moderate, healthy growth. So far, no one has moved away or has any desire to do so.

July 4, 1901   Centralia, Mo.   J. D. Guengerich

Some of our friends thought we were going to a wilderness, but it don't look like it; we have 42 scholars in our school district enrolled.

Nov. 19, 1903   Kalispell, Mont.   Mrs. Katie Eicher

We rejoice to read of our Amish friends who have moved to new localities, from rather crowded areas, and have found satisfactory homes and living conditions and that native citizens of the localities have expressed themselves glad to have them move in. We hope that the true light to the world may be kindled there by the Amish moving in. Reading on down the line we notice a few of them were fishing on Sunday and from other sources we hear that native citizens expressed themselves surprised to notice these plain people using tobacco. This causes us sadness.

Mar. 26, 1953   Belleville, Pa.   No name

Moving; motivations: Menno Keims are moving back from Illinois to Haven, where Menno grew to manhood, as the climate in Illinois does not agree with Menno or his horse, so Menno told me last fall.

Feb. 9, 1950   Hutchinson, Kans.   Delila Beiler Nisly

A group of Amish families from Portland settlement have already moved to Pike Co. and Amish families from other districts are also moving to Pike Co. The Portland group moved because of the school situation in Ind. Complications in church matters were given as the reasons for this group's decision to move.

Dec. 11, 1947   Bluffton, Ind.   Sarah Schwartz

Our official relocation committee is again on the go, this time as far as Mississippi. . . .

Dec. 12, 1963   Back Bay, Va.   J. H. Miller

There seems to be a great unrest amongst the people some are moving away, some are trying to get loose to get away some have made purchases in other localities and again given it up, but not many are having their minds on going to one certain place. So we hardly know what is in the heart of men.

Jan. 27, 1921   Haven, Kans.   C. C. Schrock

D. E. Miller changes his mind so often that we thought we would quit writing to the Budget about him going away till he is at the place where he intends to go so they are in Glen Flora, Wisc.

May 12, 1921   McMinnville, Ore.   Mrs. R. A. Miller
                                       Miss Elva Christner

230

Those pamphlets from Michigan raised considerable fever among some of our fathers.

    March 3, 1904   Burton, Ohio   R. J. Byler

People are all well in general, except some people seem to be attacked with some kind of a fever, but you ask a doctor and he will tell you it is nothing but the "Genuine Alberta Fever." He can not give any medication for it, the only proper way is to go and find out for yourselves.

    Nov. 4, 1910   Milford, Neb.   A. B. C.

Five families are about to emigrate to North Dakota. . . . As they are going to a place where there is no church of our faith, there will be special communion services before they leave at their request. We are glad to see that they desire church privileges, and with the presence and blessings of the Lord in their new homes.

    Mar. 3, 1903   McVeytown, Pa.   J. K. Hartzler

Moving, pros and cons: Will write a few points for those that are looking around for a good location for a colony for the Amish Mennonites. We know that it is risky to move to new countries where we do not know much about it. Many people have lost nearly all they had, by risking to move in new countries, some of them would be glad to move back if they could sell out. Others have been taken in by land agents and have lost heavily.

    Dec. 30, 1914   Plain City, Ohio   Benjamin Frey

It is surprising to a great many people about Fauquier Co., Va., that the Amish Mennonites all at once are getting so restless, and all going to leave as soon as possible.

    Mar. 29, 1900   Kempsville, Va.   A Church Lover

All the talk among the Amish here is: "Wonder when we can sell out?"

    Oct. 4, 1900   Midland, Va.   L. J. Swartzentruber

Nobody hates worse to move than I do, Nobody! None-the-less, there appears to be a move in the 'offing'. Due to circumstances beyond our control, it seems to be our lot, as a church, to make another move. Since we came back here 5 years ago most of us have put up buildings, and have made improvements as needed, and did a lot of work, without any special plans of moving away so soon, but so it is. Words fail me to express my distress in this matter or the fellowship of our small group. But a church can be too small and so it is in our case. All we needed was a few more

families of like precious faith.
Feb. 13, 1980   Purdy, Mo.   Mrs. Alvin Kropf

I think we can draw a good lesson from moving. The old saying is - - a rolling stone gathers no moss - - but a setting hen doesn't grow fat. Also we can take a spiritual lesson. Some may be content to stay in the same stage and not concerned about moving on, but Christ teaches plainly that we must deny ourselves and follow Him. So if we are led to move on, let us consider it prayerfully.
Feb. 8, 1962   New Paris, Ind.   Amos M. Schrock

A good bit of moving will be done the next few weeks, with a good many people moving out of the valley because farms just cannot be gotten here as it seems to be full everywhere, and being walled in with mountains, much like the cities of ancient times, we cannot expand like other settlements. There are many young people here, married a number of years, who still are not able to get a farm.
Mar. 24, 1949   Belleville, Pa.   D. Y. Renno

While visiting in Indiana last fall many would say to me, "I would not like to live there, I am sure." Why? They would answer, "because it is such a back woods." Friends, 'tis for that reason we like it here. For all about us are things of beautiful nature, not made with hand. Even though I regret it, the land is fast improved and soon these acres shall be cultivated as elsewhere, as far as eye can see will be fields of grain. "Tis well, God made it so, and let us not despise it. Neither then should we despise our woodlands, because that too was the work of God. It pains us to have people speak lightly of our home, the woodlands, the beautiful flowers, the hills, the streams with fishes, which are all dear to us because to us this is home and freedom.
Mar. 16, 1905   Biggs, Mich.   Maidalene Hershberger

We have a man in our neighborhood, who, after living in North Dakota about 10 years, sold out and left in search of a better place. He traveled by the overland route with his family, through nearly all the states between the Mississippi River and the Rocky Mts., farming one year in Oklahoma and one year in Texas, and finally came back to this state to stay. Pretty good evidence that North Dakota is all right.
Jan. 24, 1901   Grass Lake, N.D.   S. Y. Zook

We have the cars nearly all unloaded. They all seem to like the country so far, but I tell you we have fine houses, they are worse than Illinois hogstables. The crops had been very good last year.

Jan. 16, 1896   Gibson, Miss.   J. C. Miller & Henry Eash

We were expecting there would be a lot of land for sale in Kansas, after Lauber, the Amish prophet, had predicted a famine, but it seems it didn't go very deep.

May 8, 1902   Millersburg, Ohio   Yost K. Byler

Please stop Alvin Beachy's paper till he knows where he is going to locate.

Jan. 1, 1903   Whiteson, Ore.   Pete Whiskers

Moving time for farmers: Undoubtedly many of you westerners wonder why everyone waits until April 1st to move. Upon sale of a property an agreement is drawn up that the place will be open to the purchaser by April 1st. This also affects a large percentage of renters. Sometimes a long list of moving are effected by the first party moving before the others proceed to their new homes.

April 7, 1949   Lancaster County Briefs   Jonathan B. Fisher

There will be a lot of people that will have to move by Spring and some of them have no places yet.

Jan. 4, 1934   Arthur, Ill.   Budget Readers

Many people are moving this spring and some have not found places yet.

Mar. 5, 1936   Shipshewana, Ind.   Miss Polly A. Miller

Moving is the order of the day; about 60 families are moving. Some are moving here from other places; some newly married couples, and others changing places.

Mar. 20, 1902   West Farmington, Ohio   Joel J. Yoder

Moving to foreign countries: After reading the Lynnhaven Gleanings last week, one wonders what this other country has that is drawing these Amish families out of the U.S. Of course, we all know that this country is moving at too fast a pace, which is probably the reason they are leaving. But it seems that these Central American countries can change rulers every few years, and often times for the worse.

May 9, 1963   Hicksville, Oh.   L.

Moving within the United States: This is our first experience of ever living close to the sea shore and is very pleasant indeed.

Feb. 14, 1901   Kempsville, Va.   Simon D. Hershberger

As near as we can tell, there are 17 families moving from Holmes and Tuscarawas counties, to Geauga Co., this win-

ter and spring.
>Mar. 7, 1901   Berlin, Ohio   S. Summy

Thirty families have moved in here since Jan. 1st, 1901. How is that for Geauga Co.?
>Apr. 4, 1901   Middlefield, Ohio   Samuel J. Miller

If I am not mistaken, it will be fifty years next month that my parents emigrated from Somerset Co., Pa. to Johnson Co., Iowa. There were eight in the family and we came all the way on a two-horse spring wagon and were on the way 24 days.
>Oct. 1, 1903   Amish, Iowa   C. D. Yoder

We have learned a great many lessons since we are in the west and they have cost us dearly but I hope we may be better fitted for God's use in the future than in the past. We have learned by experience that it is unwise for our people to change locations, only in colonies, and we have sold our home here so as to get where there is a church of our Mennonite faith. We like this country fine but we never had the courage to invite any of our own people here on account of land being so high in price. It is selling from $150 to $200 per acre.
>Feb. 25, 1909   Glendale, Ariz.   D. Y. Hooley

To those thinking of coming out here, it is not entirely a bed of roses, as there are sandstorms, ants, and the blistering heat, if I may call it that.
>April 24, 1947   Phoenix, Ariz.   Christian L. Mast

To those thinking of coming out here, it is best not to come unless you have some money saved, as work is scarce unless you are a skilled hand or work on ranches and farms.
>April 3, 1947   Phoenix, Ariz.   Christian L. Mast

We wish some more people would come and settle here, so we could have a church. We are the only Amish family living in Midland Co. Come and see the beautiful country while it is yet cheap, and while you have a good choice, like the old saying, "The early bird catches the worm."
>Sept. 3, 1909   Brier, Mich.   J. M. Bontrager

Visitors are so numerous here that the people have to borrow bigger carriages to bring them from the station. There must be something that draws them, either the good country - - or the nice people; but just come on, we have plenty for you to eat.
>Nov. 11, 1909   Bayport, Mich.   Simon D. Gnagey

[A signed article of five paragraphs about the Amish colony of Dayton, Colorado, giving a favorable report. It was signed by the following: N. S. Beachy, Mrs. N. S. Beachy, J. H. Yoder, Miss N. M. Mullet, and Mrs. D. S. Bontrager.]
Nov. 25, 1909

There were nine cars of household goods unloaded during the last ten days and eight of them were of Amish Mennonite people, coming from North Dakota and Oklahoma. There are eleven families of our people here, and we expect more soon.
Dec. 9, 1909   Wild Horse, Colo.   H. S. Nissley

We feel quite jubilant on account of the fact that Eli Hochstetler and family have settled here. Bro. Hochstetler is an ordained minister and he and his brother, Andrew, both from Ness. Co., Kans., have each purchased forty acre farms, near Ordway, and we hope soon to have a good sized Amish settlement here.
Aug. 00, 1910   Ordway, Colo.   Amos Stutzman

There is a peculiar fever among the people around here, it is called Brown Co., Ohio fever. There are about a dozen going down there tomorrow. It is about 25 miles west of Cincinnati.
Oct. 7, 1914   Shipshewana, Ind.   J. K. Miller

We are the only remaining Amish family living in Southwest Texas and in order of getting in connection with our church again, we expect to move to Nappanee, Ind. by spring....
Nov. 25, 1914   Palm, Texas   J. J. Miller

There are three families of New Amish unloading their cars here from Arizona.
Feb. 28, 1917   Bay Minette, Ala.   J. K. Fisher

News is a little scarce here, as most of our colony are making ready to move away.
Nov. 15, 1916   Bay Minette, Ala.   J. K. Fisher

I am glad to hear that Moses A. Coblentz is making arrangements to locate a colony somewhere in the south.
June 1, 1922   Bay Minette, Ala.   J. K. Fisher

So many people are going to Florida, which makes one most wish to be there also for the winter.
Dec. 18, 1924   Fairview, Mich.   Mrs. M. S. Zook

Joe Coblentz will have sale tomorrow. They will leave

before long for Mississippi to make that their future home.
>> Nov. 21, 1929   Hartville, Ohio   Clara Yoder, Edith Stutzman

A truck load of men are going about 40 miles from here to-morrow to look at an island in the Chesapeake Bay. Some are thinking of moving there if the location suits them.
>> Aug. 18, 1932   Cheswold, Dela.   Effie D. Mast

There are 9 Amish families here and a lot of young boys and girls and many Mennonite people from different places, most of the young people have work on the celery fields, and in the packing houses.
>> Feb. 7, 1935   Sarasota, Fla.   E. J. Miller & wife & son

Wm. Miller's three emigrant cars from Thomas, Okla. arrived here on Friday morning and were unloaded the same day. Livestock consisted of 16 head of horses and 10 cattle.
>> Mar. 10, 1938   Topeka, Ind.   Mrs. Ida Gingerich

Travel; domestic: B. K. Smoker expects to have public sale in in October, then he and his family want to go traveling a year, by the overland route with horse and wagon.
>> Sept. 9, 1909   Norfolk, Va.   Simon D. Hershberger

The Nappanee bus was going to stop in Geauga last night on their way to Niagara Falls.
>> Aug. 25, 1932   Middlefield, Ohio   Miss Katie Borkholder

We have been having Sunday School and Church services the last three Sundays. The first Sunday there was an attendance of 52, the second Sunday 61, and last Sunday there were 93 present, so you can see there was quite an increase in the church, which was made by more people coming down from the north. Last Sunday evening we had an open air meeting at Pinecraft out in the yard. It concluded in singing and prayer. Pre. Emanuel Swartzentruber and Jake Frey spoke.
>> Feb. 11, 1937   Sarasota, Fla.   Mrs. Bob R. Miller

I will let the readers of the Budget know that we all got through from Hartford, Kans. to this place, O.K. I arrived on the 2nd inst. with my emigrant car. I had a little trouble along the road to keep the bums out of my car.
>> Mar. 29, 1900   Wellman, Iowa   J. P. Swartzendruber

We also were in Independence Hall where the Declaration of Independence was signed and walked across the huge Delaware River bridge which is two miles in length and held up by cables. It really is a sight worth seeing. I never before realized that there were so many different animals in the world. There are some other people talking of going before long.

Aug. 13, 1936   Cheswold, Dela.   Effie D. Mast

Bro. Jonathan Shrock will start for Atlanta, Ga., tomorrow, where he will spend the winter for the benefit of his health.

Dec. 26, 1901   Goshen, Ind.   D. G. Schrock

Travel; foreign: The articles by the cattle attendants on their trips to Europe are very interesting, but I haven't much desire to make such a trip myself as I would be afraid to be on the water. Our son is across now, and as near as I can figure it out, he is 10,000 miles away.

Feb. 28, 1946   Haven, Kans.   Jonas L. Keim

I enjoy reading Bro. Fisher's letters, as he asked me to go with him when I was in Pennsylvania. I often wish to be with him. [Did Fisher travel alone by necessity?]

Nov. 26, 1908   Millbank, Ont.   J. R. Ebersol

Will say that the letters of Jonathan Fisher, who is now in Germany, are very interesting to me as he has been visiting in the land where my grandfather was raised.

Dec. 10, 1908   Oakland, Md.   Dan C. Schlabach

We arrived here on May 20, after sailing for 53 days, a distance of over 13,000 miles. The voyage was an ordinary nice one. We had it a little rough in the North Atlantic and in the extreme South Pacific oceans. We were in plain view of the extreme eastern part of S. A. for over 24 hours. The prettiest sights were in the Magellan Strait, which was lined with mountains having high peaks, covered with snow. After leaving the strait we sailed for 22 days without seeing either land or ships. We enjoyed the trip very much even though we did have some hardships. [The trip covered the distance between Newport News to San Francisco. They made a short stop at Punta Arenas, Chile.]

June 18, 1908   San Francisco, Calif.   Amos Brenneman

[P. A. Yoder provided a 3 column description of a trip to the Hawaiian Islands. Yoder also supplied information about his trip around the world.]

Sept. 24, 1908

[Jonathan Fishers books about his travels were mentioned.]

April 1, 1909

The travels and detailed accounts in THE BUDGET by Raymond and Willie Wagler of Kansas created widespread interest. This was increased with their speaking engagements after returning home. This trip took place in 1938 and 1939 just before World War II. With the foreign relief work after the war and new vistas in mission work, foreign travel came to be accepted as something much more common and everyday. The Waglers probably received as much publicity from their travels as anyone of Amish or related groups. Jonathan Fisher traveled farther and longer, and wrote articles for THE BUDGET, but he did not keep speaking engagements in the U. S. as did the Waglers. The first installment by the Waglers appeared on October 14, 1937.

Traveling and visiting are two of the highly valued activities. A Sugarcreek scene.

Music and Singing   32

Among the Amish, the matters of music and singing did not present many options. Singing in unison in church services was regular practice, with limited four-part singing at the young people's weekly or biweekly singings. Instrumental music was not an option.

The Amish Mennonites more readily adopted the four part singing. With the change of language from German to English, the transition from singing in unison to four-part followed. On the matter of musical instruments, most Amish Mennonites did not approve of their use or ownership by members, and certainly not in the meetinghouses.

The Mennonites displayed a range of attitudes. The Mennonites of Swiss background at first did not favor the use of musical instruments, while those of Dutch background generally looked with favor on them. The more progressive a group, the more readily it accepted the use of musical instruments in the homes. It seems that their wide acceptance in the homes makes it but a step to their use in public worship services.

Singing; acappella and unison: Is now sunset, and I'll go to the Church of Christ this evening. They have a nice service and also don't use musical instruments at services. [The scribe was in Mineral Wells, Texas for health reasons, bathing in mineral water for rheumatism and other ailments.]
May 13, 1937   Mineral Wells, Texas   Ervin J. Miller

Last evening, a singing was held at "Ikey" Huyards for last winter's German pupils of the Groffdale district. Considering their ages, their singing was to be highly commended. "Ikey" seems to have the knack of bringing out their talents in singing.
June 5, 1941   Lancaster County Briefs   Jonathan B. Fisher

Up at the place of the old Corinthian church the ruins of the old amphitheater is impressive. At this place Paul spoke, but seemingly of a more encouraging nature than at

Athens. Paul remained a long time and established the Church of Corinth. While on world tour I spent two nights and part of two days there. I attended the old Eastern Church services. They still sing in the old Gregorian chant similar to our Old Order Amish. It produced a homelike feeling even if the wording was not understood.

Oct. 25, 1945   Lancaster County Briefs   Jonathan B. Fisher

[J. W. Yoder explained in a letter that the Gregorian chants originated in about 570 A.D, during the time of Pope Gregory.]

Oct. 18, 1951   (No location given)   J. W. Yoder

[John F. Glick explained in a letter that "There are approximately 40 tunes suitable to sing in the services in *Lieder und Melodienbuch*, and 18 tunes suitable for use with the *Ausbund*. He mentioned that there were no tunes for 364, 419 and 762 in the *Ausbund*. He described some of the faster, newer songs as the "catch me if you can" type.]

Mar. 30, 1961   Gap, Pa.   John F. Glick

[There was objection to publication by J. W. Yoder of songs from the *Ausbund* with the tunes used by the Old Order Amish. J. W. Yoder had listened to some singing of hymns from the *Ausbund* and had supplied shaped notes. Objections by Glick were threefold: a) It was not officially accepted by the Amish. b) He used Mifflin County tunes. c) It was an attempt to standardize the tunes for the Amish.]

Jan. 30, 1964   Gap, Pa.   John F. Glick

They have started a singing here in our church with Brother L. C. King as teacher. It was needed badly. I hope it will be a success.

Oct. 7, 1926   Bennet Switch, Ind.   Polly King

A gospel singing is to be held in the woods near Steve Fisher's home ... everyone welcome.

Sept. 13, 1934   Gap, Pa.   Mrs. B. K. Stoltzfus

The event was most for the choristors of the various districts of the Mennonite Lancaster Conference to improve the singing. Is something entirely new. [The instructors were D. W. Lehman of Harrisonburg, Va. and Clarence Fretz of near Philadelphia.]

July 28, 1949   Lancaster County Briefs   Jonathan B. Fisher

Unclassified: The Jewel brothers, two young Evangelists, held a series of meetings in our town of Topeka, closing with a

240

blizzard of music.

Sept. 29, 1904   Topeka, Ind.   Cor.

To Joseph J. Zehr, I will say, anyone wishing to hear a good graphophone and about 60 good records, this is the place to stop.

Sept. 26, 1907   Croghan, N. Y.   Lena R. Moser

[Ezra Kanagy stated his understanding that the *Ausbund* refers to the New Birth on page 744, verse 34.]

May 1, 1958   Belleville, Pa.   Ezra Kanagy

Three song books used by the Amish. Most of them use the *Ausbund,* shown at the center.

Mutual Assistance 33

This section gives some insight into community and mutuality in terms of helping each other. Sometimes this was exchange help, such as in threshing rings. On other occasions it was helping someone due to illness or some difficulty. This help, however, did not remain only within the community, it also evidenced itself in terms of various forms of service beyond the community.

One of the forms of aid which helped as well as cheered many people were the dime showers. They had their beginning around the turn of the century when the 5 and 10 cent stores were popular. This latter is mentioned to remind the readers that a dime donated then was of considerable value. A few people began announcing showers for others anonymously, usually by a scribe reporting in his letter that he was requested to announce a shower for a particular person. A proliferation of dime showers in 1937 forced the Editor to require the person announcing the shower to identify himself to the readers.

Mrs. Sol Hostetler of Hartville, Ohio (TB June 24, 1937) was the recipient of a shower. She "hoped" that the Editor would grant her space enough to give the name of each person making a contribution. The Editor's response was: "We regret that it will not be possible to publish the list of names and addresses. There are nearly seventy names in all."

Bees and frolics: We hope to have a wood Bee Tuesday. Hope the weather will be favorable.
> Dec. 11, 1924   Fairview, Mich.   Mrs. M. S. Zook

A chicken picking bee was held at the Dan Miller home Wednesday. 78 chickens lost their lives.
> Jan. 31, 1924   Mylo, N. D.   Two chums

There was a well attended husking bee at Howard Jacksons last Wednesday. They husked nearly seventy acres for him. Mr. Jackson is gaining from his fall but is far from well.
> Nov. 15, 1934   Mark Center, Ohio   Miss Sue Mast

A group of 21 women and girls gathered at the Dan Eash home near Honeyville and canned 299 quarts of fruit and vegetables for the camp boys and they expect to can some more later on if possible.

Aug. 13, 1942   Topeka, Ind.   Mrs. Ida Gingerich

Tobias Hershbergers took down an old house about three-fourth mi. west of them on Rt. 2 and hauled the lumber home. Fri. eve. they had a nail-pulling for the young folks which turned out to be quite a success with 26 or 27 attending.

Sept. 29, 1976   Pulaski, Iowa   Mrs. David J. Stutzman

Wednesday evening a group of around 40 boys and men cut corn by moonlight for Joe E. Miller, he being unaware of it until the next morning when a shock of corn stood on the walk.

Oct. 21, 1954   Conewango, N. Y.   Mrs. Menno E. Miller

There were about 80 or 90 men of this community that went to the home of Earl Yoder on Wednesday and husked corn for him, and the corn was almost all husked until noon, and then they went and husked Noah Troyer's corn.

Nov. 10, 1932   West Liberty, Ohio   Maude E. Peachey

Last Friday about fifty menfolks gathered at the home of Sol Ropp and helped him shuck corn. They shucked 2000 bushels. There were about 34 women there and assisted Mrs. Ropp in cooking, quilting and sewing.

Dec. 1, 1932   Kalona, Iowa   Katie, Laura and Wilma

The writer had a carpet rag sewing Tuesday of this week. 33 women and girls were present. They sewed 32½ pounds.

Aug. 13, 1925   Kalona, Iowa   Mrs. A. S. Miller

A sled load of women folks attended the quilting at Joe Whetstones....

Jan. 28, 1920   Burton, Ohio   Cor. and Ida Miller

The apple pealing at D. S. Beachy's on Tuesday evening was well-attended.

July 28, 1920   Norfolk, Va.   Jacob B. Swartzentruber

We geschwistert have a wood cutting planned for Mommy and Lizzie tomorrow.

Mar. 25, 1987   Ethridge, Tenn.   Jacob J. Gingerich

Rudy Millers had a log rolling and quilting yesterday.

Dec. 14, 1899   White Cloud, Mich.   Two Readers

We understand they had a sewing and wood chopping for widow Healdings last week one day.

Nov. 30, 1899   DeGraff, Ohio   Cor.

There was quite a good turn-out at the husking bee at preacher Jonathan Kurtz's last Thursday. 21 came in the morning and 4 more in afternoon. He had 313 shocks and till 3 o'clock it was all husked out, the fodder all tied and the corn nearly all in the crib.

        Nov. 23, 1899   Topeka, Ind.   J. E. K.

A wood cutting bee is announced for tomorrow for Mrs. S. Detweiler and family. They are getting the wood in M. S. Steiner's woods, and Mrs. M. S. Steiner will have a rag sewing tomorrow.

        Mar. 6, 1912   Fairview, Mich.   Mrs. M. S. Zook

A stone hauling bee was to take place today at Jacob H. Peachey's but on account of the rain it was postponed for next Tuesday, when a large stone pile is to be removed that was gathered by early settlers to clear for farming and now will be used for filling up in other places where improvements can be made.

        June 2, 1915   Allensville, Pa.   S. L. Byler

Yesterday they had a corn husking for Noah Slaubaugh as he is not able to work anything he is nursing a very sore hand.

        Nov. 24, 1921   Kalona, Iowa   Mrs. Lydia Chupp

A wood sawing bee was had in Jonathan Hartzler's timber.

        Feb. 9, 1905   Mottville, Mich.   J. A. Hartzler

An old-time quilting will be held tomorrow, at the home of Mrs. I. Chupp.

        Nov. 25, 1909   Garnett, Kans.   Mrs. S. S. Beachy

An old-fashioned apple cutting was held at the home of L. L. Knepp, Tuesday evening.

        Sept. 23, 1909   Garnett, Kans.   Mrs. S. S. Beachy

Mrs. Israel Kauffman is slowly improving but Mr. Kauffman is not well. Twenty-two women and girls were there one day recently. The girls cleaned their house and the women sewed for them.

        May 28, 1913   Kishacoquillas, Pa.   Bertha E. Peachey

M. J. Bontrager had a hauling bee yesterday, to haul stone for the new house he intends to build the coming summer.

        Feb. 15, 1900   Shrock, Ind.   J. M. Bontrager

Menno Miller had a bee yesterday to haul gravel and to do some concreting in the afternoon.

        June 2, 1921   Middlefield, Ohio   E. M. Hochstetler

Simon Lehman is going to have a bee on Wednesday to reshingle his barn.

Oct. 26, 1899   Lowville, N.Y.   J. K. Schwartzentruber

Rob Troyer had a frolic to haul lime stone last Saturday afternoon. There were seventeen teams present.

Nov. 27, 1912   Troyer Valley, Ohio   A. C. S.

On the 18th will be a frolic to take up potatoes for Leon Smoker. He has been in the hospital for seven weeks with a broken leg. He was loading his milk and slipped and fell, breaking his leg.

Sept. 18, 1941   Gap, Pa.   N. N.

There was a frolic at Mrs. Lydia Brennemans last Thursday. Eleven women were there to help hoe and plant and clean house.

July 7, 1927   Kalona, Iowa   Mrs. Eliza Miller

Mose P. Miller expects to have a frolic to put up hay next week.

July 2, 1953   Apple Creek, Ohio   D. N. Petersheim

Today E. D. Smuckers had a frolic to cut wood and there was a lot to cut.

Nov. 3, 1915   Maryville, Ind.   J. E. Hershberger

A general house-cleaning "frolic" will be held at Benjamin Troyers next Monday.

Nov. 15, 1900   Goshen, Ind.   Goshen Scribe

Building frolics: Steven Esh had a frolic on Thursday to demolish a lot of old buildings which will not be needed after the new barn is finished. Quite a high time was had by the boys, as the place was pretty well stocked by rats.

June 27, 1901   Gordonville, Pa.   John H. Kauffman

There was a frolic for the raising of a straw shed at the Yoder Bros. farm this forenoon.

June 7, 1923   Shipshewana, Ind.   Mrs. Harvey Glick

A barn raising will soon be called at Andrew Millers.

April 22, 1909   Shipshewana, Ind.   B. E. Miller

Jacob Trumeaux had a barn raising yesterday; they raised it with a 16 horse power engine. They broke the derrick, and the hands all jumped for safety.

June 24, 1909   Louisville, Ohio   M. S. Miller

A band of approx. 70 menfolks were working on the new house today that was erected at Chris N. Schwartze's.

There were men helping from Adams Co. Ind., Camden and Reading. A load was helping there from Quincy on Friday. The old house was destroyed by fire and now 9 days later they have the new house up and enclosed, with the wallboard hung and perfataped downstairs. Chrises are staying at their bro. and sis., Emanuel N. Schwartzes since the fire.

Feb. 25, 1987   Reading, Mich.   Samuel J. Schwartz

There was a big barn raising at Eli J. Millers Tuesday. There were around 180 present with the women folks. Lunch was served for them also supper. They also had a few good wrestling matches in the evening.

June 28, 1923   Plain City, Ohio   No name

A dozen or more men started on Wednesday P.M. to build a house for Pre. R. W. Benner and by Saturday they moved into it. Benner is not well.

Feb. 2, 1950   Sarasota, Fla.   E. J. Miller

Community and beyond: Some of the Budget scribes are doing fine work in advising and helping the readers along to send to the unfortunate in Europe, in a way that we shall find out where it went and how much it was appreciated. So let us be liberal and share some of our surplus that the good Lord has again blessed us with the past season. What has happened to others may also some time come over to our country. Our saved up wealth may be of little or no value to some of us then.

Jan. 9, 1947   Elverson, Pa.   B. F. Stoltzfus

[For more on this topic see the chapter "Church and Outreach".]

Dime showers: [The dime showers had their beginnings at the turn of the century. The B. E. Miller shower of 1901 was one of the most publicized, and may actually have been the first one. The B. E. Miller family lived in northern Indiana. Their house burned and they lost four of their children, ages 8 - 15 years. The bodies were laid in one coffin. There was an outpouring from the readers. The April 18, 1901 issue carried 2/3 of a column listing contributions and a "Thank You" from the Millers. The total received was $586.34.]

It seems as though some people are dissatisfied about the bountiful help that Ben E. Millers and family received; but dear friends, just think for a moment whether you would

like to spare a part of your family for all that Ben received.
I hope not one person that donated didn't do it with a willing
heart, otherwise he had better not done it.

Mar. 21, 1901   Shipshewana, Ind.   E. M. Hochstetler

We would like to get up a dime shower for Susie Miller of
Centerville, Mich. Route 2. She has been sickly for the last
few years and not able to earn anything for herself, and has
doctor bills to pay.

Sept. 15, 1932   A Friend

There have been many dime showers announced in the
Budget during the last few years. But I venture to say,
that if necessity required a dime shower for anyone, it is
necessary for Mr. and Mrs. Miller. He is past 75, and she is
nearly 72 years old and both practically helpless and from a
financial standpoint, they have practically nothing.

Aug. 22, 1940   Kalona, Iowa   Joe Bontrager, Sr.

Being a poor, young girl, I thought it would be nice to try
and cheer her up by having a shower for her. [She was
describing elderly Florence Walls, who had multiple
sclerosis.]

Sept. 25, 1947   Berlin, Ohio   Sara Weaver

[The Editor continued to get numerous comments concerning the dime showers. He reported it this way: "Practically all of them say that they would not like to see the
showers stopped altogether, but that they think it has
been carried a little too far."]

Nov. 2, 1939   Editor's Corner

Lately a number of persons have been getting around that
rule [of supplying their names] by simply implying that
money and other articles of value should be sent, without
actually mentioning it. So, in the future, we will publish no
such announcements unless we may also publish the name
of the person asking for the shower.

Mar. 26, 1942   Editor's Corner

I think it would be more according to the gospel not to go
to extremes about dime showers but mention the needs of
the people and remind others what a blessing it is to be
well and have enough to pay their debts. It wouldn't be
necessary to have just one day set to sent contributions
and not just a dime each but according to how ones sees fit,
whether it be a penny or a dollar, or five dollars.

June 17, 1937   Meyersdale, Pa.   No name

As you say, maybe some did not deserve what they got and maybe some were not in need. I know of one case where a party got about $80 through a dime shower and people of that community said they were not in need; not only that, but if they were in need their preachers would see to it that they got help. As far as the Old Order Amish are concerned they will help their needy, and I know the Mennonites, also, make that a rule. Others have the privilege of getting help when necessary, from Uncle Sam if they conduct themselves properly.

Oct. 26, 1939   Editor's Corner   [Writer's name not given.]

I got 118 letters and it amounted to $66.73. Now, shouldn't I feel thankful for that? It paid all my expenses and a little besides. I can't tell you people how much I appreciated it and how thankful I feel toward all those that took an interest in my dime shower.

June 10, 1937   Middlefield, Ohio   Lizzie J. Weaver

I received 76 letters, a book of Bible Knowledge, a cushion top, stamps and $23.55 in cash. We just feel the Lord directed and led you in this shower. We wish to say a hearty thank you.

Mar. 4, 1937   Allensville, Pa.   Mary R. Yohn

I am almost ashamed to write what all we received, but as so many wanted me to, I will try to as nearly as I can. A tray, scrap bucket, 2 ready-made caps, 2 single bed blankets, 6 pair pillow slips, sheet, tablecloth, 2 scrafs, 3 teatowels, 9 towels, 6 washcloths, 4 pair stocks, 1 ready-made apron, 5 small aprons, table cover, 19 handerchiefs, 4 pudding pans, 1 lb. butter, 1 qt. chicken, green berry set, 2 tablespoons, 6 teaspoons, 2 packages of noodles, some 30 dimes, 4 nickels, 6 quarters, 1 half dollar, a $2.00 money order and a $2.00 check and some $1 bills and many nice pieces of goods. We will thank you all again for your kindness and sympathy toward us.

ar. 18, 1937   Garnett, Kans.   Mrs. John L. Plank

[A dime shower was announced for Mrs. John Kempf, whose husband died and left her and 10 children, the oldest of whom was 14 and still in school.]

Sept. 7, 1939

Former Amishman appeals: I want to write to all my relatives and do not know of a better way of reaching them than through the columns of the Budget. Hope the editor will insert this soon.

I am not able to move around a good deal, but am not able to do any work at all. At present my youngest daughter is very sick with typhoid fever. The oldest daughter is also beginning on the same disease. We have the doctor twice a day. My wife is compelled to be up all the time; she sleeps a little in her chair. We can not afford to hire any help. We are completely helpless; I don't see what will become of us. I was well-to-do as long as I could work at all, I have many rich relatives who could and would help us if they could see how badly off we are, and I now appeal to them, for the love of mercy to come to our aid. When I was young my brother was drafted into the army, in 1864. He had always been weakly, and I sent him all I could raise - - $250 - - to hire a substitute. Now that I am in actual distress I want to ask those who can to help us. I do not see how a Christian can refuse to help another, even if he does not belong to the Amish Church. God is no respecter of persons. God helps all who deserve help. Christ loved mercy and gave it freely, even Lazarus was not beneath him.

July 4, 1901   Chehalis, Wash.   Moses Yoder

Government subsidies: The Amish claim to be a self-supporting group, therefore we should be careful we do not accept any subsidy or support money from the government in any form or manner.

Mar. 28, 1957   Charlotte Hall, Md.   John F. Esh

[For more on this topic read the chapter, "Taxes and Benefits". That section covers Social Security, etc.]

Insurance association: Could an insurance association be formed by the readers of the Budget, with the editor the president of the association? When a loss would be met with each reader would be taxed a certain per cent to meet the loss. Let us hear through the Budget what the readers think about it.

June 6, 1901   Weatherford, Okla.   A. B. Miller

Miller did not find any respondents who took his proposal as a serious one, via THE BUDGET. It might be pointed out that it probably would have been an unworkable plan, based on the fact that at times more than one-fourth of the readers were in arrears on their subscriptions to THE BUDGET, without facing the prospect of potential assessments for a health plan.

Names and Nicknames 34

The total Amish population has been reliably estimated to be in the range of 88,000, including children. The number of Amish Mennonites added to this would push the population over the 100,000 mark. This group of people, however, do not reflect the diversity of surnames which one would expect to find in a similar segment of American society as a whole, or from a city of 100,000 population.

The survey of surnames of subscribers given in this chapter reflects this. Sixty-percent of the subscribers use only thirty-two surnames. It must also be kept in mind that many subscribers today do not fall in the category of Amish, Amish Mennonite or Mennonite. No attempt was made to estimate the percentage. Therefore one must be careful what conclusions are drawn about the diversity of surnames among the Amish and Amish Mennonites who are among the forty-percent of subscribers not having one of the thirty-two surnames listed.

Because of the small number of surnames, and the tendency to use a very select group of given names, duplication of names occurs over and over. This duplication confuses identification. In order to simplify identification they often resort to the use of nicknames. Middle initials are exceptionally important for mail and legal purposes. Some even resort to the use of two middle initials.

The use of middle initials shows some variation. Probably the most widely held practice is that of taking the letter of the father's first name as the middle initial. For instance, the author's father is named Simon, so the author became Elmer S. Yoder. Much less widely practiced is the use of the first letter of the mother's name, or perhaps her maiden name. The latter would probably be found more in the East, such as Lancaster County.

On some mail routes where duplication of first and last names as well as initial is common, an additional initial is used. The additional one chosen is usually from the other parent. An example is the former Amish Bishop Daniel J. F. Miller of Hartville. His father's name was Joe, thus he became Daniel J. Miller. But to set himself apart from other Daniel Millers in the community, he took the first letter of his mother's name, Fannie, and became Daniel J. F. Miller.

Additional identification: The "Old Levi" gma is to be held at "Old" Noah Swartzentrubers, Nov. 18. The "Old Sam" gma is to be at "Sam Sammies" Nov. 18.

        Nov. 15, 1956   Beach City, Ohio   No name

The Amish here had a lunch counter at the Sim Joe Davey Yoder sale last Monday. . . .

        Nov. 23, 1961   Mifflintown, Pa.   Ray Weaver

Heiny Dave Yoder had another sick spell. . . .

        June 10, 1954   Sarasota, Fla.   No name

Old Sam Yoder is not quite as well the last week. . . .

        Jan. 18, 1914   Latour, Mo.   Sarah F. Hershberger

Little Amos Miller who was in a wreck several weeks ago, is getting along fairly well.

        Feb. 11, 1932   Thomas, Okla.   Eli S. Bontrager

Duplicates and initials: . . . there are three persons by the name of John D. Miller on our Fredericksburg, Ohio, list. A few weeks ago one of them moved to Dalton and it has taken several weeks and some assistance from the Fredericksburg postmaster to finally get the right John D. Miller's address changed.

        April 23, 1942   Editor's Corner

The question has been asked why we put Resaca on our address. We do that to avoid getting our mail mixed up as much as we can, as there are four Eli Beachys here. . . .

        Jun. 8, 1944   Plain City, Ohio   E. N. Beachy

There are many Stoltzfus families with the same given name, none however to exceed those by the name John. There are fourteen married John Stoltzfuses in this vicinity, possibly more. Each, as a rule, has a different middle initial, however there are two John P's and John E's.

There are many of us who dislike the new, more popular and worldly given names. There's nothing in a name, but it's the spirit back of it. Those desiring new names can find them in the Bible. Even in the New Testament there are some of which Linus is an example. See II Timothy 4:21. The name is already used in the Kalona, Iowa section. The

Linus referred to is supposed to have been the first Christian bishop in Rome.
Nov. 11, 1948   Lancaster County Briefs   Jonathan B. Fisher

Not everyone takes of the middle initials of persons, which would be a great help to enable one to know whom the persons spoken of or written about may be. The application of the middle initial is different in the west than here. The western folk use their father's given name while our way is to use the mother's maiden name. By the former method one may more readily know who is being referred to.
Jan. 6, 1949   Lancaster County Briefs   Jonathan B. Fisher

And while we're on the subject of names, how would you like to be the mail carrier on Rural Route No. 4 out of Millersburg, Ohio? There are seven Moses Yoders living on that route and three of them are named Moses J. Yoder. In order to make it possible for the carrier to distinguish them, one signs his name Moses J. J. Yoder, another is Moses J. S. Yoder, and the third is just simply Moses J. Yoder.
Feb. 9, 1950   News item on page 1.

The item about the Mose Yoders on a Millersburg, Ohio route made me think of the Dan Schwartz's in this vicinity. There are Dan L., Dan A., and Dan O. Schwartz on Route 1, Berne. So be sure to use the middle initial when writing to any of them. Last week a letter from Ohio, intended for Mrs. Dan L. Schwartz, was put in our box. No middle initial was given. The following are on the Geneva route: Dan J., Dan J. O., Dan D. and Dan M. Schwartz.
Mar. 2, 1950   Berne, Ind.   Sarah Schwartz

I wonder if any settlement has more different names than there are in these some thirty-five church districts, including what we call the Marshall districts. We have at least 54 different last names among us Old Order Amish folks.
May 17, 1951   Harve, Ind.   Eli J. Troyer

[Two items from the Editor's Corner. Someone informed him by letter that . . . in one church district there are ten Sam and ten John Stoltzfuses. The Editor added as a matter of curiosity on his part the question of why the name Paul is seldom used among the Amish. Other good Bible names such as Matthew, and Luke are almost never used, while Samuel, John, Moses and Daniel are overworked.]
Mar. 25, 1954

Among our group here of 38 families, we do not have a single person named John and also not one Miller family, which is rather unusual among the number of persons here, which amounts to well over 200. Of course there are members of Miller families, but no family head by that name.

May 19, 1960   Montezuma, Ga.   Mrs. Enos W. Yoder

[From the Editor's Corner comes the following information about the duplication of names of subscribers on two Millersburg, Ohio mail routes:

Route 4		Route 5	
6 subscribers	Dan Miller	4 subscribers	Abe Miller
3	Eli Miller	6	Dan Miller
3	Levi Miller	5	Eli Miller
3	Abe Yoder	3	David Miller
3	Albert Yoder	3	Andy Miller
3	Andrew Yoder	5	John Miller
5	Dan Yoder	3	Jonas Miller
5	Moses Yoder	4	Andrew Yoder
		3	David Yoder
		6	Eli Yoder

Jan. 19, 1961

The Mespo area has long had a large variety of Amish names, all living here at one time. Some new ones have been added more recently to make a total of 26 or so, different last names in this vicinity. Isn't this unusual or does it occur elsewhere, too?

May 14, 1980   Mesopotamia, Ohio   Katherine M. Byler

Nicknames: [Urias Yoder of Grantsville, Md. requested the address of "Chicken" John Yoder.]

Nov. 19, 1903   Millersburg, Ohio   Katie and Annie J. Yoder

Wonder how Fletch and Flutch Miller of Stark Co. enjoyed themselves in Holmes Co.

Feb. 4, 1926   Charm, Ohio   No name

[Some nicknames found, without giving the date for each, were as follows:]

Fritz Yoder	Monty Hostetler
Dan Pencil	Andy Gump
Push and Spike Bontrager	Huligan Bontrager
"Cold Water" David	"Gap" Dan
"Gloy Benj"	"Lame John"
"Honey" Dan Yoder	"Henner Dannies"
"Waxey Sam"	"Gopher"
"Fishworm"	"Wild Bill"
"Punch"	"Rope" Sam
"Pit Joe"	"Glotfelty"

"Yuppie" John Hostetler is working for Enos Swarey's....

Oct. 13, 1955   Mifflintown, Pa.   Ray Weaver

"Wild young men were referred to frequently as "Billys".
Sept. 2, 1954   Page 1

[An article appeared under the heading "What's In a Name?" and a part of it is quoted below. It was written by Preacher Abe J. Yoder who moved from Burton, Ohio to Hartville, Ohio about the time he wrote this article. No address was given in THE BUDGET.]

We say we are a plain people, we want to be recognized as such, especially in time of war. What all does this plainness include? Is there such a thing as having a name that is plain or not plain? I believe we do well to consider this matter, therefore I will give my own view - - you can take them for what they are worth.

We say there isn't much in a name, they are merely for identification. Yet I think we will agree that it isn't so simple as that. Names are revealing - - they tell us not so much of the child, but much more of the parents who give the names.

To hear that a child is born is too common a thing to attract much attention - - but the name - - that's different! We listen carefully, then, in many cases, we ask to have it repeated slowly, then we attempt to pronounce it, and begin to wonder if the child was named after a movie star or just where the name might have originated. We also wonder if the parents were trying to imitate the world, or maybe just trying to outdo the neighbors, or if they thought the name would gain social standing for themselves or the child.

I have been in very poor homes where there was not quite enough to supply bodily needs, but the children had such high-sounding names that one could imagine they were from the upper crust in society. I hope you will pardon my illustration, but it reminds me of the time when I was a little boy and played with stick horses. If I heard of a horse that took the blue ribbon at the state fair one of my sticks soon had their name.

I have wondered how far some people look into the future when naming their children. Surely they want their children to grow up. Should not then a child be given a name that is fitting for an adult? "Shirley" and "Patricia" will be outgrown by the time the children are big enough to milk a cow. Can you picture a grey-haired Amish Bishop and his wife named Larry and Patricia? There may be men filling our pulpits now who wish they had names more fitting for preachers.

Aug. 5, 1954   No address given   A. J. Yoder

The article in last week's Budget "What's in a Name?" is well worth reading or re-reading, especially to those who may sometime be required to select a name for their children. Few Amish parents would think of going to see a movie, but some will name their children after movie stars or other worldly heros. Would it not be more scriptural to give them bible names or name them after friends and relatives which we think a lot of.

Aug. 12, 1954   Aylmer, Ont.   David Wagler

About names: I too like the common names the best, but as I go through the Martyr's Mirror and back of the Ausbund I find names that are not so common among our Amish people. I think a lot depends upon the motive of giving the names we do.

Jan. 10, 1901   Middlebury, Ind.   I,

A number of correspondents have commented on the fact that Amish babies have recently been given names that were heretofore unheard of among the sect.

We don't want to make any comment one way or the other on the propriety of such names, but if the rural carriers were consulted I am sure they would be heartily in favor of a wider assortment of names.

Jan. 19, 1961   Editor's Corner

I see from comments that others, too, have noticed the new-fangled names which are creeping into the Amish localities. Can you picture some cute little girl, but now grown to a grey-haired mother or grandmother, answering to the name of some heathenish, famous movie star. If we expect our children to grow up into honorable, upright persons, would'nt it be better to name them after such persons.

Of course, it's like the editor pointed out, a good thing can be overdone. Variation would be better, but why not limit it to virtuous Christian names. There are many Amish communities where you never find a Mark, Paul, Timothy, Philip, Solomon, Matthew, Rhoda, Lois, Priscilla, etc. Anyone wishing to start something new, would have plenty of opportunity without resorting to Hollywood.

Feb. 2, 1961   Aylmer, Ont.   David Wagler

Surnames of subscribers: [Based on a survey of the subscription list in June of 1989, it was discovered that 60% of the subscribers used thirty-two surnames. It was further noted of the surnames used by at least 1% of the subscribers, the number was reduced to sixteen. That means that only sixteen surnames were used by 51% of the subscribers to THE BUDGET.

For purposes of efficiency, the variations of spelling of some of the surnames were grouped together, at the risk of offending some people. For instance, Hershberger includes also the Herschberger; Hochstetler includes Hostetler and other variations of the name; Bontrager includes Borntrager; Burkholder includes Borkholder; Schlabach includes Slabaugh and other variations; Schrock includes Shrock, and Kauffman includes Kaufman.

The surnames will be listed in order of occurrence, followed by the percentage of the total subscribers using that name. Admittedly the .03% is perhaps an arbitrary cutoff point, but in another way of stating the case, it means that all of the surnames have more than fifty subscribers using it.

Surname	Percentage of total	Surname	Pecentage of total
Miller	14.73%	Kauffman	.09%
Yoder	9.36%	Wagler	.08%
Troyer	3.67%	Coblentz	.07%
Hershberger	3.13%	Wengerd	.06%
Hochstetler	2.51%	Detweiler	.05%
Byler	2.36%	Stoltzfus	.05%
Mast	2.23%	Zook	.05%
Bontrager	2.11%	Eicher	.05%
Weaver	1.69%	Keim	.04%
Gingerich	1.67%	Helmuth	.04%
Schlabach	1.60%	Fisher	.04%
Schrock	1.49%	Peachey	.04%
Raber	1.25%	Schwartz	.03%
Beachy	1.18%	Chupp	.03%
Graber	1.15%	Stoll	.03%
Stutzman	1.05%	Swartzentruber	.03%

It must be emphasized emphatically that these statistics refer to the subscribers of THE BUDGET in June of 1989, and are not presented here as reflecting accurately Amish population throughout the Americas. In a nationwide census of all Amish, it is almost certain, for instance, that Stoltzfus would rank higher than it does on this list.]

Twins and triplets: [Some names of twins and triplets were discovered in scanning the issues since 1890. They will be listed with a minimum of comment. It must be remembered what was stated earlier about births, that in most births reported, the names of the babies were not included. This explains partly the shortness of the following list.

Mary & Mattie King   Katie & Barbara Lapp
        Aug. 5, 1954

Jonas M. Coblentz twins: Andy and Amanda
        April 28, 1955

Linda and Lucinda
        Dec. 8, 1955   Plain City, Ohio   Jonas E. Beachy

Triplets of Mr. and Mrs. William Chupp of Goshen, Ind. Leora, Leanna, Leoto.
        Aug. 1, 1957

Twins born to Mr. and Mrs. Donald Yoder: Tryphena Grace and Tryphosa Beth.]
        Sept. 21, 1977   Altamont, Tenn.   The Petres

Harvesting grain on an Amish farm near Sugarcreek, Ohio.

Despite the predominance of agriculture as a means of livelihood there has been a diversity of crafts and skills among the
Amish, Amish Mennonite and Mennonites. The diversity has
been increasing, and the number of persons earning a livelihood
from other than agriculture is growing. There are Amish church
districts, such as several in Geauga County, Ohio where about
50% of family heads are engaged in occupations other than agriculture.

This trend away from agriculture is not looked upon with favor
by the larger Amish community. A respected Amish spokesman
of Holmes County, Ohio stated that the lunchbucket is the
biggest threat to their community. He implied that other Amish
leaders agree with him.

The following excerpts will show some of the diversity as well
as some of the attitudes expressed. One must guard against
assuming that because a scribe or person referred to possessed a
skill in the area expressed that it was his source of livelihood. Some
of the excerpts express attitudes, rather than indicate occupation.

Beekeeping: Our bees have been very busy already. C. E. and
son, Harry, have hived three swarms, and one swarm left.
They are both novices in the bee business but as long as
everything goes alright, they do well, but when the bees
don't behave properly, they call for grandpa J. C. Beachy.
May 11, 1933   Westover, Md.   Mary Miller

Craftsmenship: Another feature which differs much from former
years is one not being at all commendable of the good olden
time days, is that of the working tradesmen. For instance,
the brick layers and masons done twice as much work in a
ten-hour day as that of the present one in their 8 hours. A
brick layer at 75 cents an hour showed more activity than
those of the present time. Even merely back in 1941, a
bricklayer got his $13.68 for eight hours work, and generally
laid 1000 bricks. It's stated that now they get $18.96 a day

and on average laying only 540 bricks. This compares much
to other tradesmen's work of other kinds.
May 5, 1949   Lancaster County Briefs   Jonathan B. Fisher

To Sam Swartzentruber, how are you enjoying making
hats. I hope fine.
May 26, 1932   Mt. Eaton, Ohio   Dan C. Miller

Joe Kauffman and his gang are about done on their barn
southwest of Huntsburg.
June 16, 1938   Middlefield, Ohio   A. J. Hershberger

There is a splendid chance here for a first-class blacksmith.
Horseshoeing costs 50 cents a shoe, (new shoes) and other
work in proportion.
Feb. 8, 1900   Nampa, Idaho   J. H. Detweiler

The cheesemaker has reported that some people think that
he should make good products from bad milk only by praying.
Aug. 6, 1896   Troyer Valley, Ohio   Reporter

I would like to hire a good hand to work at slate roofing
next summer, I will pay fair wages, and introduce the hand
to my customers. After next summer, I would sell my tools
cheap, and quit the business. That is a good chance for a
new hand, and a good place for a slater. Too much work is
the reason I want to quit the business. I would rather be
where there is no work, and plenty to eat.
Jan. 19, 1893   Emma, Ind.   Ferdinand Miller

J. J. Yoder is supplying Gibson with brooms this year. He
is quite an adept at broom making.
Mar. 6, 1902   Gibson, Miss.   Katie Yoder & Lena Lawless

There is about 500 acres of celery planted and looking fine.
Some celery will be ready to cut by Christmas. We are
hoping there will be some more coming down here to spend
the winter, in sunshine with us. [Henry and Freeman Miller
were working on the celery farms near Sarasota, Fla.]
Nov. 28, 1929   Sarasota, Fla.   Henry and Freeman Miller

Factory: The basket factory is going to start in a week or so
again, then vacation will be over for some of the girls
around here.
April 27, 1933   Hartville, Ohio   A Reader

John Coblentz, who had been working for E. C. Hershberger for 22 months quit on account of thinking he can make
more money working in the shops, but says the shop work
is harder work. Mr. Hershberger is in need of a good man

at wages from $65 to $100 per month house rent free.

Nov. 4, 1920   Hartville, Ohio   A Reader

Firing: Was it? F. J. Gingerich, who had been operating our village creamery the past seven months, has recently been deprived of that position, his successor being Mr. O'Neal, of Iowa Falls.

Nov. 9, 1899   Florence, Iowa   Amos D. Zook

General comments: Miss Cora Miller is selling books around the country.

June 13, 1901   Smithville, Ohio   Tobias L. Miller

Sister C. S. Swartz is assisting the writer with their butchering this winter for the Norfolk market.

Dec. 24, 1908   Norfolk, Va.   Lizzie Z. Smoker

The raggary has been booming for the past several weeks and the housewives are unusually busy sewing rags. . . .

Aug. 28, 1912   Allensville, Pa.   S. L. B.

Mrs. Tillie Summy is busy spinning flax. There were about 200 people there last Thursday to see her at work, most of them being high school students from Berlin. Mrs. Summy is 88 years old.

Dec. 18, 1930   Salisbury, Pa.   Nettie M. Yoder

I am working in a fernery. There are many ferneries here in Apopka. They call Apopka the Fern City. The ferns are mostly shipped all over the United States.

Nov. 3, 1927   Apopka. Fla.   Menno F. Kauffman

Miss Elmeta Stutzman is working up at Wellman taking pin feathers out of turkeys.

Nov. 22, 1934   Kalona, Iowa   Velma Gingerich &
Maude Brenneman

Andrew Ropp expects to enlarge his deer park this fall; he is getting too many deer and elks for his pasture. He has 8 elks and 9 deer at present.

Oct. 26, 1899   Pekin, Ill.   A. H. M.

Our gold mines are starting up again, with two new factories, one at Belfort, what is known as Mt. Tom, and the other at Pine Creek, that will make five in all.

Aug. 16, 1900   Croghan, N.Y.   Joe J. Zehr

You can hear people blasting stumps in every direction. They haul them to market to make tar and turpentine. They get $2 per ton for the stumps.

Mar. 8, 1916   Bay Minette, Ala.   J. K. Fisher

We are living on a ranch, eight miles square, owned by the Swiss Land and Cattle Co., who own about eighty thousand head of cattle. They have numerous ranches; this is one of their best; it produces about eight hundred tons of hay each year, for which they pay me $2.00 per ton. I am employed by the Co. to irrigate the meadows and put the hay in stacks, through the winter I have the hay fed to the cattle, what cattle is fed here, which is about 2,000 head each winter.

June 18, 1903   Bordeaux, Wyo.   A. B. Troyer

Will say to my cousin that sister Katie is getting along fine, devoting most of her time to church work, as school is out. She had a nine months school at $50 a month and has the same school at $52 for next year.

June 20, 1907   Garden City, Mo.   M. A. Gingerich

The writer is also tired of working sixteen hours a day and will move on his farm and will raise calves and squealers.

Feb. 7, 1907   Topeka, Ind.   Alvin E. Yoder

[One scribe did not think it in the best interest of the Amish or farmers to ride, either on horseback or on the equipment, while doing the farm work. He felt it was much more appropriate to walk.]

May 27, 1909   Ashland, Kans.   Daniel S. Troyer

Girls: Levi J. Lee, of Arthur, Ill., was here trying to get a girl to work for them but couldn't find any to suit him. The girls are rather scarce in this part of the country.

May 30, 1907   Loogootee, Ind.   Misses Katie & Lovinne Graber

Working girls seem to be scarce. Were looking for girls for Island Lake summer resort.

June 25, 1936   Mio, Mich.   Mrs. E. S. Troyer

There are a lot of people looking for Amish girls to work for them.

Sept. 14, 1939   Burr Oak, Mich.   Sue Troyer

About a half dozen families want to hire girls for next summer, but they are not to have in this vicinity, as they are too scarce: wages, $1.75 and $2.00 per week.

Jan. 22, 1908   Hutchinson, Kans.   Eli Helmuth

Hired hands: Andy J. Yoders are having an 85 year old hired hand to haul their coal this fall.

Nov. 18, 1926   Dalton, Ohio   Two Sisters

A number of farm hands started work at their respective

261

places. The "farm help" problem is a hard one to solve in our community as well as in a great many others. If the next ten years will take as much farm help away as the last ten have done, who will then run the farms? Is the work on the farm too hard, too unsystematic, too unattractive or are the "wages" the reasons why help is so scarce?

April 7, 1920   Walnut Creek, Ohio   Local news

I have at present 3 gangs of Mexicans grubbing for me. They live in tents, they do all their cooking and baking over a little fire on the ground and then they will sit on the ground around the fire and eat their rudely gotten up meals with more pleasure and satisfaction then we often do.

Mar. 18, 1914   Tuleta, Tex.   D. L. Schrock

M. E. Brunk wants a young married man, who is not afraid of work and has good control over his children, to farm his place. He has a good house and a fine place to live?

Aug. 5, 1909   Wolf Trap, Va.   L. B. Good

Hired hands will be quite scarce if the weddings will not come to a close soon.

Jan. 17, 1901   Kalona, Iowa   John A. Glick

Hired help is scarce. The boys all left for the west and the girls are as scarce as white crows. Everybody wants a hired girl; someone please send a car load here. [Probably means a freight car.]

Sept. 7, 1897   Bowne, Mich.   J. Y. M.

[A description of a cooking wagon and threshing crew.] . . . a house 10 X 22, built on a wagon. It is intended to be used during threshing season, "to board the hands." Machine owner furnishes all the hands, 15-20, and 8-10 teams. The owner of grain pays 8 cents per bushel for the service.

June 11, 1896   Carrington, S. D.   H. H. Miller

More hands is what we must have as soon as harvest commences. Come on, boys, you need not be afraid, you are sure of a job as soon as you get here, that is if you show any ambition at all. We have enough of the other class now already. A good hand, or a man that is not afraid to do something, can get $30 to $35 per month from now on. By the day, wages will be from $1.50 to $2.00. In threshing time a good separator man can easy get from $3 to $5 per day; a good engineer from $4 to $5 per day; a fireman, $2 to $3; band cutters, $2 per day. A man with a team, $3 to $4 per day and a man that does not care and will not mind

his business can easy get his walking papers.
July 25, 1901   Island Lake, N. D.   R. L. Bontreger

Many readers of the Budget will notice the letter and may think that we can not supply them all with work, but you may be surprised at your arrival at our depots, seeing the platforms standing full of farmers, watching for a crew of hands, as high as a dozen for one man or farmer, as there are lots of farmers that must have a dozen or more hands. I say again to those that are not afraid to work: "Come on."
July 25, 1901   Island Lake, N.D.   R. L. Bontreger

About 20 boys of Clinton, have gone to North Dakota to work in the harvest fields.
Aug. 27, 1903   Goshen, Ind.   Amanda M. Maurer

A bunch of boys from around here intend to go to Kansas and North Dakota this summer for harvest.
April 7, 1927   Montgomery, Ind.   Harvey Wagler

Labor Unions: [A statement of the Amish position on labor unions was given. According to Deacon Moses Mast, joining a labor union was a test of membership.]
July 18, 1946   p. 1 and 6.

Monotony: The main disadvantage at Boonsboro [a Civilian Public Service camp.] was the grind of the daily task of digging postholes in rocky soil; same job, every day, every year. My best regards to the men at that camp now.
April 11, 1946   Montgomery, Ind.   David L. Wagler

Salesperson: It is a nice thing to be a general agent. There was one of our young people selling the book of the famous hero, Admiral Dewey and his deeds. Of course they all get rich, for he jumped his job and is digging potatoes.
Oct. 26, 1899   Lowville, N.Y.   Chris Schwitzer

Wages and salaries: Farm labor can be had at 75 cents per day and board. Woodchoppers at the sawmill on the ridge are getting $1.50 per day and carry their kettle.
Mar. 9, 193   Elverson, Pa.   Amos J. Stoltzfus

I wish some young boys would come to this country, for hired help is very scarce; farmers are paying as high as $25 a month, and then they can't get all the help they need, but if any should come, I would advise them to bring a girl along, for they are just as scarce as boys.
June 14, 1900   Lowville, N.Y.   J. K. Swartzentruber

Menno Keim has hired Sim Swim for the coming summer,

at $22 at month and a horse kept.

Jan. 31, 1907   Middlebury, Ind.   Martha Keim

We are always glad to see young people come to this locality, but do not like to see them leave, as young people are rather scarce here. Wages are much higher here than in the east, on account of the scarcity of young people. I was offered $2.50 per week from now until next fall.

Jan. 3, 1901   Reading, Minn.   Miss El. V. Gingerich

Farm hands are as scarce as the "Proverbial hens teeth." Some farmers are offering $30 per month and then cannot get hands.

Feb. 12, 1903   Kalona, Iowa   A. D. Zook

The writer is busy planting his father's corn this week as help is very hard to get at present. Wages are good - - $20 to $25 per mo., or $1 per day and upwards.

May 21, 1903   Arthur, Ill.   S. D. Beiler

Many of the newer nonfarm Amish homes have the appearance of this one in Ohio.

Outward Views 36

The outward view is the term used to include some of the perceptions and thoughts expressed by the scribes about things outside their community. As members of their churches and communities, they looked out on the rest of society and the world. One of the words frequently used by the more conservative groups is "outsiders", meaning anyone not in their church group. The author preferred "Outward View" as a more suitable chapter title than "Outsiders". It also serves as an umbrella for some related topics.

Attendance at other services: Yesterday we were to Mobile, Ala. and heard Billy Sunday preach a sermon. His tabernacle has a seating capacity of 7,000 people, but was not full. They say some days it is crowded to its full capacity.
> Jan. 20, 1927   Bay Minette, Ala.   H. J. Mast

Quite a number from here went to Robbins Lake last Sunday, to see the baptizing of a number of so-called converts.
> July 16, 1904   Mottville, Mich.   Grandpa

Yesterday evening a number of young folks attended a colored revival, which is an interesting thing to look upon. A splendid sermon was delivered, getting three converts.
> Sept. 7, 1922   Princess Anne, Va.   Mary Miller

Foreigners: A trolley road is being built from Lancaster to Christiana, along the Pella Turn Pike, a distance of 20 miles. The work is done by foreign labor.
> Aug. 10, 1905   Ronks, Pa.   A. L. Beiler

Last week one morning several cars standing on the track near the round house caught fire and burned to the ground, they belonged to some "Dagos", working on the railroad at that place.
> Mar. 12, 1903   Clarion, Iowa   TOPSY

It is reported that there are 100,000 Japanese on the Pacific Coast; they are a detriment to the white laboring man, and it is feared by some it will cause war.

Jan. 16, 1908   Los Angeles   Amos R. Kurtz

Hobos: No doubt there are a large number of unemployed whites here at present, but it must be remembered that southern California is the "Mecca" of the professional Hobo during the winter season. During a recent night journey from Fresno to Los Angeles I found the right of way dotted with the camp fires of these "Gentlemen of the road", wending their way southward to still further swell the ranks of the unemployed. A large percent of these men will not work when employment is plenty, and when work is scarce they raise a big clamor.

Jan. 16, 1908   Pasadena, Calif.   S. S. Miller

Indians: I noticed one man in writing said that he had been in Oklahoma and Indian Territory and saw so many Indians; that some were civilized, others partly civilized. I will say, you may think they are but partly civilized, but you go and undertake to beat them in trading or buying and you will think they are as smart as anyone you ever saw, while there are many that can't talk English yet, but they are smarter than you think. Some of the nicest men we have here are part Indian.

Oct. 1, 1903   Lenapah, Indian Territory (Okla.)
E. C. Hershberger

Integration and discrimination: Calvin Halobaugh and Harvey Metzler each hired a colored man from North Carolina for the summer. They proved to be good hands and gave good satisfaction so far.

July 16, 1903   Columbiana, Ohio   Peter Metzler

Segregation in itself is not so bad, but discrimination is very bad. God is no respecter of persons - - why should we be? Can we all imagine how it would feel to be always crowded back and pushed down, just because your skin is a different color? Would we be willing to "sit where they sit", as Eze. did among the captives? We can never win anyone for Christ unless we have His compassionate love in our hearts.

Nov. 8, 1962   Salisbury, Pa.   Mrs. Irwin Beachy

The U. S. attitude of Christians towards Negro Christians is known all over the world, and it badly affects our witness.

May 23, 1963   "Japan Witness"   Lee Kanagy

Speaking of the Negro, I have not yet been convinced that

a Negro does not have the same mentality as a white person on the same social level. If the Negro would have had the same education privileges as the whites have for the last few generations, then moral, social, educational levels would probably be equal also, but they have been depressed with little chance for advancement.

Mar. 5, 1964   Blountstown, Fla.   Edward Yoder

I believe in the present confusion we are reaping what was sown in times past. It was the white man that started and profited from the slave trade and the present trouble seems to be a carry-over from the days of slavery. I can easily believe that Negroes in the South are different but maybe it is because they are brought up in a different environment. It is hardly fair to judge an entire race by what a few say or do.

When we lived in southern Ohio, there were several respectable farmers in the community who were negroes. Once, on our way to town, we broke a shaft on the buggy and had to ask one of these farmers for repairs to fix it. The service he gave was excellent, and equal to any I have ever received. His farm looked well-kept and prosperous. As far as I could see, or find out, these people were no different than the average American citizen except that their skin was black.

Dec. 13, 1962   Aylmer, Ont.   David Wagler

... as I looked down this line I saw something I had never seen before -- white and colored sitting side by side the full length of the counter. Then I thought of the old buildings outside giving way to newer and better ones and of the old system giving way to a new and better one -- right before my eyes. Surely God is no respecter of persons.

Dec. 21, 1961   Fentress, Va.   Ira E. Miller

The question often arises whether the Negroes have a soul or not? and according to my knowledge they have. I don't think it depends on the color or the tribe of people, for there is no respect of persons with God. Ro. 2:11 [The scribe gave an interesting story of Cuff, a Christian slave in the South.]

Feb. 20, 1918   Burton, Ohio   No name

I am rather disinclined to discuss such questions, as the very discussion of them keeps the question alive, and some people will think that it is still questionable whether the

Negro has a soul or not. I fully agree with what our Burton scribe said. . . .
Mar. 6, 1918   Kalona, Iowa   J. F. Swartzentruber

I am thankful to the correspondent of Burton, Ohio about Negroes having souls as well as we. It is my honest conviction that they are worthy in the sight of God, as he is no respecter of persons regarding race or color.
Mar. 6, 1918   Bay Minette, Ala.   J. K. Fisher

Speaking of the Negro, and speaking kindly - - not criticizing, they do not have the "natural ability" of the white man. I realize such a viewpoint is not accepted by many, and the talk is all about the "environment", etc. as to being the cause of what the Negro is today. To be sure that is part of it - - but not the whole story. The Negro is a descendant of Ham's son, Canaan, whom God cursed (Gen. 9:25). After the flood these descendants of Ham are supposed to have gone South and from them came the Negro in Africa, while the others settled in other parts of the world. No one could say that except for the "curse of God" one group did not have an equal opportunity to become civilized and progressive. The White Man did. He increased in wisdom, made great inventions, etc. The Negro probably was much less civilized when he was taken into slavery several hundred years ago than he was when he left the Ark. Whether that be the effects of the "curse of God" or simply a lack of ability for self-advancement we as Christian brothers are duty bound to seek to help him to a higher station of life - - especially the Spiritual.
July 21, 1960   Lynnhaven, Va.   J. J. Hershberger

We could not help but note with some concern, several recent articles in religious periodicals, concerning the racial fracas at Albany, Ga. Evidently the northern citizen is given a slanted biased view of the situation, and we firmly believe that the average southern Negro would be satisfied in his setting. The North is given a picture of slavery, and suppression, which we as southerners do not agree with. Yes, the Negro is in need of evangelization, and the soul of the redeemed darkie is just as precious in the sight of God as any other person, regardless of color or race.

The Negro in general is not interested in integration, and we believe that politics has played a strong part in all this controversy. Yes, we need to use our influence to convince the dark man of his sinful ways, but do so if you can. When the sin of illegitimacy was pointed out to one of them, he refused to accept it and said he knows he is right, for the Bible teaches us to be fruitful and multiply.

Oct. 25, 1962   Montezuma, Ga.   Mrs. Enos W. Yoder

Law enforcement: The English have been very good to us "Mennonites". At times some young men were out molesting teams and such things, but the natives soon took care of us. We feel there are lots of English who would be greatly offended if we were to drift away from our accepted way of living.

Feb. 6, 1964   Ethridge, Tenn.   John B. Zook

Perceptions; varieties of: I have to marvel sometimes at the words of wisdom some non-Amish folks say concerning us plain people. This certain Amish farmer was out in his field one nice day, working with his horses. A car stopped out by the road that passed his field. Probably a salesman, thought the farmer to himself. But as he approached the car he discovered that he was wrong. The man was from Texas.

"You know," said the stranger to the plain-dressed Amish farmer, "I was just standing here watching you, sitting there behind your horses with everything so quiet and peaceful; no tractor roaring in your ears. And I just thought to myself, that man must be close to God."

July 12, 1989   Sugarcreek, Ohio   Lester Beachy

The hocke or natives around here say they thought the Amish were different and now they know for sure as some were baling hay last week. This hay was still in wind rows from last fall and nice and green underneath yet.

Mar. 25, 1987   Pine City, Minn.   The Borntregers

I doubt if there is another place in the world like Big Valley, with so small an area, and so many people of different denominations. Those who live there are not aware of how the outside looks in on them. I often wonder why some of the forefathers settled there, as it is one of the hardest places to farm that I know of. And isn't it strange that so important subject as religion should cause so many divisions?

Feb. 21, 1963   Stillwater, Pa.   John Renno

We built reservations for the Indians, ... let's build the 11 Amish counties down near Lancaster into an "Amish Reservation" where we could send our leaders to study

"How to live and let live," by following some of the simple teachings of God Himself. [A letter addressed to Governor Tine of Pennsylvania from Edwin O'Brien, operator of a scenic dining room in Waverly, N.Y.]
Mar. 26, 1953

The South: Would like to mention a few of the peculiar ways of the natives here. They use only one horse, if any, and do their plowing with it, but they only scratch the soil a few inches deep then fertilize it. Even the corn stalks and grass they burn off before they plow it; they think it spoils the soil, and keep plowing would spoil it so it would not yield at all. That shows their ignorance in farming. I think if the northern people would settle in and farm right it will be a spendid country, if they will not take the Yankee style.
Feb. 21, 1907   Bay Minette, Ala.   Laura E. Kauffman

The Texas fever is very high with some, but I think it can be broke with about a year's treatment of Colored and Mexican.
Jan. 17, 1907   Jet, Okla.   Mr. & Mrs. C. J. Bontrager

Uncertainty: A young man from Washington, D.C. has been interviewing every Amish family, wanting to know all about our way of farming and the reason for coming to these parts, but confessed to us that is not his exact reason for coming down here. That makes us wonder what is going on. He says he goes to college at night and works for the Army in daytime.
Feb. 9, 1950   Mechanicsville, Md.   Mrs. Benj. J. Yoder

One meets up with some rather amusing circumstances sometimes, like the time when the little boys asked if he was one of the Smith Bros., referring to the picture on the Smith Bros. cough drop box. [The scribe also described an incident involving Eli and Floyd Brenneman, Abe Kinsinger and Homer Coblentz. A young boy walked up to one of the Brenneman boys, nearly touched his beard, and asked, "Is that real?"]
Feb. 5, 1953   Meyersdale, Pa.   Mrs. Enos J. Maust

Jonas Kauffman returned home, Tuesday, from his trip to Texas. Abraham Yoder and Jacob Beachy who accompanied him stopped off in Mississippi and are expected home today. While they were in Houston, Texas, they were mistaken for South African Boers.
Sept. 3, 1903   Arthur, Ill.   Wm. L. Mast

270

Urban people: Those Wooster Ohio ladies reminded me of a Chicago lady that never saw a cow milked, so she made up her mind that she would milk one. She set the pail under the cow then took hold of the cow's tail and commenced pumping, but she did not get the results she was looking for.
July 7, 1902   Chappell, Nebr.   D. J. Kaufman

I wonder what the city people think of Amanda D. Miller's bare feet.
Aug. 7, 1902   Welshfield, Ohio   A SUCKER

Welfare, poverty: A couple weeks ago there was a piece in the paper from Mesopotamia, Ohio about Amish children getting free meals at school. I agree with what you wrote. My children, they pack their lunches most of the time. We could also get free meals, but I don't think its right to live off of welfare. There are some here in Adams Co. that get their meals free. Some worldly people talked to me about it and said they were so surprised to see Amish get free meals. I don't think there's any Amish family so poor they can't feed their own children. Church is here to help if it has to be. Is this giving the Amish people a good name to live off of welfare?
Nov. 10, 1976   Geneva, Ind.   Mrs. Henry H. Schwartz

There is a universal cry of hard times in all the world. It is hard to obtain money, and yet, there never was so much money as at present. But it is being collected - - gathered in heaps - - by the powerful few, while the limited means of the masses are dwindling lower and lower. The poorer classes witness the absorption of wealth by the money kings, with feelings that are being aroused to the point of desperation by the sense of their inability to secure what seems to them a more equitable distribution of the things of this world. James 5:1-6. But what shall we do as citizens, neighbors, and Christians? This is the question of great importance now. Inspiration long ago foresaw our situation. We have to read only two verses further in James' letter to find the counsel we need. James 5:7-8.
Mar. 9, 1933   Gap, Pa.   Aaron E. Beiler

An adequate sampling of the comments and discussions by the scribes relating to nonresistance, experiences about the draft, war, and the way of love is much more difficult than for some other sections. The chronological arrangement for wartime experiences and comments was chosen so that the readers can sample it without the breaks necessary to categorize by war periods, etc.

Attitudes: Heroism, some people cannot feel content with performing some heroic deed, at different places in the county they burned all the German books they had in the school.
May 1, 1918   Burton, Ohio   D. D. Miller

In a recent edition of our daily paper I chanced to read an article that was listed under the People's Forum column, which showed quite plainly this certain writer's opinion of the Conscientious Objector. To a certain extent I could not help but agree with him. He made the expression that some of the plain people are constantly fighting among themselves, perhaps with their tongues, but they actually refuse to take military training or fight for their country. It is now needful more than ever for the Christian man or woman of today to heed the words of Christ in Matt. 5, where he tells us to let your light shine before the world that they may see thy good works.
Mar. 5, 1942   Gap, Pa.   John F. Glick

Each and every church today can swing the sharp tongue at the other to cut the other down, and no one gets anywhere. We are all far too much in the fix of the blind carpenter.
Oct. 23, 1952   Editor's Corner

In regards to "Blackmail" which was recently issued, the family concerned recently received another unsigned letter from the same party, and apologizing for accusing members of the family of being involved in affairs which proved to be false. Can the guilty member remain in this stage and partake of the Lord's Supper? God will some day decide on this matter.

Jan. 21, 1954   Oelwein, Iowa   Emanuel Miller

If you think publishing this letter will cause more heat than light, do not publish it because I think the Budget is not made for a mud-slinging center. [It was a letter about salvation and freedom from sin, and not the regular type of letter. It was published.]

Feb. 10, 1955   Salisbury, Pa.   An Old Order Amishman

In regard to the "Pinecraft Bench", it is merely a bench that sits outside a grocery store for the convenience of people waiting for the bus, and for retired folks who like to sit out in the pure air that God gives us to breathe. But sometimes some people who like to gossip, and listen to gossip, also spend their time there. Those are the ones who know it to be true, but is publishing it in a newspaper the way God tells us to do if a brother sinneth? [The scribe must be referring to what some people refer to as the "gossip bench."]

April 21, 1955   Sarasota, Fla.   No name

It is probably a coincidence that the Golden Rule should be found in the 7th chapter and 12th verse of Matthew, but nevertheless it should be practiced 7 days of the week and 12 months of the year.

Feb. 4, 1960   Lynnhaven, Va.   J. J. Hershberger

It isn't necessary to blow out the other person's light in order to let your light shine.

Aug. 2, 1962   Shipshewana, Ind.   J. B.

Conscription, conscientious objection, alternative service, military; Chronoligical sampling of comments and experiences:
When I read the Budget, I saw an item dated Mar. 11th, from Great Bend, Kans., was written by A. B. Miller. I would like to know whether your name is Adam and if your father's name was Jacob. If that is the case, I am the man that got an overcoat from you when you came back from the Civil War.

April 7, 1904   New Wilmington, Pa.   Abraham Kurtz

There are in LaGrange County many Amish, Dunkards, and Mennonites and a few Quakers. These people are certainly entitled to their religious belief whatever it may be.

They are noncombatants and because they are such Gov. Roosevelt questions their right to live in a free community. [This is one paragraph of an article appearing in THE BUDGET and reprinted from the *Lagrange Democrat*. The article was about Roosevelt and noncombatants.]
> Nov. 1, 1900   News item

The threatened war with Mexico appears to be at an end, for which we feel to give God the praise, and also feel grateful to our President for the action he has taken to avert such a crisis which was staring us in the face. We trust all is over. We have quite a number of Mexicans round us, but apparently seem not to be of such a fighting nature.
> Aug. 23, 1916   Tuleta, Tex.   C. C. Schrock

Sorry to note our beloved United States so near on the brink of war with some of our foreign nations.
> May 16, 1917   Tuleta, Tex.   C. C. Schrock

I guess it is everywhere talked about the war. We do not take any daily papers and I do not believe in them, but we hear so much talked we heard lately that every man from 21 to 31 years of age have to enlist or pay fine. Now us married women lets pray to God to help us to keep our husbands with us.
> May 23, 1917   Arthur, Ill.   Mrs. Jake L. Beachy

But we can be thankful yet that our government will exempt those belonging to religious creeds that do not believe in war.
> June 6, 1917   Mark Center, Ohio   M. D. Glick

Last night after services special prayer meeting was held for the dear brother Ottis Bontrager who had to leave today for Camp Custer.
> Nov. 28, 1917   Fairview, Mich.   Mrs. M. S. Zook

Several brethren of the different churches here made a trip to Camp Mead, Md., over Sunday to see the boys, who are always glad to see the friends come.
> July 17, 1918   Belleville, Pa.   Rudy J. Kanagy

Two of our boys are in war, Elmer is in France already. We had several letters from him since he is across the waters. We have not heard from Harry for over a week he was at Camp Levenworth, Kans., the last we heard.
> Aug. 28, 1918   Chappell, Neb.   Mrs. S. C. Yoder

I was inducted into the army about March 5, 1918, and was

274

first sent to Camp Greenfield, Ga., where I remained more than five months and, of course, had some very hard trials. The officers tried to make me work as a soldier, and when I refused to work under the military establishment they threatened to shoot me, to hang me, etc.; but after hearing my reasons for not working, some of the officers were very kind while others did not want to see it that way. [John J. Yoder wrote additional letters which were published in THE BUDGET.]

June 3, 1919

It seems as though, "Peace on earth, good will towards men," is being utterly ruined in the Old Country today when we read and hear about the great disturbance which now exists. They must suffer with the unjust which also includes women and children. In I Esdras chapter 1 (Apocrypha), we read of the various kings that reigned at that time and did evil in the sight of the Lord

June 13, 1940   Gap, Pa.   John F. Glick

A non-resistance meeting was held at the Warwick River church Saturday night and all day Sunday with the Brethren J. L. Stauffer and Chester K. Lehman of Harrisonburg.

July 11, 1940   Oyster Point, Va.   Mrs. S. H. Glick

Quite a few of this community received a questionnaire of late which is quite a problem to all of us, but with the help of a Higher Power we hope exemption of military training will be possible.

Nov. 14, 1940   Gap, Pa.   John F. Glick

A conscientious objectors meeting was held at the Bishop David Fisher home last Friday, attended by several authorities from Washington, D.C., also some neighboring friends. Possibilities were discussed of attempting to keep our "boys" out of the camps, as there is a labor shortage on farms, and they are needed for agricultural work.

Aug. 7, 1941   Gap, Pa.   John F. Glick

A class is being trained in first aid, two nights a week, at the school in Kempsville, of which a number of our people are taking advantage after being urged to do so, considering we are in a dangerous location if our country was air-raided and since we do not want to help in any way in the production of war material, we were asked if we were willing to aid anyone injured in our immediate community.

April 23, 1942   Lynnhaven, Va.   Mrs. Enos W. Yoder

[The Editor drew attention to a full column of explanation about The Civilian Bond Purchase Plan.]
July 16, 1942   Editor's Corner

Around 90 Amish boys had to take their examinations last week. We heard that 13 didn't pass.
Jan. 25, 1945   Middlefield, Ohio   Emma M. Borkholder

Several of our boys had to take their physical but failed to pass. That makes 6 of our congregation that were turned down. 3 were in CPS camps and were sent home. In one way that does not look so good for our young boys but I suppose they were glad to be released.
Feb. 15, 1945   Harper, Kans.   H. E. Hostetler

A group of 240 of our plain young men and boys of our county were to Philadelphia Mar. 8th for their physical examinations. About half were of our sect.
March 15, 1945   Lancaster County Briefs   Jonathan B. Fisher

At this time we are faced with a peace-time draft. Something which we people of America have never experienced, and what will the outcome be? If we stop and think in what condition the countries in Europe are that have compulsory military training, and how many of their governments have been destroyed, it would seem that we would not want it. Jamieson says the draft is a peace move. I doubt it very much. [Jamieson was a regular columnist featured in THE BUDGET and other newspapers.]
Aug. 12, 1948   Burton, Ohio   Abe Yoder

Regarding the subject of writing our congressmen to advise them what laws they should make. I wonder if it is consistent for us as nonresistant people to take part in the affairs of the government. We do not believe war is right and don't help to elect the officials who prepare for and engage in war. How can we therefore give advice on how they should run their affairs? Wouldn't it be much more scriptural to admonish them into repentance, pointing out that war itself is evil, no matter in what way it is carried on.
Feb. 7, 1951   Piketon, Ohio   D. W. L.

[D. J. Stutzman submitted a lengthly letter opposing universal military training which was a hot issue in 1951 and 1952.]
Jan. 17, 1952   Millersburg, Ohio   D. J. Stutzman

It appears to the writer that the hospital is a good place for some I-W boys. On the other hand it's not too good for the weaker ones. Most all kinds of people work here, and some of the boys take advantage of it. Some of our Amish boys have gone as far as buying a car, but to my joy one of the boys told me he intends to sell his car and come back to what he has lost.

Sept. 30, 1954   Cleveland, Ohio   Jacob J. Yoder

I don't want to interfere with anybody's religion or start an argument and the like, but I think every church should work with their own I-W boys instead of depending on another church to do it for them, as far as the draft board is concerned.

Oct. 14, 1954   Cleveland, Ohio   Jacob J. Yoder

. . . much has been written in various papers about the opportunities which the present I-W Service gives us. But seldom have I seen that any attention has been called to the dangers involved for the youth of our plain churches. Highly respected men from nearly all our Amish communities have given me their opinions on this matter and practically all of them are gravely concerned and are not too well satisfied with the present conditions.

Sept. 22, 1955   Aylmer, Ont.   David Wagler

["Amish Youth Sentenced in Draft Case" was an article about Joni L. Petersheim, 22, of Hazelton, Iowa who was sentenced to 2 months in jail and fined $5000 for draft evasion.]

July 4, 1957

[The kidnapping of Daniel Dale Gerber of Dalton, Ohio, 21 year old PAXMAN, working under MCC was reported. He was one of 3 workers in Vietnam which were kidnapped. Daniel has not been heard from since the kidnapping.]

June 7, 1962

I can say "Amen" to David Miller's (Okla) remarks where he stated: "If you are of draft age and consider Oklahoma City as a place to spend your 2 years of I-W service, be sure you are a Christian before you go there. This is very important."

Mar. 14, 1963   Belleville, Pa.   Ezra Kanagy

A lot of talk is going on and advertising being done around here on "fallout shelters." Some folks are building them or have built them. The shelter we are interested in is far removed from any radio-active material here on earth. It is eternal in the heavens.

Sept. 21, 1961   Shippensburg, Pa.   Nelson Baer

Convictions on draft violations: [Benjamin Kauffman of Fredericksburg, Ohio elected to go to prison rather than be drafted or serve in a hospital in lieu of military service.]
June 26, 1958   p. 5

[Abraham Y. Bontrager of Hazelton, Iowa was sentenced to Federal Penitentiary "because he said his religious scruples forbade him to use electricity or other modern conveniences." His status as a CO was not in question.]
Jan. 9, 1958   p. 6

[Levi L. Hershberger of Wooster and Eli J. Miller of Applecreek, Ohio took a 3 year prison term in lieu of I-W work.]
Feb. 11, 1960   p. 1

[Paul A. Miller, 23, ended up in jail, when he quit a draft-assigned job at University Hospital in Cleveland because he had to work on Sundays.]
July 28, 1960   p. 2

[Three Amish men were convicted on Selective Service violations and given penitentiary terms. They were Benjamin C. Yoder and David W. Miller of Applecreek and Daniel M. Swartzentruber of Beach City, Ohio.]
Sept. 15, 1960   p. 1   Sept. 22, 1960   p. 5

Capital punishment, Cleo Peter's case; Coblentz death: [Noah J. B. Miller reported on the funeral of Paul M. Coblentz, age 25, who was murdered while attempting to flee and obtain help when his wife was threatened by two intruders. Miller stated that it was "believed to be the largest Amish funeral ever held in Ohio, a crowd estimated at about 2500 people gathered at the Mose Coblentz farm in Holmes County, Monday, for the funeral of Paul Coblentz, 25, who laid down his life in an effort to aid his young wife (Dora) in a struggle with lawless drunkards."]
July 25, 1957   p. 1

[The men convicted for the brutal murder of Paul M. Coblentz, were Cleo E. Peters and Michael G. Dumoulin. The latter was sentenced to life imprisonment. Peters was sentenced to die. THE BUDGET contained some short news items about the trial nearly every week from Dec. 1957 until May of 1958. Governor O'Neill commuted Peter's death sentence to life imprisonment. It was reported that numerous Amish wrote the Governor and others, asking that Peters' life be spared.]

I hope everyone read the letter from Switzerland last week regarding the death sentence for the Coblentz slayer. Will we as Amish be left blameless in the matter if we do not present a written request to the authorities, asking that his life be spared. Such a request, to carry any weight, would have to be signed by the affected parties and by the church officials. There is still time to act. [Peters had originally been scheduled to die in the electric chair, April 10, 1958 but it was postponed.]
          Mar. 20, 1958   Aylmer, Ont.   David Wagler

All the Old Order Amish I talked to were interested in Cleo and most of them said they had written the governor asking that Cleo's life be spared. [This statement was included in an article by Edwin E. Espenshade, Minister in the Oldest Order River Brethren Church, with the title of "My Visit with Cleo Peters."]
          Feb. 11, 1960

[Paul Hummel and Urie Shetler reported visiting Peters in the Penitentiary and wrote of his conversion.]
          Dec. 25, 1958   p. 6

It has also been my thought here of late that it certainly is too bad there is no one here to give services of God in the Plain Way. [Written by Cleo Peters in a letter to Budget readers. He was incarcerated in Columbus.]
          May 5, 1960

The . . . scribe touched on a touchy subject when he mentioned capital punishment among non-resistant people. . . . For my own self I believe that since God alone is the author of life, we should to Him alone reserve the right to take life. Then too, I have as yet not been able to bring myself to the place where I can say, "It's all right for the other man, but not for me, whether he be a Christian or not."
          May 26, 1960   Lynnhaven, Va.   J. J. Hershberger

Civilian Public Service: [The Editor invited the boys in each Civilian Public Service camp (CPS) to select a scribe. Letters appeared from approximately thirty camps. Some scribes wrote regularly; others only occasionally. CPS was a form of alternative service during World War II.]
          July 24, 1941

Federal court cases: [During World War I patriotism was running at a high pitch in many communities. Liberty bonds were promoted with great pressure. The Amish and many Mennonites could not with good conscience purchase them. Amish Bishop Manasses E. Bontrager of Dodge City, Kans. put his counsel as a minister in a letter to THE BUDGET, of which he was a scribe. His counsel on war bonds led to a court trial of both Bontrager and the Editor, S. H. Miller. Neither case was reported in THE BUDGET. For a good account of it read Erv Schlabach's book, *A Century and a Half with the Mennonites of Walnut Creek* (Strasburg, 1978). The part of the Bontrager letter that led to the indictment is as follows:]

How are we meeting the great problems confronting us? Shall we weaken under the test or are we willing to put all our trust in our dear Savior? Are we willing to follow His footsteps? Our young brethren in camp were tested first; let us take a lesson of their faithfulness. They sought exemption on the ground that they belonged to a church which forbids its members the bearing of arms or participating in war in any form. Now we are asked to buy Liberty Bonds, the form in which the government has to carry on the war. Sorry to learn that some of the Mennonites have yielded and bought the bonds. What would become of our nonresistant faith if our young brethren in camp would yield. From letters I received from brethren in camp I believe they would be willing to die for Jesus rather than betray Him. Let us profit by their example they have set us so far, and pray that God may strengthen them in the future. Many people can't understand why we don't help defend our country.

May 15, 1918   Dodge City, Kans.   Manasses E. Bontrager

[S. H. Miller was an Amish Mennonite minister as well as editor of THE BUDGET. For including the Bontrager letter in the paper, a five count indictment was issued against him on July 7, 1918, charging him with violation of the 1917 Espionage Act. He was imprisoned less than a day and fined $500 and was to pay court costs of $145.93. The case was The United States vs. Samuel H. Miller. An account is given in *Mennonite Life*, May 5, 1975.]

Politics: He is a man of honesty and integrity of character; an influential citizen, and served several terms as Trustee of

280

his township. He is Republican in politics, and he and his family are members of the Omish Church. [One paragraph from a biographical sketch appearing in THE BUDGET, "Old Citizens." There were four paragraphs about Benj. I. Hochstetler.]

Oct. 4, 1890   Local news

Public position: The Mennonite Church position on war was adopted by General Conference, August 29, 1917. It appeared in THE BUDGET. A committee of three brethren was appointed to deliver the document to the proper authorities in Washington. The three were D. D. Miller, Aaron Loucks and S. G. Shetler.]

Sept. 5, 1917

Security and nonviolence: [The use of watchdogs was mentioned frequently. One example of "sicking a dog" on robbers was found. The scribe mentioned that "the premises were safe from bums and peddlers as long as he (the dog) was around, but his one fault was of being a little too vicious at times." Two intruders had broken into the sugarcamp where the scribe and his dog had hidden themselves. After they were in and had agreed what they will take, in the words of the scribe, "Quietly I said, 'Go get em Max.' Everything seemed to explode. With a roar Max was on them. ... we had no more syrup stealing trouble after that."]

Aug. 20, 1980   Huntsburg, Ohio   Uria R. Byler

Rudy Rader, I can not agree with you that Christians should vote to keep the "bottom from falling out of our good old U.S.A." Our power lies, not in our vote, but in our God. He is the one who originated government and He is still the power that rules over government.

Nov. 7, 1940   Kingston, Md.   Mary Miller

Puzzles and Riddles   38

The number of puzzles and riddles in THE BUDGET went through several cycles. The careful reader will notice that the excerpts in the sampling are concentrated in two major periods. Some of the puzzles and riddles were included in the regular letters and others were mailed directly to the Editor.

This volume can do no more than abide by its goal of being a "sampler". A compilation of all the puzzles and riddles found on the pages of THE BUDGET would probably be of interest to many of the readers, but this task will remain for someone else.

One of the persons submitting a Bible quiz had included two questions for which the answers were supposed to be found in the 6th and 7th Book of Moses. This led to greater care in printing the questions prior to having the answers in hand. The Editor defended himself in the following words, "And if you are still hunting for the Book of Moses, blame that on Mr. Miller, too. We simply copied what he gave us."

The peak of interest in puzzles and riddles seems to have been reached in the mid and late 1930's.

> We now have about 20 problems which were sent in by the readers.
> Nov. 4, 1937   Editor's Corner

> We have been having some exceptionally difficult problems the last few weeks so I'll give you a little breathing spell by publishing one that is comparatively easy to solve.
> Mar. 30, 1939   Editor's Corner

> What makes more noise than a pig squealing under a gate? [Answer: Two pigs.]
> Feb. 12, 1913   Pulaski, Pa.   Jacob Mast

> The question is, if I put six ears of corn in a bushel basket and a rat carries out two ears each night for three nights, how many ears of corn will be left in the basket? My answer is six ears of corn will be left in the basket. Of course every

time the rat leaves the basket she takes two ears along.

Aug. 14, 1912   Troyer Valley, Ohio   Lizziann I. Hershberger

A man had $100 to invest in livestock. He learned that he could buy hogs at $3 each, sheep at 50 cents each, cows at $10 each, and he bought 100 head. How many of each did he buy?

June 2, 1921   Editor's Corner

A stranger gave a merchant a $50.00 bill in payment for shoes which cost $3.65. The merchant paid the stranger the difference in money and put the $50.00 bill in the bank. Later, the banker found that the bill was counterfeit, so the merchant had to pay the banker $50.00 in good money. How much did the merchant lose?

Dec. 30, 1937   Editor's Corner

What goes when a wagon goes, stops when a wagon stops, is of no use to the wagon yet the wagon can't go without it? [Noise]

Nov. 18, 1937   Editor's Corner

What are the best materials for slippers? [Banana peels]

A man was 38 years old when his son was born. How old will the man and his son be, 18 years from now, if the man was twice as old, 18 years ago, as his son is now? Answer given: The man will be 76 years old and the son would be 38.

Mar. 10, 1938   Editor's Corner

A prisoner received a visitor and the jailor asked what relation the visitor was to him. The visitor answered, "Brothers and sisters have I none, but this man's father is my father's son." How is the visitor related to the prisoner? Answer: The visitor was the prisoner's father.

Jan. 6, 1938

I think the little folks are doing good, have only one objection and that is the riddles, would rather see Bible questions. ["So would I", was the response of the Editor. There was a period of several years in the second decade of this century that children were given the privilege of submitting puzzles and riddles. For a time there was active participation.]

Feb. 19, 1913   McMinnville, Ore.   Alvin M. Beachy

A tall girl, named Short, long loved a certain Mr. Little, while Little, little thinking of Short, loved a little lassie, named Long. To make a long story short, Little proposed to Long, and Short longed to be even with Little for his

283

shortcomings. So Short, meeting Long, threatened to marry Little, which caused Little in a short time to marry Long. Did Short love Little less because Little loved Long?

     May 8, 1941   Topeka, Ind.   Lizzie S. Miller

. . . so many puzzles and riddles appear in the Budget that a person just can't keep up with them. About the only puzzle or riddle I know is: How do you say Spark Plug in Dutch? [Glick responded in the June 21 issue, with the answer, "spark plug." He said there is no word for it in the Pennsylvania "Dutch".]

     May 24, 1951   Gap, Pa.   John F. Glick

A two-horse carriage used in some communities.

The Amish and Amish Mennonites recognized the value of the proverb that "All work and no play, makes Jack a dull boy." But this belief was not expressed by frequent favorable use of either the term recreation or avocation. For the large majority of readers, the words conjured up images of golfing, expensive yachts, lounging in the sun or dining in lush and expensive places.

There were many who were highly skilled in woodcrafting, quilting, embroidery, and metalwork, and which did it as a hobby. The term which they would probably have selected to describe why and what they were doing would have been "pastime." Hunting and fishing might have been considered as part of the "play" that keeps Jack from being a dull boy, but it would hardly have been labeled as recreation. Since most of the hunting and fishing was done on their farms and in the neighborhood, they did not need to address the issue of "recreation."

The same people who had this aversion to the terms recreation and avocation certainly enjoyed them. For them, recreation, even though not going by that term, took the form of hunting and fishing, traveling and socializing. The order of importance to all adults would probably have been the order of socializing (visiting), traveling (short and long distance), hunting and fishing. Some of the activities that could have been placed in this section are found in Everyday Life and Social Affairs.

Ball games: I was surprised when I read in the Ft. Wayne news, having a ball game on Sunday. Calling themselves Amish Giants. Read Matt. 5:16. Let your light so shine.
> May 21, 1931   Archbold, Ohio   Jos. S. & Jannie Short

In regards to the Fort Wayne news, I might add with the Archbold, Ohio scribe, that it is most embarassing to many readers of our weekly paper to read of such news as ball playing on Sundays. ...I would urge that all parents, ministers, or members of a Christian faith would strongly disprove it. May those so-called Amish giants be transformed into humble "Davids".

May 28, 1931   Norfolk, Va.   Levi Bontrager

The Amish Giants beat the Centerville ball team last Sunday....

Aug. 13, 1931   Fort Wayne, Ind.   Savilla

Circus: The John Robinson circus is expected to come to Goshen the 7th suppose there will be a lot of time and money wasted then that day in Goshen, don't expect they will see me there. I think time and money could be spent in some better services than spent it by going to shows.

July 7, 1921   Goshen, Ind.   Susan Miller

Fishing: A number of the middle aged men went out fishing last week one day. Alphi Hostetler was quite unlucky as he was in the act of sneezing his artificial teeth took a dive into the water.

Sept. 13, 1934   Oyster Point, Va.   Mrs. S. H. Glick

A severe epidemic of a certain type of communicable disease has struck the community. The disease is no respecter of persons, affecting old and young, the rich and poor, and the spry and feeble alike. I may say that thus far, I have had but a touch of the malady, and unlike many cases, this touch did not develop into a chronic condition nor has there been a recurrence to date. There seems to be but one cure and that is temporary, namely, in the words of Galsworthy, "I must go down to the sea again." The sea in our case is Lake Erie and the mouths of the creeks and rivers draining into it; and the remedy seems to consist mainly in dangling a worm in the right place so as to lodge it in a fish gullet. I understand that most of the action required to do this lies with the fish and not with the worm or the fisherman.

July 18, 1957   Aylmer, Ont.   Joseph Stoll

It seems most people don't work here on Saturday, at least my boss don't, so I usually grab my fishing rod and head for Lockhart Lake and those shell crackers really grab the bait. Yes suh, that's the time I forget all bout my cares and worries.

June 14, 1962   Zellwood, Fla.   Abe J. Weaver

Fishing stories were soon on the go among our group from old fishermen. One saying, "When I am home working I am 69, and when I am in Florida fishing, I am only 10."

Nov. 1, 1945   Sarasota, Fla.   Mr. & Mrs. Addona E. Mullet

Now for the benefit of anybody contemplating a fishing trip on Delaware Bay, I want to give them some advice as it would have been a great help to me if I had known a little more than I did. Be sure to go with a trustworthy gang, as some gangs are mighty tricky. And figure on getting up early in the morning as the fish are rather wild and they try to slip up on them before daylight. If you want any information go to the captain, you can trust him. Watch the old fishermen, they are tricky.

Sept. 17, 1953   Centreville, Mich.   John M. Bontrager

Hiking: Last week Tobe and Aden Yutzy decided to climb to the top of one of the peaks of Shade Mountain. They thought it would be only a short walk to the nearest peak, but the short walk turned out to be a twelve mile hike, and now they advise anyone who has trouble working up an appetite to try to climb Shade Mountain.

May 15, 1953   McAlisterville, Pa.   Emery A. Weaver

Hunting Debated: Tomorrow the hunting season will open, which is a big day. I like to go hunting about once a year and we always get fresh meat too. I go to the hog pen. That is the best place to go hunting. I don't need any license and what I like the best of all, the neighbors always come and help put up the meat, pick the bones and make the sausages. I am feeding a few hogs that I think will do for my hunting this fall.

Nov. 15, 1934   Shipshewana, Ind.   Enos Glick

Hunting season will soon be here, starting next Sunday, and many will be disregarding the Lord's Day, but our people were given a warning last Sunday from the pulpit which we hope will be heeded by all.

Nov. 12, 1931   Mio, Mich.   Mrs. E. S. Troyer

The following arrived here last Saturday in a Reo truck; Wm and Martin J. Overholt, Lancaster, N.Y., Moses D. Kurtz, Levi D. Schlabach, John and Jerome Overholt from Stark Co., Ohio. They are camping here and have pitched their tent near N. E. Yoder's premises. Much of their time is spent in hunting, especially nights. They intend to leave for Moyock, N.C., where they will spend some time in hunting before extending their trip to Florida as they intended to do. They have three dogs, 11 guns and a complete camping outfit.

Dec. 18, 1924   Princess Anne, Va.   Mary Miller

Hunting is the order of the day. Nearly everybody is out in the woods.

Nov. 27, 1912   Exeland, Wisc.   Manasses Bontrager

Bennie Fisher, of Intercourse, in attempting to shoot a cat took wrong aim and shot three chickens. I presume the baby boy that came to stay with them made him somewhat excitable.

Apr. 19, 1900   Ronks, Pa.   John L. Fisher

The Hunting season has closed and how it does "ache" some of our hunters to see poor "cotton tail" hop for 11 months and 10 days more.

Dec. 20, 1900   Pleasant Valley, Ohio   SNOWFLAKE

John Keim has such big boots that while chasing a rabbit, his boots fell one way and John the other.

Nov. 16, 1899   Charm, Ohio   Jacob & Eli J. Mast

The people had a scare made up that the rabbits have sore throat, but that was all wind, the people can eat all the rabbits they want to. (We presume you mean all they can get. Ed.)

Feb. 18, 1897   Arthur, Ill.   M. F. Yoder

Some Amish are taking advantage of the private fishing ponds and go fishing when the owners are in church and even do not ask. It costs money to keep a pond stocked with fish.

May 14, 1980   Berne, Ind.   Sarah Schwartz

Hunting of birds: Hunters are quite plenty and lots of ducks are being killed.

Jan. 2, 1902   Iowa, La.   J. J. Keim

Blackbirds are plentiful as six thousand were shot at Eli Hershbergers one evening this fall.

Nov. 7, 1929   Arthur, Ill.   Mrs. Enos S. Yoder

... some men had a real crow shooting bee the two last Saturday nights, near Norwich, Kans., 15 miles northwest of here in a Catalpa Grove about 400 yards wide and ¾ mile long. They claim they shot 5,000 crows. There is no bounty on the crow, so they put them all on one pile, 4 feet high and 12 feet long and burned them. The crows are plentiful. If they killed 5,000 they can kill 5,000 more before we miss them much. The Government should not allow us to raise so many crows.

Feb. 15, 1934   Conway Springs, Kans.   A Sun Flower

288

Hunting large game: The deer season opened last Thur., Sept. 20. Quite a few from this vicinity went to Eastern Oregon to hunt mule deer.

Oct. 4, 1934   Harrisonburg, Ore.   Mrs. Alvin Kropf

As has been the custom for sportsmen, a deer supper will be shared with the less fortunate hunters on Tuesday evening. [Served jointly by lucky ones, others attending will bring other dishes.]

Dec. 6, 1962   Montezuma, Ga.   Mrs. Enos W. Yoder

Many deer have been slaughtered since the season is open in this section. Also several bear in the mountains. One was shot by two boys, 14 and 16 years old. They fired 20 shots and 14 hit the bear before he dropped. He was coming for the boys. They must have been pretty brave.

Dec. 19, 1929   Johnstown, Pa.   Budget Readers

The season for deer hunting was closed on Wednesday, our hunters meeting with grand success, no less than seven of the finest specimens being captured by the nimrods of Belleville and vicinity....

Dec. 29, 1915   Belleville, Pa.   Rudy J. Kanagy

Yesterday morning a party of "Nimrods", all happy and gay, armed themselves with guns, jack knives, hoes, shovels, dogs and plenty of ammunition, with a pair of mules and a wagon, all started in pursuit of a coyote. They found a hole in the ground; hoes and shovels were soon applied and dogs were kept on the watch nearby, and what do you think they found - - the other end of the hole.

Oct. 25, 1906   Normanna, Texas   C. C. Schrock

A women was in the shop and said her husband was out hunting and pouring out a cup of coffee when some deer came running and one jumped right over him, upsetting his coffee.

Dec. 17, 1986   Winesburg, Ohio   David E. Miller

Panthers are said to be prowling about the woods three miles from here among the several camps. Everyone is anxious to get them, but they have not been captured.

Sept. 19, 1901   Jerden Falls, N. Y.   A Reader

Hunting small game: Our small game and water fowl season opens on Sat., Sept. 25, but poor me I probably won't be able to make it out to a duck blind the first morn. Maybe we will just kill a couple tame ones.

Sept. 29, 1976   Desboror, Ont.   Joe Stutzman

I could never figure why anyone would want to spend a lot of time and money on ammunition just to get a few cents worth of meat. Surely it would be cheaper to raise it or buy it. To me, the best kind of hunter is the one who goes without a gun to watch and appreciate the wildlife and things of nature. [The above followed an outburst over the disrespect of a hunter for shooting a heron at one of their nearby lakes.]
     Nov. 15, 1962   Aylmer, Ont.   David Wagler

To the Aylmer writer: People don't all have the same idea of what is sport. If he had lived on the Kansas prairie the jackrabbits would probably have made a hunter out of him. Also not all hunter's meat is so expensive. Son Mart left the house about half past 5 in the morning and by 8 o'clock he had an 8 point buck. Results were we had about 65 lbs. deer hamburgers, several messes of steak and some meat to boil. Time, two and one half hours, five dollars for license, 21 cents for shell. Not very expensive at present meat prices.
     Nov. 22, 1962   Centreville, Mich.   J. M. B.

Thus far 18 foxes have been killed in Adams Co., on which a $5 bounty was paid. The pelts bring about $5 or $6 apiece.
     Mar. 2, 1944   Monroe, Ind.   Sarah Schwartz

John K. and Jack went out hunting one night last week and caught three possums, skinned them and sold the meat to the colored people.
     Jan. 7, 1932   Sarasota, Fla.   Bill and Dutch

The young men of the Yoder community had a big rabbit chase Wednesday. One section was taken in at a time. The men were scattered with trucks. We went over seven sections. Some over 200 rabbits were shot. No coyotes were seen.
     Jan. 19, 1928   Yoder, Kans.   Mahlon Beachy

Jack rabbits are plentiful. M. J. Troyer, D. A. Miller, D. D. Borntrager and the writer's father killed 62 in 3 hours time last Wednesday, and the day before they killed 35 rabbits.
     Jan. 24, 1912   Bucklin, Kans.   Daniel & Jacob Borntrager

Threshing millet and hunting rabbits is the order of the day. Over 100 rabbits were caught around here the past week.
     Dec. 3, 1908   Nineveh, Ind.   Elmer S. Hochstetler

On the 6th inst. we had a rabbit hunt; there were 106 rabbits killed now boys in the east, beat that if you can.
     Dec. 18, 1902   Ransom, Kans.   John J. Lehman

Hunting, roundups and chases: The men in this community were having a fox chase Saturday. Had 3 foxes in the ring but they all escaped and they didn't get that panther either.
      Jan. 1, 1948   Millersburg, Ind.   Mrs. Ida Miller

The fox drive yesterday in this vicinity was a fair success, a big crowd had gathered, and 6 foxes were captured.
      Nov. 29, 1934   Middlefield, Ohio   E. M. Hochstetler

A week ago today a large group of men met in the Partridge community for a coyote round-up, but it turned out to be more of a Jackrabbit hunt. I guess there were between four and five hundred rabbits brought in.
      Feb. 6, 1947   Hutchinson, Kans.   David A. Hostetler

There was a coyote chase held on Thursday of last week, where they [had] 5 roundups and only saw 1 coyote and that one got out of the ring, and then the dogs got him. The lunch for the chasers was served at P. D. Borntragers.
      Jan. 24, 1935   Hutchinson, Kans.   Mrs. Sam R. Borntrager

Wednesday is to be a deer chase. This is the last one for the 1933 season as the season closes the 15th. They are expecting to have a big affair with about 40 dogs in the chase.
      Dec. 14, 1933   Moyock, N.C.   Mr. & Mrs. Will Overholt

People in this vicinity are doing chores, making firewood, chasing fox, and such like. We had our third fox chase on New Year's day, which resulted in capturing 2 live fox. The foxes were sold at the pole before the people departed. One brought $22.50 and the other $25, the proceeds of which is to be used for lunch at the roundup, and the balance goes to the Red Cross. There are two more fox chases planned, one on Saturday, Jan. 5, and the next one on Jan. 12.
      Jan. 10, 1924   Middlefield, Ohio   E. M. Hochstetler

A great wolf hunt took place here last Tuesday. About 340 men in the ring, but no wolf in the round up. There were a few in the ring, but they didn't watch the line, and consequently they broke the ring.
      March 16, 1893   Waystaff, Kans.   U. J. Miller

There was another war on coyotes and rabbits on Jan. 11th. 275 men gathered together and divided into four sides. Each side took two miles and that way took four square miles, everybody walked toward the center and you ought to have seen the rabbits run and heard the discharge of the guns when they came together. We rounded up four times and the result was two coyotes and more rabbits than we wanted to carry.

> Jan. 25, 1906   Haven, Kans.   C. V. Yoder

There was a wolf chase on Monday which closed up in the neighborhood of Dan Harshberger's. About 200 men were present but no wolf was caught.

> Feb. 14, 1912   Garden City, Mo.   Mrs. John L. Zook

Pests: . . . I hear that Noah A. Keim and Wm Keim of Mt. Hope have purchased Hi-powered rifles and are going to do some executing on crows and ground hogs this summer, and I wish them luck.

> Mar. 19 1931   Millersburg, Ohio   A Budget Reader

[Mt. Hope Rat Hunt. J. E. Schlabach's "side" and Miller's "side" were competing. Miller's side had 1400 counts. Schlabach's group had 5549 counts and was served an oyster supper by Miller's side.

Category	Points per animal	Total points
Hawks and owls	40	400 counts
Sparrows	1515	3030 counts
Rats	456	1368 counts
Mice	751	751 counts

> Jan. 14, 1892   Local news item

[A news item reported a pest hunt at Bunker Hill. Two teams of 19 single men vs 19 married men competed for one week, Monday through Saturday. Points were given for killing sparrows, rats, mice and starlings. The point breakdown was as follows:

	rats	mice	starlings	sparrows
Married men	894	91	3	5103
Single men	887	195	4	3431

Married men's total was 14,779 points.

Single men's total was 11,508 points.

The losers served an oyster supper to the victors. The names of the participants were included.]

> Nov. 17, 1938

Reptiles: A 55 inch Blue Racer snake was killed by Sylvan Sprunger 2 miles north of Berne last week. It was clumsy but the temperature was warm enough to enable it to come from its winter hibernation to bask in the warm sun.

> March 2, 1944   Monroe, Ind.   Sarah Schwartz

Bill Hochstetler is quite a snake and alligator catcher. In the past two weeks he has caught two 6 ft. cotton-mouth moccasins, one rattler, two 4 ft. alligators and about 5 lbs. frog legs.

> May 21, 1936   Sarasota, Fla.   Mrs. Bob R. Miller

Andy Z. and a number of other boys went out the other day and caught a big rattle snake. It was six feet long and they skinned it dried the hide and it sure looks nice.

> Jan. 7, 1932   Sarasota, Fla.   Bill and Dutch

Last week Erwin Yoder, Henry and Bob Miller and the writer went turtle hunting on the Miahka River. We returned with 16 turtles, the largest one weighing 20 pounds.

> Jan. 21, 1932   Sarasota, Fla.   Frank Overholt

Alligator hunting is a great sport here on a dark night, with a lantern to shine the alligator's eyes, so that the gators cannot see to run away; in this way a person can go right up to them and shoot them.

> Nov. 2, 1899   Grandin, Fla   Henry Lehman

Hunting alligators is all the go at present; the big ones are caught for hide, while the young ones are sent north for pets or amusements. Anyone wanting a pair, send in your order.

> June 29, 1899   Iowa, La.   C. C. Schrock

Seaside: A crowd of young folks of this community spent a day at the ocean. They all report a pleasant time.

> Aug. 21, 1912   Fentress, Va.   SUNNY SOUTH

Last Thursday a number of our colony went to the beach to take advantage of the bathing season and all reported a good time.

> July 23, 1913   Norfolk, Va.   Iddo D. Yoder

Trapping: Trapping is all the go. Furs are shipped from here nearly every day.

> Dec. 21, 1899   Iowa, La.   C. C. Schrock

Travel: Misses Katie Kurtz and Leah Yoder made a pleasure trip to Barberton and Akron on Thursday.

> July 20, 1899   Smithville, Ohio   Lucy A. Yoder

About 60 persons from this place enjoyed the excursion to Washington D.C. on the 13th, 80 cts. for round trip, a distance of 50 miles.

> July 20, 1899   Midland, Va.   Mrs. S. S. Beachy

Weekend: Others vacationing over the weekend include.... [One of the early uses of the term "weekend".]

> June 10, 1954   Hartville, Ohio   No name

Winter: The young people had quite a time coasting Saturday night here by our place. It was an ideal night.

Jan. 22, 1925   Fairview, Mich.   Mrs. M. S. Zook

The young people are having fine sport coasting these days.

Feb. 16, 1928   Fairview, Mich.   Mrs. M. S. Zook

The young folks are taking advantage of the ice nowadays and skating parties are the order of the day.

Mar. 13, 1912   Minot, N. D.   Two readers

An Amish meetinghouse and horsebarn near Springs, Pennsylvania.

Records and the Unusual 40

The title accurately describes the subjects of the excerpts in this chapter. The items were not checked against *Guinness Book of World Records*. The scribes were taken at their written word, even though a few accounts might seem to be marginal and close to the "tall story" category.

Farm animals: I don't want to "blow", but as Yankeedom is a place where milk and cheese flow, I will give the number of pounds of milk that one cow gave during the month of May. A cow belonging to J. S. Ford gave 2,057 lbs. of milk, giving as high as 71½ lbs. in one day.

June 19, 1902   Burton, Ohio   R. J. Byler

Seen an item written June the 29 from Mattawana Pa., stating that David Allgyers have in their possession a Rhode Island Red hen that lays four eggs a day. I wish someone would give more information about it to the Budget. We also have Rhode Island Red hens but none to lay 4 eggs a day and I would like to get some of that laying strain.

June 29, 1922   Shipshewana, Ind.   D. J. Glick

A Rhode Island Red hen belonging to Mr. Solomon Schlabach layed an egg measuring 6¾ X 8³/₄ and upon breaking the shell another hard shell was found on the inside.

Feb. 7, 1924   Oakland, Md.   E. B.

A veal calf, seven weeks old, purchased by Clint Porter, meat dealer in this place, from Archie Plank, that weighed 210 pounds when butchered last Wednesday afternoon, was found to have two full sized hearts. The hearts were exactly alike in every respect and connected so that each performed the same function.

June 24, 1926   West Liberty, Ohio   Maude E. Peachey

Field crops: [In a local potato picking contest, according to the scribe, in the Conestoga "section", four pickers picked more than 2000 bushels. The previous record had been held by Norman King at 563 baskets. The baskets held ½ bushel, but the exact number of hours in which the picking was done was not given. The name of the runner-up was not given.]

Sara, daughter of Henry F. Stoltzfus, picked 631 baskets.
Stephen R's daughter _____, picked 630 baskets.

    Oct. 31, 1940   Lancaster County Briefs   Jonathan B. Fisher

[The four best records of corn cutting were given by a scribe. Each of the four was given a peck of choice seed corn.]

Levi T. Weaver of Millersburg, Oh, 175 shocks 8 X 8 with 3 stalks to a hill and he also made the tie hills.

Christ F. Beiler, Gap, Pa. 450 shocks with 2 stalks to a hill, 6 X 6.

Mose K. Blank, Gap, Pa. 400 shocks with 2 stalks to a hill, 6 X 6.

Levi J. Raber, Millersburg, Oh. 250 shocks, 7 X 8, 2 stalks per hill.

    Jan. 31, 1946   Millersburg, Oho   C. S. Miller

Husking of 25 acres of corn in 2 hours. 135 men and 31 wagons. It was for Milo D. Hochstetler, a polio victim.

    Nov. 17, 1949   Nappanee, Ind.   No name

It is said by truthful Amish men that were there this summer since thrashing, that one man thrashed 346 bushels of oats from three acres. I have not heard whether there were any better yields than that. [He was writing about the Midland, Mich. community.]

    Sept. 23, 1909   Topeka, Ind.   J. M. Bontrager

The writer did his first threshing for 1910 last Thursday, at Jacob Albrights. Who can beat that for early threshing?

    Jan. 25, 1910   Brunner, Ont.   E. Nafziger

Some potatoes have been dug already and are a heavy crop. A few potatoes that I measured were 15 to 18 inches in circumference, one way, and 12 to 14 the other.

    Oct. 4, 1900   Gadshill, Ont.   Jacob Iutzi

Sam Byler found an ear . . . which had 20 rows of kernels and 72 kernels in a row. [Found in Moyock, N.C.]

    Oct. 22, 1925   Norfolk, Va.   J. K. Fisher

Garden plants: Talking about string beans, today we had our first mess of so called yard long beans. "Yes that's how long some get," we had some measured 42" already. And they aren't too old for good at that length either.

Sept. 22, 1976   Leola, Pa.   Dorothy D. Stoltzfus

John J. Bontrager and wife, while visiting in Kansas, saw and helped measure a monstrous watermelon stalk, or rather the root, above the surface of the soil by actual measure, measured 10 inches in circumference, from which grew nine vines, of which one was 1½ inches in diameter. By actual count there were 43 eatable melons on these nine vines, with about as many smaller ones. This single stalk covered a space of ten rods square.

Dec. 15, 1904   Middlebury, Ind.   M. G. Stoltzfus

[A mangal weighing more than 24 lbs. and a carrot 3' 10" long were reported by an Ontario scribe.]

Nov. 29, 1900   Brunner, Ont.   Ella Nafziger

[A cabbage head weighing 14 lbs. and 3' and 11" inches in circumference was reported.]

Nov. 15, 1900   Kenmare, N. D.   D. M. Troyer

The writer has a radish in her garden that measures 26 inches in circumference and is still growing.

Oct. 4, 1900   White Cloud, Mich.   Fannie & Ella Kauffman

[A sweet potato of 12 lbs. actual weight was reported from La.]

Jan. 8, 1903   Iowa, La.   J. M. Shwartzendruber

Trees: The writer has a peach tree 20 ft. high and 36 ft. wide, when not loaded with peaches. Where is the peach tree that will beat that?

Oct. 4, 1900   Berlin, Ohio   S. Summy

Crows: I will give you a "believe it or not" crow story. At Raga, Kansas, about 20 miles from here, is a Catalpa grove crow roost. Under the direction of the game warden they loaded 410 booms of dynamite and 6 pounds of steel shot and wired and hung them on the trees. Then they touched it off by electricity. They have estimated that they killed over 100,000 crows.

Mar. 23, 1944   Harper, Kans.   H. E. Hostetler

Sausage: Noticed in the last issue about a sausage that was 56 ft. 6 in. long. We thought this could hardly be beat but the other day we learned that I. J. Hershberger, of near this place, beat the record by 23 ft. 6 in., making a sausage 80 ft. long. It required 32 quarts of meat to fill the casine [sic] and the sausage weighed 59 pounds, all from one hog.

Dec. 24, 1908   Burton, Ohio   Levi Schmucker

This chapter will give the reader an opportunity to follow some activities by seasons. These activities could very well have been included in other sections, but this arrangement permits an imaginary seasonal trip without interruption. Please remember to observe the date and the location in order to get the greatest value and effect from your reading. The seasons will be taken in natural order rather than alphabetically.

Spring: Spring is here with all its sweetness.
May 7, 1931   Fort Wayne, Ind.   Savilla

Work among the men is steaming tobacco beds and plowing when the weather permits. Women folks are busy cleaning house and tending baby chicks.
April 13, 1933   Ronks, Pa.   Lancaster Co. Bunch

The work among the women is moving into the summer kitchens and cleaning house.
June 4, 1925   Applecreek, Ohio   A Reader

Sales are the order of the day now, as one or more take place every day.
Mar. 17, 1920   Bird-in-Hand, Pa.   Annie M. Newhauser

The work among the women folks is making garden and cleaning house and taking care of little chicks.
May 19, 1920   Shipshewana, Ind.   Barb and Amelia Bontrager

Planting peppermint and sowing oats is the work of the men, and cleaning house and making garden for the women.
April 26, 1916   Topeka, Ind.   Laura E. Kauffman Yoder

Farmers were busy getting their wood buzzed last week.
Mar. 21, 1917   Morocco, Ind.   Fannie F. Helmuth

Cleaning house is the main subject talked about by the women everywhere.
May 1, 1912   Goshen, Ind.   J. E. Smucker

Working on the road is the order of the day among the farmers.
June 12, 1912   New Wilmington, Pa.   Jonathan D. Byler

Cultivating is the order of the day among the farmers, while women are busy cultivating gardens and cleaning house.
    May 27, 1914   Thomas, Okla.   E. J. Miller

Boiling syrup and attending sales is the order of the day.
    Mar. 29, 1910   New Hamburg, Ont.   Cor.

Ben Weaver was out one day after his mail box, which the water took about 4 miles down the creek.
    April 7, 1904   Nineveh, Ind.   Martha D. Stutzman

Breaking sod and going to timber after fence posts is the order of the day among farmers.
    Mar. 24, 1904   Calhan, Colo.   Mrs A. F. Yoder

Trimming hedge and getting ready for field work is the order of the day.
    Mar. 16, 1905   Gridley, Ill.   Joseph Yoder

Slashing brush is the order of the day.
    Apr. 24, 1902   Macksburg, Ore.   A. N. Mitchel

Sugar making and taffy pulling is the order of the day.
    Mar. 27, 1902   Goshen, Ind.   Two Sisters

Cutting thistles in the beet field and blocking beets is the work of some people now.
    June 7, 1934   Prattville, Mich.   Mrs. A. D. Miller

Summer: Corn is about all planted, and cultivating is the order of the day.
    June 25, 1903   Wellman, Iowa   S. D. Guengerich

The young folks are sewing and planting garden and taking care of chicks.
    June 30, 1927   Conneaut Lake, Pa.   A Reader

Picking huckleberries is the order of the day, which are very plentiful this year, but other fruit is very scarce.
    July 16, 1903   Middlebury, Ind.   Ira L. & Annie A. Schrock

Working on the road is the go now and is needed also cleaning and weeding truck.
    June 24, 1914   Mio, Mich.   M. S. Zook

Work among the women folks is cooking for threshers and planting their early fall gardens and taking their matured vegetables in store for winter use.
    Aug. 8, 1935   Sullivan, Ill.   Mrs. Chris. Helmuth

Women folks are taking care of gardens and cooking for the harvesters.
    June 30, 1932   Hutchinson, Kans.   Just Me

There was a thrasher's meeting at Menno S. Eichers last night. We enjoyed ice cream and what goes with it.

July 27, 1977   Seymour, Mo.   Mr. & Mrs. Mahlon Schwartz

Cleaning garden and picking strawberries is the order of the day among the women folks. Cultivating corn and making hay is the order of the day among the men.

July 2, 1919   Centerville, Mich.   Mrs. Lizzie D. Bontrager

Threshing, suckering and cutting tobacco and digging potatoes is the work among the men, while the women are sewing and quilting. . . .

Sept. 1, 1921   Gordonville, Pa.   Sylvia Stoltzfus

Hoeing garden and canning fruit is the work among the busy women.

June 16, 1915   Hydro, Okla.   Miss Malinda Swartzentruber

Filling silos is the order of the day among a good many farmers.

Aug. 30, 1916   Halstead, Kans.   A. A. Zook

Filling silos, cutting corn, thrashing, boiling apple butter, and canning is the order of the day.

Sept. 20, 1916   Mattawana, Pa.   Two Readers

The waters of the old swimming hole in the Conestoga in Hartz meadow are being troubled every evening by crowds of boys from the whole neighborhood as it has been every summer for more than 50 years.

Aug. 1, 1917   Elverson, Pa.   Elsie Stoltzfus

Last Tuesday about 30 people of our neighborhood went huckleberry picking, but did not have very good success in the forenoon, but we made up for it in the afternoon.

Aug. 2, 1911   West Branch, Mich.   Katie Miller
                                         Nancy and Katie Jantzi

Well digging seems to be the order of the day among some of the farmers.

Aug. 2, 1911   Latour, Mo.   Sarah E. Hershberger

Threshing timothy is the order of the day which is a fair crop.

Aug. 14, 1912   Mt. Hope, Ohio   S. E. T.

Plowing for wheat is the order of the day among farmers.

Aug. 28, 1912   Thomas, Ind.   Noah M. Mast

Stilling peppermint is all the go in this neighborhood.

Aug. 19, 1914   Honeywell, Ind.   Noah S. Yoder

Women folks are busy drying and putting up peaches.

Aug. 19, 1914   Garnett, Kans.   Mrs. S. S. Beachy

Picking and canning huckleberries is at hand. Huckleberries are quite plentiful, although there are not as many as last year. I had about three bushels to can.

Aug. 5, 1909   Fairview, Mich.   Mrs. M. S. Zook

Garden truck is doing well; have early cabbage large enough for use; also beets, etc.

July 1, 1910   Garden City, Mo.   Mary A. Gingerich

Huckleberries are plenty; on Tuesday morning the K.V.R.R. train had 49 passengers, enroute to the huckleberry land.

Aug. 9, 1906   Belleville, Pa.   M. P. Zook

Broomcorn cutting is the order of the day. The fields are spotted with broomcorn "Bums."

Aug. 28, 1902   Arthur, Ill.   Maggie Kohli

Fall: Weather is moderate, but warmer than cold, and very dry. Crops are suffering for want of moisture. Flies, bugs, Grasshoppers and insects of all kinds are plentiful.

Sept. 26, 1935   Hutchinson, Kans.   C. C. Schrock

Flies seem to be a regular pest since the cool and wet weather....

Sept. 27, 1934   Jessup, Iowa   Mrs. Ida Gingerich

Livestock is all housed up for the winter now, and farmers have pretty well settled down to the winter job of doing chores, keeping the fire going, and attending the livestock sales.

Nov. 26, 1959   Chesley, Ont.   Sam Yoder

Farmers are busy making soybean hay and some have started to husk corn.

Oct. 6, 1932   Fentress, Va.   S. D. Kurtz

The work among the men is husking corn. They appreciate the women very much in the corn fields. Some are husking with the machines.

Nov. 10, 1932   Applecreek, Ohio   A Reader

Cane stripping is here too. Several are planning on having sorghum made to take the place of sugar.

Oct. 13, 1942   Gap, Pa.   John F. Glick

Men folks are busy cutting corn and cleaning ditches.

Oct. 5, 1933   Fort Wayne, Ind.   Rosa Chupp

The work among the men folks is filling silo while some are busy snapping cotton.

Oct. 15, 1925   Weatherford, Okla.   Mrs. Geo. Yoder

The large department store is selling cheap at present. A. A. Schrock and wife and the scribe were in town today and got a supply of winter sewing.

Sept. 30, 1901   Shelbyville, Ill.   Laura E. Kaufman

The work among the men folks is sowing wheat, husking corn, and topping kaffir corn. The work among the women is doing the fall sewing.

Nov. 5, 1925   Dodge City, Kans.   Elizabeth A. Yoder

Some women are cleaning house, while others are boiling apple butter.

Oct. 12, 1922   Rhodes, Mich.   Mrs. T. J. Bontrager

Butchering is going on about everywhere.

Dec. 14, 1922   Charm, Ohio   Mary Bontrager

Buying and selling farms seems to be the order of the season.

Oct. 23, 1918   Atglen, Pa.   Mary E. Stoltzfus

Cutting corn is the order among the men folks and moving in their winter houses is at hand for the women.

Oct. 13, 1915   Plain City, Ohio   A Reader

Preparing for weddings and attending them is taking up considerable of the time of some people some being burdened with invitations to three weddings in one day.

Dec. 15, 1915   Bird-in-Hand, Pa.   John H. Kauffman

Putting up cowpeas and digging potatoes is the order of the day among some of the neighbors.

Oct. 25, 1911   Garnett, Kans.   Mrs. Moses Hershberger

Picking winter apples making cider and boiling apple butter is the order of the day.

Oct. 15, 1908   Newton, Kans.   J. R. Miller

Filling silos and cutting corn is the order of the day....

Sept. 23, 1909   Garden City, Mo.   Henry J. King

Making apple butter and hulling clover is the order of the day.

Sept. 22, 1904   Kokomo, Ind.   G. W. North

Butchering and making brodewarst for visitors is the order of the day among the farmers.

Dec. 5, 1901   Charm, Ohio   Menno J. Mast

Winter: Hauling saw logs and cutting firewood is the work at present.

Feb. 15, 1900   Archbold, Ohio   A. A. Yoder

302

Yesterday the scribe helped to butcher . . . and cleaned all the casings for 5 hogs.

Feb. 14, 1912   Shelbyville, Ill.   Laura E. Kauffman

Work among most of this Amish colony here is getting ready for the market.

Jan. 31, 1924   Norfolk, Va.   Mrs. E. J. Troyer

Shoveling snow and feeding the stove is the order of the day.

Feb. 5, 1925   Elk Lick, Pa.   Annie M. Bender

Buzzing wood is the order of the day among the farmers.

Jan. 8, 1925   Westover, Md.   Mrs. Ira M. Zook

Farmers are busy hauling logs, putting up ice and attending sales which are getting quite numerous.

Feb. 21, 1924   Burton, Ohio   No name

People are busy butchering, making candy and getting ready for Christmas.

Dec. 22, 1927   Dublin, Ohio   H. L. Mast

The work among the women is sewing and quilting and also keeping the household things straight, while the men are butchering, making wood and doing chores.

Mar. 8, 1928   Uniontown, Ohio   Isaac and Elsie Lapp

The work among the men folks is keeping the stoves warm while the women are busy sewing.

Dec. 12, 1929   Kidron, Ohio   Chums

The work among the men folks is sawing logs and buzzing wood.

Feb. 3, 1921   Shipshewana, Ind.   Anna Weirich & Lydia Miller

Choring and getting firewood and going to town is the work among the men folks.

Feb. 16, 1922   Midland, Mich.   Mrs. A. D. Miller

What the women folks are working in Monterey? They are shoveling coal and ashes a good part of the time these cold days.

Jan. 23, 1918   Bird-in-Hand, Pa.   Annie M. Newhauser

This evening I moved my bed from one corner of the room in the room in the middle of the room and hung some quilts at the windows as I am short of firewood and we have to look our for winter this time of year.

Dec. 1, 1915   Meyersdale, Pa.   S. S. Summy

Staying in the house and making fire is the order of the day.

Jan. 24, 1912   Shipshewana, Ind.   Two Budget Readers

Shredding corn, cutting hedge, sawing wood and attending public sale is the order of the day among the farmers at present.

Feb. 21, 1912   Garnett, Kans.   Enos D. Yoder

Putting up ice is the order of the day among the farmers.

Jan. 21, 1909   Lowville, N.Y.   Jacob G. Stoltzfus

Look out for some spotza before long as Eli Kauffman bought a supply of buckets yesterday at Middlebury to catch the sweets as they run from the trees.

Mar. 5, 1908   Shipshewana, Ind.   B. E. Miller

Butchering is the order of the day. The writer's folks butchered three hogs yesterday. Today they are killing four for Andy Zehr. Tomorrow they will be at Work for C. S. Zehr and next day for F. E. Eicher; so you see the people in Iowa still have plenty to eat.

Mar. 16, 1905   Manson, Iowa   Mrs. J. C. Zehr

I expect the young folks have to do without ice cream next summer, as there has no ice been put up yet this winter.

Feb. 20, 1896   Garden City, Mo.   E. K. Zook

The teaming on the Saginaw Bay was very handy this winter; the teamsters did not need to be afraid of breaking through the ice, because it was 25 to 26 inches thick. Ice cutting was hard work by hand this year.

Mar. 13, 1902   Elkton, Mich.   H. E. P.

Butchering and stripping tobacco is the order of the day.

Feb. 1, 1900   Gordonville, Pa.   Martha Kauffman

Eating cornbread and brodewarst is the order of the day.

Feb. 27, 1902   Beemer, Neb.   Jacob Iutzi

Putting up ice and attending sales is the work among the farmers. Sewing and patching is the work of the women.

Mar. 15, 1916   Shipshewana, Ind.   Guess Who

Butchering and braking (sic) ponies is the order of the day.

Jan. 14, 1914   McMinnville, Or.   TWO SISTERS

Moving will soon be the order of the day.

Feb. 18, 1914   Barrs Mills, Ohio   Local

Some of our friends may wonder what people are doing here. Cutting saw logs, cord wood, kiln wood and cedar posts and hauling same is the order of the day.

Jan. 7, 1909   Central Lake, Mich.   Mrs. Susan Weirich

Social Affairs   42

Social affairs is a broad term including many activities. The social affairs named in this chapter are not intended to cover the intermingling and visiting resulting from formal church services, weddings or funerals. Those will be dealt with elsewhere. By social affairs is meant the gathering of small or large groups for singings, for picnics, parties and eating together. It includes some designed to be of help to persons during the time in which the socializing takes place. Travel is included in social affairs, whether short trips of one day or for extended periods of time.

The subheadings are not in alphabetical order in this chapter. The arrangement used permits better clustering of related activities.

Singings: The "singing" was probably the most common social and religious function among the young people, socially. They were generally held on Sunday evenings. Some were held during the week if there were visitors or there was some other special occasion, such as a farewell. The Old Order Amish young people still have their Sunday evening singings. The Beachy Amish Sunday evening services are changing from the "singing" to topics, preaching, informational programs and various forms of nurture. Prior to 1930 singings were common among Amish Mennonites and Mennonites as the Garden City and Waynesboro entries below show. These same groups were the ones which referred to some singings as social singings. The Amish did not so name them. A singing among the Amish might be identified in one of three ways: a young folk's singing, an old folk's singing, or a combination young and old folk's singing. Whether singings were large or small depended more on the size of the Amish community than on other factors such as weather. There have been some communities where the singings were held biweekly, rather than weekly.

> Last night we attended the singing. (Mill Creek at Christ Millers) It is estimated that there were about 325 young folks there.
> Jan. 14, 1932   Bird-in-Hand, Pa.   Roman Schmucker

The young folks had their social singing here last Friday evening, which they have every two weeks. There were 62 present. They sang very good, and everybody seemed to enjoy themselves.

Oct. 20, 1932   Garden City, Mo.   Mrs. Anna Yoder

Five social singings took place last month and were all well attended.

Oct. 11, 1916   Waynesboro, Va.   Tillie

There were three singings last Sunday night; at Joe G. Gingerich's, Joe Gunden's and Geo P. Miller's, and all were well-attended.

Aug. 29, 1907   Kalona, Iowa   Katie

Crowd, Bunch and Doings: Since the Amish did not have formal "socials" as did the Amish Mennonites or Mennonites, they needed some term other than social to describe gatherings other than their singings. It appears that "crowd" was such a word. Another word was "party" but used in a wholesome way and not with the modern perversion of associating it with alcoholic beverages and sexual misconduct. The use of "doings" and "bunch" was also common.

The young folks had a crowd on Friday evening. They expect a ball game Easter Monday, if the weather is favorable.

Mar. 31, 1932   Plain City, Ohio   Madison Bums

There was a crowd at George L. Yoders last Sunday.

Mar. 10, 1921   Hartville, Ohio   Two Chums

A bunch of young folks from Wellesley spent Sunday at Elora Rocks.

July 26, 1923   Brunner, Ontario   Cor.

There was a doings held at Pre. Daniel J. Millers.

June 15, 1925   Hartville, Ohio   Miss Fanny Yoder

A surprise party was held in honor of brother Alvin's 22nd birthday. Oysters were served to 48 that were present. Seventeen of those present stayed overnight.

Jan. 25, 1934   Sugarcreek, Ohio   Sarah Mae Miller

There is to be a party at Emanuel Hochstetlers Tuesday evening. A few weeks ago there was a well attended party at Leffy Millers. We sure had a swell time.

Jan. 14, 1932   Uniontown, Ohio   A Budget Reader

The young folks are having quite a few parties, lately.

Feb. 17, 1921   Burton, Ohio   A Reader

Varieties of Activities: The following excerpts give some additional evidence of the wide variety of activities engaged in by the young people.

> The young folks in the three churches exchanged names on Christmas day. Last Sunday evening after the singing the presents were exchanged which caused a lot of fun. I guess there were 76 names.
>
> Jan. 18, 1934   Kalona, Iowa   (No name)

> A pound supper was given at Willie Kauffman's last Tuesday evening.... About 30 were present....
>
> Mar. 1, 1906   Wayland, Iowa   Mrs. Mattie Roth

> A box supper was given at the Mulberry schoolhouse last Friday night; the proceeds amounted to a little over $14.00.
>
> Nov. 23, 1899   Weatherford, Okla.   A. B. Miller

> Box socials are all the go now.
>
> Nov. 6, 1912   Topeka, Ind.   Alvin E. Yoder

> The young people had a pound supper and Valentine box social at Dan Wittmers Saturday evening and was well attended.
>
> Feb. 26, 1925   Hartville, Ohio   David Detweiler / Herman Stoll

> Sam K. Stoltzfus had an ice-cream supper for employees and some friends on Thursday evening; also a fine lot of fire works.
>
> July 11, 1901   Gordonville, Pa.   John H. Kauffman

> The young folks enjoyed the Belgian hare supper at Eli Nislys last Sunday evening.
>
> Sept. 25, 1902   Hutchinson, Kans.   Eli Helmuth

> There is an oyster supper to be held at D. Hartzlers on Saturday evening.
>
> Nov. 9, 1899   Smithville, Ohio   Lucy Yoder

> Last night being Easter, the young folks had an egg-fry at Joe Lengachers and it was well attended.
>
> Mar. 31, 1932   New Haven, Ind.   Anna Zehr

> The ball game at Jacob Z. Kuepfers on Ascension Day was exceptionally well attended and enjoyed by all. There is to be another ball game at Joe Z. Kuepfers on Whit Monday.
>
> June 9, 1938   Milverton, Ontario   (No name)

> Upwards of half a hundred young Amishmen congregated at the home of Joel Stoltzfus a young farmer a short distance north of Honeybrook on Monday and enjoyed a day of real

sport. This all day event took place on the Talbot farm recently purchased by D. N. Glick and tenanted by Mr. Stoltzfus. The feature of the day was an interesting game of cornerball, in which all took an active part. The young men present represented Amish families from both the Pequea and Conestoga and those from the one valley vied with those of the other valley in the corner match ball. Those from the Conestoga Valley won the honors of the day. Every last man greatly enjoyed the sport. Mr. Stoltzfus gave his guests a sumptuous dinner. In the near future the Amish maidens also set apart a day for merriment.

April 18, 1917   Elverson, Pa.   Elsie Stoltzfus

The young folks had a ball game at John N. Yutzy's Monday afternoon.

May 31, 1923   Plain City, Ohio   Lizzie & Sadie Miller

There was a wiener roast at Fred and Amos's shack Thursday evening.

June 14, 1934   Hartville, Ohio   Just Me

The young folks went fishing on Ascension Day but did not catch very many fish as they were too wild.

May 27, 1926   Alma Detweiler & Mary Ann Yoder

A taffy pulling was held at the home of Fannie S. Beiler Friday night, and about 50 young folks were present. . . . Everybody enjoyed it.

Sept. 7, 1933   Ronks, Pa.   Katie Lapp

The young folks enjoyed a sugar stew at the home of C. K. Hostetler on Wednesday night.

Feb. 22, 1910   Denbeigh, Va.   Mrs. S. H. Glick

On Tuesday evening the Stranger Aid was held at Sam Rabers where they had a square dance, also had one at Mose Troyers on New Years eve.

Jan. 14, 1926   Charm, Ohio   Saloma & Sevilla Wengerd

Joint Activities: There were joint activities, involving both the young people and adults. Such activities were viewed by many as beneficial for both groups. The first excerpt reported an outdoor picnic.

Those who favor this church function think it is a means of getting our young people to associate together without becoming involved with worldly or questionable society, the older people having a watchful eye over them.

Aug. 18, 1921   North Lima, Ohio   Joseph Metzler

A basket dinner was served yesterday in Galen Yoder's pecan grove for the . . . strangers and our group. It was enjoyed by all.

July 29, 1954   Montezuma, Ga.   Mrs. Sol W. Yoder

The spelling at Dumb Hundred school house was attended to overflowing last Friday evening. C. C. Miller was the champion speller.

Jan. 30, 1902   Kalona, Iowa   Subscriber

Visiting / Entertaining: Without question, one of the most frequent activities was that of visiting, or from the standpoint of the hosts, entertaining. This was true within their immediate community as well as within the larger community. Some of the groups resulting from these gatherings were extremely large by the standards of the 1980's. It must be remembered that most of this entertaining took place within the confines of the dwelling houses, not some rented public buildings.

I guess I am getting in line with Enos Glick of Ind. I have butchered a beef and a pig last week, and now I am ready to wait on visitors.

Jan. 24, 1935   Middlefield, Ohio   E. M. Hochstetler

About thirty young people took dinner at Manasses Brenneman's, Sunday.

May 10, 1910   Kalona, Iowa   Maggie Miller

About twenty guests took dinner at the home of Mrs. L. E. Kauffman last Wednesday.

Jan. 14, 1909   Topeka, Ind.   Mary E. Riehl

Pearl Stutzman and a number of others accompanied Edith Mast home after church last Sunday. The reason they went they knew they would get chicken for dinner.

Dec. 3, 1908   Fairview, Mich.   Mrs. M. S. Zook

Young roosters taste pretty good and we ate quite a few. Anybody is welcome to come and help us eat them.

July 27, 1939   Nappanee, Ind.   Lizzie Ann Borkholder

Noah E. Yoders of Norfolk had 34 guests for dinner on Sunday.

Dec. 24, 1931   Belleville, Pa.   S. D. Peachey

There were forty-seven persons gathered at Emanuel C. Yoder's last Saturday evening in honor of Mrs. Menno Zook. Oysters were served and a jolly good time was had.

Nov. 23, 1899   Topeka, Ind.   J. E. K.

During this past year there were 246 different visitors at Eli Borkholder's, and lots of them were there several times.
Jan. 9, 1902 Nappanee, Ind. Mary E. Berkholder
          Amanda W. Yoder

About 49 people ate dinner at Eli Millers on Thanksgiving, mostly young folks. There was also a well attended singing at the same place in the evening.
Dec. 1, 1932 Lynnhaven, Va. Jemimmia Yoder

The Indiana Jolly Bunch took supper Saturday evening, at the F. R. Schrock home.
Oct. 13, 1932 Plain City, Ohio Andrew J. Yoder

I learned through a reliable source that strangers from three states were seen in our little community last week, none of whom ventured back in the sticks far enough for us to get a glimpse of them.
Sept. 18, 1952 Enon Valley, Pa. Jacob Z. Yoder

The visiting season is coming to a close and the Yankee people will all be gone ere long.
Mar. 1, 1900 Baden, Ontario Jacob Iutzi

Adult Activities: The adults were not left without their own types of activities, as can be seen in the comments above about visiting. There were also singings and social gatherings for the old folks.

There was a well attended young and old folks singing at Peter J. Gingerichs last Sunday evening.
Mar. 29, 1945 Ethridge, Tenn. Amanda M. Yoder

The sewing for old folks is to be next Wed. Nov. 16 at the writer's place, and is also there for the young folks in the evening.
Nov. 10, 1955 Hartville, Ohio Nancy Coblentz

An old folks singing was held at the writer's home on Saturday evening. They did not happen to get up a big crowd like the young folks sometimes do, but judging by the late hour at which they retired it must have been enjoyed by all. After singing they were supplied with such things as apples, cakes and cider to supply the wants of the inner man.
Feb. 8, 1900 Gordonville, Pa. John H. Kauffman

A good many elderly folks spent the evening at Ben Yoders on Sunday.
July 7, 1927 Bird-in-Hand, Pa. Aaron L. Beiler

There was an old singing at Dave Plank's last night, but

wasn't very well attended on account of the rain.
Aug. 31, 1933   Garnet, Kans.   Mrs. Barbara Beachy

The old man singing was held on Wednesday evening at Enos Yoders. There were only 15 there, as the weather was so bad.
Jan. 24, 1935   Sugarcreek, Ohio   No name

An "old man" singing was held at Mahlon J. Hochstetlers....
Jan. 18, 1945   Millersburg, Ohio   No name

There was an old folk's singing held February 12 at the Joe S. Bontrager home in honor of the above named. There were 131 present. We were glad to have them all.
Mar. 1, 1934   Haven, Kans.   Miss Betz S. Bontrager

Outings and Transportation: Some of the places and events of interest took them beyond the confines of their own communities. Others were caused by the "outside" being brought into their community very suddenly. The four concluding excerpts give some insight into the forms of transportation used other than buggies and automobiles.

Some of the young folks were to the Lynnhaven River where 26 Negro young folks were baptized.
Sept. 28, 1933   Norfolk, Va.   Jemimia Yoder

This afternoon a number of our people attended the Methodist baptizing services at the Kaskaskia river, there were twenty-nine immersed.
June 10, 1914   Shelbyville, Ill.   Nettie M. Hostetler

The main topics of conversation at present are the weather, baseball, and air mail flyers. One came down about 2 miles west of Troy lately on account of fog and stayed till the next morning.
Oct. 22, 1925   Burton, Ohio   Levi Miller

There was a crowd at Mony Daves on Sunday, but was not so well attended on account of two airplanes that came down Saturday evening, and nearly everybody anxious to see them.
June 9, 1932   Fredericksburg, Ohio   Ida Miller

A wagon load of young people enjoyed ice cream and melons at the writer's home Saturday evening.
Aug. 20, 1908   Denbeigh, Va.   Mrs. S. H. Glick

A sled load of young folks spent Sunday evening at S. J. Swartzendrubers.
Feb. 15, 1910   Pigeon, Mich.   S. Albrecht, Ed Gunden

311

There were a truck load of Indiana people up here at Wm. Hochstetler, there were 20 of them and there were some neighbors there, 52 in all, had 8 gallons of ice cream.
June 29, 1922   Centreville, Mich.   Cor.

On Tuesday evening . . . a party (of nine) took an enjoyable cart ride.
Aug. 23, 1906   Hearing, Va.   Sunny South

Mutual Assistance and Socializing: The kinds of activities which merged socializing with some form of aid or assistance were limited only by the ingenuity of the persons in the communities. The reader can sample the wide range of such activities from the following excerpts.

Thursday evening a bunch of young folks gathered at the home of Mary Fisher. She is making straw hats, so they helped her to strip the straw. After the straw was finished, lunch was served at about 11 oclock.
June 15, 1933   Ronks, Pa.   Katie Lapp

A rather unusual quilting was held at John Kings near Bird-in-Hand on Saturday in honor of their twin girls, Mary and Mattie. Five pair of twin girls were invited.
Aug. 5, 1954   Ronks, Pa.   Lydia F. Beiler

Joe Borntragers had an apple "snitzing" last Tuesday night, which was fairly well attended. All were treated with cakes, pies and watermelons after the "snitzing".
Sept. 8, 1932   Fairbank, Iowa   Miss Fanny Yoder

There was a wood chopping and a quilting at Andy Bylers on New Year's Day and also an oyster supper in the evening.
Jan. 14, 1926   Burton Station, Ohio   Susie N. Mast
                                            Amelia Stutzman

Last eve. a corn shocking was held at Johnny Millers for the young folks. Chris Schwartzs had a corn husking bee last week one eve. and we plan to have a wood ranking tomorrow eve.
Nov. 9, 1977   Norfolk, N.Y.   Eli Troyers

The husking party, which was held at Simon Zooks, of Earlville . . . was largely attended by young folks from Upper Pequea, Millcreek and Groffdale to the number of seventy. After husking three hundred and fifty shocks, they made for the house, where supper was ready for them and after supper they went to the barn and had a jolly time.
Nov. 12, 1903   New Holland, Pa.   Rufus K. Allyger

312

A lot of young folks gathered at Jacob Stoltzfus' on Wed. afternoon and husked his entire crop of 13 acres of corn. After supper was over they proceeded to the barn floor, where the time was spent in playing (or dancing as some call it) until a late hour.

Feb. 8, 1900   Gordonville, Pa.   John H. Kauffman

A tobacco stripping party was held at Ben Smokers on Wed. evening. About 250 lbs. of tobacco was sized and a lot of fun was had in the bargain. N. S. Beiler thought it was the best crowd he met in a long time.

Feb. 8, 1900   Gordonville, Pa.   John H. Kauffman

About 35 neighbors and friends attended the strawberry capping at E. S. Millers, Monday evening. Ice cream and cookies were served.

June 9, 1932   Princess Anne, Va.   Jemimia Yoder

One evening last week the young people had a "lathing party" at Henry Hertzlers. They report a good job, however some of the ladies who are not used to doing carpenter work had sore fingers the next day.

Nov. 15, 1906   Substitutes of Two Sisters

Quite a number of our young girls attended a rag bee at Jr. Shrags, Saturday afternoon. The boys made their appearance in the evening and did ample justice to the good things.

Dec. 21, 1899   Baden, Ontario   Cor.

A "comfort tying" for the young folks was held at Alpha Peacheys....

Mar. 1, 1945   Norfolk, Va.   Henry M. Yoder

A seed potato cutting was held at Mahlon Weavers on Tuesday evening for the young folks.

Feb. 28, 1946   Norfolk, Va.   Henry M. Yoder

There is supposed to be an apple coring at Mosey Bontragers Wednesday evening, Sept. 2.

Sept. 3, 1936   Fairbanks, Iowa   Polly Gingerich

An apple and pear peeling was held at Melvin L. Yoders....

Sept. 13, 1945   Norfolk, Va.   Henry M. Yoder

A bean hulling was held at the home of Sylvanus Stoltzfus last Friday evening. The folks also shelled a lot of corn for mush after the beans were hulled. On account of the muddy roads some of the people had to be taken home in a machine. A few others were lost and found again by the aid of the flashlight.

Oct. 11, 1916   Elverson, Pa.   Elsie Stoltzfus

313

Outings Beyond The Community: Many outings of a day or two can be documented. Some of the more prominent ones found are represented in these excerpts.

The writer and Jonathan Fisher returned from the seashore last Saturday all safe and sound, for which we are thankful to the Giver of all good. We were well pleased with our trip and enjoyed ourselves very much, although the time passed too soon. It is a wonder that not more of our folks go to the seashore as it is a delightful place, but full of temptations for the unwary.
Aug. 22, 1901   Gordonville, Pa.   John H. Kauffman

About 16 of the young folks went to the coast this week for a few days.
Oct. 4, 1934   Harrisburg, Ore.   Mrs. Alvin Kropf

On Tuesday the following spent the day at Bowers Beach bathing and swimming. (Seven families were named)
July 12, 1934   Dover, Dela.   Mrs. Jacob M. Beachy

Quite a number of young folks spent Saturday in Nelson Ledges.
June 10, 1937   Burton, Ohio   Clara Slabaugh

Five of the boys went to the mountains on horse back last Sunday, for some western cowboy sport and think they got it.
Oct. 5, 1922   Glastone, N.M.   D. C. B.

The young people of this place intend to make a pleasure trip to Castle Rock next Monday.
April 7, 1904   Arnold, Kans.   Susanna Chupp

The writer and twelve more took a free train ride on Whit Monday to Friendsville, which is about sixteen miles along the railroad they all seemed to enjoy the trip. We went in the morning and till 5 oclock in the evening we were back to Crist Beitzel's and Mrs. Beitzel had a good supper ready for us till we came.
June 13, 1901   Bittinger, Md.   Sarah M. Schrock

On Whit Monday a party of fifteen of us took a drive of seven miles over a fine road, with grand scenery, to Mt. Carmel, an elevated point, from which a really noble view of the surrounding country can be obtained. We enjoyed our picnic dinner, singing and the view very much, and returned in the evening.
June 14, 1900   Aurora, W. Va.   M. J. and S. J. Miller

A sleighing party of about 20 young people went to Elam

Horsts on Monday evening, they took oysters and cake with them and had a good time, at least I think they had, for they did not get home till after 2 oclock.

Jan. 8, 1903   Wooster, Ohio   T. L. Miller

Longer trips: The short trips mentioned above consisted of only one part of the mobility and movement. The moving of families from one community to another will be clarified under the heading Mobility. The traveling mentioned here arises from social and recreational motivations. Some of the final excerpts reveal the responses of several scribes to what was considered to be the excesses of a few. The reader should be reminded that the small minority engaging in the excesses mentioned received more attention than the large majority who engaged in visiting in an acceptable fashion but without the publicity of those who misused the privilege and tradition.

Many of the boys around here have the Somerset fever at present. Six expect to leave for that county tomorrow, and a few more expect to go later. There are a few however that have recovered.

Feb. 19, 1903   Gordonville, Pa.   John H. Kauffman

Menno S. Zook and wife and Emanuel Peachey and wife of Allensville, Pa., arrived here last Wednesday to visit friends and relatives here a short time. The trip of about 120 miles was made in two days with 2 horses in a top buggy.

Nov. 22, 1934   Springs, Pa.   Nettie M. Yoder

The writer was visiting a little over three months in Geauga and Holmes counties, Ohio, and enjoyed it very well.

Dec. 26, 1901   Topeka, Ind.   Mattie E. Miller

It is estimated that about $560 were paid for car fare between this and Mifflin counties the past fall and this winter, by the Amish people, who went visiting.

Feb. 21, 1901   Gordonville, Pa.   John H. Kauffman

We returned home on Thursday evening from 2 weeks visit in Illinois and found the children all well, we thank God for his protecting care over us, we visited at 70 different homes and enjoyed our trip very much.

July 4, 1935   Kokomo, Ind.   Mrs. Jonas B. Beachy

We called on or visited with around 450 different families, attended church services about 55 times, were at 7 weddings and 7 funerals. (Gone for 6½ months)

Feb. 19, 1942   Thomas, Okla.   Mr. & Mrs. Joe Bontrager

On the 26th, J. B. Augsburger and I bought round trip
tourist tickets, good for about 9,000 miles.

    July 23, 1903   Salem, Ore.   Peter F. Burkholder

John D. Stoltzfuses arrived home ... from their 13,000 mile
trip to the West Coast and return via the southwest.

    Sept. 2, 1948   Lancaster County   Jonathan Fisher

I will say a few words of my 34,000 mile trip.

    Sept. 3, 1903   Milford, Neb.   John D. Eicher

Middlefield at the present time, as well as other towns, has
its boom; and as Geauga county has lots of cheap homes,
and good for speculation, it has a tendency to bring home-
seekers, visitors and curiosity seekers to this county, and
usually they stop at this place first, as the electric line
terminates there.

A word to the wise should be sufficient. The people are
always welcome, but should use a little judgment and bear
in mind that all going to one place and making their stopping
place in town is imposing upon a man's patience and good
will. It is no unusual occurrence for some of our Amish
brethren who live in town to serve from forty to fifty meals
per week, and give lodging to eight or ten at one time, while
their are many other open-hearted brethren living within
ten minutes walk from the station who would be glad to
have you come and share with them, thus relieving others
already over-crowded, which we think would make it more
pleasant for all.

We hope this article will not offend or keep anyone away,
nor be misconstrued, but take it in the right spirit, as it is
intended.

    Dec. 5, 1901   Middlefield, Ohio   AN EYE WITNESS

We are expecting some more western boys to visit through
here, as there are lots of letters awaiting them here.

    Jan. 16, 1902   Gordonville, Pa.   John H. Kauffman

The Yankees seem to be quite numerous over here, although
I have not seen very many yet.

    Dec. 26, 1901   Baden, Ontario   E. J. Gingerich

Nappanee was flooded with visitors during this past week.

    Oct. 26, 1899   Nappanee, Ind.   M. H. Hostetler

Ohio girls are getting fat, living off the Missouri people,
are they?

    Jan. 16, 1902   Round Prairie, Ohio   Ellen King

There are several young men from Canada and also from Indiana and a few of our boys at home in this neighborhood, going from place to place as if it were a privilege to entertain and feed numbers. Their jollity, hilarity, and levity of conversation would be less questionable if less stimulated. Their conduct in towns along the road and at public gatherings is such as to cast shadows on their characters. The influence for good by such church members must necessarily be of low order. I trust the boys will not take offense, but heed a friendly warning and conduct themselves as becomes young gentlemen.

Mar. 22, 1900   Kalona, Iowa   A Friend

An Amish minister's roll-top desk and study room.

The scribes formed the network of reporting news via the pages of THE BUDGET. The scribes were acquainted with numerous people in other communities. Since the correspondents submitted their news in the form of letters, they often included some personal responses to other scribes. These exchanges will be called social banter. The word banter means playful teasing or joking. Several instances of direct personal attack were found, but those will not be included under this section. Reference to the latter will be found in the chapter, "Editor and Scribes."

Animals: Did you ever hear an insect talking? One "spoke" to me in an orange tree this afternoon. Interpreted into the English language, a wasp said something on this order, "Please don't bump your hat against my house." And I was very respectful to her language.
April 5, 1962   Zellwood, Fla.   Dan E. Hershberger

Our doctor is quite a generous stork. He left triplets at a certain home north of town.
Mar. 24, 1920   Walnut Creek   Local news

Ben and John J. Byler were to New York State the first week of deer hunting there, but I guess they aren't quite smart enough for those New York deer, so now they want to try their luck on the dumb Pennsylvania deer the next few weeks.
Dec. 6, 1956   Fredonia, Pa.   A. J. Hershberger

To the Bowling Green scribes, we have heard you have had quite a bit of company through here, but didn't think it took an 18 room tourist house to take care of them all.
Feb. 2, 1950   Portland, Ind.   M. G.

To the Portland, Ind. scribe, that 18 room tourist home you mentioned is a tourist home for Martins (birds) only. We have been able to take care of all other tourists in the homes this far.
Feb. 9, 1950   Bowling Green, Mo.   No name

Eli N. Millers got 500 unexpected visitors Sunday morning. The mailman delivered them, and turned out to be Leghorn chicks.

April 18, 1935   Hutchinson, Kans.   No name

The Board of Alderman have served legal notice on Messrs Hog and Goat to leave the town by July 2nd, which I think is a grand move as they are roaming all over town and doing a lots of mischief. Mr. Goat even got on the wagon and relieved the writer of part of his dinner.

July 4, 1907   Bay Minette, Ala.   E. N. Beachy

The writer won a horse last week by buying a ticket for 30 cts. He was a "wind splitter," I'll bet the horse could go 1 mile in 29 minutes and 63 seconds. After having him for 5 days I sold him for $9.00.

Dec. 28, 1899   Lowville, N.Y.   J. K. Schwartzentruber

Alcohol and tobacco: I saw in the paper that horses eat tobacco in Colorado. I guess it means loco instead of tobacco, that is a raisin weed. I think it is bad enough if men chew tobacco and costs enough for them to furnish it for themselves, instead of getting it for the horses.

Sept. 11, 1912   Surrento, Colo.   Emma L. Miller

E. S. of Eagle's Grove, Iowa, you make a good guess. I am guilty of using tobacco; I used it on a horse to kill lice, and if necessary, would use it on myself for the same purposes.

Aug. 20, 1903   Calhan, Colo.   Abner F. Yoder

We have a man in our town (however not a Mennonite) who came home late at night, and in the habit of filling the coal stove, took a pail of coal and emptied it into the rocking chair. The fire was out the next morning. He did not get his medicine in our town though.

Nov. 6, 1912   Topeka, Ind.   Alvin E. Yoder

Economics: Ye Eastern broiler raisers - - If the market should take a sudden slump, you might know why, as I am putting 500 on the market today. Watch the market, not the squirrels.

June 7, 1951   Thomas, Okla.   Joe Bontrager

Farm crops: It is not very dangerous anymore here, as the corn is done shooting ears. Some stalks have shot 4 or 5 times, but will not shoot anymore on account of being frozen too much.

Oct. 2, 1902   Wilmot, Minn.   Jonas B. Jantzi

Household: Recently Grandpa got quite a laugh out of his women here. We had company over the holidays, some of these forgetful ladies left some diapers lay here. As grandma wanted to be very generous she cleaned and washed them for them. But when they sorted the wash, they somehow got one of these diapers in with the dish towels. Now a few days ago one eve. after they had wiped the dishes, they found out they used a diaper to wipe them. Did I get a laugh out of that. . . . Of course I would have sent them home as was.

Jan. 30, 1980   Heuvelton, N. Y.   Rudy S. Yoder

Mishaps: Pre. Bontrager had quite an experience about fifteen miles northeast of here; where he went to hold services, Saturday. It is well for our ministers, as well as other people to have a piece of baling wire with them, in case they run against a stump and result in a broken sleigh.

Jan. 13, 1910   Fairview, Mich.   Mrs. M. S. Zook

I was surprised to read in the Budget that Bill, in sending a letter home tried to post it in the fire alarm box in Chicago. His family must surely have thought they were in danger of fire upon receiving the letter. I never thought Bill would make such a mistake as that. I have known Bill for a long time; I and Bill were partly raised together. I don't mean raised to manhood, but had our tempers raised together many times.

Nov. 22, 1906   Adams, Mont.   G. D. Chupp

I guess Turner will keep his muffler closed the next time he goes through Akron.

June 23, 1921   Uniontown, Ohio   Pete

Mississippi seems to be a good sleeping country, as a little woman fell asleep and fell from the bench, the other Sunday evening in the singing. Nobody was hurt.

Jan. 30, 1930   Kiln, Miss.   Emma Coblentz

A few girls had the misfortune of coming in hard contact with a fence post, but it didn't do the post any damage.

Dec. 19, 1929   Winesburg, Ohio   Budget Readers

I was disappointed for not seeing the Huntsburg scribe U. R. B. there and learned that he was not able to attend, due to his latest mishap. He had so many narrow escapes throughout his lifetime, tho he was lucky enough always to come through in one piece and with the right end up. I heard that someone suggested putting him in a wooden cage for his safety.

Aug. 27, 1980   Mt. Eaton, Ohio   Eli E. Weaver

320

Puzzle: To John R. Yoder (scribe) your question about grammar is a bit tricky, but I would say, The yolk of an egg is yellow" instead of "is white" or "are white". Ha! I'm smarter than you thought.

Oct. 19, 1977   Mendon, Mich.   Mrs. Lonnie Yoder

Regional rivalry: To Levi Miller of Lockwood, Ohio, if you will re-read the statement about the poorhouse you will see that it says I have often heard the remark made that if Geauga Co. only had a roof it would make a good poor house. It is the truth that I did hear that remark, but as for me starting it, that is wrong, as I was quite young when I first heard it said. 50 or 55 years ago some of the farms were in a run-down condition with dilapidated buildings, and most of the families were renters. I did not mean that as a slur against anyone.

Mar. 2, 1950   New Wilmington, Pa.   Y. J. Byler

There is a good prospect for corn and a man said to me, "Kansas can raise the prospect and Iowa can raise the corn."

July 2, 1942   Haven, Kans.   Leander S. Keim

Wonder if Joe Overholts of Va. are about ready to leave that place again? Guess they are so busy picking strawberries that they haven't time to leave yet by this time.

May 24, 1923   Uniontown, Ohio   No name

S. S. Summy, are you done making sugar? We will all come down there and eat "spotza". Come up and see us.

Mar. 29, 1911   Berlin, Ohio   Mrs. Daniel Middaugh

Those cow buyers from Stark Co., . . . were not much in need of a job of work but after driving over the country and seeing what shape some of the corn fields were in, they thought it would be well to offer their service to hoe corn; but not seeing any ears above the ground they thought perhaps the Geauga corn grows like peanuts or potatoes with the good fruit under the ground, so they made up their minds theyhad better not tackle it for fear they might ruin the crop.

Aug. 30, 1906   Lake, Ohio   V. P. Y.

Relationships: Oh, boy, I'm in trouble. Today is our 35th anniversary, and as so often happens we aren't as prepared as we would like to be. Now what does one do at the very last minute, that doesn't look as tho it was done at the very last minute. Move over, Rover, it looks as tho I'm in the doghouse along with you again.

Sept. 29, 1976   Virginia Beach, Va.   John H. Miller

321

By oral reports I guess a few Eastern people think the Oregon people are on starvation. Don't know but I guess we have been too slow to find out something like that. Think it would be very nice if they would try and take a turn at being a good Samaritan to the poor.

Jan. 13, 1938   McMinneville, Oreg.   Magdalena Yoder

A certain young "Valley" boy also attended (an Old People's singing). He is engaged as a farm hand in our country at present. Upon being asked who his parents were he said, "Dem Mam und Dat sei bu."

Aug. 31, 1944   Lancaster County Briefs   Jonathan B. Fisher

Abe Miller played a cute trick on his family last Sunday. When greasing the buggy in the morning he left one of the nuts off the hind axle and when they had gone a little ways the wheel came off and down they went. Abe, you should not be so forgetful the next time.

Aug. 24, 1893   Troyer Valley Items   GERMAN T-P

I think "chip of the old Block" has given himself the right name, as I am personally acquainted with him and his father; only I think the chip has turned out to be worse than the block, net far ungut, Jake, kum aus wieder.

July 13, 1899   Armington, Ill.   Timothy

There is a young Kansas "Jumper" here; he told me to put a good piece in the Budget about him, and I don't know anything, only he sleeps to long on Monday mornings, that he does not get home till sun-up.

July 13, 1899   Worthington, Minn.   J. J. Yoder

There are certain parties that would better mind their own business and not others.

July 30, 1903   Pleasant Valley, Ohio   O. K.

Talkativeness: E. N. Beachy, of Bay Minette, Ala. has given good advice to those people who are so talkative, telling them what they should talk about. It is certainly the practice of many people to scatter so many truthless stories, which the Gospel strictly forbids. Who did Christ say is the father of lies?

July 18, 1907   Arthur, Ill.   Lewis D. Yutzy

It's dangerous to be in the corn fields these days as ears fly in every direction.

Nov. 30, 1899   Hutchinson, Kans.   CITY LAD

We have many letters to answer, and have been almost

322

covered up with false reports and ridiculous talk, which causes many unnecessary questions. Altogether I have spent about twenty days in answering inquiries, therefore did not get time to answer our friendship letters as we had like to. [The two questions and accusations most frequently raised were that the country is so full of snakes it is not safe to go out, and that it gets so hot that men and teams cannot work.]

Dec. 19, 1907   Bay Minette, Ala.   E. N. Beachy

It is said: "You never make a success peddling excuses, for you will find that the people are all well supplied."

Feb. 16, 1950   Thomas, Okla.   Joe Bontrager

The young bald-headed man, who combs his hair over the bare spot, should not kick when the grocer puts the largest potatoes on top.

Mar. 13, 1902   Baltic, Ohio   PANSY

In my opinion the most dangerous person I ever met was the one that sits on two-thirds of what he or she thinks during the conversation and then spouts out in all directions behind our backs.

May 9, 1946   No location given   David D. Yoder

About every so often someone tries to "get even" with another person by making malicious statements about them in letters for the Budget. I try to be on the lookout for slanderous remarks and omit them before print - but occasionally some slip through. [Editor's remarks in Editor's Corner.]

July 10, 1941

Travel: Now it's my turn on Levi. He has been around and has had a lot of experiences to relate. While on their way to Paraguay on a boat they were getting close to the equator. Levi was talking to the captain. "Is there some way that you can tell where the equator is?" "Oh sure," replied the captain. "Just look through this here telescope." As Levi was getting situated on the scope the captain reached up and pulled a hair out of his head and held it in front of the scope. "Can you see the line?" asked the captain. "Oh yes," said Levi, "and I can see a camel walking across the cable." Now really, Levi should have known that camels don't have six legs or even that lice don't get super big down there. Yet in the excitement he also didn't realized what a louse would look like crawling on a hair through a telescope.

July 23, 1980   Rexford, Mont.   Ora N. Miller

323

E. S. Miller of Va. in a recent letter of correspondence, asked if about all the Florida suckers have left. In reply I will say that by the time this letter is printed, about all the tourists have left....
May 31, 1945   Sarasota, Fla.   E. N. Beachy

The tourists usually get a great enjoyment in fishing when the mackerel come, but they played a trick so far this spring, and very few were caught. Someone asked a colored lady, "When do you suppose the mackerel fishing will be good?" The colored lady answered him, "When all you northerners go home."
Apr. 9, 1942   Sarasota, Fl.   Mr. & Mrs. Dan Headings

Young people: Some boys think it a good idea to take water melons along on Sunday evening, when they go to see their girls to eat as a midnight lunch. For particulars ask Ray Bontrager.
Sept. 24, 1908   Fairview, Mich.   Minnie Miller

Friend Kanagy, of Belleville, Pa., you are mistaken if you think I was out there on a "dear hunt". I want you to know there are plenty of "dears" here in Lancaster Co., yet, and they don't seem to be very wild either.
June 13, 1907   Gordonville, Pa.   John H. Kauffman

I will say to the woman, north of Madisonburg, who told around last fall that I went after a wife already, that I am not in a hurry yet: will wait till your husband is dead and then I can get one in a short time.
Mar. 31, 1904   Smithville, Ohio   T. L. Miller

To Barbara Helmuth of Madison, Co., Ohio we heard you are married; hope you have a husband both gentle and true; with plenty of money and always willing a kind deed to do.
Jan. 31, 1917   Intercourse, Pa.   Lily of the Valley

Weather: There were several weddings last week, which was probably the cause of the cold spell we had. [Four couples were named.]
Dec. 9, 1909   Davidsville, Pa.   Levi J. Kauffman

We were informed by a reliable source in Canada that they would send us a box of snowballs for a bu. of sunshine. Well, we had a bushel of sunshine ready to put the lid on but we shall wait to send it until the snowballs arrive in good condition.
Mar. 8, 1962   Zellwood, Fla.   Dan E. Hershberger

In a former issue we noticed a correspondence from John K. Erb of Slocum, Nebraska, in which he says that must be a queer country, when people come to church wearing straw hats and overcoats. I have all along thought there was something wrong with the people there.

July 25, 1901   Baden, Ont.   A Reader

I noticed in the Budget that "Gid Jub" mentioned the blizzard, and that it was almost impossible to go from house to barn. That don't surprise me, for it goes hard enough with him to go to the barn when the weather is nice. Most of the people went to their barns regular through the blizzard.

May 19, 1904   Grass Lake, N. D.   ZERO

Words and Wordiness: I have long been fascinated by the simplicity of government and legal rhetoric. If one of our government officials or lawyers were to ask the Lord to give us this day our daily bread, I am told it would sound something like this. "We the undersigned do hereby, respectfully petition, request and entreat that due and adequate provision be made, this day and the date hereinafter subscribed for the satisfying of the petitioner's nutritional requirements and for the organizing of such methods as may be deemed necessary and proper to assure the reception by and for said petitioner of said quantities of baked products as shall in the judgement of the aforesaid petitioners constitute a sufficient supply thereof.

Aug. 3, 1977   Mountain View, Ark.   Melvin L. Yoder

[Describing a trip to Indiana.] Here it was where all of children got our limited "eddicashun," sutch as reedin', riten', spellin', 'rithmatik, and so on. I bekame putty good in vokabularry, (it seems to me this word is not spellt rite) any way I meen spellin! I nearly alwase got the most head marks in my klass, and I don't remember, mebby when I was not in the klass. Bruther Dave, eh was reedin' nearly all the time while at home and he kunt understand why he duzzent no more than he duz. Well - - as I sed: hees my Brother.

Another thing I diddint quite get at skule, and that was whare to poot all the diakrittikal marks! such a periots, commis, and so forse, exkorse all mistakes, if any.

Oct. 16, 1947   Thomas, Okla.   Joe Bontrager

I have an uncle that used to torment and tease his poor,

meek and innocent little nephew when a boy and he still likes to jest me sometimes. He said he thinks I am not fit to take over "Briefs". By the way Uncle Aaron, do you remember one of the first times you read the Scriptures in church, how you stumbled and fumbled over the words and the people wondered if you were going to be fit for a Deacon. All in fun!

Mar. 28, 1946   Gap, Pa.   Successor to JBF

Unclassified: To John Glick - - What's going on in Lancaster co? You don't need news from all over the country for your Briefs. Why don't you respect what happens in your own community.

April 11, 1946   Montgomery, Ind.   David L. Wagler

I guess the people around Hartville got sore eyes, from watching the airstrip ambulance which was supposed to come to Hartville but failed to come.

April 28, 1921   Hartville, Ohio   Two Readers

Farmers laugh on the other side of their face since the city folks commenced eating meat again, especially those who did not dispose of their hogs during the boycott.

Feb. 25, 1910   Cherry Ridge local

The French language is more easily understood over the telephone than the English language, providing you understand French.

June 25, 1913   "off the Electric Wire"

That man who went out on Sunday morning to poison gophers had better stayed in the house and talked with the baby.

June 12, 1912   Bucklin, Kans.   S. N. Stutzman

Special Days 44

The yearly calendar of the Amish, Amish Mennonites and Mennonites included numerous special days. Very few of the days were other than religious in nature. The special days with a religious focus centered around the life of Christ and biblical precepts, such as Thanksgiving. Special days relating to events within the denominational history are few, and among the more conservative groups, nonexistent. The founding of the Swiss Brethren on January 25, 1525 has not become a special day. The division of the church in 1693 which led to the formation of the Amish Church has likewise never become a special day. The "lunch pail" worker must make some decisions about national holidays which the farmer can largely avoid.

Ascension and Pentecost: Quite a few people attended the gospel meeting at Maple Grove on Ascension Day and some were at the Welsh Mt. Mission at a similar meeting.
> May 28, 1925   Elverson, Pa.   Lena Stoltzfus

On Ascension Day, the Sam Yoder church was held at Andrew J. Troyers.
> May 24, 1923   Mt. Eaton, Ohio   A Reader

A number of young folks gathered at the home of Mr. and Mrs. Dan Wagler on Ascension Day.
> June 7, 1911   Millbank, Ont.   Peter E. Boshart

The Mennonite Sunday School conference held in the Kaufman Church on Ascension Day, was largely attended the house was full and all took an interest in it.
> May 23, 1907   Davidsville, Pa.   Levi J. Kaufman

There was a large crowd at Troyers Hollow on Whit Monday.
> June 4, 1931   Millersburg, Ohio   A Budget Reader

[An Indiana scribe mentioned a gathering on "pinsta" Monday. Whitmonday is the day after Pentecost, and is also referred to by the Amish and Amish Mennonites as "Pinksta-Moantag", sometimes simply called "Pinsta".]
> June 1, 1961   Topeka, Ind.   Ida Miller

Christmas: There will be Christmas exercises held at Clinton (Amish) Church on X-mass.
> Dec. 28, 1900   Goshen, Ind.   K. A. Z. E.

I fear many think Christmas is just for a "good time" as they call it. Let us try and spend the day to honor God instead of all the worldly amusements. We are just a few days from New Years; then we may turn a new leaf, but if we look over the past and see the blots on the past year. Let us try and do better in the year ahead of us.
> Jan. 9, 1902   Wayland, Iowa   Lavina Gerig

We have just celebrated the one thousand nine hundred and second anniversary of our blessed "Lord and Master", and have today thought of that great and precious gift that God has presented unto the world, one that is able to save that which was lost.
> Jan. 1, 1903   Nappanee, Ind.   G. W. North

We had a Christmas tree here on Christmas eve, and had a nice time; the children all came home; there were twenty six of us in all ... each one had a few presents and had the tree just loaded with presents, popcorn and candy, and it looked nice, too, and then we had a big supper; had four chickens roasted, had oyster soup and lots of other good things, too numerous to mention.
> Jan. 22, 1903   Jet, Okla.   Miss Katie C. Bontrager

Santa Claus went down the old road in an automobile on Wednesday. Perhaps he went to Philadelphia to order his Christmas goods.
> Dec. 9, 1909   Gordonville, Pa.   John H. Kauffman

The Amish had services on X-mass.
> Jan. 22, 1913   Shelbyville, Ill.   Laura E. Kauffman

I was alone over the holidays, and spend my 90th X-mass with joy. I had a rooster to go on, which helped me to have a good time.
> Jan. 19, 1916   Berlin, Ohio   M. T. Miller

As we see at this time of year so many of our people spell and write the word Christmas thus (Xmas) which is one of the most foolish abbreviations of the English or any other language on record. Dear friends we should consider and take this matter to heart and not regard it as a joke, we must understand that to abbreviate any name implies a certain lack of respect. Abbreviations and short cuts at the right time and place are all right, but if our Christmas is intended as a tribute to Christ, our beloved Saviour we surely ought to be able to take time enough to write out the full word Christmas.

Jan. 1, 1920   Belleville, Pa.   Rudy J. Kanagy

On Christmas Day was the wedding of Mose and Edna Troyer.

Jan. 3, 1935   Hartville, Ohio   Ellen Byler

I came to the conclusion that there were more than 3 wise men coming from the East. 3 entered while others waited outside, and presented their gifts. "I do believe the remaining ones outside were all involved in prayer in honor of Baby Jesus." [Em Miller suggests that the 3 gifts represent "Die drei zeita", "Die drei tag von Jesus im Grab", and "Glauba, Hoffnung and die Liebe." Translated the "The Three Times", "The three days of Jesus in the Grave", and "Belief, hope and love."]

Jan. 12, 1956   Shipshewana, Ind.   Em Miller

While jolly Saint Nicholas must have had a good thing in mind in helping the poor, the name "Santa" seems to fit better to this pagan holiday and to see the mass of people and number of Santas, surely this must be the season of Santamass.

Dec. 27, 1962   Princess Anne, Va.   John Kanagy

Easter: Today is what we call "Good Friday", when our dear Saviour was crucified, and shed his blood for you and for all of us. Let us remember why this is called "Good Friday."

April 26, 1900   Middlefield, Ohio   John B. Sommers

We had an interesting Sunday school on Good Friday afternoon and a singing in the evening which was well attended, it was held at Lewis Swartzentrubers.

Apr. 10, 1918   Greenwood, Dela.   GUESS WHO

Most of the congregations out here are having church on Good Friday.

April 21, 1927   Kalona, Iowa   Verna Boley

It looks as though we shall have a white Easter. I guess we'll have to fix the bunny's nest on the porches or some place so it doesn't snow on him. Treat him well and he will treat you.

April 18, 1935   Fair Oaks, Ind.   Alta Miller

Epiphany: To-day some Amish keep old Christmas, others kept it yesterday and before 1900 they always kept the 6th, so I will keep them both to make it sure.

Jan. 13, 1915   Meyersdale, Pa.   S. S. Summy

Fasting, day of: Thursday is to be a day of fasting and prayer and there were services at Sycamore.

June 5, 1918   Latour, Mo.   S. E. Hershberger

In obedience to the rulers of our land we had church services today in the Niverton meeting house conducted by Moses Beachy and Daniel Yoder.

June 5, 1918   Elk Lick, Pa.   Mrs. John D. Yoder

We had a "fast day" on Thursday.

April 19, 1962   Garnett, Kans.   Susie Beachy

Halloween: Some of the boys did not forget it was halloween last night. We seen quite a bit of the effects of it today.

Nov. 10, 1921   Fairview, Mich.   Mrs. M. S. Zook

Thursday evening a Halloween masquerade party was held with Eli Miller for the Amish young folks. A good time was had by all.

Nov. 7, 1929   Burr Oak, Mich.   Mrs. August Wickey

Many are breathing a sigh of relief that Hallowe'en is past again. Would be a good idea for the government to take that festive eve off the calendar and to abolish all Hallowe'en pranks. One of the most shameful acts was the burning of Dave E. Miller's buggy near Maysville. He is critically ill.

Nov. 6, 1947   Berlin, Ohio   Sara Weaver

The day probably originated from some Christian source because it is called Hallow-e'en (evening), and in the German version "Abend vor dem allerheiligenfest."

Oct. 20, 1949   Berlin, Ohio   Sara Weaver

Halloween passed by with a minimum of pranks. Several small ghostlings rapped at the door, but a bit of candy appeased them.

Nov. 3, 1960   Middlefield, Ohio   Enos Miller

Hallowe'eners were busy here. They burned 14 shocks of corn for John Hostetler and 18 for Joe Yoder, and dumped 100 gallons of fuel for me. They took a hack belonging to Eli Yoder and a spring wagon and buggy belonging to Ura P. Gingerich. The sheriff got them and made the eight boys push them home. . . .

Nov. 8, 1962   Ethridge, Tenn.   A. M. Yoder

I don't think Christian people should take any part in Hallo-

ween. Ghosts and witches (associated with Halloween) are not Christian, but are of evil. Real witches (and we have many of them in America today) have supernatural power with the devil.
> Nov. 10, 1976   Windsor, Ohio   Mrs. John J. Overholt

Independence Day: I sometimes hear people say, "I am going to the 4th." I never need to go to it, it always comes to me. Today I have been to the 4th, just the same as those that were in town, and I was weaving a carpet all day.
> July 10, 1902   Wooster, Ohio   T. L. Miller

Quite a few expect to spend the fourth at the lakes.
> July 5, 1910   Fairview, Mich.   Mrs. M. S. Zook

The 4th of July is past and we all feel relieved, as the bang of the fire cracker is over for another year, at least. It was estimated that there were one thousand people here, to see the parade, attend the ball game and see the fireworks in the evening. A lot of money spent uselessly, that could have been put to better puruose [sic].
> July 12, 1910   Belleville, Pa.   Cor.

Labor Day: Bathing was fine at Ocean Park this week.... There was a number of people in bathing on Labor Day. [The scribe then names 19 Amish visitors among those at the beach.]
> Sept. 14, 1922   Norfolk, Va.   W. J. Overholt

Leap Year: I presume the rush of weddings is practically over with. As many regard Leap Year as the unlucky year. I haven't found anything in my Bible to that effect.
> Jan. 4, 1940   Topeka, Ind.   Mr. & Mrs. Dan A. Yoder

I will give the Budget readers a question. How is it about my birthday? I was born in 1832, on old Christmas Day. Now in 1900 my birthday is not on old Christmas Day any more and it will not be on that day as long as I live.
> Jan. 25, 1900   Meyersdale, Pa.   Elias Gnagey

Can one help find Elias Gnagey to a birthday as he has lost his one, and his years must go by as long as he lives.
> Feb. 15, 1900   Grantsville, Md.   Emanuel Hershberger

New Century: I will ask the readers of the Budget, does the year 1900 belong to the nineteenth century or the twentieth century?
> Dec. 14, 1899   Amish, Iowa   D. B. Swartzendruber

D. B. Swartzendruber of Amish, Iowa, I think the 31st of

331

this month will make the nineteenth century full, and Jan. 1st will be the first day of the twentieth century.

Dec. 21, 1899   Arthur, Ill.   Levi J. Lee

In regard to the beginning of the nineteenth century, it certainly begins when we write 1901. 1900 begins on Jan. 1st, but it being a leap year and presidential year it's hard to tell when it will end. [The Editor reminded Byler that he was mistaken, that 1900 is not leap year.]

Jan. 4, 1900   Millersburg, Ohio   Y. K. Byler

People are debating the 19th and 20th century question now-a-days.

Jan. 11, 1900   Sharon Center, Iowa   David C. Byler

Suppose we were to start a new record of time, what would we put down, Jan. 1st, 0, or Jan. 1st, 1. It depends on how this was done in the start as to whether the 19th Century is full or not.

Jan. 11, 1900   Grantsville, Md.   Emanuel Hershberger

Many people are looking forward to the first of next month for the fact of it being the beginning of a new century. What will the next century bring forth? Will it be a repetition of discovery and invention of this wonderful century so soon to close? [This scribe was under the impression that the new century begins with 1901. The letter written was dated Dec. 26, 1900.]

Jan. 3, 1901   Flanagan, Ill.   H. E. Grieser

Only a few more days, and we will write "1900". Only one short year, and the 19th century will be a matter of history. Many wonderful inventions were made during the past century, and if the world should stand another century who can tell what it might bring forth. Not all readers of the Budget will see the opening of the 20th Century, but let us hope those who do not, will have opened to their visions far better things than the opening of the 20th Century.

Jan. 4, 1900   East Lynne, Mo.   Eli Hostetler

An enormous big quilting bee was held at the home of C. Gascho last Saturday. A large crowd of young people gathered there on Saturday evening and some remained until Sunday, and report a jolly good time. It was the largest quilting party ever heard of in the present century. [Notice the date.]

Feb. 1, 1900   Baden, Ont.

New Year: On Tuesday night we were all awakened out of our sleep by the Norfolk whistles; they were whistling for New Year; also a lot of cannons were fired, and they certainly made an awful racket.

Jan. 16, 1902   Kempsville, Va.   Simon D. Hershberger

A number of women gathered at the home of Mrs. Noah Schrock, New Year's Day and had a carpet rag sewing. A business meeting was called at the Mennonite Church on New Year's Day. Annanias Hensler was elected trustee.

Jan. 8, 1903   Greentown, Ind.   J. F. Slabaugh

In a few days we write 1907. With the new year come new duties, new responsibilities; may we be able to discharge our duties and meet our responsibilities in the spirit that becomes those that profess to be the followers of the meek and lowly Lamb of God, and be fruit bearing branches of the true vine.

Jan. 3, 1907   Smithville, Ohio   A. K. Kurtz

By the time this gets in print, we will have bidden good-bye to 1963, and its trials and its blessings. What does 1964 hold for us? I believe that God in his mercy saw that it wouldn't be good for a person to know into the future, or be able to foretell the future.

Jan. 2, 1964   Back Bay, Va.   John H. Miller

Wishing everybody a Peaceful and Merry Xmas and a Happy New Year!

Dec. 25, 1947   Campo, Colo.   Mrs. Delbert Miller

Several from this vicinity attended the Sunday School meeting which was held at the East Chestnut St. Mennonite Church, Lancaster, on New Year's Day. A very interesting program was enjoyed by those present. It is estimated that the meeting was attended by at least a thousand people.

Jan. 9, 1930   Gap, Pa.   Mrs. B. K. Stoltzfus

Thanksgiving Day: Tomorrow, we have our 25th annual S. S. Meeting on Thanksgiving Day.

Dec. 6, 1934   Mio, Mich.   Mrs. E. S. Troyer

The custom of observing annually a day of prayer and thanksgiving we owe to the Puritan fathers of our nation. Through all the years we have observed it with unfailing remembrance of the divine source of our blessings, the Almighty Ruler of our destinies. With gratitude we offer today our Thanksgiving, and invoke the continuance of the

Heavenly benediction upon our nation, land, our institutions, our homes, and all our lives.

Nov. 29, 1934   Gap, Pa.   Aaron E. Beiler

Thanksgiving is over and all seemed to have enjoyed it. We had plenty of rabbits and some had oysters for dinner. I had the best of all which was sourkraut and speck.

Dec. 6, 1911   Berlin Items

Status and roles did not change very much among the Amish and Amish Mennonites during the 100 years of THE BUDGET. Undoubtedly this stability is the reason that not more reference to them was found. The views expressed in the final three excerpts of the first section should be read carefully.

Attitudes expressed: M. D. Yoder rented a big farm. I guess he thought he was going to have some help, but now he says its only a girl, so he took his brother, Ben, in as a partner.
<blockquote>Oct. 29, 1903   Plain City, Ohio   E. J. Miller</blockquote>

After a good many men have been killed by aeroplane flying, and others are still at it, the women folks are getting crazy, or almost so, to go up in the air. Several young women have taken out sky pilot's license with the intention of trying their luck.
<blockquote>Aug. 9, 1911   From an editorial in THE BUDGET</blockquote>

Will take this way to let the old maids of our church districts around here know that we have planned for them to go to Ephrata Clothing Center on Mar. 10.
<blockquote>Feb. 11, 1954   Bareville, Pa.   Barbara Zook</blockquote>

I wonder how many of our women are guilty of having usurped authority in the home so as to advance from the Old Order to a more liberal church, or are the direct cause of sending their children on ahead?
<blockquote>Aug. 2, 1962   Shauck, Ohio   Reuben I. Harvey</blockquote>

Raymond Byler was still not able to preach for us, today, so Mrs. Byler used part of that time to repeat her talk she gave at the sister's meeting at conference. Of course the men folks were permitted to listen in. It was edifying to all of us.
<blockquote>Aug. 26, 1954   Blountstown, Fla.   M. B. Yoder</blockquote>

Women scribes did expound on Scriptures, something not permissible in the church. [Meaning that they expounded

on Scripture in THE BUDGET.]
Dec. 6, 1906   White Cloud, Mich.   Mrs. Elizabeth Stutzman

I wonder who could answer this question? Why so many more women than men are Budget scribes? In one of the Budgets this month we counted 41 women and only 14 men scribes, not counting the letters where names were omitted.
July 22, 1954   Belleville, Pa.   Ezra Y. Peachey

While shredding corn at Eli Klopfenstein's the hay caught fire from a spark from the engine, and all his outbuildings, including the windmill are burned down. By the thoughtfulness of his wife all his implements were saved; thus we see a woman's brain is not inferior, but superior to a man's.
Nov. 21, 1901   Noble, Iowa   Miss Nebel

I was disappointed the way events turned out. I supposed he was king at least in his own home at his age. King Ahasuerus did not go to the dog house when his Queen refused to obey; I would suggest they have that book of Esther for devotions in the near future. [A response to John H. Miller of Virginia Beach, Va. who stated that he will probably be in the dog house because he forget to get a present for his wife on her birthday.]
Oct. 13, 1976   Danville, Pa.   John Renno

Weather has been a little on the fair side the last while, however it is cool. The weaker sex will soon be turning their thoughts to gardening while the stronger side will amble to the fields to prepare the soil for spring seeding.
Feb. 4, 1954   Bayside, Va.   Mrs. E. W. Yoder

Differences in wages and work: There are about twenty boys and girls here from Holmes Co. to husk corn. The boys get 3 cents per bu. and the girls get about 75 cents per day.
Dec. 11, 1902   Plain City, Ohio   Mrs. Anna K. Yoder

Yes, Menno says it pays to raise girls when they earn just about as much wages as the boys, and that is what they do for working in town, and the work is not as hard as it is at home on the farm.
July 24, 1902   Wilmot, Minn.

The work among the men folks is threshing while the women are busy canning fruits and vegetables for winter use.
Aug. 16, 1923   Plain City, Ohio   A Reader

The work among the men is planting corn. . . . The women

are kept busy canning strawberries and cherries. . . .
June 1, 1922   Montgomery, Ind.   A Reader

Husband and wife relationships: Am in the bread baking now as the Frau can't see to mix the ingredients. So far we are making out.
April 16, 1980   Meyersdale, Pa.   Noah Wengerd

I had not intended to write to the Budget this week, but my wife wants me to. So, to keep peace in the family, I will write again. I guess most of the men folks know how it is.
Aug. 19, 1948   Manitou Springs, Colo.   Andy D. Kurtz

Leah Hochstedler has a Tupperware party tonight and mom, along with most of the neighborhood women, are attending. I asked mom if I could go along. I could see it was hard for her to tell me no, but rules are rules. And she reminded me that I got to go to Truman's auction last night and she didn't.
Oct. 20, 1976   Mountain View, Mo.   Melvin L. Yoder

I pity the men who have to leave here just because their women are so dissatisfied; I should think that they could stand it if the men can, who have to work so hard, and as everything is so plentiful; potatoes are a good crop and are also very nice, tomatoes are plentiful and watermelons are also ripe. I think after the people get used to the soil once, they can raise almost anything here.
Sept. 23, 1909   Fairview, Mich.   Mrs. M. S. Zook

A fatal mistake in the use of the "rod of correction" is in the theory that only one of the parents is qualified to the use thereof. We have known many cases where the father was a type of "executioner" and the mother a "sympathizer", an arrangement which is always fatal.
Jan. 23, 1964   Lynnhaven, Va.   J. J. Hershberger

As the Monroe, Ind. scribe mentioned about a strange woman in their neighborhood, there is also one in this neighborhood, whom I think would be better off if she would go to her home and stay with her husband, instead of walking the roads.
June 22, 1939   Greenwood, Dela.   Mrs. Olive Miller

Most widely known and traveled: Jonathan B. Fisher, who passed away at his home in Bareville, Pa. Friday, was probably more widely known than any Amish who has ever lived, both among this own sect and the non-Amish people

as well. [Fisher's obituary appeared in this issue.)
Feb. 26, 1953   Editor's Corner

... we read that he was the most widely known Amishman who ever lived. If that means among people in general I will agree, but if it means being seen among our sect, I'd mention a certain bishop who traveled over 400,000 miles by rail and stood and preached in nearly all of the Amish settlements in the U.S. and Canada. [The author inquired of numerous knowledgeable Amish people about the identity of this person whom the scribe did not name. The unanimous response was Bishop Eli Bontrager of Ind. His name has also appeared as Bontreger.]
Mar. 12, 1953   Fredericksburg, Ohio   Mose P. Miller

Women's work: The work among the women folks is getting ready to move and clean house.
Mar. 31, 1921   Belleville, Pa.   Mollie M. Yoder

Women's work:
    The gardens need hoeing,
    The lawns need mowing,
    The chicks need attention - - -
    Very well knowing,
    There's house cleaning and sewing.
April 29, 1937   Harrisburg, Ore.   Mrs. Alvin Kropf

Mrs. Noah Harman is helping to saw down trees; but she isn't the only one. Is she, Lizzie?
Sept. 17, 1903   Denbeigh, Va.   Cor.

Sam Yoder and two sisters, Sallie and Emma, went to Grass Lake, to join a thrashing crew. Sallie and Emma are Mrs. Renno's cooks, and if he furnishes the goods the girls will put up a good meal.
Sept. 17, 1903   Surrey, N. D.   I. M. Yoder

I've noticed a sign in a diner which says: "If your wife can't cook keep her for a pet and eat here." No doubt many girls now days marry and don't know how to cook. Also among the Amish in Penna. many girls grow up now days and couldn't build a wood fire in the kitchen range and successfully bake bread, or milk cows, since the gas ranges and milkers have been adopted to do the work with.
Mar. 16, 1950   Belleville, Pa.   D. Y. Renno

Status: A few of the most important of the young folks of Middle Pequea were in Chester Co., over Sunday. The writer, of course, wasn't in it.

April 21, 1904   Gordonville, Pa.   John H. Kauffman

I had intended to buy a small property through here some-place, but according to A. J. Kramer's letter, Madison Co. must be the place to make the $ roll. I believe I could also scratch $50 together, but Abe didn't say how much money he had besides the $50. But I know that it is of no use for me to attempt to move to Madison Co. as one of their mem-bers said only the first class people would move there, and I know that I am none of that class. Abe, I just wonder how you got there, maybe you moved there while they were asleep.

Mar. 12, 1903   Middlefield, Ohio   E. N. Beachy

E. N. Beachy, of Geauga Co., I was glad to read your letter in last week's Budget. You would better come and locate here, as we have first second and third class people here, and some that don't amount to much at all.

April 9, 1903   Summit Mills, Pa.   S. Summy

I had the privilege to attend the funeral of a millionaire in Mexico.

May 28, 1953   Hartville, Ohio   Abe Yoder

I met a millionaire the other day and feeling myself too small to talk to him, he turned to me and said, I appreciate your news column.

Nov. 30, 1977   Laurel Hill, Pa.   A. M. Shirk

I will say to Mrs. Levi Miller, of Limon, that is right, I think the poor have just as much business in Colorado as the rich, the difference is, the rich can do as they please, and the poor have to do the best they can, and, I think mostly the poor people will want to go to such a place to get themselves a home.

Aug. 28, 1912   Wild Horse, Colo.   A Friend

I noticed in the Plain City Advocate that Nick Miller writes that he likes his location and that he wears a broader hat since he is boss over five men.

Aug. 2, 1906   Plain City, Ohio   A. D. Mullet

The Amish have been known to be self-reliant in respect to taking care of their own people, whether it be medical costs or actual physical need such as food and shelter. Among the matters of taxes and benefits, the one that caused the greatest amount of discussion, as judged from THE BUDGET, was that of Social Security payments and its benefits. Comments about other forms of insurance and benefits took a back seat to Social Security.

Government subsidies: The Amish claim to be a self-supporting group, therefore we should be careful we do not accept any subsidy or support money from the government in any form or manner.
> Mar. 28, 1957   Charlotte Hall, Md.   John F. Esh

The government wants to reward farmers to "sit in rocking chairs and watch the fields go back into woods." A bank connotes thrift and industry. The "soil bank" embodies waste and idleness.
> Oct. 18, 1956   Fairfax, S. C.   Mrs. Alvin Kropf

Personally I believe we would all be better off if the whole farm program had been dumped in the ocean 15 years ago. [Miller was writing in response to the peanut acreage allotments south of Hydro and the large sums of money the allotments commanded.]
> May 9, 1963   Thomas, Okla.   David Miller

Why not change the name politicians have given it (Social Security) and call it an Aid Plan, an Old Age Aid Plan. What about the money given farmers to plow under crops, etc.? Are these subsidies Farmer's Aid?
> Sept. 20, 1956   Portsmouth, Va.   Emanuel E. Troyer

Social Security payments and benefits: Certainly the Social Security Tax is disapproved by many and taxes as a whole are getting to be almost a burden, but maybe we are not thankful enough for our many blessings, whether we deserve them or not, in order to pay our many taxes whether we feel we owe them or not.

June 1, 1961   Wooster, Ohio   A. S.

I suppose someone could be found who could take the Bible and prove that it is a good thing for a farmer who is making good money to take all the handouts he can get from the government, even if he must be a little careless in the way he handles the truth - - but that it is wrong for a poor old man who hasn't enough money to buy a mule or to buy a shelter large enough to cover his death bed, to take any money from the government even though he has a perfect legal right to it. If someone could not be found who would try and prove this with the Bible, then it is about the only thing I heard of in the last few years that has not been attempted over the air, the press, and pulpit.

Sept. 20, 1956   Portsmouth, Va.   Emanual E. Troyer

We are a religious group (Old Order Amish) and do some charity work and fill our income tax report in a group instead of individually. So the federal government classes us as a religious organization and in reality have federal income tax exemption (which we did not ask for) and automatically the Social Security question is not mentioned.

Jan. 26, 1961   Ashley, Ind.   David Yoder quoted in Editor's Corner

Income tax paying time is here again and the social security question again. I can't understand why we pay a tax of which a large part goes for war purposes and a tax that goes to help those that need it we don't want to pay. Why seek exemptions for self-employed and not for laborers? Maybe I just don't understand it right.

The Lord used Nebuchadnezzar to work out his will and called him my servant. Could it not be possible that the Lord saw the plight of some of our poor people and made a way for them to live without being on charity, with some of the unpleasant results from it.

Jan. 19, 1961   Centerville, Mich.   John M. Bontrager

I learn that at a meeting of a number of Bishops it was decided to advise their subjects not to pay Social Security tax, hoping by such means to create enough influence among lawmakers in Washington to get the law changed and to get exemption from the Social Security tax. They also advised their subjects that there was a lawyer who offered to take the case without charge.

Dec. 14, 1961   Centerville, Mich.   J. M. B.

We read in the Budget how people feel about Social Security. Would the people that are so against it all agree to put aside a certain percent of money to be given to the widows each month? [The Editor was quoting from a letter mailed to him, and signed, "The Widows", Ind.]

July 26, 1962   The Editor's Corner

[The letter above by the widows drew this response.] Furthermore, if our churches should now lay aside their old customs of supporting our own needy families and look to the government for support, we would not only be dishonoring the teaching of the Bible (Isa. 1:17 and many other passages in scripture) but we would also be losing one of the oldest foundations of our old faith which was already established in Europe long before the American nation was settled. [Noah's letter occupied more than an entire column and appeared in The Editor's Corner. Noah wanted it to be clear that more than the preachers are opposed to Social Security.]

Aug. 2, 1962   Millersburg, Ohio   Noah J. B. Miller

Social Security exemption: [During the 1950's at least ten news articles appeared in THE BUDGET about the Amish and their search for exemption. Nineteen articles appeared in the 1960's.]

Technology 47

One of the most formidable problems faced by the great majority of THE BUDGET readers was the rapidly increasing number and kinds of mass-produced consumer goods. Such products became available in increasing quantities and at unit prices making them preferable to many home-made things. The difficulties with the Ordnung have revolved around these technological matters more than with any other single facet of life.

Airborne: There was quite an excitement here on the 18th, when four balloons passed through here, that had started from St. Louis. They even scared the chickens.

      Oct. 25, 1910   Fairview, Mich.   Mrs. M. S. Zook

This week something passed thru this neighborhood just about a mile south of us which the people never saw before and it was an airship. [She also states that "It was something I never hoped that I see."]

      June 6, 1917   Middlebury, Ind.   Miss Polly Yoder

A balloon, which left Chicago on the 4th, arrived here Sunday morning, tearing up fences and damaged one barn. In this age of balloons and automobiles when man or beast is not safe in house or barn for fear of being hit by one of those monsters. Nor is it safe out doors for fear of a monkey wrench or some other tool falling on him and causing loss of life and damaging property. I think it would be a good idea to have a storm cellar to crawl into if he sees one approaching and save himself. The Atlantic Ocean would make a good sporting ground for them. They would not be so apt to have their ropes and anchors caught on fences and trees.

      July 23, 1908   Brunner, Ont.   Elia Nafziger

Two more airplanes passed over this part of Mayes Co. again last week which make four that have gone across here this month.

      Sept. 11, 1918   Pryor, Okla.   Ida and Ada

An airoplane passed our house last week one day, it was a sight to see.

Sept. 4, 1918   Hollsopple, Pa.   Mrs. Noah Kauffman

Last Tuesday a group of 8 airplanes went through here. They looked like a flock of large birds.

May 12, 1927   Prattville, Mich.   Mrs. A. D. Miller

Isn't it almost unbelievable regarding the new record made by a lone man in a plane circling the earth in 73 hours and 3 minutes? Then also the Superfortresses a few weeks ago with 160 passengers coming to Washington from Tokyo in just a little more than 31 hours.

Aug. 14, 1947   Lancaster County Briefs   Jonathan B. Fisher

On July 30, 1909 Orville Wright broke all speed records in a flight of 10 miles in 14 minutes and 52 seconds. Compare this with today. Sound travels 700 miles per hour, but man flies swifter than sound! If the earth stands another 30 years and the wisdom of man increases like it did in the past 30, I am made to wonder what sort of place it will be to live in.

Aug. 23, 1951   Gap, Pa.   John H. Glick

Who would have thought it possible to put a rocket on the moon, as the Russians claim they have. Maybe they did and maybe not, but seems we're living in a time the impossible can happen.

Oct. 1, 1959   Belleville, Pa.   Ezra Kanagy

Well, the Russians have scored another first - - or so they say. They claim to have shot a man around the world in a "space vehicle", and brought him back to a safe landing. The journey took something over 90 minutes, as reported, and attained a speed of 18,000 miles per hour. Meanwhile Khrushchev is crowing like a rooster (You know what I mean) all puffed up and full of glory.

April 20, 1961   Lynnhaven, Va.   J. J. Hershberger

Atomic energy: Now they are talking about using the atomic bomb for power instead of destruction. Well, we don't know just what will happen. Fifty years ago if someone would have told us that we would have horseless farms and do everything with gas, we would have thought they might be a little off in their upper story, but now there are lots of horseless farms in Kansas.

Oct. 18, 1945   Harper, Kans.   H. E. Hostetler

[THE BUDGET carried a news item entitled "Amish Settlement Disrupted by Atomic Plant." The Amish moved to other communities.]
Aug. 21, 1952   Piketon, Ohio   David Wagler

Automobile: Nappanee has now eight automobiles and one run-a-bout. The News says: "The automobile fever seems to have struck here all at once, and the end is not yet.
Aug. 25, 1904   Nappanee, Ind.   Yost I. Yoder

The mail carrier on R. No. 2 purchased a new automobile which he uses to deliver the mail; the first time he used it he was afraid to put on more power, so he had to get out and push it up hill.
May 3, 1906   Goodwell, Neb.   Mahlon, Ella and Lucretia

We heard that an automobile was purchased in the neighborhood.
June 23, 1908   Maximo, Ohio   Three Sisters

Automobiles are numerous here, and a person meets many of them on the piked roads. Some of them are very expensive machines.
Mar. 11, 1909   Lemon City, Fla.   Michael Schrock

This cold snap does not scare the automobiles all, still some are traveling the road yet.
Nov. 25, 1914   Maple Valley, Ohio   Eli Hershberger

The latest in doing delivering was when Mr. Gerber hauled pigs in his auto, with his wife to watch them. That's what we call Q.D. in Canada for farm work.
July 7, 1915   Zurich, Ont.   Cor.

Orie Yoder, our drayman has purchased a auto truck to do his draying.
Oct. 4, 1916   West Liberty, Ohio   Maude Peachey

Levi M. Yoder has purchased a new Packard auto, it is said his son Chester had her speeded up to 70 mile per hour on Sunday.
Aug. 9, 1916   Belleville, Pa.   Rudy J. Kanagy

One of the quietest Sundays for a long time was realized on the 1st when the small number of teams which traveled the road exceeded that of machines, the government having asked the citizens not to use gasoline on Sundays. This shows what a vast amount of people are out merely for pleasure on the sacred day.
Sept. 11, 1918   Elverson, Pa.   Elsie Stoltzfus

We have enjoyed our trip so far and had good luck coming to Florida without changing tires, and in 3 tires we still have Ohio air.

Jan. 28, 1926   Tampa, Fla.   Mrs. Sam M. Miller

Computers: At the same meeting at Elmos, another topic was presented for us to think about, and that is the long-range effects of the Computer Age on our churches, and what we ought to be doing to stay clear of the dangers. The question was raised as to how an earlier generation was able to sense the profound effect the automobile would have on society and on the churches, so that it was decided not to allow the ownership of cars. Are we in the same point today in the computer revolution, having already accepted their fore-runner, the calculators?

June 11, 1986   Aylmer, Ont.   Joseph Stoll

Electricity: Electric lights have been installed in the Oak Grove church and grounds. May we hope that the spiritual light of the church may be brought to the same standard of perfection as has been the natural light by the installation of the electric motor.

June 23, 1915   Smithville, Ohio   A. K. Kurtz

Farmstead: Will Eash will have a cement water tank made, today, that is to last as long as the world stands. People are getting wise when they get things made that last to the end of time.

June 29, 1899   Inman, Kans.   S. Y. Yoder

I expect everybody would like to know what a silo is, that David Hostetler, of East Lynne, Mo., is building. Let us have him explain what it looks like and what it is used for.

Aug. 10, 1899   Middlebury, Ind.   M. H. Hostetler

Sometime ago one of the Budget correspondents wanted to know what a "Silo" was. Surely that person does not take a farm paper or is not posted much on practical farming and stock raising. Let him refer to some farm paper and surely the question will soon be answered. The Budget is a good paper in its line, but I think every farmer ought to keep a farm paper also, to post himself in the advancement of practical farming.

Aug. 31, 1899   Hopedale, Ill.   A Budget Reader

Eight incubators are in operation in this neighborhood; you ought to see the chicks jump out of the shell.

May 1, 1902   Iowa, La.   C. C. Schrock

346

Field work: In Minnesota I thought I would lose my hat when I saw the first corn planter, as I had never seen one before and did not know what they looked like.

> July 18, 1901   Milverton, Ont.   David Schwartzentruber

J. T. Himes purchased a McCormick corn husker this fall and has been husking for some of the farmers around here, besides his own crop; yet it remains to be decided whether it is a paying investment to husk by machinery, as the majority of our farmers still prefer the old way in preference to the husker, as this is the first one having been introduced among the farmers here.

> Dec. 4, 1902   Allensville, Pa.   Benjaman Y. Zook

Some farmers are making use of the corn binders, which throw out the corn on bundles, ready to shock; it makes very nice work in fodder corn or sugar cane, and saves a good deal of work.

> Nov. 13, 1902   Kempsville, Va   Simon D. Hershberger

Today Noah Johnson . . . became the victim of one of those man-slaying machines, called corn shredders. He lost his right arm and is suffering very much; this evening the reports are that the case may be fatal.

> Nov. 21, 1901   Nappanee, Ind.   G. W. North

Mart Overholt is working for Sill Slabaugh through threshing. He has a new 30:50 Flour City tractor and a 56 inch Grey Hound Machine.

> Aug. 3, 1922   Mogadore, Ohio   No name

Farmers are busy this week building sheds for their combined machines.

> Sept. 1, 1927   Conway, Kans.   Cor.

Naturally, the chief cause of growth is mostly due to the automatic pick up baler devised by the modest, plain Mennonite Eddie B. Nolt. It is claimed his income tax is $90,000 annually. [The above was under the heading "New Holland Machine Co. affiliated with Sperry Corp. of NY.]

> Oct. 16, 1947   Lancaster County Briefs   Jonathan B. Fisher

Motorcycles: John Roggie and Alexander Miller each purchased a new wheel.

> April 18, 1901   Needy, Ore.   Miss Sarah Yoder

On Tuesday evening we were startled by getting a glimpse of two flying motorcycles passing over the macadamized road through our town at break neck speed. People who were privileged to see the foolish act claim the speed was nearly a mile a minute.

April 25, 1917   Manchester, Ind.   J. Albert Zepp

Phonograph: A Graphophone entertainment was given at the school house.

Sept. 19, 1901   Jerdan Falls, N.Y.   A Reader

Telephone: The new telephone line is completed to this place and Shanesville, with the exception of the instruments. When the line is placed in operation we will be in communication with nearly all the principal cities in the United States, as connections will be made with long distance lines at Canal Dover.

June 29, 1899   Sugarcreek, Ohio   Local news item

There will soon be a telephone line through here, "then there will be some more talking done."

Jan. 16, 1902   Metamora, Ill.   Reader

The writer is getting a telephone; the posts and wires are up, but the phone has not yet arrived. Then we can talk to Flanagan, Gridley and Meadows, and to almost every house within eight or ten miles, without going out of the house.

Mar. 7, 1901   Flanagan, Ill.   Joseph Yoder

Tractor power: Edwin J. Yoder whose farm joins the town of Topeka, has purchased a Happy Farmer tractor built at LaCrosse, Wis.

Jan. 29, 1919   Topeka, Ind.   W. W. Hartzler

Eli Tice and Fred Miller are operating Fordson tractors on the farm of Mr. Hudgins, a trucker of this place.

June 29, 1922   Princess Anne, Va.   Jonas E. Miller

Bert McMikles bought a team from Charley Smucker a few weeks ago. Horses are in good demand and bring good prices, as many farmers are going to let their tractors stand idle this spring on account of expense.

Mar. 10, 1932   Prattville, Mich.   Mrs. A. D. Miller

Farmers in this section had a great opportunity to do a lot of farm work the past week, especially those with tractors. There are farm tractors buzzing all around us here in this neighborhood, but we just slowly and easily shuffle in behind and "let 'em buzz."

May 11, 1944   Gap, Pa.   John F. Glick

Unclassified: I have heard my parents mention when screen doors were first introduced, they being considered a luxury

at that time. Now we regard them as essential.
April 20, 1950   Bayside, Va.   Mrs. E. W. Yoder

Levi Slaubaugh, our local blacksmith, has come up with an unusual piece of footwear. I am unable to say exactly how it is made but I understand that borum was joined in some way to the bottom of his overshoes. At any rate, Levi can run over icy roads, while other people must travel at a snail's pace, or skate.
Feb. 19, 1959   Aylmer, Ont.   David Wagler

Of the new inventions, there is no end. Now signs in quite a few of the cities say, "Speed is checked by radar." Don't know how it works, and don't want to drive fast enough to find out.
Mar. 5, 1953   Fairfax, S. C.   Mrs. Alvin Kropf

Contractor S. A. Robertson is making good headways in constructing the farmer's canal. There are 36 teams working on it this week.
June 29, 1899   Iowa, La.   Cornelius Schrock

[Someone responded to the use of kerosene lamps and the danger of accidentally putting gasoline into the tank, or was it the early lamps using bottled gas?
Flicker, flicker, gasoline.
    Where, oh where will the lamp be seen?
Up above the world so high,
    With its owner in the sky.
May 29, 1890   Page 1

An Amish buggy with Timken roller bearings, airfoam rubber seat, and complete equipment - - except for horse, is going to be sold to the highest bidder by R. P. Schrock, who operates a buggy shop on the west side of Walnut Creek. [Twenty had been installed with bearings and axles designed by Timken Roller Bearing Co., but all of them broke. Schrock designed a new axle, which was made according to his specifications. It was pulled behind a jeep for 1036 miles for testing, and it met road tests.]
May 3, 1951   Editor's Corner

Oh how different things were then, about sixty years ago. They had no machines, everything was done by hand. A plow with a wooden moldboard, a one-shovel plow and a harrow made of poles pinned together were their farming tools. They had no mowers, horse rakes, reapers or threshing machines. Didn't even have cook stoves.

When I was fifteen years old the grass was cut with a scythe and raked by hand. The grain was cut with a hand sickle by men and women. There were no factories to make the clothes of the goods. Wool was spun and woven by hand, as was also flax. There being no sewing machines the sewing had to be done by hand with the needle.

After my marriage I left Pennsylvania, loading what little goods I had on a two-horse wagon, and went to Indiana, stopping in Lagrange Co. Was on the road eighteen days. Here I took up 160 acres of timber land. Had money enough to buy a cow and a pig. Hunted a place to build, cut down trees and put up a little shanty in which to live. Traded one horse for a yoke of oxen and the other to get four acres cleared. When Sunday came we hitched the team of oxen to the wagon and went barefooted to meeting. My first granary, smokehouse, and chicken house were made out of a big hollow sycamore tree. Everything was done by hand, no machinery to work with. Did all my farming with the ox team. We were poor newcomers but well-pleased with our home.

Dec. 5, 1907   Haven, Kans.   D. D. Miller

The author's father and his 10-20 McCormick Deering tractor in the early 1930's.

Transportation 48

Transportation, even for the Old Order Amish, has undergone considerable changes. They still rely largely on horsedrawn vehicles for local highway transportation. Public transportation is widely used for travel to distant places. An increasing part of travel, both short and long-distance, depends on the hiring of private individuals with automobiles and/or vans.

Buggies and springwagons: Winds were so strong Sunday night that it wasn't safe to be out riding in a buggy. A few of the young folks stayed till Monday morning at the Tobe L. Yoder home. . . . [One who tried to travel on Monday morning had his buggy toppled.]

Jan. 23, 1964   Topeka, Ind.   Mrs. Jerome Hochstetler

Recently I heard some discussion about the flags required on vehicles in Ind. As far as I can see, those flags do not represent anything of any kind but are supposed to be for the safety of the people on the road.

Feb. 20, 1964   Centreville, Mich.   J. M. B.

There are quite a few that have hazard or blinker lights operating their buggies or carriages at night. In fact they are putting them on about as fast as supplies come in. In my opinion they are a good improvement in night driving on the highways. Seemed our greatest danger with buggies on the highway at night was from fast-moving traffic from the rear, especially when other traffic with bright lights was approaching from in front. Me thinks about the only excuse for not seeing these lights now, would be sleeping or drinking.

June 18, 1962   Belleville, Pa.   Ezra Kanagy

[A news item reported that an Indiana man was fined for reckless driving with horse and buggy. He was cited for "endangering traffic because of driving at an unreasonably low rate of speed." The driver's attitude was, 'I paid for a license for the buggy which permits me to drive on the

351

highway." He pleaded ignorance to a clause in the reckless driving law which says either unreasonable fast or slow driving constitutes an offense.]
Jan. 9, 1958

Horses balking: While Mrs. Wilson McGill was returning from church recently, the horse took flight at an automobile, overturning the buggy. Mrs. McGill was seriously hurt.
July 16, 1903   Mottville, Mich.   Grandpa

Overland travel: A few weeks ago the writer and D. Plank made a trip to Shaffer, about 65 miles from here, to get Mr. Plank's corn lister, harrow and corn sled. We made the trip in two days and part of a night.
May 12, 1904   Arnold, Kans.   Y. J. Miller

Jonas J. Yoder and wife and Elias Yoder and wife intend to make an over-land trip to Howard and Lagrange countries, Ind. in a few weeks.
Aug. 30, 1906   Arthur, Ill.   Lewis D. Yutzy

Mr. Nisly and wife and John Schrock of McPherson Co., left for Oklahoma, Thursday morning, by the overland route.
Aug. 16, 1900   Hutchinson, Kans.   Eli Helmuth

Amos Troyer went back to his home in Ohio on horseback.
Jan. 3, 1901   Flanagan, Ill.   Mary A. Slagel

Elmer Kurtz and wife and Mrs. Kurtz's mother are at present visiting among relatives and friends here. They are on the way, moving from Colorado to Georgia by wagon. Next week they expect to resume their journey.
July 4, 1901   East Lynne, Mo.   Eli Hostetler

Prairie "schooners" from the east can be seen passing through here every day on their way west to help harvest the big wheat crop....
July 4, 1901   Hartford, Kans.   SUNFLOWER

Andrew M. Coblentz arrived here last Friday from Tuscara-was Co., by the overland route. He intends to husk corn.
Oct. 17, 1901   Plain City, Ohio   TWO BOYS

Noah Harmon and family arrived here, Sunday morning, from Louisiana, and will make this their future home. They took the overland route as far as Alabama, then sold their horses and wagon and took the train for this place.
July 23, 1903   Denbeigh, Va.   Mrs. Noah Harmon &
Mrs. S. H. Glick

Railroads: I crossed one of the roughest pieces of railroad of any time since I came to this state. It was marvelous to ride on such a rough road without any accidents, as many accidents happen on the Southern Pacific, between Eugene and the California line. From Eugene to Riddes, a distance of 120 miles it took us 8 hours to make the run; uphill and downhill; two engines all the way.

Aug. 8, 1901   North Canyonville, Ore.   Charles E. McGowen

Roadways: Roads are getting to be quite an important factor. People used to drive over the prairie anyplace.

June 29, 1899   Iowa, Nebraska   Cornelius Schrock

Our road is in bad shape at present so many holes that if you try to dodge any you just hit others. . . . I'm surprised that horses don't break legs running through them, especially at night.

Mar. 26, 1980   Middlefield, Ohio   Mrs. Elmer J. Mullet

Some people get disappointed that live back off the paved roads, when they put a load on the sled and then get to the pavement. They find it bare, consequently they have to unload.

Mar. 1, 1934   Middlefield, Ohio   E. M. Hochstetler

The roads are just like a floor, but last Sunday the 5 they were so bad the mud getting stiff, that several broke their single trees while going home from church.

Mar. 22, 1916   Latour, Mo.   Sarah E. Hershberger

A beginning has been made to pike the old road in the vicinity of Weavertown.

Nov. 13, 1913   Ronks, Pa.   John H. Kauffman

About 5 or six autos are passing this road, they make the dust fly.

June 17, 1914   Bay Minette, Ala.   John E. Borntrager

It is reported that a new oyster shell road and a street car line will be constructed from Norfolk to this place.

Mar. 22, 1900   Kempsville, Va.   D. D. Hershberger

Harvey Carson is hauling milk to Creston. I should think it would shake into butter sometimes, the way the roads are.

Mar. 1, 1900   Smithville, Ohio   T. L. Miller

The roads are so bad, people can hardly drive with a team; they have to put four horses to a buggy; that is bad enough, I think, if you have to clean buggy wheels every few steps.

Mar. 26, 1903   Kalona, Iowa   David Graber

We have a road that they call "pike", but it is a "mud pike".

They have it fenced up so no one will stick in it again; a two horse wagon got in and it took eight horses to pull it out. That is the kind of pike we have. The road dried off fast this week.

Mar. 26, 1903   Wooster, Ohio   T. L. Miller

Varieties of vehicles: Will say to the eastern people, if you want to see people go to church in a grain tank, or see the young folks go to a singing in the hay rack, come to N. Dakota, and they even upset yet at that.

April 26, 1916   Mylo, N. Dak.   Miss Mattie Hostetler

The author's parents with their Chevrolet in the early 1930's in Somerset County, Pennsylvania.

354

Trials and Temptations 49

The following excerpts are a sampling of some of the struggles and trials of the scribes and readers. The chapter on accidents includes many that could well be included here. That life was not easy is reflected in these excerpts and many others that could have been used.

Some trials: Have you ever tried doing a good deed and every-
think goes wrong? Such was the case of Mrs. Wallace Byler
on Tues. She went to do laundry at her daughters the Paul
Millers, who were sick with flu. She took her own wringer
along, knowing theirs didn't work. While washing she
found out it was the gear box and not the wringer that was
bad. She did the drip-dry laundry and took the rest home,
so she made arrangements to go to her son Paul's. While
getting the wagon to cart it over she discovered a wheel off,
and while she was making arrangements to haul it on the
wheelbarrow, Wallace appeared on the scene. Soon there
was power and water and everything turned out nice and
clean.

     Jan. 7, 1987   Belle Center, Ohio   Mrs. Jonas Coblentz

This community was saddened by the tragedy, which took place at Ray R. Miller's on Sun. evening. Ray's bro. Jake, who lives across the road had gone out to the barn, to give more hay to the cows, and on returning to the house, he saw that Ray's house was on fire. He pounded on the door, which could be what wakened Ray, who then woke Leona. They slept upstairs and both jumped out the window. Ray received a big gash in his leg, cutting a main artery, which needed surgery that night. He also had burns and Leona had cuts and burns.

    All was tried that could, to get the children, but smoke was too thick to get in. Rays were left childless when Robert (age 4 yrs., 10 mo., 4 days), Karen (age 3 yrs., 7 mo., 23 days), Barbara (2 years., 3 mo., 15 days), and Rosanna (1 yr., and 26 days) died in the fire. Funeral will be on Wed. at Roman M. Millers.

All will be buried in one grave, but each having its own casket. They cannot be viewed.

Feb. 25, 1987   Guys Mills, Pa.   Mrs. Crist Miller

[A. A. Coblentz of Hartville, Ohio had been at home with 2 grandsons while the others were at a funeral on Thanksgiving Day. The following is a response to A. A. Coblentz.] You stated that you had a lonely day on Thanksgiving Day. I will tell you it was a memorable day for me also. A year ago on Thanksgiving my wife was buried and on Thanksgiving Day, 1924, my second wife was buried, and my first wife nearly the same date in 1901, and besides 3 children, and 2 stepsons, makes 8 deaths in my family. I say with Job - - the Lord has given and the Lord has taken and Blessed be the name of the Lord.

Dec. 27, 1934   Nappanee, Ind.   J. J. Miller

A tragic thing happened in this area Wed. eve. Since the Amish children ride the school bus and some of the non-Amish children have head lice, some of the Amish families also got them. At least 5 or 6 families out here have had them. One of Andy Miller's children came home from school and Fannie found a few in one of the children and to be on the safe side they all soaked their hair with kerosene and then washed them with shampoo. Sylvia, age 12, got too close to the lamp and her hair caught fire. By the time they got it out most of their hair was gone. They both had first and second degree burns on their face, hands and back.

Jan. 16, 1980   Clymer, N.Y.   Mrs. Walter Troyer

Mr. Zook's family has certainly had their share of trouble recently. About eighteen months ago his wife died, and last summer his barn was destroyed by lightning. On top of this all comes this dreadful accident of Sunday, a sad substitute for a marriage feast. [An accident at a railroad crossing in Lancaster County, while he and his daughters were on their way to a wedding.]

Apr. 2, 1903   Middlebury, Ind.   John E. Bontrager

Weather and the Heavens 50

Of all the topics and matters mentioned in THE BUDGET, weather would probably rank at the top or near the top. It is very likely that more letters open with comments about the weather than any other single topic. It should be understood that a rural and farm oriented people would be interested in the weather more than urban people. Knowing that these people had their roots in the soil and depended on it for a livelihood should then lead to an appreciation of their comments on the weather, rather than criticism.

Clothing: Last week one of the school boys dared to wear a straw hat to school, but he also took ear muffs along!
Mar. 19, 1980   Windsor, Mo.   Linda and Susan Mast

Dog days: Locusts are here and their buzzing shows us that the nicest part of summer is past, and dog days are here, and if all are like most have been so far, we won't be sorry when they are past, too.
July 27, 1977   Burton, Ohio   Mrs. Roman Schmucker

Drought: We are in the midst of a drought the like of which was experienced but once here, since 1880, and that was nine years ago; those people who came here with almost nothing to start with, and expected to become rich right away, are now in a sweat to get away, and there are many chances to make good investments.
July 23, 1908   Yoder, Colo.   A. F. Yoder

A certain farmer was cutting oats and dropped his wrench and it dropped in a crack in the ground it went so deep he had to go home get a shovel to dig it out, so you can think the ground is dry.
Aug. 6, 1919   Archbold, Ohio   No name

The eclipse is over; dog days are ended and the drouth is broken....
Sept. 8, 1932   Prattville, Mich.   Mrs. A. D. Miller

I expect the eastern people thought that was Kansas dust which they received a few weeks ago, but that came from the west. It didn't look like our ground. It wasn't windy here at the time. The dust came down like fog. Many children in the west got pneumonia from the dust.

April 18, 1935   Haven, Kans.   Mrs. Wm. C. Yoder

We hear of the great drought and dust storms and the armies of grasshoppers the people in the West are suffering from. We people who have plenty to make a meal and living from cannot feel thankful enough that God is still bringing rain and the blessings from above although we know not what might be ahead of us.

July 23, 1936   Belleville, Pa.   No name

Corn does not amount to anything. The grasshoppers got it all, also garden vegetables, and they are now taking the leaves from the trees. Some trees are just as bare as they are through the winter, such as mulberry trees and hedge which they like the best. They are sure a hungry bunch.

July 30, 1936   Hutchinson, Kans.   Joe S. Bontrager and wife

Our country had the driest summer in 100 years. The potatoes dried up under the extreme heat of the sun. The vegetables also were spoiled by the dry weather. Even the wet meadows all dried up this year so that the farmers have no feed for their cattle. Many cattle and hogs had to be slaughtered for the reason of feed shortage.

God is passing a hard judgment over us. The heavy burdened people have fear for the coming winter. We Christians pray that God may keep us in his trust and keep us through His power. He has delivered and kept us so wonderfully through the sorrows and trouble in the years gone by that we believe He will also in the coming distress give us our daily bread.

Oct. 30, 1947   Haven, Kans.   Leander Keim

Heat and cold: [Eli Beachy reported a big freeze in Hawthorne, Fla., the coldest in a decade, which killed more than 1 million orange trees.]

Feb. 21, 1895

The cold and stormy winter is expected, as the weddings are coming in early and plenty.

Nov. 12, 1908   Charm, Ohio   A Buckeye

Providence has shared us with such nice, cold weather before the snow, that many ice houses could be filled with nice clean ice.

Jan. 21, 1910   Gordonville, Pa.   Benuel Fisher

Wonder what will come next: This is one of the funniest countries I ever saw. Last Sunday some people came to church in their shirt sleeves, while others came with their overcoats and strawhats on.

July 4, 1901   Slocum, Neb.   John K. Erb

With pretty good sleighing and the thermometer down below zero makes one realize that king winter is here to reign for some time at least.

Dec. 20, 1910   Lagrange, Ind.   Artie Yoder

Forty-two years ago last Monday was the time when we had the frost in Ohio. All the wheat froze, the fruit, potatoes, and even the corn froze. I remember that all the talk for a few days was that we would starve, but the Lord provided a way for us to get through.

June 14, 1911   Berlin, Ohio   M. T. Miller

Men folks are planting corn and kaffir with overcoats on.

May 2, 1917   Garnett, Kans.   No name

We are having unusually warm weather the last week. It was from 105 to 110 in the shade every day all this week. The warmest we had for so many days in succession since I'm in Okla., 8 years if I remember right. But we hear it's very hot in other places also, so we can't get away from it, and want to be satisfied as the Lord makes it. We also need rain again, but is not as dry here as it is around us or in some states the way we hear.

July 23, 1936   Thomas, Okla.   Eli S. Bontrager

. . . left Iowa. . . . Got as far as Silver Creek, Nebraska where we stayed overnight. We stopped rather early on account of the dust storm. It was very hot and dry coming through Nebraska, being the hottest day on record there, 116 in the shade. We were all tired and glad to get to bed but couldn't sleep on account of the dust and heat. It was a pitiful sight to see how the crops were suffering from the heat. Acres and acres of corn just dried up from the heat. What was left the grasshoppers were destroying. Carloads of cattle were being shipped out on account of dried up pastures. [The scribes were describing a trip from Iowa to Nebraska for a "stay".]

Aug. 6, 1936   Manitou, Colo.   Lydia Yoder, Amelia Bontrager, Emma Helmuth, Sarah Kaufman

Northern lights & meteors: I am wondering how many people witnessed the strange lights in the sky last Friday night? Scientist said the rays were caused by the "northern lights". Some disbelieved the scientists and agreed among themselves that they were signs of the times, coming of the last days, according to the Bible.

    Aug. 1, 1946   Berlin, Ohio   Sara Weaver

The meteor that fell in July, at the line between Aligan and Kent Counties, was a wonderful thing, it struck almost the whole state. The people nearby found three pieces; one weighed 62 lbs., one 58 lbs., and the third 48 lbs., and it contains valuable metals.

    Aug. 31, 1899   Browne Co., Mich.   J. V. M.

Praying for rain: I will ask the readers, "Is it wrong to pray for rain?" If we still have plenty to eat but much of the food must be bought.

    Sept. 3, 1953   Haven, Kans.   Leander Keim

Sayings and superstitions: Someone should have loaned the Groundhog an umbrella; but it seemed that everybody was afraid and we will have to stand about six weeks more of winter.

    Feb. 14, 1895   Glasco, Kans.   Cricket

Wonder if those post holes in N. D. that L. S. Yoder wrote about were froze? [L. S. Yoder had written about freshly dug post holes in North Dakota that were blown from location by the strong Dakota winds. Yoder was passing on a tall story.]

    May 6, 1897   Arthur, Ill.   M. D. Miller

The groundhog will surely see his shadow today; according to the old saying, there will be six weeks solid winter yet.

    Feb. 15, 1900   Arthur, Ill.   Levi J. Lee

Sam Kauffman was in town on Wednesday with a straw hat on. No wonder it got so warm the next day.

    Feb. 22, 1900   Davidsville, Pa.   Levi J. Kauffman

By the way the wind whistles and roars at present, we would judge that the groundhog is a more reliable weather prophet than our old friend, Sol Yoder, of Belleville.

    Feb. 21, 1901   Reedsville, Pa.   Samuel H. Byler

Last Monday was ground hog day, when he saw his shadow all day, and according to the old maxim he retired to his abode again where he will remain for 6 weeks and we will enjoy that length of winter yet.

Feb. 12, 1903   Kalona, Iowa   A. D. Zook

Well the ground hog saw his shadow, and now we will have six more weeks of cold weather. I have lived 85 years and I can not tell whether this saying is true or not.

Feb. 7, 1912   Berlin, Ohio   M. J. Miller

The lion has been roaring the first day of March, and if the old legent [sic] become true we will hear the lambs bleat before the fool's day enters in.

Mar. 4, 1914   Walnut Creek, Ohio   No name

The ground hog could see his shadow very plainly on Sunᵈ ·y if there were any ground hogs here, which there aren't, anyway the old rule about having six more weeks of winter isn't very reliable in Oregon.

Feb. 13, 1941   Harrisburg, Ore.   Mrs. Alvin Kropf

Having heard in the past that there are only four Saturdays in a year wherein the sun doesn't shine, I kept track the past year, and according to my records there were only four completely sun-less Saturdays.

Jan. 9, 1964   Fairfax, S. C.   Mrs. Alvin Kropf

Snow and rain: When we left Illinois last fall we rather thought we would strike a country that wouldn't be so muddy, but we found Johnson, Co., equally as bad; the only difference is that here it is yellow, instead of black.

Mar. 21, 1901   Amish, Iowa   Boyd Smucker

We noticed in last week's issue of the Budget that the Oklahoma people were so unfortunate as to have ripe strawberries under snow. We certainly would help you get them out if we were there.

May 23, 1907   Fairview, Mich.   Mable Bontrager

Singing was held at Levi Miller's last Saturday evening, and was quite well attended, but some were scared away on account of the rain. Some of the boys went without their buggy tops, and of course had to stay somewhere all night.

June 3, 1910   East Lynne, Mo.   Cor.

I hear more of people stuck in the roads since the snow is going away than I did when it came.

Feb. 20, 1918   Apple Creek, Ohio   Mrs. S. J. Yoder

We had wet weather for some time. It has done a great deal of damage. David S. Yoder put a wash boiler out in the yard and inside of twelve hours it had about one foot of water in it.

Sept. 3, 1919   Greenwood, Dela.   Val Bender

The spring birds are whistling their merry old tune and the frogs are croaking for spring to come soon and the farmers are waiting for the roads to dry up.

Mar. 17, 1921   Hartville, Ohio   Peter Stauffer

There was a strange happening on Tuesday that not often takes place. At noon when in the midst of the snow storm, there were several sharp flashes of lightning and heavy peals of thunder. What this was for, or what sign it may be, we poor pilgrims do not know.

April 10, 1924   Bird-in-Hand, Pa.   Annie M. Neuhouser

[J. D. Mishler was asked if it is true that people in Oregon need two suits of clothing, one for the forenoon and one in the afternoon, so the one could dry while the other is worn. A further question was how one would get to town, or any other place in the winter because of the heavy rains. His response was that he had not met any such people who wear two suits.]

May 28, 1896   Eugene, Ore.   J. D. Mishler

Storms and winds: November was one of the roughest winter months ever known of in this country, and on the 27th was one of the worst storms ever known in the northwest. It commenced snowing on the 26th and with a strong wind from the north. Wind kept getting stronger and getting colder and on the 27th it was a raking blizzard, so a person could do no out-door work and lasted until about three o'clock A. M. on the 28th. No damage was done here except the roof of R. A. Yoder's house was blown off and some broke up. A. J. Yoder, who was staying there, had a narrow escape down the stairway before the roof was lifted off over his head. His pants, which were hanging on the bed posts, containing a pocketbook with $11 of money, were blown away. The family fled to the cellar and kept warm until the storm was over. But we were thankful to the Lord that no lives of men or beast were lost in this vicinity.

Jan. 21, 1897   Grass Lake, N. D.   J. A. Yoder

During the thunderstorms in 3 days, last week, lightning struck nine barns, and of that number only one caught fire. There were also a number of shocks of wheat struck and burned.

July 19, 1900   Gordonville, Pa.   John H. Kauffman

362

God again displayed his power by sending a hurricane through the central part of this state on Tuesday night, destroying many buildings and wind mills, and many trees were broken down.

June 19, 1902   Miner, Ill.   H. S. Hostetler

The Amish church house, which had been blown from its foundation, has again been put in place.

July 3, 1902   Fisher, Ill.   Anna Yordy and Lena Schrock

We are sure hurricane Donna needs no introduction. The eye of the storm passed through here about 5:00 Monday morning. It has made a lot of extra work for many people, but probably the absence of electric current was felt most heavily at the time.

Sept. 22, 1960   Princess Anne, Va.   J. Elmer Yoder

By noon it was really snowing and blowing. Someone called it a "risser schnee" (snow coming through all the cracks).

Feb. 18, 1987   Middlebury, Ind.   Eli Gingerich

Sugar season: The sugar water season so far has been very poor, some trees are already drying up, having given very little sap. The old saying that "if the ground is frozen deep will mean much sap," does not hold out this spring.

April 10, 1912   Goshen, Ind.   J. E. Smucker

The heavens: I was surprised lately to learn that a "flying disc" was seen only a few miles from my home. I had supposed that these were seen up among the clouds where they could not be seen plainly, but not so in this case. The man's wife, being awake about midnight, happened to glance out the window, saw something unusual, so she awakened her husband and they dressed and went out in the yard where a golden-like disc about the size of a dinner plate flew around in a sort of rectangular path about 15 feet above their heads, never going farther away than the houseyard fence. They watched it about half hour and said it was still there when they went back to bed. These are people whose word is not be doubted.

Jan. 6, 1949   Millersburg, Ohio   C. S. Miller

"Stars for June" [A news column rather than a letter.]

June 4, 1959   Aylmer, Ont.   David Wagler

Thunder and lightning: Yesterday, while the boys of J. S. Miller - - Menno and Simon - - were in the field plowing corn, a thun-

363

der storm came up and lightning struck the plow, splitting one singletree, killed one horse and shocked the other one and boys very hard. All were unconscious at first, but are getting along pretty well again.
        July 4, 1901   Grantsville, Md.   Emanuel Hershberger

On the way home from Mexico City we had the unusual experience of a heavy rainstorm in the desert, south of Cd. Jimenez. Hailstones roared upon our car, lightning flashed almost continually and great bolts of electricity streaked all over the road and the desert around us. The hail cracked our windshield and one bolt of lightning came down beside us and stayed standing, a pillar of fire, for about a minute until it slowly faded out. The storm occurred right before sundown and lasted for several hours.
        Feb. 18, 1987   Cuauhtemoc, Chihuahua, Mexico
                                      Peter & Susan Hoover

Use of words: We had some awful nice rains lately.
        July 7, 1932   Sugarcreek, Ohio   Sarah Mae M. Miller

The thermometer run down one below zero on Saturday morning.
        Jan. 2, 1918   Walnut Creek, Ohio   Valentine J. Miller

Jack Frost came through here in a hurry Monday of last week. He stayed away for a long time but he came down from the north and left black marks on his tracks. The ground was frozen ice could be seen and a few snow flurries and all tender vegetables is bowing its head as the consequence.
        Nov. 4, 1914   Maple Valley, Ohio   Cor.

Zodiac: According to the Almanac, everyone born in a certain month will be thrifty, clever and honest, love the truth, but are quick to anger and are apt to have cancer. If they are born in another month they are friendly, can give good advice, and are intelligent in everything except they have a weakness for strong drink and women. If the stars had anything to do with it, then everyone born in a certain month of the year would be natured alike.

    I wonder if it would not be good to notice the church almanacs to see whether they are free from such worldly superstition? I suppose the people who make these almanacs get their material from some almanac company, but I believe they would be glad to omit such things if they knew their readers wanted it that way.
        Dec. 23, 1954   Aylmer, Ont.   David Wagler

I will verify the truth of the statement made by Val D. Miller of Lynnhaven, Virginia that observance of the moon-signs is a form of idol worship. [The above statement was made under the heading, "Signs of the Zodiac."]

April 13, 1950　　No address given　　John D. Mast

[John B. Mast submitted an entire column under the title, "Ancient and Modern Superstition Concerning the Heavens."]

July 13, 1939　　Meyersdale, Pa.　　John B. Mast

A chair built by Jonas "White" Stutzman of Holmes County for use by Christ upon His second Advent. Stutzman expected to witness the return in 1853.

This chapter includes excerpts which serve as a sampling of views and comments on the larger world as well as of the future. These excerpts help to give a better perspective of what the scribes were saying about various matters of concern and interest during the one-hundred years.

Americas: This country was settled by peace loving people who came here for the love of freedom and to worship God as they saw fit. South America, on the other hand, was settled by people interested in making money, discovering gold mines, etc. consequently, that continent has progressed very little compared to ours. When we, our people, strive only after money, honor, power, and ease of living, then our progress will come to a stand-still and we will lose our heritage, the plain, simple and God-fearing life which has been taught us by our forefathers.

> Aug. 8, 1946   Montgomery, Ind.   David L. Wagler

North America has prospered and has progressed much faster than South America, in the hundreds of years. A writer claimed that the difference was caused by the fact that the people migrated to S.A. in search of gold and wealth, but many of those that came to N.A. came in search of freedom to worship God.

> July 31, 1952   Berlin, Ohio   Sara Weaver

Calendar and time: Suppose daylight saving time has gone into effect in many places. Haven't heard of it being an issue in these parts. They say the idea comes from an old settler who wanted to lengthen his blanket, so he cut off one end and sewed it onto the other end. It does just about that much good.

> May 14, 1953   Fairfax, S.C.   Mrs. Alvin Kropf

It looks like Dacatur, Berne and many other towns and cities of Indiana will go back on Daylight saving time, as it is called, but to me it is only man-made.

Oct. 28, 1954   Berne, Ind.   Sarah Schwartz

The towns around here have turned their clocks back one hour in order to have daylight saving time, although they could not turn back the time.

Oct. 4, 1951   Topeka, Ind.   Mrs. Ida Miller

This morning Ontario changed over to daylight savings time. We have never been able to understand the advantage of this. It appears to be an attempt to find a painless way of getting up an hour earlier.

May 2, 1957   Aylmer, Ont.   David Wagler

On our calendar is printed, "Birth of John the Baptist" underneath today's date. (June 24) One must wonder how someone arrived at that opinion.

July 2, 1980   Hazelton, Iowa   Mrs. Felty Yoder

Eclipse: [Wagler wrote that "on this day the sun, moon, and the five planets visible to the naked eye, are all close together and set within an hour's time." He explained that on Feb. 4 will be an event so unusual that it has not happened for hundreds, possibly thousands of years.] Some people appear to be certain that this denotes an unusual catastrophe. Although possible, it is unlikely. It is, however, unusual that the eclipse begins in Indonesia, which right now appears to be a boiling point in world affairs. It is possible that a war will begin there and like the eclipse, head for North America.

Feb. 1, 1962   Aylmer, Ont.   David Wagler

Europe: [The following is a response to the drowning of two PAX men in Greece; Simon Miller of Iowa and Eli M. Miller of Mt. Eaton, Ohio.] The community was shocked to hear the sad news that came on Saturday from the Old Country, ...

July 29, 1954   Kalona, Iowa   No name

Beeny, meeny, miney mo,
Catch the Kaiser by the toe,
 When he hollers make him say
I surrender - - - U. S. A.

Dec. 4, 1918   Manchester, Md.   J. Albert Zepp

Global perspective: "Driving a stake to China" meaning that in driving a stake directly into the ground it would come out on the other side in China." Question raised: What angle must the stake be started at to reach China? Must know your longitude and latitude.

April 4, 1957   Ephrata, Pa.   D. B. Stauffer

A letter from Cyprus, Sat. from my former intimate friend of Palestine, gives an account of their experiences and persecution endured by the Haganah Jewish soldiers.

My personal sympathy had been for the Jews, but due to the hardships of the Swiss colony under the Jews a lot of sympathy for them has waned. Some of them were cold-bloodedly killed. Wouldn't wonder if the Jews would be losing out and subdued by the Arabs since England has now given up reign in Palestine.

May 20, 1948   Lancaster County Briefs   Jonathan B. Fisher

[F. M. Lehman reconstructed "Mother Shipton's Prophesies" to what occupied 102 lines of a full column width. Mother Shipton lived in England during the 1400's. Lehman indicates that it foretells the automobile, the submarine, the airplane and the Balfour Declaration.]

Sept. 5, 1940

We are glad to notice the interest taken in behalf of the starving in India. Accompanied with our prayers and the blessings of God our mites may do considerable towards elevating [sic] the terrible suffering in that famine stricken land. But in connection with this, the thought occurs, that if Great Britain would use its millions, which is worse than wasted in that unjust war in South Africa, for the relief of its starving subjects in India, but little outside aid would probably be needed. [He probably meant alleviating instead of elevating.]

Mar. 1, 1900   Glass Lake, N.D.   Eli J. Bontreger

As it is going today some people are afraid the world is about to come to an end others think it is the will of God to carry on such a war as is raging in Europe today while I think it is exactly against his will.

Dec. 16, 1914   McMinnville, Ore.   A. M. Beachy

We again hear and read in the newspapers of the terrible disasters the European war is bringing onto countries. We as Christians and Americans are fearing it may be only a matter of months or even weeks until we hear those dreaded words, "American is at war." [The above was the first response found by the author to the outbreak of conflict triggered by Hitler's invasion of Poland.]

Sept. 14, 1939   Thomas, Okla.   Mary Mast and Susie B. Yoder

[The author could not find a single reference to Pearl Harbor in the Dec. 11, 1941 issue, even though many of the letters included were written on Dec. 7 and several on Dec. 8. In the next issue, Dec. 18, of the 41 letters included, only two letters mentioned Pearl Harbor - - one from Harrisburg, Ore. and one from Gap, Pa.]
            Dec. 11, 1941   Dec. 18, 1941

The signs of the times indicate either a revival of religion or a revolution of panic and terror - - perhaps both. A large number are pleasure seekers and deserters of the Holy Sabbath. On Sundays there are the base ball fans, moviegoers, restaurant patronizers of gambling machines, and pastime game addicts, fishermen, etc., who look forward from Sunday to another to enjoy their pleasures. Then too, there are the intemperate, eating and drinking, and night-frolicking, which totally take away spirituality from these pleasure-seekers, who in their working hours are not fit for work, and who are not ready for the "great day" when it finally overtakes them.
            Mar. 12, 1942   Lancaster County Briefs   Jonathan B. Fisher

Now that the war is over, it often comes to my mind what a western bishop said in his sermon shortly after the war. He said if the Christian people will not take this for a warning or chastisement and live better, some kind of epidemic or severe sickness will come. In other words, he meant that if the consequences of the present war will not bring people nearer to God, something else shall come that will. Possibly this after war epidemic is on its way already, as some 30 cases of typhoid fever are reported throughout the county.
            Sept. 13, 1945   Gap, Pa.   John F. Glick

The Bible gives the justice meted out to the erring nations and again the love and blessings of God to those who seek to walk in ways. The Bible charts the course of history from beginning to end.
            Nov. 22, 1945   Lancaster County Briefs   Jonathan B. Fisher

We realize that the war is over in Europe, but there is still Japan. Many of us also remember of the influenza epidemic that followed World War I, and the thought often comes to my mind - - What will it be this time? Is it possible that medical education has so far developed that serious maladies or epidemics can be exterminated? All medical education cannot change the views, plans and ways of God Almighty.

If it is His will, epidemics will surely come.
> May 24, 1945   Gap, Pa.   John F. Glick

We sincerely hope favorable results will follow the peace conference at San Francisco, where so much pains were taken to work out a program to avoid future wars. The results will depend upon you and me and all peace-loving humanity.
> July 12, 1945   Lancaster County Briefs   Jonathan B. Fisher

What will the Peace Conferences mean to us? Will they mean permanent peace? Time will tell.

At the San Francisco Conference, not one session was opened with a prayer as was the custom in all such meetings before, and with Congress, all on account of one delegation from one country, and there were about fifty countries represented there.
> July 9, 1945   Burton, Ohio   Abe J. Yoder

Unemployment in this vicinity is on the increase. Rubber factories are slowing down. Many carpenters are out of work. War clouds are gathering on the horizon.
> Jan. 12, 1961   Middlefield, Ohio   Enos Miller

I can't help but feel pity for Eichmann - - though he indeed is charged with a terrible crime.
> April 13, 1961   Lynnhaven, Va.   J. J. Hershberger

Judgment, God's: I heard say that at some places they are wishing for wheat to freeze. It is awful. I wonder if God will not sometime let them know that there is one All Powerful. Oh let us trust Him more from whom all our help cometh.
> Feb. 22, 1934   Mio, Mich.   Mrs. E. S. Troyer

There is nothing more certain than death, nothing more horrible than Judgment, nothing more terrible than eternal punishment in the lake of fire and brimstone, with weeping and gnashing of teeth forever' and nothing more glorious than heaven. If we think of these four things, continually, the rest of our lives, the devil will lose his power over us. [This was the final paragraph of 15 on the subject.]
> Mar. 1, 1934   Paris, Illinois   John B. Mast

Last days: Frankly speaking, I would much rather have lived in the days of the Martyrs than now, for Satan, "as an angel of light" is much more to be feared than as a "roaring lion." I am convinced that we are in the last days - - - days when the enemy of our souls is making an all-out effort (his last

one) to deceive the very elect of God.
Feb. 14, 1963   Lynnhaven, Va.   J. J. Hershberger

All of India is in an uproar this past week. The astrologers say the end of the world is coming on Monday, Feb. 5 (if it does you probably won't read this anyway). They have as their gauge the fact that five of the planets are within 13 degrees of the sun, which happens every century or so, but they say this is different because there will also be a total eclipse of the sun at the same time.

Feb. 8, 1962   Stillwater, Pa.   John Renno

No doubt such it was before the flood and all was destroyed, but 8 souls. So it will also be in this world; when the Lord says enough is enough, then He will put a sudden stop to all this foolishness on earth and send His son to straighten things out and then we'll all take what we get.

July 24, 1952   Gap, Pa.   John F. Glick

I once heard the statement that in the time of Christ the most conservative men were the most deluded; so we need to be on our guard. The devil doesn't care how a person misses heaven just so he can get us to miss it. If he doesn't succeed in getting us to drift with the world, he tries to get us self-righteous.

April 29, 1948   No address   A Brother

This world, or rather its people, are going "fast". Sooner or later God will make an end of it. It's only the "Salt of the Earth" that's keeping it and not the worldly-wise, worldly-minded ones.

April 14, 1949   Lancaster County Briefs   Jonathan B. Fisher

We hear so much about churches drifting and by traveling around some you can see for yourself that there is some truth about it, and by all appearance we must believe that we are in the last days.

June 10, 1943   Mylo, N.D.   R. L. Bontrager

If a person takes just a little time and checks up on scriptures, you'll find them nearly all fulfilled. After all we don't realize what really is ahead of us. But I actually believe we will see different times in the future regardless.

Feb. 8, 1940   Fairbank, Iowa   Emanuel Miller

Sugar rationing, gas rationing, and signing up for crops, etc. give some people reason to believe that we are nearing those days. I do not believe we are yet there because the

Bible says in that chapter: This mark shall be in their right hands or in their foreheads. Possibly we are nearing those days.

July 9, 1942   Gap, Pa.   John F. Glick

Another reason we believe this age is drawing to a close is because of the six dispensations. The first one closed in judgment when Adam and Eve were driven from paradise to earn their bread by the sweat of their brow. The second closed with the flood, God saving only a remnant. The third closed at the Tower of Babel, by the confusion of tongues. The fourth closed with the children of Israel in Egyptian bondage and slavery. The fifth closed with seventy years of captivity under King Nebuchadnezzar. The six will close in Judgment as the other five have closed, only it will be the most sorrowful one ever come upon the world. Christ said, "A time of trouble such as never was and never will be hereafter." Matt. 24.

Mar. 1, 1934   Paris, Illinois   John B. Mast

We need not look away from our so-called Christian Churches for fault. Do not think for a minute that the world only is wicked read about King Nero in Martyr Book part 1, page 8 to R. If anybody can show more ungodliness than Nero did, I don't know what they would have to do. Famine came in that time. In Luke . . . it says: "There shall be signs in the sun and in the moon, and in the stars, and upon the earth distress of nations, with perplexity, the sea and the waves roaring." We find these fulfillments the natural darkness of the sun which occurred May 19, 1780, with the moon in the blood the following night, and the stars from heaven that the people were overwhelmed with the distress of nation which occurred Nov. 13, 1833 in parts of the United States. [This statement was a response to the government programs introduced by President Roosevelt.]

July 5, 1934   Hazelton, Iowa   C. M. Bontrager

A French Prophet Astrologer of the 16th Century (1503-1566) had predicted the rise and fall of Hitler and Mussolini as well as World Wars I and II. This prophet, Michael de Natredame, predicted that in the first few weeks of 1960 Russia would send birds over America "with wings and breath of fire," and the battle would last 11 days and it would take 11 months to bury the dead. The paper stated that they hoped this time the prophet was wrong.

Mar. 19, 1959   Fredericksburg, Ohio   D. H.

News of this community is not plenty and my mind dwells on the welfare of our undying souls, as I firmly believe that the great judgment day is not far off, read Matt. 24; II Thess. 2:7 to 10.

Jan. 16, 1918   Midland, Mich.   Menno D. Miller

One world government: [Discussion of the Trilateral Commissions with a negative viewpoint, and particularly the ownership of land in the United States by foreigners.]

July 16, 1980   Cashton, Wisc.   Joe C. Borntrager

Occasionally we see some comments about the Trilateral Commission and a one world government. A lot of things could be going on that we ordinary people don't know about, however. I have always been inclined to take such stories with a grain of salt. My thoughts go back to one of the first men who was supposed to represent the beast and it was all figured out how the letters of his name would come out to 666. After he was elected president for the fourth time, a lot of people started wondering if there might be something to the story. His name was Franklin D. Roosevelt, but he went the way of all flesh. Since that time quite a few others were similarly labeled. A few years ago it was Henry Kissinger and now it is David Rockefeller.

July 23, 1980   Bloomfield, Iowa   David Wagler

Population: At this time the earth is probably more thickly populated than ever before. And what is worse, there are fewer Christians - - or we might say fewer church-going people - - than there have been for centuries. Why is it so?

April 22, 1948   Loogootee, Ind.   No name

Postal Zip: Some think the zip code number is uncalled for. But another year will be needed to get the benefit. I say, use it if known.

Jan. 9, 1964   Sarasota, Fla.   Mose B. Miller

Space: We pick up the paper and see in bold type that a U.S. scientist predicts a trip to the moon and back will be commonplace by 1980. We hear about nations arguing who can blow whom the highest. I am thankful I can say with David, "God is our refuge and strength, a very present help in trouble."

April 11, 1963   Shreve, Ohio   Wayne Weaver

The Russians think they have accomplished quite a feat by putting a man and a woman in space for a few short hours.

June 27, 1963   Aylmer, Ont.   David Wagler

Last Wednesday morning, Sept. 19, at about 5:30 o'clock fast time, I noticed a small red glow in the southeastern sky, about 1 ft. wide and 3 ft. long, according to my measurements, and a little to the east of that I noticed a star getting much brighter until it seemed to explode out of a smokestack, and casting a yellowish red-colored cloud, over a wide radius. In about 5 minutes everything disappeared, including the star and the red glow to the side of it. Now what was it? Might it have been a satellite blowing up (someone asked if I saw pieces fly), or was it a star, or some sign?

Sept. 21, 1961   Belleville, Pa.   Ezra Kanagy

Russia: A recent morning paper reports Khrushchev having made about the most sensible speech I ever heard him make.

July 25, 1963   Lynnhaven, Va.   J. J. Hershberger

According to Bible prophecy, Russia will some day march on Palestine with many horses. The Dead Sea has a vast amount of minerals stored in it, which other nations covet. [He claimed that horses sent over after WWII to Poland were confiscated by the Russians.]

June 14, 1962   Fentress, Va.   N. H.

There is a threat to Christianity spreading over the world and it is called Communism. If the Lord tarries, it may yet sometime take over this country and we know it is heartless. Nothing is too awful for the communists.

July 23, 1980   Bloomfield, Iowa   David Wagler

Just why the Russians are called Reds, I am unable to state, but in the 6th chapter of Rev. verse 4, we can read about the red horse and the power thereof. Makes a person study.

Oct. 14, 1948   Gap, Pa.   John E. Glick

Second coming of Christ - - prophecies and predictions: We seem to be living in an era when the jugglers of figures, numbers and even letters of the alphabet, are having their day. By adding a bit of scripture-wresting, a picture can be portrayed to appear real and life-like, but without the latter wouldn't have even "a leg to stand on." A person with imagination may well be able to set up practically any combination of letters, the initials or name of a man, and come up with the three-digit number mentioned in Revelation prophecy.

Sept. 29, 1976   Ephrata, Pa.   D. B. Stauffer

[After discussing the marks and numbers on the labels of merchandise that have appeared in the year previous to writing, the scribe concludes with the following.] Some thought this was a forerunner of the mark of the beast and a new world order that evil men would like to establish, which we believe the salt of the earth has prevented thus far.

Oct. 20, 1976   Blackville, S. C.   John Kanagy

[The Name of the Beast by Rev. Nicholas Elia . . . Minister of Gr. Orthodox Church, Lancaster, Pa. was discussed positively by a scribe. It can be summarized as a = 100, b = 101, c = 102 and z = 125. Based on this H = 107; I = 108; T = 119; L = 111; E = 104; and R = 117. The total of the six is 666.]

July 31, 1941   New Holland, Pa.   S. J. Farmwald

In the July 21st issue, a statement and diagram was given as to who is the mark of the beast described in Rev. 13:16-13. I have two other diagrams, which someone has declared and described as being the mark of the beast. One is the Pope of Rome and the other is Franklin Delano Roosevelt. Whether these are wise or unwise statements we are hardly able to say.

Aug. 28, 1941   Lynnhaven, Va.   Levi Bontrager

[A prophecy alleged to have been made by the German monk Johannes about the year 1600, received wide attention during World War I. An article from *Pathfinder* was reprinted in THE BUDGET. It occupied more than 3 columns of small print. After an explanation of twelve paragraphs, the statement is made that ". . . so runs this noted prophecy. It fits the kaiser and his war like a glove. . . ." But also noted was the fact that ". . . the most vital portions of the prophecy remain still to be put to the test, however."]

Jan. 30, 1918   [p. 2; + 3 column reprint]

Since the Kaiser's downfall, someone has discovered a record of it in the 11th verse of the 11th chapter of the 11th book in the Bible. Read it and see for yourself, in I Kings 11:11.

Jan. 8, 1919   Manchester, Md.   J. Albert Zepp

The earthquake in California last week gives us evidence to believe the coming of our Lord is near.

Mar. 16, 1933   Elverson, Pa.   Mrs. Katie B. Stoltzfus

Surely the whole world is in distress, with the awful horrors of war and following in its wake the destructive agents of famine and pestilence and the great political unrest being manifested throughout the universe, one must think that the time of the end cannot be far.

The war seems to have come to an end about as suddenly as it started. Some of the world's greatest men are in conference with each other discussing plans for world wide peace and safety for all mankind, forever. Oh that all God-fearing people may take warning. The Apostle Paul in his 1st epistle to the Thessalonians, after telling them of the second coming of Christ, says "For then they shall say, Peace and safety; then sudden destruction cometh upon them." I Thess. 5:3.

Jan. 1, 1919   Allemands, La.   Samuel J. Beachy

Oh what a pity that satan has so much power at present to deceive so many people, for the end is coming, when we should be prepared to meet our God. Those feelings strike my heart often in my old days, for I know the end is coming fast.

Aug. 11, 1920   Shipshewana, Ind.   John E. Bontrager

A fellow off the road stated to my father a few weeks ago: "The world will not stand more than ten years."

Aug. 29, 1940   Gap, Pa.   John F. Glick

Trust by "outsiders": Recently one of our Amish men had business dealings at Macon, a city about 50 miles north. He asked if the purchase must be cash, or if he would be given some time, whereupon the answer was cash. Then the dealer asked him if he was a Mennonite, and of course the reply was yes. Then he was told, you may pay for it when ever you say. Do we deserve the trust that is placed in the plain people?

Dec. 19, 1963   Montezuma, Ga.   Mrs. E. W. Yoder

United States: As we enter the 80's the prophets are painting a rather gloomy outlook for the coming decade financially and morally, but the up look is as bright as ever. Let us ever look up, for our redemption draweth nigh.

Jan. 9, 1980   Uniontown, Ohio   Enos Miller

As of today our country is in a terrible mess, high taxes, murder, crimes and dictatorship to certain extent. Under the circumstances, I wish to pass my opinion in the latter affair. There are firms now that who will furnish turkeys to the extent that all you do is feed them. You also have the same chance on feeder cattle and hogs. We shall see the time when they have this setup well enough under way that the farmer won't have anything for himself. It can easily develop into government control. You then will raise and do as ordered, and will end up in a dictatorship. Am I right or wrong?

June 13, 1957   Middlebury, Ind.   Em Miller

I wish we would all read and study the 1st and 2nd and 58th chapter of Isaiah. It makes one wonder if there was ever a time or nation who had more gold and silver, more chariots and horsepower than our nation. When were the chariots swifter or more sought after than today? Do we hold the work of our own hands as vexation and vanity as Solomon says, or can't we give our whole heart to God because of them.

July 24, 1952   Fredericksburg, Ohio   William J. Keim

[The very conservative magazine, the *Defender Magazine*, was quoted and referred to by some scribes. The following is an example.] Like Gerald B. Winrod put it: "Only a small percent of the people really understand the true character of the sinister agencies which are trying to destroy civilization and blot Christianity from the face of the earth."

June 13, 1935   Oelwein, Iowa   Joe Borntrager

I am convinced that the Supreme Court is erring in their interpretation of what the constitution of our country is supposed to say. [This comment was in respect to the decision to ban formal prayer on public school property.]

July 5, 1962   Lynnhaven, Va.   J. J. Hershberger

The news of the ruthless shooting of the President came as a great shock to everyone here, and also to the nation and world. I know that God permitted it, and don't know why, but it did something to the nation, and I hope it was for the good.

Nov. 28, 1963   Stillwater, Pa.   John R. Renno

I wonder how many of my friends were as shocked as I was when the sad news was flashed from Dallas last week. The Lord had a hand in it and if it was for our good or not time will tell.

Dec. 5, 1963   Hartville, Ohio   Gideon Stoll

This chapter contains excerpts considered worthy to be included but not falling appropriately in any of the previous categories. They are included here for your enlightenment and pleasure.

Amish in the news: None of them had applied for ration books in any classification (sugar, gasoline, oil or tire). The Amish, said Joseph L. Davis, raise their own honey for sweetening, they drive horses and buggies and they go to bed at sundown. [Bontrager took this from a newspaper clipping, "Amish Farmers Lose Nothing by Rationing."]
  Feb. 11, 1943   Thomas, Okla.   Joe Bontrager

Animals: We also saw in the Belleville Times while plowing in a field near Lewistown, Pa., Beaver G. Thomas found a turtle upon which was carved the letters C.C. 1492. S. M. supposed it to be carved by Christopher Columbus upon his first trip to America.
  June 29, 1922   Allensville, Pa.   M. P. Zook

This has been a beautiful March day. The birds are happy and their sweet songs has a tendency to make us older people feel glad. I for one do enjoy the coming of the sweet songsters, a harbinger of spring.
  Mar. 31, 1920   Atwater, Ohio   Leah J. Harris

The Berlin folks report that they have a white robin up there, that surely ought to denote people at Berlin. In 1881 there was a man by the name of John Opliger preached in his sleep west of Berlin and he said then there would be a white bird come to Berlin, but don't know what he meant it was for and this man had no education whatever maybe this is the white bird he spoke of.
  April 7, 1921   Bunker Hill, Ohio   Mrs. Daniel Middaugh

A chicken with four legs was hatched at the home of Jacob Borts in town last Monday, but it did not live. Two of the legs were in the proper places and the others protruded from under each wing. Mr. Borts thinks this new variety would have been a great success as a scratcher.

April 19, 1916   West Liberty, Ohio   Maude Peachey

I was informed that Fred Loucks, the practical bee-keeper, is trying to cross his bees with lightning bugs (June bugs) so that his bees can see to work night and day.

June 14, 1900   Lowville, N.Y.   J. K. Swartzentruber

Potato bugs are great sinners, because they go around and destroy the farmers potatoes. They don't keep the Sabbath holy; they even work on that day.

July 23, 1896   Walnut Creek, Ohio   E. N. Beachy

Snakes milked a cow while she stood in the water. [Quoted from a story in the Holmes County Farmer.]

June 26, 1902

It sounds "way off" to be trotting a horse up hill and singing, "Nearer My God to Thee."

July 11, 1901   Pleasant Valley, Ohio   B 4.U.

Here is a true fish story that did not work out so profitable. Some time ago, a certain Amish farmer near Churchtown took off at least part of a night on a fishing trip. While the hired boy was also absent the forepart of the night, the wife heard a racket in the barn, but being alone with her children, she did not investigate until the boy returned. He found a fresh cow hanging dead on a gate. She had tried to jump over the gate to her calf.

June 28, 1951   Elverson, Pa.   B. F. Stoltzfus

Last week we had a nice young pup (blue heeler) come to our place. He looked well taken care of so we tried to figure out why someone would not want such a dog. As time went on we knew why; he is absolutely deaf; how would you stop him from chasing a cow when you want him to stop? I guess time will tell what to do.

Feb. 18, 1987   Grandin, Mo.   Freeman A. Byler

Domestic relationships: A man and his wife were driving along a highway. Noticed a farmer in his field with a nice team of two big horses hitched to a wagon. Man said to his wife, "Look how nice they pull together. Wouldn't it be nice if you and I could pull together like they do?" The wife said, "We could if we had but one tongue between us."

Nov. 7, 1946   In a local news item.

379

Concerning Jonas Beachy's letter in last week's, about some Stark Co. young folks who were at their place and got up during the night and set their table. Well, one reason we could not sleep was the strong coffee which was served at supper time and thought maybe we could set the table to pass the night and also get breakfast in good time in the morning, and not be late for church. It wasn't set like they usually do in Madison, so we were kind enough to get up and put it in place again. Sure enjoyed the weekend.

April 28, 1955   Hartville, Ohio   Nancy Coblentz

Health: There are three species of grip; the strong man's grip, the doctor's grip, and grip, as a physical disorder. Let us quote praise to the first, cheer to the second, but sympathize with all who are subject to the latter.

Jan. 17, 1901   Havelock, Iowa   J. C. Burkey

Humorous: The water system in Berlin is nearing completion, which reminds me of an incident which occurred while the 90 ft. water tank was being constructed. Mr. M. Miller was standing a short distance from the tower, watching a man working at the top of the tank. After he was finished with his task he slid down into a little platform not far below. Mr. Miller didn't notice that a platform was there and thought the man was falling. Miller fainted.

Nov. 25, 1948   Berlin, Ohio   Sara Weaver

A local driver got a chuckle out of 2 little boys Saturday. They came out of the Town & Country Store in Kidron, with 1 pint of ice cream, but only one spoon. Their faithful little dog was along. One boy held the pint of ice cream while the other boy got a big spoonful of ice cream. The first boy ate part of the spoonful, the second boy ate part of it, the balance going to the their small dog, all off one spoon.

March 11, 1987   New Bedford, Ohio   Melvin E. Hershberger

Don Ward, a local taximan, is not exactly bashful. Last evening he asked the girl behind the counter at the west union Dairy Freeze if he gets a tip for being so old. She asked, "Do you want a tip?" He said, "Yes." She said, "Plant your potatoes early."

March 11, 1987   West Union, Ohio   Atlee J. Hochstetler

The little daughter of Junior Schwartzes decided to eat a moth ball when they were calling at the Sammie R. Borntrager home one Sunday not long ago. She didn't seem to show much results except I suppose she was disinfected

good on the inside.
Dec. 27, 1962   Hazelton, Iowa   Mrs. J.M.S.

Our neighbor was in at the local IGA store and bought some $20 of groceries for their family of seven. He remarked that the lady just behind him had $22 worth of dog food. The time may be here that we have to be careful when we talk of a "dog's life." It just could be better than some children or human's life.
July 30, 1980   Aylmer, Ont.   Simon Wagler

Legal / trials: Myrtle Crabtree, 14, was fined $16 and sent to jail in default, for whispering in church. This should be a warning for others, as the law is very strict in regard to misbehavior or disturbance, either in or outside of the church, during services.
Feb. 27, 1896   News item about a girl in Portsmouth, Ohio.

The young scalowag that shot through Jake Farver's window last week, would better be a little careful or he might get where the dogs can't bite him.
July 9, 1896   Farmerstown, Ohio   Ike, the Dauber

Names: Approximately seven months ago a cabbage farmer from the States was visiting Double Head Cabbage. He thought perhaps the farmers would raise cabbage with two heads. But of course he did not find any cabbage farmers in the village. The strange name for this village comes from a Cabbage Palm Tree which looks much like a coconut Palm Tree. The Cabbage Palm does not grow cabbage heads....
Sept. 29, 1976   Double Head Cabbage, Belize   Floyd Stoltzfus

Anti-Can't Class. [Name given a Sunday School class.]
Feb. 18, 1914

Psychological: A certain dairy farmer over in Holmes County was thinking one thing and doing another. After he was through milking his cows, instead of carrying the milk to the milkhouse and run it through the separator he carried it to the hog stable and poured it in the trough for the hogs not discovering his mistake until the hogs had it all.
Oct. 30, 1912   Local news item.

I was blasting stumps too today and had to lit one twice, but I tell you friends it will make a man think when blasting stumps after this.
April 5, 1916   Bay Minette, Ala.   J. K. Fisher

Riddles / puzzles: Do all readers know where the word News

originated? Findings from the north, east, west and south constitute the N-E-W-S.
Jan. 16, 1918   Manchester, Ind.   J. Albert Zepp

OPTIMIST
'Twixt optimist and pessimist
  The difference is droll
The optimist sees the doughnut
  The pessimist sees the hole.
  July 8, 1910

YOUR MIND
Great minds discuss ideas
Average minds discuss events
Small minds discuss people
[This saying was followed by 12 inches of discussion.]
  May 17, 1945   No address   Felty S. Yoder

Dr. Yoder has been trying to teach the Creek hay tossers a new wrinkle: he says, "make hay while the sun shines, is an advice often needed. "Make love while the moon shines," is oftener heeded.
  Sept. 17, 1896   Bear Creek, Wyo.   W. M.

Rumors: A rich man by the name of Thauston of South Carolina, owns 5300 acres of well improved land here in Madison Co. about 7 miles from our settlement, and we heard he sold 4000 acres to a Toledo man and he sold it to Amish Mennonites of Canada. I would like to find out if this rumor is true. We also heard that all the Amish Mennonites will leave Canada.
  June 23, 1920   Plain City, Ohio   E. R. Yutzy

Thought I'd write and let people know we are still here. Rumors were going around that we're all moving away. Don't know of anyone who has plans to move. Satan is very busy because he knows he has little time.
  Oct. 27, 1976   Kendallville, Ind.   Mrs. John H. Schwartz

Technology: Two weeks ago, I reported that there were 38 aeroplanes passing over us in 45 minutes or so; since I have heard of several people that counted as many as fifty and more. These people lived in different parts of the county and it was while some that were above us and made such a noise that others passed to the N.W. of us. One idea of the noise they made can be gotten from Mrs. C. J. Swartzentruber who thought it was thundering and went to the garden to pick beans before it should rain; about half the planes had flown over her before she discovered the source of the "thundering". The people here are having a laugh occasionally at her expense, but she always helps.

July 7, 1921   Princess Anne, Va.   Jonas E. Miller

Joe McDavis got lost one night last week, and it wasn't very dark at that; but I guess it was because he had the two big wheels on one side of the buggy. You want to look better next time, Joe.

July 25, 1901   Iowa, La.   Jacob Keim

Then and now: Fifty years ago men wore whiskers, square hats, ascot ties, red flannel underwear, big watches and chains, chopped wood for stoves, bathed once a week, drank 10 cents whiskey, rode buggies and sleighs, worked 12 hours a day, and lived to a ripe old age, and also paid a reasonable price for land.

Now, men have high blood pressure, wear no hats, and some have no hair; shave their whiskers, shoot golf, bathe twice a day, drink poison, play the stock market, ride in airplanes, seldom go to bed the same day they get up, are misunderstood at home, work 5 hours per day, play 19 hours a day and die young. Also pay from four hundred to a thousand dollars an acre for land.

Fifty years ago stores burned oil lamps, carried everything from a needle to a plow, trusted everybody, never took an inventory, placed orders for goods a year in advance, and always made money.

Now stores have electric lights, cash registers, elevators, never have what customers want, trust nobody, take inventory daily, never buy in advance, have overhead markups, mark down, quota, budget, advertising, stock control, annual and semi-annual end of the month and economy day sales, and make a dollar day, rummage, founder's day, little money for the tax collector. What will it be in Twenty Hundred if the world is still in existence?

Feb. 16, 1950   Gap, Pa.   John F. Glick

Tramps: Tramps were quite numerous in town of late. One morning last week, M. I. Hostetler and a _____ tramp happened to be at the same place for breakfast, and somehow the tramp failed to get enough to eat, and consequently called at several other places to get breakfast. Mose followed him, telling the people that he had his breakfast, etc. and ordering the tramp to leave town, etc. After the tramp had breakfast at five different places, and had his stomach well filled, etc., Mose succeeded in starting him towards the North Pole, etc.

March 23, 1893   Local Sugarcreek news

Young Mennonite preacher and his wife in Mo. near R.R. had many tramps. Finally asked each one to chop wood or do some other work before the meal. In the course of time they decided to have special meetings. Bishops in charge made arrangements, set the day and called the preacher.

Then one evening another stranger knocked at Grandpa's back door having just gotten off the train a half mile or so down the tracks. This man too, asked for a bite to eat, so Grandpa kindly asked him to split some wood while Grandma prepared something for him to eat. He gladly split the wood, then Grandpa told him of the meetings at the meeting-house that evening and invited him to go along. He accepted the invitation and, behold! When they got to church the stranger was the visiting preacher! That was one of those proverbial "most embarrassing moments".

May 11, 1961   Amelia, Va.   LeRoy Hooley

Vegetation: It is claimed that at Danville, Ky., a small group of shittim trees has been located, the same kind of wood from which Moses was commanded to have a certain part of the ark of the covenant made.

Jan. 9, 1947   Lancaster County Briefs   Jonathan B. Fisher

Our garden has turned out some funny-looking carrots. One has to wonder what is next. We only dug up about a half dozen; and two of those are shaped like the bottom half of a man and a woman, complete with two legs each! We probably won't eat them!

July 23, 1980   Mesopotamia, Ohio   Katherine M. Byler

"It Grew in Holmes County"

The largest log ever seen in this vicinity was hauled to this town yesterday by Elmer Syler, a local lumber dealer. The enormous piece of timber is sycamore, ten feet long and twelve feet in diameter at the butt end. It was cut on the Nickolas Speer farm about 10 miles west of here, in Holmes County. Mrs. Syler hauled the log to Baltic by means of an engine. He has decided to mount the log in his lumber yard as a curiosity. [News item from "Holmes County Farmer"]

July 1, 1910

Unclassified: Have you heard of the goat man from Macon, Ga.?

384

He claims to have traveled most of the U.S. with his goats. On Wed. he made his appearance in Hephzibah, twenty goats pulling two steel-wheeled wagons loaded with "JUNK" (His belongings). He claims to be a preacher but the only followers seem to be the six nanny goats tied behind the second wagon.

Jan. 24, 1963   Hephzibah, Ga.   Jerry and Thelma Yoder

There were several boys that wanted to go to the movies unseen, so before going in they stood on the side walk looking this way and that way until they felt sure no one saw them. Then they ducked into the door. But they were seen. They failed to look straight up.

Sept. 1, 1960   Belleville, Pa.   Ezra Kanagy

A farmer near Ragen had a narrow escape last Saturday while gathering roasting ears. He was standing on top of a thirty foot ladder leaning against a stalk of corn, when he accidentally fell, and when within ten feet of the ground had the presence of mind to cling to a nubbin until a neighbor drove under him with a load of hay and saved his life.

Nov. 1, 1906   Wisner, Neb.   L. H. Lantz

A parking lot in Sugarcreek on a summer day.

Index

This index deals primarily with topics and subjects mentioned by the scribes in the excerpts included in this volume. A short index of Pennsylvania German words/phrases or Anglicizations follows the main index.

An index of the names of scribes was considered. It was not undertaken for various reasons. It would have been far too time consuming. To make it accurate would have called for considerable work in genealogy. There would almost certainly have been many duplications and omissions, due to sometimes using full first name and at other times only initials. The names of some changed during the time they were reporting. For instance, Mary Miller was a scribe before she was married, and after her marriage she signed as Mrs. Enos W. Yoder. She was honored for sixty years of writing, about half of that time in Virginia, with an address of Lynnhaven and later Bayside. She served about thirty years in Montezuma, Georgia. If the author had not known her personally, her name might well have appeared several times in such an index.

386

390

Pennsylvania German words/terms, expressions and/or Anglicizations used in this volume. For greetings and closing of letters see pp. 170 - 171.

Some words or phrases used in Pennsylvania German style, other than what appears in Chapter 28, "Language and Vocabulary". This list does not include expressions common to the general public, unless applied differently.

Author Information

Elmer S. Yoder was born near Salisbury, Pennsylvania to Simon L. and Lydia E. Yoder. He lived with his parents near Kempsville, Virginia until 1950 when he married Esther J. Yoder of Stark County, Ohio. Elmer and Esther are the parents of three children: Dorcas, married to Nelson Eberly; Elwood, married to Joy Risser; and Jason, married to Donna-Marie Francis. The Yoders have seven grandchildren.

Yoder is an educator and was a teacher for thirty-two years in both elementary and high school. Nine of the years were in Christian schools and twenty-three years in public. He has also served more than thirty years on boards of Christian schools, on four levels; elementary, high school, Bible institute and college. He earned his bachelors and masters degrees at Kent State University.

Since 1956 he has served as an ordained minister in the Conservative Mennonite Conference, and served both the Marlboro and the Maple Grove Mennonite Churches of Hartville.

Currently he is Editor of *Brotherhood Beacon,* the official publication of the Conservative Mennonite Conference. He serves as the Conference Historian and Chairman of the Conference Historical Committee. He also serves as Chairman of the Stark County Mennonite and Amish Historical Society, as well as holding positions on numerous committees and membership in several professional organizations. Yoder has written five books, among which is *The Beachy Amish Mennonite Fellowship Churches* (1987).

One of his hobbies is photography. Several slide presentations have been developed, among which is "Sermons from Barns", and shown more than 100 times. The varied ministry of the Yoders has its outlet through Diakonia Ministries.